Studies in Renaissance Literature

Volume 27

LORD HENRY HOWARD (1540–1614) AN ELIZABETHAN LIFE

Born the second son of the poet Earl of Surrey, Henry Howard was a Cambridge scholar, courtier and crypto-Catholic intriguer of suspicious repute; after falling in and out of favour with Elizabeth I, he eventually became the most important adviser to James I. This detailed reassessment traces his career through its various vicissitudes. In particular, it places him in the context of scholarship on Renaissance humanism and its varied interactions with the different styles of argument and persuasion that Howard used, often to no avail, to improve his position in these dark times for those of his faith. The book will appeal to all those interested in the intellectual, religious or political history of early modern England.

DANIEL ANDERSSON is a fellow of the Max Planck Institut für Wissenschaftsgeschichte, Berlin.

Studies in Renaissance Literature

ISSN 1465-6310

General Editors
David Colclough
Raphael Lyne
Sean Keilen

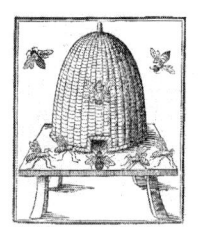

Studies in Renaissance Literature offers investigations of topics in English literature focussed in the sixteenth and seventeenth centuries; its scope extends from early Tudor writing, including works reflecting medieval concerns, to the Restoration period. Studies exploring the interplay between the literature of the English Renaissance and its cultural history are particularly welcomed.

Proposals or queries should be sent in the first instance to the editors, or to the publisher, at the addresses given below; all submissions receive prompt and informed consideration.

Dr David Colclough, School of English and Drama, Queen Mary, University of London, Mile End Road, London, E1 4NS

Dr Raphael Lyne, Murray Edwards College, Cambridge, CB3 0DF

Dr Sean Keilen, The College of William and Mary, Williamsburg, VA 23188, USA

Boydell & Brewer Limited, PO Box 9, Woodbridge, Suffolk, IP12 3DF

Previously published volumes in this series are listed at the back of this volume

LORD HENRY HOWARD (1540–1614)
AN ELIZABETHAN LIFE

Portrait of Henry Howard, anonymous 'British' follower of Hieronymus Custodis, 1594 (Courtesy of the Mercers Company).

LORD HENRY HOWARD (1540–1614)
AN ELIZABETHAN LIFE

D. C. Andersson

D. S. BREWER

© D. C. Andersson 2009

All Rights Reserved. Except as permitted under current legislation no part of this work may be photocopied, stored in a retrieval system, published, performed in public, adapted, broadcast, transmitted, recorded or reproduced in any form or by any means, without the prior permission of the copyright owner

The right of D. C. Andersson to be identified as the author of this work has been asserted in accordance with sections 77 and 78 of the Copyright, Designs and Patents Act 1998

First published 2009
D. S. Brewer, Cambridge

ISBN 978-1-84384-209-5

D. S. Brewer is an imprint of Boydell & Brewer Ltd
PO Box 9, Woodbridge, Suffolk IP12 3DF, UK
and of Boydell & Brewer Inc.
668 Mt Hope Avenue, Rochester, NY 14620, USA
website: www.boydellandbrewer.com

A catalogue record for this title is available
from the British Library

The publisher has no responsibility for the continued existence or accuracy of URLs for external or third-party internet websites referred to in this book, and does not guarantee that any content on such websites is, or will remain, accurate or appropriate.

This publication is printed on acid-free paper

Typeset by Tina Ranft
Printed in Great Britain by
CPI Antony Rowe, Chippenham and Eastbourne

CONTENTS

Abbreviations — xi
Editorial principles — xii
Preface — xiii

Introduction — 1

1. 'The knowledge of good letters'.
Birth, Education and First Years at Cambridge — 9

2. '*Tanta assiduitas*'.
A Scholarly Life at Trinity Hall — 30

3. 'Beware of to much arte'.
Between Cambridge and Audley End — 54

4. 'The skill of Philenus'.
Teacher, Polemicist, Papist — 81

5. 'In some sort communicat with daunger'.
Survival, Success and Defeat — 106

6. 'Somewhat closely carried'.
Rhetoric and Astrology — 127

7. 'No termination but *in vocativo*'.
Failure, Votary and Civilian — 144

8. '*An nobilitas perdatur per infamiam?*'
From Conspirator to Kingmaker — 168

Conclusion — 179

Appendix I Henry Howard's Epicedion for Nicholas Carr — 182
Appendix II A Note on Edification — 186

Bibliography — 192
Index — 218

Ars longa, vita brevis
Seneca, after Hippocrates

ABBREVIATIONS

BL	British Library, London
BLO	Bodleian Library, Oxford
CSPD	*Calendar of State Papers, Domestic: Elizabeth I*, eds R. Lemon and M. A. E. Grenn, 12 vols, London, 1856–1872
CSPF	*Calendar of State Papers, Foreign: Elizabeth*, eds J. Stevenson *et al.*, 23 vols, London, 1898–1969
CSPSc	*Calendar of State Papers relating to Scotland and Mary Queen of Scots, 1547–1603*, ed. J. Bain, 13 vols, Edinburgh and Glasgow, 1898–1969
CSPSp	*Calendar of State Papers, Spanish*, eds G. A. Bergenroth *et al.*, 13 vols, London, 1862–1869
CUL	Cambridge University Library
DBI	*Dizionario Biografico degli Italiani*, Rome, 1960–
DHI	*Dictionary of the History of Ideas*
DUL	Durham University Library, Special Collections
HMC, Hatfield House	Historical Manuscripts Commission, *Calendar of the Salisbury Manuscripts*, London, 1888
HUO	*History of the University of Oxford*
JHI	*Journal of the History of Ideas*
JWCI	*Journal of the Warburg and Courtauld Institutes*
LP	*Letters and Papers Foreign and Domestic of the Reign of Henry VIII*, eds J.S. Brewer, J. Gairdner and R.H. Broadie, 21 vols, London, 1862–1932.
LPL	Lambeth Palace Library
MLN	*Modern Language Notes*
TNA: PRO	The National Archives, Public Record Office, Kew
STC	*Short-Title Catalogue*
VCH	*Victoria County History*

EDITORIAL PRINCIPLES

Where no accents are given in a transcription of Greek, the original is also lacking them. I have corrected the accentuation for Greek printed in early modern books or manuscripts where it is faulty. For Renaissance Latin texts, there has been no normalization of orthography (other than *i/j* and *u/v*), but I have repunctuated in order, where the sense is clear, to make the Latin intelligible; where I have some residual doubt as to the precise sense, I have left punctuation out. I have neither repunctuated nor changed the orthography (except that I have normalized *u/v*) for transcriptions of French, English or Italian passages. These editorial rules apply unless there is some indication to the contrary. Contractions have been expanded silently, unless there is a possibility of dispute (as, on occasion, with the ampersand, unless metrical considerations require otherwise) and where the original has some marker of a contraction, that marker has been silently abandoned (e.g., 'm.o.' becomes 'm<agistr>o' and not 'm.<agistr>o'). Pointed brackets indicate an editorial supplement of varying degrees of certainty and square brackets indicate paleographical uncertainty. All translations are my own; no translation is given of poetry, or of very doubtful passages.

PREFACE

This book has been much improved by the warm vigilance of Jill Kraye. It has been in large measure due to her that I have begun to understand how much the intellectual content of history is acquired through and inheres in its editorial activity. She has also encouraged me by example to stem the rising tide of first person singular pronouns in scholarly prose; *tanta assiduitas* makes for *quanta humilitas*. The work's debt to the Warburg Institute and its library will, I trust, be apparent, albeit that this book slots itself into that tradition of intellectual history more fitfully than I would have liked. My abiding interests have been rhetoric, religious phenomenology and the history of science: each of these has its own temptation to ignore the sort of philological history that the best of Warburg scholarship exemplifies, and the Institute has helped me to ignore these temptations.

The student of early modern culture is heavily dependent upon libraries, and few are as well-organized and intellectually vital as the Herzog August Bibliothek, Wolfenbüttel. Thanks also go to the rare books room in the University Library at Cambridge and the Special Collections department at Durham University Library. An award from the Deutsche Akademische Austauschdienst afforded me the opportunity of spending a long period of uninterrupted research time at the Bayerischer Staatsbibliothek in Munich, during which my knowledge of Renaissance natural philosophy was very considerably deepened. In similar fashion, a generous grant to attend l'Institut de l'Histoire de la Réformation in Geneva allowed me to gain a broader intellectual perspective on the English Reformation, so often studied somewhat parochially. A generous research fellowship at the Max Planck Institute for the History of Science, Berlin, has provided additional time and space to complete the book. Anne Moss gave me a book on dialectic, and Diarmaid MacCulloch some advice on the history of liturgy. John Bossy, who is also writing a book on the Elizabethan Henry Howard, and I have corresponded amicably, and he kindly sent me a draft of his article on Howard and Sir Philip Sidney. Some

Preface

of the material in this book has previously appeared in article form in *History of Universities* and *Notes and Queries,* and Oxford University Press (the publisher of these two journals) is thanked for having granted permission for this re-use.

Many have given generously of their time and effort in discussing particular ideas or texts and I am most thankful for their labours: in particular, Steven Vanden Broecke, Crofton Black, Kristine Haugen, Eckhard Kessler (despite my losing the keys to his institute, twice) and Irena Backus. Susan Brigden and Stephen Clucas offered additional encouragement and suggestions, and were more than tolerant of my more than occasional typographical infelicities. Rhodri Lewis provided ebullient intellectual support. Richard Serjeantson, fellow labourer and humanist, has always laughed at my jokes, and never my ideas: *quid plus?* The anonymous reader's report from the exemplary Boydell & Brewer encouraged me to recast the book into a biography (rather than the more rebarbative thematic structure that an earlier draft possessed). More personal obligations have been incurred to my mother, Stephen Little, the National Health Service, Jason Yiannikkou, Peter Chadwick, Alex Heylin, George Fraser Black and many men in and around the Royal Vauxhall Tavern. Michael Comber, who did most to consolidate my desire to spend time with ideas and texts, died before I could offer him anything in exchange for the passion and seriousness which he inspired in me, as in so many of his pupils. To all these friends and colleagues I am deeply grateful. I only hope my gratitude outweighs their disappointment and my own.

Matri Optimae

Introduction

THE SIXTEENTH century witnessed profound shifts in the role of the nobility in cultural life. The various aristocracies of Europe, in response to both military and social changes, needed to provide innovative justifications for their position and prestige. It is a commonplace observed in scholarship on the Renaissance that the growth of the interest in the recovery of the Classical past, at least in its guise as humanist educational ideal, was closely related to this redrawing of the intellectual foundations of the hegemonic map. At first sight, it is hard to understand why these two factors should be so linked. The story is normally told in something like the following terms. Throughout the medieval period, a compact had long obtained between military distinction and noble rank: the notion that one's leader in peacetime should be also one's leader on the battlefield ran deep. Although the realities of kingship often put this idealizing compact under strain, the notion was far from being merely an ideological fiction that must be 'unmasked'; this emperor had clothes – and armoury. Technology was soon to alter this alignment (though the precise scope accorded to such innovation is naturally a matter of dispute for those who detect a whiff of technological determinism here).

Historians have long noted the increasing cost of waging war in the fifteenth and sixteenth centuries, with each new siege artillery innovation stimulating equally expensive developments in fortification. This meant, among other things, that war had soon become so costly that it was an option open only to the heads of Europe's emerging dynastic states (perhaps a better term than the oft-misunderstood 'nation states'). In turn, so the traditional account has it, this left a considerable lacuna in the self-image of the aristocracy, which was widened by such factors as the increasing displacement of the cavalry by infantry. Those who failed to see which way the ideological wind was blowing were left, like Don Quixote, tilting at windmills. One remembers with poignant fondness the noble Pierre Terrail, whose distaste for the ignoble arquebus did not prevent him from being shot dead by a Habsburg bullet.

Lord Henry Howard: An Elizabethan Life

There are many qualifications to so crude a picture, and the flood of social and economic history of the 1970s provided a good deal of such nuancing. One thinks, in the context of England, of the productive controversy that attended the years following Lawrence Stone's *Crisis of the Aristocracy*.[1] More recently, with the cultural turn in early modern history, scholarship has tried to be rather more precise in defining the English reception of educational programmes of humanism and in quite what sense the relation between education and ideology actually worked in practice. Still more recently, scepticism about Anglophone exceptionalism, that perennial bugbear of British history, has generated an 'intellectual turn' to match the earlier cultural one, causing a confluence of literary and political history which has led to some productive work grounded in the close reading of texts: philology in its wide Italian sense.[2] This, after all, is how the boys of Tudor England were themselves taught to read, and not only boys, but princes, whose more ideologically focused pedagogy which, alas, cannot be reconstructed for Howard (though if it could, we would doubtless be able to arrive at an account of noble humanist pedagogy that emphasized as much the construction of the expectations of the noble's discursive communicants as the passivity of the learning experience). It is reassuring, to say the least, that historians study texts in a way their authors would recognize. This transformation, under the influence of these ideological and political factors, of the enthusiasms of the early *Quattrocento* Italian humanists into a university curriculum and then into a culture of textual attentiveness and increasingly sophisticated standards of argument across the disciplines is one of the most extraordinary achievements of the Renaissance. It is, furthermore, to this story that the current work, *sotto voce*, speaks.

For Lord Henry Howard, these narratives of nobility and intellectual endeavour were complicated by religious and financial factors. He was a noble sympathetic to the stances of humanism and to the Catholic faith in a period during which England was far from fertile soil for either enthusiasm. Most work, indeed, of any intellectual distinction in the 1560s and the 1570s was produced by asylum-seeking exiles to the Continent: the Marian congregations in Geneva, or, from a different intellectual and confessional tradition, Edmund Campion or Richard Stanihurst. It was Howard's nobility and his strong attachment to the possibility of secular power within England that kept him, unlike his sim-

---

[1] Lawrence Stone, *The Crisis of the Aristocracy 1558–1641*, Oxford, 1967.
[2] See, e.g., David Colclough, *Freedom of Speech in Early Stuart England*, Cambridge, 2005.

Introduction

ilarly minded cousin, Charles Arundell, from seeking refuge across the Channel. This relative absence of engagement with Continental thought takes its toll on his writings. One might argue that the rather low level of philological sophistication in his works is capable of internal explanation in each case: his work on natural philosophy is a manuscript for his sister outside the university milieu and his attack on the Presbyterians a few years later explicitly eschews the more elaborate point for point refutation in favour of a more epideictic treatment; his attack on astrology is deliberately broader in argumentative scope and intended audience than the Latin works upon which it depends. For all that, the traditional notion that he was the most learned of the nobility of his time, if true, only casts a rather dim light on the rest of that class.

No full biography of Howard under Elizabeth has yet been produced, and yet he was the second son (and after his brother the Duke of Norfolk's execution, the chief scion) of the noblest family in England, by comparison with whom the Tudors appeared Welsh upstarts. Howard is clearly an important figure, whether in rumour or reality, for the various intrigues that attended the confused mapping of confessional allegiance on to political faction. He also had ever before him the example of his father, Henry Howard, Earl of Surrey, with its abiding question of how to deal, both politically and intellectually, with so great, and yet so tainted, a legacy. Howard's response, as we have noted, was considerably complicated by the requirements of a conservative religious position and his decision to remain as a student and teacher of Cambridge University, a decision that assisted with some aspects of his father's legacy while placing others on hold.

The reader will soon appreciate how persistent a figure he was in the various abortive palace revolutions of Elizabeth's reign. This book concentrates on the first fifty or so years of his life. The last decade of Elizabeth's reign is not only one of the longer periods of Howard's life for which there is, at least until the end, little in the way of documentary evidence, but it is also the most barren from a cultural or intellectual standpoint. His 1590 tract on female rule is closely connected to his university training, as are, to different degrees, and in different ways, his earlier works; but beyond 1590 it is a rather different story. Furthermore, the reader may consult exemplary studies by Paul Hammer and Linda Levy Peck that pick up Howard's biography from the middle of the 1590s at the date of his greatest involvement with the Earl of Essex.[3] We will soon

---

[3] Linda Levy Peck, *Northampton: Patronage and Policy at the Court of James I*, London, 1982 and Paul Hammer, *The Polarization of Elizabethan Politics. The Political Career of Robert Devereux, Second Earl of Essex, 1585–1597*, Cambridge, 1999.

have the benefit too of Pauline Croft's eagerly awaited biography of Robert Cecil, which will cast light on the 'secret correspondence' between Cecil and King James VI, in which Howard played a pivotal role. An attempt has been made, therefore, to avoid reduplication of scholarly labour.[4]

Without losing focus on other aspects of Howard's life, the book gives special attention to his intellectual biography. There remains so much work to do in the intellectual history of the Elizabethan period that we need such case studies as a means of orientating later and more ambitious work. Accordingly, the book makes the case in detailed fashion for the relevance of the basic building blocks of Renaissance university education ('the arts course') for understanding concept and expression, the philosophy and literature, of the period. Some parts of the arts course were naturally more 'porous' with respect to other areas of discourse than others, and so disciplines such as rhetoric feature in all areas of the book. We are particularly fortunate with Howard in that we know that he spent so long at Cambridge, and that so many of his works are clearly intelligible only with a knowledge of the argumentative manoeuvres that he learned there. These in turn inform the immediate political contexts of his life.

It remains a hallmark of much scholarship on Renaissance English culture that the immediate intellectual context has often been lost to later scholarship in the rush to construct a canon of 'great authors' or 'great thinkers' who were involved in some sort of Olympic-torch-like tag race from one to the other. This is still very much true at the undergraduate level, where one may gain the impression that there is a canon of Renaissance English prose writers that runs from Hooker to Bacon to Burton to Browne, with their canonicity running through them like a scarlet thread. It is the purpose of more careful scholarship to illuminate these 'great' texts with the arts course texts (usually written in Latin) with which these authors were in fact in dialogue, giving the scarlet thread back to Ariadne. The centrality, however, of humanism (that cultural movement obsessed with the recovery and recreation of the Classical past) to much of the intellectual activity in this period cuts across any such supposed illumination – for humanism was a phenomenon which had roots as strong *outside* the university milieu as those within it.[5] The characteristic techniques of humanism simultaneously limit and enable the 'new' historiography of Renaissance intellectual history.

---

[4] Too late to be taken into account for this book, John Bossy informed me that he has found Howard's notes on Edmund Campion's *Reasons* in Castle Howard. The author was similarly unable to treat the late-discovered mss. of Howard in the Finch-Hatton collection.

[5] Michael Pincombe, *Elizabethan Humanism: Literature and Learning in the Later Sixteenth Century*, London, 2001, is a careful study which emphasizes the variety of meanings in the

Introduction

They both limit the precision with which we can track the progress of ideas (according to one paradigm of Renaissance intellectual history at least) from person to person and country to country, but also enable a rather different means for the dissemination and reformatting of those ideas across a range of material and social arenas.

This is all the more evident with 'vernacular' humanism, where the connections between idea transmitted and idea received were loosened not only institutionally but also linguistically. For Howard wrote as much in English as in Latin. Humanism, in its vernacular guise, becomes a series of stances and slogans, and much less a particular series of patterns of arranging words, with particular stylistic preferences. Howard's work on natural philosophy, for example, is a simple, vernacular text. Closely modelled on the *De naturae philosophia* of Sebastian Fox Morzillo, it is aligned with a humanist drive to expound and extend the text, but also in some ways at odds with it. In particular, he attempted (in what appears to be his only original contribution to his vernacularization of Fox Morzillo) to graft on to Aristotle a series of Platonic and Ciceronian references. This is probably best explained by the position of both of these authors in mid-Tudor Cambridge, though our evidence for philosophy in this university at this period is meagre.

The centrality of reading, annotation and composition to intellectual activity in the Renaissance is not in dispute, though achieving agreement on precisely the scope of this centrality has not been easy. 'Grammatica', the most basic of the disciplines of the trivium, had close connections with composition in the late medieval and Renaissance periods. It was a liminal discipline within the arts course, since it was mostly taught at the grammar schools. We need to understand the basic building blocks out of which Howard constructed his persuasive discourses. His annotations, originally dating from perhaps the end of the 1560s and continuing until perhaps 1585, tell us much about what he found interesting in the texts he annotated, but it is hard to see how his annotations differ from earlier or later practice. Where it is possible to draw closer connections between theory and practice is in his 1577 encomium of Elizabeth, the *Regina fortunata*, and this difference resides precisely in Howard's attempt to show his noble proximity to the queen rather than his patronage-seeking distance. (This is an issue, consonant with the earlier remarks on the refashioning of the aristocracy in this period, that will recur continually in Howard's biography.)

cluster of 'humane' and 'courtly' attitudes that rub shoulders with each other in Elizabethan uses of the new humanist learning. Pincombe goes far in the direction of the vernacular material at the expense of the university context and so provides, not wholly without justification, an intellectually more bleached version of humanism. The current work tends, for obvious reasons, in a rather different direction.

The strongly pronounced Renaissance taste for structural elegance over narrative drive as a literary virtue may be seen in some of Howard's own aphoristic comments on literary composition. In the same way, the epicedion that Howard penned on the death of his Cambridge colleague Nicholas Carr conforms clearly to various prescriptions from the textbooks on poetics and imitation, and is a highly-wrought and self-conscious affair.

Howard's early involvement with the struggle for place under Burghley encouraged him to engage in an published dispute that richly exemplified the resources of the next key discipline of the arts course, dialectic, which taught the art of proper argumentation. Its manoeuvres illuminate Howard's religious tract on Presbyteriansim, a text that can only be fully understood, however, through an awareness of Howard's confessional slipperiness (his sudden conversion to the Protestant cause under James I has long been a chief reason for his poor reputation among historians of Tudor and Stuart England). Various pieces of evidence suggest that his willingness to compromise his faith, especially in the 1570s, had very definite limits. In addition to his enthusiastic backing of highly elaborate prayers (which were perhaps to be set to music), we have a letter to Francis Walsingham that explains very clearly that he will refuse to stop celebrating private mass. Much of the debate about Catholics in sixteenth-century England has focused on the more extreme positions, but there has been a new resurgence of interest in the 'church papists'. Howard was clearly at the more Catholic end of the church papist spectrum though, if this is so, we need to explain his authorship of the 1574 defence of the Elizabethan settlement. Over and above biographical explanations (such as a request from Lord Burghley to write the work), we can look to the relationship between religious phenomenology and ecclesiology. The role of dialectic as a means of settling the dispute between the two parties was subject to certain limitations because, as a brief comparison with the more formal argumentative manoeuvres of a university disputation from 1573 shows, it is questions of differing temperament and perspective that are truly determinative of the problems between the Presbyterian and the Conformist parties.

Howard's attempts at preferment were not notably improved by his penning of the religious tract, and his entire career in the 1570s may be best understood as an attempt to navigate a difficult conduit for the clever and ambitious in early modern England, that between the universities and the court. Bad luck, and poor judgement, afflicted his dealings with the Earl of Oxford and his involvement with Queen's marriage plans. After the collapse of his hopes, yet again, he was forced to write his attack on astrology. Howard here deployed the resources of rhetoric to transform the Latin cri-

Introduction

tiques of astrology that he had read. By adopting a more obviously rhetorical approach (and by penning the work in the vernacular) he produced a far more wide-ranging piece of persuasion than any account of it which views it purely as a contribution to the history of astrological critique would be able to do. Once again, however, his intellectual activity landed him not preferment but in prison.

The principles of organization of Howard's main contribution to the literary history of England in the 1580s (his works of devotion) are for the most part those of liturgy rather than arts course disciplines, and Howard was propelled into the private sphere, never again venturing into the medium of print of the disasters of 1583/4. As the 1580s gave way to the 1590s, he did find a new form of political influence available to him by the dedication to Elizabeth of two further manuscripts, his nugatory translation of the Emperor Charles V's advice to his son, and the more substantial work on female rule. This latter work is both a culmination of and farewell to the Cambridge curriculum. While it has largely been viewed, where viewed at all, as a contribution to 'Renaissance feminism' or political theory, it would be better to suggest, in keeping with the 'arts course' focus of the book, that it is more responsibly (that is to say, historically) analysed as being as much in the tradition of displays of those techniques of legal argumentation that Howard both learned and taught at Cambridge almost thirty years earlier.

The 1590s were above all, for Howard, the decade of the Earl of Essex, his relationship with whom, however, to the extent that I have been able to reconstruct it, seems rather different in its approach to the politics of learning or humanist counsel than the one Howard affected earlier. By the time of the accession of James, and Howard's transformation from 'Lord Harry' to the 'Erle of Northampton', the ground had moved beneath Howard's feet: a ferment of intellectual change was altering the relationship of courtly career to humanist achievement that had been so notable a feature of the Elizabethan reception of the ancient world. One wonders how much he cared. After all, he appears to have thrown himself with some gusto into the virtuous duties of political administration and the pleasures of wealth accumulation. Nothing of any intellectual substance survives from Howard's years under James. Perhaps the most lasting achievement of these years was the construction of his grand residence on the Strand, Northampton House, where, on 15 June 1614, just nine years after it was built, Henry Howard died of a 'wennish tumour' on the thigh.[6]

[6] See now Manolo Guerci, 'The Strand Palaces of the Early Seventeenth Century: Northumberland House and Salisbury House', unpublished PhD dissertation, University of Cambridge, 2007.

It has been argued that 'in the case of scholastic faculty psychology, notions of "will", "reason", "passion" are not thought by the end of the Renaissance to convey objective facts about human nature and its physiological affinities, but are seen as words which designate in an organized fashion interrelationships which can only be analysed – and perhaps which only exist – in discourse'.[7] Such a view certainly conveys something of a trend noticeable within sixteenth-century texts. This move is inextricably linked to the prevalence of certain humanist traits: historicization, a taste for philology and for wider notions of what counts as *evidence* in a given discourse, leading to the endless contextualisms of history and the birth of social sciences in the seventeenth century.[8] Howard's works continually use this 'humanist' style of exposition and argumentation. This highly rhetorical version of these techniques of discourse served him well throughout his career, though we should be mindful not to reduce his learning to a mere tool of careerist expedience. The transformations of humanism created, in time, a culture, a set of ways of thinking and arguing and reading. It is to be hoped that a secure grasp of his life, and of the political and religious ambages to which he was subject, will enable the reader to better understand such argumentation; for persuasion and argument were crucial in both the public and learned worlds in which Howard played so interesting a part.

---

[7] Ian Maclean, *The Renaissance Notion of Woman: A Study in the Fortunes of Scholasticism and Medical Science in European Intellectual Life*, Cambridge, 1980, p. 87.

[8] The various interesting questions of evidence across the different disciplines in this period should not be reduced to an obsession with whether or not the Renaissance had a concept of internal evidence, thereby hindering the development of the scientific revolution (see, famously, Ian Hacking, *The Emergence of Probability*, Cambridge, 1975, p. 37).

Chapter 1

'THE KNOWLEDGE OF GOOD LETTERS'
BIRTH, EDUCATION AND FIRST YEARS
AT CAMBRIDGE

THE Lord Henry Howard was to play many roles throughout his long life, some traditional – courtier and man of religious devotion – and others less so – prisoner, scholar, efficient administrator, patron and, perhaps, murderer.[1] Throughout these frequent changes of stage and scenery, one thing, at least, remained constant: the importance of the written word.[2] Unlike his more militaristic brother, Thomas, he sought advancement and favour through literary productions, each with different audiences in view. The central tenet of the rhetorical education of which he was a beneficiary was that the 'writer' should always think of his audience and adjust his matter accordingly. Of course, too much thought for one's audience might be misread at the time as a lack of consistency or hypocrisy.[3] Even the future

---

[1] For the allegations of murder (relating to the death of Sir Thomas Overbury in 1613, and hence beyond the scope of this book), see the spirited summary in Anne Somerset, *Unnatural Murder: Poison at the Court of James I*, London, 1997. A drier (but judicious) presentation of the evidence may be found in A. Bellany, *The Politics of Court Scandal in Early Modern England: News Culture and the Overbury Affair, 1603–1660*, London, 2002.

[2] At least for the Elizabethan period, for '[f]rom 1600, once his position at court became more powerful, he stopped producing manuscripts; instead, the flow was reversed and a rich procession of dedications came his way': H. Woudhuysen, *Sir Philip Sidney and the Circulation of Manuscripts 1558–1642*, Oxford, 1998, pp. 102–3.

[3] This is perhaps even more true of Howard's biographers of later years: see, for example, the entry in the *DNB* sub nomine. This tradition, however, started early: see, for instance, the seventeenth-century chronicle [Michael Sparke], *A Historicall Narration of the First Fourteen Years of King James*, London: Richard Cotes, 1651, p. 5: 'Now Henry Howard, youngest son of the Duke of Norfolk, continuing a Papist from his Infancy even unto this time, beginning to grow eminent, and made heretofore famous for his learning, having been trained and brought up for a long time in Cambridge, by the perswasion of the King

Earl of Northampton's name, to say nothing (as others would) of his character, is not consistent in its orthography (though this was not a unique phenomenon in the Renaissance):[4] Henrye Howarde, Henricus Howardus, Henry Howarde, H. H., Henry Hωward, Henrie Hωwarde.[5] Some of these are natural enough variations from any Elizabethan hand; others, for example those that use the Greek omega, are the *jeux d'esprit* of a humanist. To suggest these name changes were simply games may, however, mislead. Indeed, within only a few months of having been granted an earldom by James I, he notes that the name 'Northampton' is as much in favour with him now as his old name 'Howard' ever was in years gone past. These were not conceits of the quill, but of identity.

The reader will soon appreciate that any attempt to pin down Howard's intellectual and ideological allegiances is no less difficult. There are serious gaps of evidence. The documents relating to his life tend to cluster at a few key moments of political intrigue, after which we hear nothing. It is a familiar rhythm to those engaged in Elizabethan biography, but it is made worse by Howard's own tendency to engage in if not outright duplicity then at least opacity about his motives and activities. He was inclined, from time to time, 'to raise a mist' and conceal, perhaps even from himself, his true orientation in matters political and religious.[6] To some, Howard's vacillations and calculated silences smacked, pure and simple, of fraud.[7] One might choose many points of departure for an

---

changeth his opinion of religion in outward appearance; and to the intent to reap unto himself more honours, became a Protestant, for which cause he was created Earl of Northampton, and had the Kings favour bountifully bestowed upon him ... This man was of a subtle and fine wit, of a good proportion, excellent in outward Courtship, famous for secret insinuation, and fortuning flatteries, and by reason of those qualities became a fit man for the condition of these times, and was suspected to bee scarce true to his soveraign, but rather endeavouring by some secret waies and means to set abroad new plots for to procure Innovations...'.

[4] Erasmus, for example, had changed his name from 'Roterdamnensis' to 'Roterdamus' and then to the more sonorous 'Roterodamus': see J. Huizinga, *Erasmus*, Basel, 1928, pp. 6–7.

[5] Examples: 'Henrye Howarde': BLO Bodley MS 616 f. 12^v; 'Henricus Howardus': BL Cotton MS, Titus C vi f. 7^r; 'H. Howarde': BL Cotton MS, Titus C vi f. 11^r; 'Henry Howard', ibid., f. 13^v; 'H. Hωwarde', ibid. f. 33^r. The Greek omega in place of a long o is not infrequent in seventeenth-century printed books; its occurrence in Elizabethan manuscripts is rare, but for one instance see Robert Southwell, Stonyhurst manuscript, f. 12^r [foliation my own].

[6] The phrase 'to raise a mist' is taken from an aphorism of Howard's: see BL Cotton MS, Titus C vi f. 283^r. It is quoted in full at p. 79.

[7] This was the view of, e.g., William Herle. Consider also the anonymous poem, 'The great archpapist learned curio', for manuscript details of which see A. F. Marotti, *Manuscript Circulation and the English Renaissance Lyric*, Chicago, 1996, p. 85 (with footnotes).

enquiry into the evanescent and Protean aspects of Howard and of their various accommodations, but biography (however uncharitable a pursuit) begins at home.

The myth of Northampton started early, but there was much more to Howard than 'Northampton', and any consideration of Howard must, in fact, start, as he often did himself, from a consideration of his clan.[8] After all, the family that is persecuted together, stays together. Even in one of Howard's darker periods, the early 1590s, he was emboldened to intervene with Matthew Hutton on behalf of his niece; the tangible benefit to Howard himself himself is hard to see.[9] Such an act was, of course, only selfless to the extent that the promotion of the Howard line was not also an act of self-promotion; still, hindsight is often cynical, since historians have the leisure to see connections that may not have been apparent at the time. Certainly, Howard as 'the Earl of Northampton' found a new life, with less trace of family clannishness: by the time that Howard had achieved his dream of power, wealth and influence, in his most inward chamber, he kept portraits of Mary, Queen of Scots, and of James I, mother and son, but the concerns of the Jacobean period should not be too far retrojected into the Elizabethan.[10] Since Howard never married – indeed, was probably homosexual – he had little personal outlet for such emotions of respect and love that he had.[11] These tender feelings, the reader should be warned, were

---

[8] Even a passage from what sounds like an 'official' biographical notice from the early seventeenth century, the period of Howard's great power and wealth, connects him with his family's misfortunes: BL Additional MS 6928, f. 285^r: '[t]his Lord in his youth being very studious and gyven to the knowledge of good letters, became for his great Learning and eloquence in the Greek and Latin tongues the Rhetoricke Reader in the University of Cambridge. Afterwards throughe his brothers misfortunes and some other disasters happening in that noble house; hee lived for the most of Queene Elizabeths dayes as a man obscured …'.

[9] King's College Archive, Cambridge, Miscellaneous Collections 18/3.

[10] So much, at least, is suggested by perusal of Howard's will: see E. P. Shipley, 'An Inventory of the Effects of Henry Howard KG, Earl of Northampton, taken on his death in 1614, together with a transcript of his will', *Archaeologia*, 42, 1869, pp. 347–78. A warning note: inventories were prepared by notaries with an interest in saleability and should be interpreted accordingly.

[11] A comment from the reader's report should be reproduced here: 'Surely in an earlier generation he would have become an important churchman; he is a bit stranded on the Reformation beach which in any case abandoned clerical celibacy'. Howard was always drawn to youthful glamorous courtiers, perhaps attempts to repossess the legacy of his father. His sexual leanings would also help to explain his dominance of the bedroom court of James I. There is no documentary evidence at all for any sexual encounters between Howard and any of his servants or other associates (contrast the numerous com-

ones that very few of Howard's contemporaries would have ascribed to the man they knew as 'the most arrant villain that lived'.[12]

***

Lord Henry Howard was a scholar influenced by humanism and obsessed simultaneously by the glamour of rank and the court. We, by contrast, must be careful to separate the courtly and the humanist and not assume that they necessarily go together. We shall see that the interplay between the scholarly and the political is reflected in different ways at different times, though it is fair to say that the desire for temporal power remained a constant throughout the years of Elizabeth's reign. Indeed, the history of his own family was enough to generate his obsession with the struggle for place.

Henry Howard, later Earl of Surrey, was born in 1517 in Hunsdon, Hertfordshire. Without him and the myth that was woven around his death, much in the cultural history of Elizabeth's reign, and beyond, would look very different. Introducer, with Sir Thomas Wyatt, into English of the sonnet and blank verse, Surrey's most important gift to posterity was his self-image: a sensitive and sometimes brooding poet who was nonetheless a man of arms and action, a soldier steeped in a nobility which opposed itself to royal absolutism. Above all, Surrey possessed a haughty demeanour of almost disturbing self-assertion. Without Surrey, there would have been no Sidney. Without the Earl of Surrey, there would have been no Earl of Essex. The splendour which burns itself out in a glorious but tragically short life: this, for the generation of Elizabeth, was what Surrey meant. How different was the phlegmatic survivor his second son was to become. That son, however, did resurrect an interest in military matters, though at a theoretical level, under James I.[13] It also explains some of what attracted him, in the 1590s, to the 'arms and letters' culture of male nobility of the incandescent Essex.

---

plaints of rape made against the Earl of Oxford), and perhaps one should conclude that he was celibate; this in turn might explain some of the prurience he was to evince about the sexual pecadilloes of others. If one follows Alan Stewart (in his *Close Readers: Humanism and Sodomy in Early Modern England*, Princeton, 1997), one would wish to push the implications of the fact that Howard (not a figure treated by Stewart) possessed two sets of chairs and desks in his most intimate withdrawing chamber (evidence taken from his will: see n. 10 above), thereby suggesting the 'homosocial' or 'transactional' character of Howard's private space.

[12] The phrase is imputed to Oxford by Howard at BL Cotton MS, Titus C vi f. 8ᵛ. For an alternative rendition of the phrase, see TNA: PRO SP12/151/46 'the rankest villain that ever lived'. At Howard's funeral, one observer commented sourly: 'sic transit gloria mundi' (so Linda Levy Peck, 'The Mentality of a Jacobean Grandee', in *The Mental World of the Jacobean Court*, Cambridge, 1998, pp. 148–68, at 168).

[13] A fact that is underemphasized by Linda Levy Peck's sympathetic account of Howard as

Surrey was his father's first-born son from his marriage to Lady Elizabeth Stafford, daughter of the duke of Buckingham. He was brought up at Windsor alongside Henry Fitzroy, illegitimate son of Henry VIII. The title of Earl of Surrey was conferred on him in 1524, on the death of his grandfather. A state visit to the court of Francis I in the same year saw him accompany Anne Boleyn, the king and the duke of Richmond, sharpening further his diplomatic and linguistic skills. In 1536, Henry Fitzroy died and Surrey aided his father in putting down the Pilgrimage of Grace. In the meantime the University of Cambridge had appointed him steward. Further war service lay ahead in Scotland in 1542, again with his father, and in 1543 in Flanders on the side of Charles V, helping him acquire control of the Netherlands.

The new style of Henry VIII's political culture of court contained many aspects that were favourable to Surrey.[14] The emphasis on youth, accomplishments and humanist prowess played to Surrey's strengths. Partially, his problem was the added element of military achievement, rendering him dangerous, capable of attracting a following – in other words, a threat.[15] In 1544 he was wounded in the siege of Montreuil, but recovered to lead the garrison of Boulogne in the next two years. Military prowess could not, however, erase the taint of the flighty Catherine Howard at court, nor could it rival the ascendancy of the Seymours. Like his second son, Surrey became a guest of the Fleet. Dynastic ambitions in the shape of quartering his own family arms with those of the King compounded his crimes. His fall could easily in retrospect have been seen as part of some confessional plot, since Stephen Gardiner had simultaneously chosen to defy the King over a matter of episcopal lands, which obstinacy cost him his place on the council of

---

competent administrator in her outstanding biography, *Northampton: Patronage and Power at the Court of James I*. Peck's drive to reassess the discourse of 'corrupt' bureaucracy at the Jacobean court fails to give enough importance to the backward-looking justifications for that power advanced by at least some of the older nobility of the period. Indeed, the intellectual interest in works of war was considerable: good evidence of this is the prevalence of duelling literature and the number of books on warfare that have been identified as belonging to Howard by Peck, 'Mentality'.

[14] A rather extreme view of this 'new style', explaining nearly everything in generational and personality terms, runs through David Starkey, *The Reign of Henry VIII: Politics and Personalities*, London, 1985. More nuanced is J. J. Scarisbrick, *Henry VIII*, New Haven, 1968. For an excellent general account of Surrey, see William Sessions, *Henry Howard: Poet Earl of Surrey. A Life*, Oxford, 1999 – this masterly biography is both elegantly written and of exacting standards of scholarship.

[15] Certainly, one interpreter fifty years later thought so. See Thomas Nashe's portrait of Surrey as above all a noble knight, skilled in the use of weapons: T. Nashe, *The Unfortunate Traveller*, London, 1968, p. 38.

protective ministers that was to reign during Edward's minority.[16] Henry Howard, Earl of Surrey, was beheaded on the scaffold at Tower Hill on 18 January 1547.[17] We have his scholarly son's testimony that the lyric, 'These stormes are past, theses cloudes are overblowen', was the last poem he ever wrote. Howard was to recall these lines forty years later in an address to Queen Elizabeth:

> Therefore I confesse with David in his thankfull sonet after long experience which made his understanding ripe, and with my father in the last thing that he wrote before his end which made his iudgme[n]t cleere: Bonum est mihi quod humiliasti me.[18]

His son Henry was born on 25 February 1540, at the village of Shottesham, in the hundred of Henstead, Norfolk, two years after his elder brother, Thomas.[19] It was a small village, forming part of the Howard

---

[16] Starkey, *The Reign of Henry VIII*, pp. 156–67, is led into a conspiracy theory. On Gardiner, see the material in *The Letters of Stephen Gardiner*, ed. J. A. Muller, London, 1933, pp. 246–9.

[17] See Peter R. Moore, 'The Heraldic Charge against the Earl of Surrey', *English Historical Review*, 116, 2001, pp. 557–83.

[18] Henry Howard, 'The Dutiful Defence of the Lawfull Regiment of Women', BL Additional MS 24652 f. 9ᵛ. The title derives from Psalm 118.71, and Howard or his scribe seems to have misquoted: 'Bonum mihi quod humiliasti me'. Howard is a writer with a particularly strong interest in structure: therefore I do not think it accidental that we have an anticipation and condensation of this phrase only a little earlier: 'I thank our blessed Lorde with Job for inrowding me under the shadow of his winges till stormes were overblowne' (ibid., 9ʳ). One recent scholar has attempted to go beyond Howard's evidence and suggest that it was actually written in the Tower of London: Peter R. Moore, 'Hamlet and Surrey's Psalm 8', *Neophilologus*, 82, 1998, pp. 487–98. Henry Howard's knowledge of his father must have been minimal, though he had an acquaintance with and perhaps appreciation of Surrey's Italianate verse: see the evidence collected by Arturo Cataneo, *L'ideale umanistico: Henry Howard, Earl of Surrey*, Bari, 1991, p. 262. William Sessions has pointed out Howard's use of his father's motto 'Sat superest' in an address to Elizabeth some forty years later at Lambeth Palace Library, MS 711, f. 20ʳ: Sessions, *Henry Howard*, p. 4 n. 3 (and for the classical ancestry of the phrase, see p. 3).

[19] This date is the one recorded by Howard himself on the commemorative stone of his hospital in Greenwich from 1613. The place is confirmed by Howard's will (see the transcript in Shipley, 'An Inventory', pp. 347–78); while the exact location of his birth is uncertain, there is a local tradition, impossible to confirm, which identifies it as the Tudor farmhouse that adjoins the currently named 'Northampton Lodge'. Details of Henry Howard's birth are not preserved but probably the rituals observed would not be quite as elaborate as those for a royal birth (for which, see 'The Ryalle Booke', ed. F. Grose, in *The Antiquarian Repertory*, London, 4 vols, 1807–1809, I, pp. 296–341; and for a splendidly vivid recreation of these rituals in the context of the birth of Elizabeth I, see D. Starkey, *Elizabeth*, London, 2000, pp. 1–5, a work to which I owe the reference to 'The Ryalle Booke'). Other accounts of christening worth comparing include, above all, TNA: PRO SP12/151/46, ff. 57–59ᵛ (the daughter of Lord Russell, son and heir of the Earl of Bedford); then BL Additional MS 45716 A ff. 112–15 (Prince, later King Edward VI); BL

Birth, Education and First Years at Cambridge

estates. No record remains of his christening, but godparents would have had to be chosen, and they were usually people of greater influence than the parents. Often children were named after their godparents, just as the son of Charles V was honoured with a godchild named Philip Sidney as part of the Sidney–Dudley attempt to weld themselves to the Spanish power. Henry Howard was given the same name as the ruling monarch and so may have had royal godparents.[20] We do not know whether his father also cast a horoscope for Henry as he had done for his first-born, but in most other respects the birth is likely to have been the same.[21] His mother, Frances de Vere Howard, was the daughter of John, fifteenth Earl of Oxford, a family to whom the Howards had long been connected. She was brought up in Castle Hedingham in Essex until her marriage to Surrey in 1532.[22] She produced several siblings for the young Henry. The eldest sister was named Jane and married into the Neville family: beyond her enthusiasm for the rising of the Northern Earls, little is known about

---

Lansdowne MS 860, f. 298 (Princess, later Queen Mary) and BL Cotton MS, Julius B xii f. 19^v (Prince Arthur, Henry VII's firstborn). These accounts should be supplemented with the mass of material on midwifery contained in D. Cressy, *Birth, Marriage, Death: Ritual, Religion and the Life Cycle in Tudor and Stuart England*, Oxford, 1997: though most of his data comes from the 1580s onward, we may assume a degree of relative conservatism with regard to such practices.

[20] Thereby allowing his father the satisfaction which his first-born had denied him, since Thomas had been born premature and hence too soon for Henry VIII to make it to the christening: LP 13.1.504. In the autumn of 1575, Queen Elizabeth had promised to be the godmother to the daughter of Lord Russell, whose name was also to be Elizabeth (BL Hargrave MS 497, f. 57^r); for two further examples of identical names of godparent and child, see David N. Durant, *Bess of Hardwick: Portrait of an Elizabethan Dynast*, London, 1999, pp. 15 and 20). Naming was usually political among the ruling classes of sixteenth-century Europe: see, e.g., the remarks of Paula Sutter Fichter, *Emperor Maximilian II*, New Haven, 2001, p. 5.

[21] One might think it likely that a Continental astrologer would have been called upon in the household of Surrey, although it may be that that fashion had to be kickstarted by Cardano's position a few years later (see A. Grafton, *Cardano's Cosmos*, London, 1999); certainly, the astrologers of the famous court of Henry VII were not English: see *Letters and Papers Illustrative of the reigns of Richard III and Henry VII*, ed. S. Gardiner, 2 vols, London, 1861–1863, II. 318. Norfolk's horoscope: BL MS Lat. 4789 f. 351^r–353^v. The horoscope does not, however, date from the time of his birth, as Keith Thomas, *Religion and the Decline of Magic*, London, 1987, p. 344, assumes; unless Norfolk's christening was like that of Sleeping Beauty, there can be little chance that the section 'de morte violenta' was contemporary! Retrospective casting of horoscopes was not unknown: see the one constructed for Sir Philip Sidney in 1570, some twenty-four years after his birth: see James Osborne, *Young Philip Sidney, 1572-1577*, New Haven and London, 1972, pp. 517–22.

[22] For details, see *DNB* sub nomine and Sessions, *Henry Howard*, pp. 202–4. Her son, Henry, never once mentions her. Perhaps the fact that she married again is relevant (to one Thomas Steyning, of Woodbridge, to whom she bore children; they lived three miles away from Framlingham at Earl Soham Lodge).

her.[23] The second sister, to whom Henry became devoted, was named Katherine. A woman of haughty demeanour and noble pastimes, she was the dedicatee of Howard's philosophical manuscript; it must have had something to do with her own interests, since had Henry been interested in favour and patronage alone, he would probably have found a more powerful and influential dedicatee than the wife of Henry, Lord Berkeley. Her educational accomplishments in Latin, Greek, Italian, French and Spanish are praised in one of the family manuscripts.[24] Interestingly (in view of the dedication) it is recorded that she was given various mathematical instruments by Queen Elizabeth, 'in which she muche delighted'. Affection, however, may be explanation enough.[25] Just like her brother she had an enthusiasm for the lute, and the chief talent was in singing, though after the execution of Norfolk she sang no more.[26] She was interested in that most traditional of noble pursuits, falconry, just at the time when it was beginning to be a rarer pastime in England.[27] Her husband's profligate ways with

---

[23] She was buried on 30 June 1593, at Kenninghall, where she had remained under house arrest (though there is a letter from her to Cecil, thanking him for having obtained for her the lease of 'Branspeth' [i.e., Brancpeth] Park, part of the confiscated Neville estates around Durham, presumably for its monetary value, rather than to exercise any ius spatiandi (BL Lansdowne MS 18, f. 191) after her brother Thomas, Duke of Norfolk, was executed and after her husband (to whom there is one letter extant, BL Additional MS 46367 ff. 35ᵛ–36ᵛ) had fled somewhat unheroically to the Low Countries, where he died on 16 November 1601 at Nieuwpoort).

[24] See *The Berkeley Manuscripts: The Lives of the Berkeleys with a Description of the Hundred of Berkeley*, ed. J. Smith, 3 vols, Gloucester, 1883–1885, II, pp. 245–9.

[25] See Katherine Duncan-Jones, *Sir Philip Sidney: Courtier Poet*, 1991, p. 74. The preface to the manuscript is at pains to suggest that 'AFFECTION' is indeed the only motivation: BLO Bodley MS 616, ff. 2–10. Contrast Lawrence Stone, *Fortune and Family: Studies in Aristocratic Finance in the Sixteenth and Seventeenth Centuries*, Oxford, 1973, pp. 244–9, for the suggestion that by the end of his life, Howard attempted to get the Berkeleys to buy the wardship of her son, even though they had already obtained this legal privilege.

[26] One of the letters to Michael Hickes that Howard writes from Trinity Hall (BL Lansdowne MS 109, f. 51ʳ) asks about instruction from a London master in the lute. For a recent study of the importance of music to sixteenth-century aristocratic culture, see Stefano Lorenzetti, *Musica e identità nobilare nell'Italia del rinascimento*, Florence, 2002, esp. pp. 65–118 and 101, where Lorenzetti cites Hoby's translation of *Il cortegiano* (Baldassare Castiglione, *The Book of the Courtier*, ed. W. H. D. Rouse, London, 1959, p. 101): 'Me thinke ... pricksong is a faire musicke, so it be done upon the booke surely and after a good sorte. But to sing to the lute is much better, because all the sweetnes consisteth in one alone, and a man is much more heedfull and understandeth better the feat manner and the aire or veyne of it, when the eares are not busied in hearing any more than one voice.'

[27] See R. Grassby, 'The Decline of Falconry in Early Modern England', *Past and Present*, 157, 1997, pp. 37–62. See also the entertaining redaction of those parts of the material collected by John Smith, a clerk to the Berkeley family, dealing with Lady Berkeley's falconry and archery in G. A. Hansard, *The Book of Archery*, London, 1842, ch. 3: 'Female Archery'.

money did not prevent her giving her scholarly brother an allowance of 200 pounds sterling a year, while allowing herself the maintenance sum of 300. It was the endebtedness of the family that forced the Berkeleys to undertake a progress of poverty throughout the greater part of the 1560s, during some of which time she resided with the duke of Norfolk. Although Howard is not mentioned among the many mourners at her funeral at Coventry in 1596, he did name two of her servants as the executors of his own will. Much less is known of the youngest sister Margaret, who married Lord Scrope, Warden of the West Marches, and who died in obscurity in 1592.[28]

The association of Norfolk, the Howards and Catholicism may be deep-seated in the popular mind, but the importance of the eastern counties in the development of the English Reformation has recently received fresh emphasis.[29] The polarization that was to be felt with increasing acuity as the century wore on created, no doubt, strains on the ground among the men and women of the humbler sort across East Anglia. In the great houses of the conservative nobility, however, things were slower to change. In any case, though Howard's childhood was disrupted several times, few of these disruptions had much obvious link with confessional allegiance; they were rather lessons for the young Howard in the choice of enemies and in cautious dealing. He passed his earliest years in Kenninghall Palace, a house built in 1525 by his grandfather to rival the dwellings of Cardinal Wolsey.[30] The fondness for architectural conceit which was to dominate Elizabethan building practice among the nobility found an early adherent in the third duke, who

---

[28] Born January 1543 Ashwell, Shropshire; baptized 30 January, Lambeth, London. Died 17 March Carlisle, Cumberland; buried 8 June, Wensley, Lancashire. Married Henry Scrope (9th Baron of Bolton, before 1566).

[29] Diarmaid MacCulloch has noted that the 'further east one goes, the more positive enthusiasm for the new religion one finds' in his *Thomas Cranmer*, London, 1998, pp. 432–3. In contrast with the traditional historiography (e.g. C. Read, *Mr. Secretary Cecil and Queen Elizabeth*, London, 1955, p. 54, says that the rebellion was 'apparently without religious coloration') that viewed Kett's Norfolk rebellion in 1549 as one fuelled by social and economic concerns, see now the arguments of Nicholas Tyacke, 'Introduction' to his *England's Long Reformation 1500–1800*, London, 1998, pp. 1–32, at 14–15; note also the comments on Ipswich of Andrew Pettegree, 'Nicodemism and the English Reformation', in his *Marian Protestantism: Six Studies*, Aldershot, 1996, pp. 86–117, at 110–11, with further bibliography. The most recent contribution to this revisionist picture is Karl Grunther and Ethan H. Shagan, 'Protestant Radicalism and Political Thought in the Reign of Henry VIII', *Past and Present*, 196, 2007, pp. 35–74.

[30] On the Third Duke of Norfolk, see David M. Head, *The Ebbs and Flows of Fortune: The Life of Thomas Howard, Third Duke of Norfolk*, Athens: OH and London, 1995.

constructed his palace around a central H.[31] The cross-bar of this letter divided the two living areas, Shelfhanger and Ewery. It was in Ewery that Surrey and his children lived. Surrey's rooms were on the first floor. The chapel was nearby and had a large complement of staff, including no fewer than six domestic chaplains.[32] Though a room called 'the old nursery' existed in Kenninghall, it is recorded as a place for their grandfather's clothes. More probably they passed their time quartered with their parents. By Henry's seventh year he had been moved into a richly decorated room with his brother, adjacent to his father's suite, while the girls were placed downstairs, next to the kitchen.

Henry Howard's father had an ambitious building programme, and it is safe to assume that the family, like others, would have spent only a portion of its time at Kenninghall Palace.[33] Nobles, and their sons, had to maintain their social credit through the expected avenues of publicity. It is likely, therefore, that had his father not fallen out of favour with both Henry VIII and Edward VI's protectors, Howard would have entered the service of the royal court. But the whiff of suspicion, combined with the reduced opportunities for service available under a ten-year-old king, meant that he probably remained in the private sphere in the marches of Norfolk for a long time.

Since there is no evidence that Howard went to a particular school, we are unable to recover a particular set curriculum. We do, however, know his tutors. Henry, like his brother and sisters, was educated successively by Hadrianus Junius, John Foxe and John White, the last of whom may have left some impact on his young charge, at least as far as his religion was concerned: Henry's later confessional orientation was not obvious at this stage in his family's history.[34] Hadrianus Junius, or Adriaen de Jonghe, was a Low

---

[31] See Timothy Mowl, *Elizabethan and Jacobean Style*, London, 1993, p. 106: 'Perversities of applied geometry are commonplace ... Sir Thomas Tresham's New Bield at Lyveden, Northamptonshire was primarily intended to demonstrate Christ's crucifixion by its cross shape and his passion by its metopes of Judas' money bag'. Further instructive examples may be found in M. Airs, *The Tudor and Jacobean Country House*, London, 1995, pp. 5–15.

[32] These details are taken from TNA: PRO LR 2/115 and 2/117, cited by Neville Williams, *Thomas Howard, Fourth Duke of Norfolk*, London, 1964, pp. 3–7, who has an imaginative recreation of this information.

[33] Other possibilities included: Mount Surrey, a Renaissance mansion on the ruins of St Leonard's Priory, destroyed by Kett's men in the rebellion, returned to the Howard line by the Crown in 1562 (see Walter Rye, 'Surrey House and St. Leonard's Priory, Norwich', *Norfolk Archaeology*, 15, 1903–4, pp. 194–5); Surrey House, a town house on the north side of Great Newgate Street; the manor house at Thetford, Castle Rising on the Wash and Framlingham Castle in Suffolk (see Williams, *Thomas Howard*, p. 262 n. 9).

[34] After all, Thomas Howard, fourth Duke of Norfolk, and Henry Howard, Viscount Bindon, though far from zealots, were both Protestant.

Birth, Education and First Years at Cambridge

Countries humanist whose interests extended to emblems and medicine, as well as the more traditional pursuits of epistolography and poetry. He had already been to England in 1544, when Surrey's father appointed him as tutor to his grandchildren.[35] Although nothing survives from these years apart from some joint Latin compositions to their father, we do not have to look very far either in time or space to discover the content of a 'deluxe humanist education'.[36] Although we possess both essays and theological compilations in Latin and Greek from the hand of King Edward VI, in addition to his *Chronicle*,[37] these compilations have been all but unstudied.[38] Consisting of brief essays on various sentential themes, they are predominantly exercises both in the marshalling of arguments and in style.[39] At one point he outlines a speech on the faculties of man:

---

[35] Junius (1511–75) resided in England from 1544 to 1554. He was salaried by Surrey and lodged in Kenninghall; further details in J. A. Van Dorsten, *The Radical Arts*, Leiden, 1970, pp. 130–4; M. Aston, *The King's Bedpost*, Cambridge, 1993, pp. 176–84 and Dirk Van Miert, 'The Religious Beliefs of Hadrianus Junius (1511–1575)' in *Acta Conventus Neolatini Cantabrigiensis, Proceedings of the Eleventh International Congress of Neo-Latin Studies*, ed. R. Schnur, Tempe: AZ, 2003, pp. 583–94. One unnoticed detail: Thomas Howard paid his respects to his old teacher by desiring that his own son should be taught from Junius' works (that, at least, is my reading of an undated letter in Hadrianus Junius, *Epistolae*, Dordrecht: Vincentius Cairnax, 1652 (incorrectly stated as 1552), p. 146: 'Proinde quum intelexissem olim uti te velle mea opera in erudiendo filio').

[36] The phrase is that of Diarmaid MacCulloch, *The Tudor Church Militant*, London, 2000, p. 34. There is an English redaction of the children's joint Latin letter at *LP* 21.1.146. It is slightly peculiar that the third Duke of Norfolk, on writing to defend himself against charges of treasonable behaviour, refers (in the context of dynastic ambitions) to grandchildren, but gets the number wrong (BL Cotton MS B I f. 94^v): 'and whereas my son of Surrey has a son and divers daughters …'. Why has Henry been omitted? This would be explained by the relative unimportance in this context of second sons. For the additional moral and 'noble' input into Henry's educational regime, see Louis B. Wright, *Advice to a Son: Precepts of Lord Burghley, Sir Walter Raleigh, and Francis Osborne*, Ithaca: NY, 1962, and Stephen Clucas and Gordon Batho, *The Wizard Earl's Advices to His Son*, The Roxburghe Club, 2002.

[37] BL Additional MS 2724, ff. 2–222 and Edward VI, *Chronicle*, ed. W. K. Jordan, London, 1966.

[38] T. W. Baldwin, *Shakesperes Small Latine and Lesse Greek*, Chicago, 2 vols, 1944, II, pp. 230–4,5 is the standard work. Peter Mack, *Elizabethan Rhetoric*, Cambridge, 2002, pp. 26–32, uses similar examples. For further discussion of the role of grammar in Howard's education, see pp. 59–78.

[39] For example, BL Additional MS 2724, f. 104^r, contains the phrase *sed non victam multis firmis certisque argumentis adversari*, with *certis* crossed out and replaced by the less monotonous (after the previous equally dissyllabic 'firmis') *validis*. Other corrections (presumably by his tutor) on the same page include mistakes over the gerund and a replacement of the phrase *cum igitur* with *cum itaque*. Not all the work has been corrected: for example, f. 156 contains σοματος for σωματος.

Every creature, and above all man (who is endowed with reason) seeks out knowledge and understanding of all things which bring him profit. This is clear from all the arts, Geometry, Music, Mathematics, Dialectic and many others. Since this is the case, all the more does he desire knowledge of those things which he knows are of most use to him: the parts of the body, the passions of the soul and virtues of the mind.[40]

This is similar to chreia developments: general truth, confirmation, elaboration.[41] It could also be described as an exercise in 'a fortiori' argumentation. The periods are not careful enough to suggest that this is predominantly a stylistic exercise. In the margin the two partes orationis *exordium* and then *narratio* and *exempla* are outlined: the other parts are not mentioned, whether deliberately or not, however, it is impossible to say.[42] In other places, there are simply lists of pros and cons ready for 'confirmatio' and 'refutatio' sections of persuasive discourse.[43] The subject matter ranges widely from elementary natural philosophy to whether humans can live without sin.[44] Howard's basic education, like that of Edward, would have been an education that attempted to make him a structured organizer of common themes, capable of considerable elaboration.

Beyond such speculative retrojections, little is known with certainty about these dark years of Howard's life at all.[45] It should suffice to say that the sudden decline in the fortunes of the Howard clan and the subsequent

---

[40] Ibid., f. 112ʳ: 'Cum unumquodque animal, praecipue homo qui rationis est particeps, appetat omnium rerum quae aliquid emolumentum afferunt, cognitionem et scientiam (quod quidem apparet ex omnibus artibus, ut Geometria, Musica, Arithmetica, Dialectica, atque aliis compluribus) tum maxime desiderat earum rerum, quas scit sibi maxime profuturas, ut membrorum corpus, affectuum animi, & virtutum mentis.'

[41] Mack, *Elizabethan Rhetoric*, p. 35 makes a similar point about the usage of the chreia in another passage of the orations.

[42] BL Additional MS 2724, f. 214ʳ contains a schematic treatment of 'rationes. amor maior causa obedientiae quam timor', which is divided up into *partes orationis* and figures of thought/speech: 'Exordium ab utilitate questionis. Enarratio meae sententiae. Confirmatio per uxoris amorem. timor deterret a malo, non hortatur ad bonum. quid amor fecerit in Alexandro Severo, quod timor in Heliogabalo. Tyrannorum exitus. quid amor in Themistocle, Epamonida, scipione, Metello Cicerone et c. Confutatio. 1 rat. Bruta animantia timent, non amant. Nego 2 sunt gradus amoris. Quid tum. 3. Leges sancita indicant metum vehementiorem esse amorem. 4 Metus trahit nolentes/ 1 Tyrannis obeditur magis amoris cause quam/ sed non bonis regibus/ 2 amor non satis potest/ fateor sed timor non sufficit, neutrum amor praestantior.'

[43] E.g., ibid., f. 214: 'Ευδαιμονια θεορητικη βελτιων της πρακτικης'.

[44] Ibid., ff. 212ʳ⁻ᵛ and 222ᵛ respectively.

[45] For an interesting conspectus of related (sometimes distantly so) material on childhood and youth in this period, see Ilana Krausman Ben-Amos, *Adolescence and Youth in Early Modern England*, New Haven, 1994.

watchful eye kept over them must have marked Howard very significantly. In 1546 his mother was interrogated at Kenninghall: an index of the coming troubles.[46] By the time that disaster struck the family, only the fortunate accident of the king's death in the New Year prevented the execution warrant for Thomas Howard, Surrey's father, from being signed. After Surrey's execution, Howard and his siblings were not allowed to remain at Kenninghall. They were removed to Reigate, at what had once been Reigate Priory (granted to Howard's grandfather by Henry VIII), where the duchess of Richmond resided when she was not in Mountjoy House in London, and she now took control of the children.[47] Here Howard remained under the tutelage of John Foxe until 1553. In 1552, Edward VI had granted an annuity of 100 pounds a year to aid the duchess with the costs of the children's education, understandable given the children's own limited resources.[48] Though it is obvious that Foxe will have continued the humanist education that Junius started (after all, he wrote a Latin grammar, of which, alas, only one page survives), he did not restrict himself to these studies.[49] He took the children on jaunts out of town to other parts of the Howard family estates.[50] Howard did not imbibe his second tutor's Protestant doctrine, and we can perhaps advert to Howard's age (and contrast the Protestantism of his elder brother).

---

[46] While Sir Richard Southwell, Wymond Carew and John Gate had gone through Frances de Vere's 'coffers and closet', and sent off assorted thugs to ransack Surrey's other residences in Norfolk and Suffolk, 'not forgetting Elizabeth Holland's [Surrey's mistress] house, newly made, in Suffolk, which is thought to be well furnished', we learn that Henry Howard and the rest of his siblings were guarded in their nursery, 'with certain women attending them': *LP* 21.2.548.

[47] For further details on the Duchess of Richmond, see Beverley A. Murphy, *Bastard Prince: The Lost Son of Henry VIII*, Thrupp, 2001, pp. 232–41.

[48] So *DNB*.

[49] The page of Foxe's Latin grammar: BL Lansdowne MS 891, f. 90 (and, more broadly, see John G. Rechtien, 'John Foxe's Comprehensive Collection of Commonplaces', *Sixteenth Century Journal*, 1978, pp. 82–9). We cannot place much faith in our sources for some aspects of Foxe's tuition: see the providential account of how Foxe came to be appointed by the Duchess of Richmond by Simeon Foxe, the martyrologist's son, in BL Lansdowne MS 388, ff. 14–15 (a preposterous-sounding invention). Since we hear no more, however, about any other tutors, I shall assume Howard and his siblings were under the Duchess of Richmond's control for the entire period 1547–1553.

[50] Or rather we have evidence that he did this at least once: Bartholomew Brewton, a rogue maritime trader, moored his boat of looted goods off Lulworth, and Foxe went aboard and then 'looked after' a parcel of valuable fabrics for Brewton: so Neville Williams, *Captains Outrageous: Seven Centuries of Piracy*, London, 1961, pp. 54–5. Unfortunately, Williams does not give a precise source for this reference and, when he retells this story three years later in his biography of Thomas Howard, he says that both Thomas and Henry Howard were involved, whereas he only mentions the elder brother in his original version.

The change of religion that came with the change of monarch a few years later meant another change of tutor for the Howard children.[51] As soon as Queen Mary was enthroned in 1553, John White, Bishop of London, was appointed to attend to their educational needs, and when in 1556 White was elevated to the see of Winchester, it is thought that Howard accompanied him.[52] There is no record of how this came about, and perhaps it was Mary herself who took this decision, as part of a review of the position of the Howards. To judge from the article in the *DNB*, John White was a rather uninteresting divine.[53] It is, accordingly, something of a surprise to open his *Diacosio-Martyrion*.[54] This work was written to refute Peter Martyr's work on the Eucharist. This is no ordinary mid-sixteenth-century defence of transubstantiation, however. Here the reader finds a range of patristic and scholastic and humanist authors, from each of whom White has extracted a text and transformed it into a poem. The metres are varied, and include elegiac couplets, hexameters and several Horatian lyric schemata.[55] It belongs, in other words, to that humanist tradition of the reformatting of prescriptive works to suit a wider variety of published contexts for teaching. The testimonia are arranged historically. Even the two parliaments of Henry VIII and Edward VI are included as authorities for White's basic proposition.[56] The parliamentary testimonia of England are, however, given particular importance since they are placed at the end of the book. They are, as it were, the last word in transubstantiation. The impact of this committed and humanist Catholic upon the adolescent Howard, an impact that may be described as both religious and humanist, should not be underestimated (even if by the time of White's removal as tutor Howard was still only eighteen). Howard's future independent reli-

---

[51] It is worth mentioning that both the girls and boys were the object of this education: see *The Poems of Henry Howard Earl of Surrey and of Sir Thomas Wyatt the Elder*, ed. G. F. Nott, 2 vols, New York, 1965, I, pp. 171–2.

[52] *ODNB* sub nomine, and repeated by, e.g., Alan Nelson, *Monstrous Adversary: The Life of Edward de Vere, Seventeenth Earl of Oxford*, Liverpool, 2003, p. 54.

[53] *ODNB* sub nomine; see also BL Lansdowne MS 980, f. 294, for a very brief biographical sketch by a near-contemporary and his comments (noted by Lucy Wooding, *Rethinking Catholicism in Reformation England*, Oxford, 2000, p. 139) on the priesthood in relation to the prince at BL Cotton MS, Vespasian D xviii f. 94; for rotographs from one of his letters to Queen Mary written at the time of his tuition of Howard, see BL Supplement to MSS IV (e).

[54] John White, *Diacosio-Martyrion id est...*, London: Cuthbert Cale, 1553.

[55] The work is highly Classicizing, with pagan terminology for Christian implements and functionaries. Note also that, at first blush, there are no crass metrical errors in the Horatian lyrics.

[56] White, *Diacosio-Martyrion*, sigs O2^v–O7^r.

gious streak was not matched by any great improvement in his financial autonomy: the only bequest that his grandfather, the third duke, gave him on his death in 1554 was Tendring Hall.[57]

***

The university of which Henry Howard was to become chancellor in 1612 was not innocent of previous connections with his family.[58] Immediately after his grandfather, Thomas Howard, third Duke of Norfolk, was released from captivity in 1553, he resumed his role as High Steward of the University of Cambridge, just as Stephen Gardiner was reinstated as Chancellor.[59] With Mary's death, and the subsequent removal of John White as Howard's tutor, a private act was passed which restored Howard, and others of his family, to the official ranks of the nobility.[60] At this point, unfortunately, another of the many gaps in our knowledge of Howard's movements opens up. Despite some uncertainty as to the date of his first residence in Cambridge, we should allow him two years of freedom from formal study between 1558 and 1560: a more likely period is five years. We cannot even be certain of his location, but East Anglia, the location of the bulk of the Howard estates, seems likely.[61] This dark period comes to an end, though briefly, with the decision of Elizabeth, or at least at her expense, as traditionally reported, to send Howard to Cambridge, specifically to King's.[62] It seems proper, against some recent historiography, to

---

[57] TNA: PRO Prob 11/37/14.
[58] Since Henry VIII, the position had been filled by a politician: see *A History of the University of Cambridge. Volume II: 1546–1750*, ed. Victor Morgan, Cambridge, 2004, p. 93.
[59] A. C. F. Beales, *Education Under Penalty: English Catholic Education from the Reformation to the Fall of James II*, Oxford, 1963, p. 22. John Dudley, Duke of Northumberland, had taken control of these offices under Edward VI.
[60] 1Eliz1n39 'An Act for the Restitution in Blood of Henry Howard, Jane Howard, and Katherine Wife to the Lord Barkley'.
[61] For the possibility of a roving base for Howard, see my earlier comments on his sister Katherine's peregrinations (as I have said earlier, Howard's mother was – at least – in Shropshire in 1543). It is reasonable to assume further private tuition, although I have found no records to indicate from whom that might have come: the search for archival material is hampered by our ignorance as to Howard's location.
[62] The tradition is mentioned in *ODNB* sub nomine. I have not been able to trace its origin, but it would appear to run counter to Howard's comment in 'Dutiful Defence', BL Additional MS 24652, f. 7ᵛ: 'I may presume to my assured comfort to take notice of your Majesties most gracious and princely care of my bringing up, during the first five yeares of your raigne [i.e. until 1563]. I was then mainteyned only at your chardge, enstructed by your appointment, and trained in your sight, at which time the tener shelles of childehood were seased with so strong a sent of your perfections, as neither can bee worne a away by tract of time, nor diminished by force of any accident. After my return from the universi-

suggest that Howard was sent to a college rather than a particular tutor.[63] This is suggested partly because its master was of uncertain relation to the queen and William Cecil's own religious position, and partly because of the obvious appropriateness of sending the young aristocrat to an institution such as the recently founded King's.

By the mid-sixteenth century, King's was a grand college. One of the more notable developments in the university from the end of the fifteenth century was the gradual increase in commoners.[64] At the time of Queen Elizabeth's visit in 1564, Howard is described as one of nine 'pensioners or commoners' in King's.[65] The fellow-commoners were not descendants of the medieval *commensales* in anything other than name. While the latter category might include the precursors of the pensioners of Renaissance Oxford and Cambridge, the fellow-commoners were at this time wealthy young boys who paid their own expenses for the communal life of college. They had a good deal of contact with the fellowship. Areas for such socializing were, however, restricted: King's had limited space, and there were strict prohibitions on the extent to which a pupil could wander round town outside of the college gates, with the gates being locked at night.[66] Indeed, there was a generalized concern that too much socializing with the wrong sort of person would have disastrous effects on the more well-born student.[67] Howard may

tie though I was but lately crept or rather swept out of the ruynes of my howse your Majestie most graciouslie admitted me to the kissing of your sacred hand, you regarded mee with pitie & relieved me with favour.' The question here is: what is the force of the word 'then' in the second sentence of this quotation? I will assume its meaning is to refer back to the years 1558–63, rather than referring to some point in a future sequence. In other words, Howard was not supported by the queen at Cambridge after 1563.

[63] J. Twigg, *A History of Queens' College*, Woodbridge, 1987, p. 91.
[64] Comparative material on the relationship between scholars and commoners at Corpus Christi, Oxford, in James McConica, 'The Collegiate Society', *History of the University of Oxford*, III (hereafter *HUO*), pp. 669–75. See also Victor Morgan, 'Cambridge University and "the Country"', in *The University in Society*, ed. L. Stone, 2 vols, Princeton, 1974, II, pp. 183–245. An overview is provided by H. Kearney, *Scholars and Gentleman: University and Society in Pre-Industrial Britain, 1500–1700*, London, 1970, pp. 15–45.
[65] J. Cooper, *Annals of Cambridge*, 3 vols, Cambridge, 1842–1853, II, p. 207. For rather better evidence of his having been there at the time of the Queen's visit see his own comment in BL Egerton MS 944, f. 21: 'Fateor enim memetipsum Cantabrigiae disertae Maiestatis tuae orationi cum tanta mentis auriumque voluptate interfuisse, ut mihi plane persuaderem ... Maiestatis labra imbre perfudisse Heliconico.'
[66] For these restrictions, see Pole's statutes in *A Collection of Letters, Documents, Statutes Illustrative of the History of the University of Cambridge*, ed. J. Lamb, London, 1838, pp. 260–1.
[67] See the entertaining, though far from exhaustive, roll call of poor behaviours (even including secret marriages) in *A History of the University of Cambridge. Volume II: 1546–1750*, ed. Victor Morgan, Cambridge, 2004, pp. 318–19.

Birth, Education and First Years at Cambridge

have shared rooms.[68] Since we do not know the precise date of his coming up to King's, we are unable to say whether some other person from the Howard estates, matriculating as a sizar, acted as a lower-born servant to Howard. This was a common pattern of service in early modern Cambridge. Indeed, little evidence from Howard's period at King's survives: as a fellow-commoner, he was less likely to leave traces than a scholar, since the latter had greater involvement in college affairs.[69] Consequently much of what follows is plausible rather than provable.

Howard's attendance at King's touches upon some issues of interest to both social and intellectual historians, chiefly that of the relationship between the aristocracy and the university. This is a theme that is writ large not only in Howard's own biography but in the preoccupation of this book with moves between different styles of persuasive discourse, different audiences and different career possibilities. By the end of Howard's life 'it seemed perfectly natural that a tutor at Oxford was able to list the lords then resident in the university'.[70] Seventy years earlier, Richard Pace's *De fructu* plea for the importance of humanist pedagogy (and hence, by extension, of the universities) for the scions of the nobility was a more innovative undertaking. We can say that Howard is among the earlier of such scions to receive this education.

The 'Commons Books' for Howard's two certain years of residence (1564–6) have been destroyed, but the records for the years immediately

---

[68] The Old Court could only accommodate the supposed number of seventy fellows and scholars by letting each chamber contain two to four persons: see H. Bradshaw, 'An Inventory of the Stuff in the College Chambers (King's College) 1598', *Cambridge Archaeological Society Commentaries*, 1879, III, pp. 181–98. It is unclear if fellow-commoners come into this category. 'Pensioners or commoners' is one contemporary social classification of King's inhabitants (Cooper, *Annals*, II, p. 207), and so fellow-commoners may have been accomodated in the Pensionary after 1573–4 (when it was constructed: J. Saltmarsh, *King's College: A Short History*, Cambridge, 1958, p. 43). Howard was attended by another 'pensioner or commoner' at the Queen's visit, who is described as his 'servant' (Cooper, *Annals*, II. p. 207). Perhaps this was the cohabitant (a potential candidate is George Lawton, who taught Norfolk's children with Howard, and who, according to the 'mundum' books, was in residence at King's at roughly the same time as Howard). There were many university hostels for arts students (see J. Willis Clark and A. Gary, *Old Plans of Cambridge*, Cambridge, 1921, p. 2): Howard may have lived in one of these. Compare this situation with that obtaining in Gonville College: C. Brooke, 'Allocating Rooms In Sixteenth-Century Cambridge', *The Caian*, 1987, pp. 56–7.

[69] Most obviously, their scholarships.

[70] *A History of the University of Cambridge. Volume II: 1546–1750*, ed. Victor Morgan, Cambridge, 2004, p. 316.

prior and subsequent to this period are still extant.[71] These lists of dining fees and menus give a range of interesting details about what sort of food was being consumed and how it was paid for. King's operated a fixed fee system: fellow-commoners for the year 1563–4 paid 20 pence a meal.[72] The accounts list different foods for 'Dinner' (the midday meal) and 'Supper' and the evening meal does not seem to have involved a greater amount of food than the earlier one.[73] The fare seems nourishing enough, but rather unvaried: one reads endlessly of legs of mutton and sides of beef, with very few vegetables. Sweets are seldom mentioned, and a reason is perhaps suggested by the entry for 'Sugar loaves bought ab Londinio' for one supper in 1566 is added later: they cost eleven shillings and sixpence, considerably more than most of the standard items on the meal.[74] The 'mundum' books, compiled by the then bursar, Christopher Thompson, contain a few scraps of information on Howard: they record, for instance, his first payment for college battels in Michaelmas 1564.[75] More tantalising is an entry on the payment for beer and (perhaps) books.[76] The ledger entry has the word 'nil' after it in the amount column. What is interesting about this piece of evidence is the fact that Thompson only names Howard, either out of deference to rank or because Howard had taken on a central role in this payment process.

Regardless of the motivation for study at King's College, his subsequent interests and works suggest that scholarly life was congenial. His tutor is likely to have been Philip Baker, the Marian provost since 1558: noblemen would not have had recourse to the commoner sort of lecturer.[77] For this

---

[71] King's College Archive, Cambridge, Commons Books, vol. 17 (1562–4, 1566–7), passim. The book finishes in the summer term of 1564, so although we know Howard was present for the Queen's visit in that year, not only had he not matriculated, but he was not even in any form of residence with the College even a couple of months earlier.

[72] Ibid., f. 2^r. The records distinguish between the payments of scholars and fellow-commoners.

[73] See, e.g., ibid., f. 241^v.

[74] Ibid., f. 276^v.

[75] King's College Archive, Mundum Books, vol. 15, f. 2^r [pagination is my own]: 'Item rec ab m^{ro} master pro comunis domini henrico howard pro integro ter^e michs xxxix s.'

[76] Ibid., f. 13^r: 'Item sol. m<agistr>o. hoddylowe tam pro byrra duplici quam simplici pro hoc termine xiii li xii s v d. Sed in Tomson recepit ab domino henrico howard et ceteris commensalibus xiii li xv s x d ut pro libr<is> [...] et sic remaneat in manibus magistri Tomson.' [pagination is my own]. Something similar appears for the next term at 13^v for the next term, and again for 1565 later on in the book (ff. 63^r and 63^v). 'Hoddylowe' is presumably a reference to one member of the well-connected Cambridgeshire Hodilow family: see W. D'Oyly Bayley, 'An Account of the Family of Hodilow', Topographer and Geneaologist, 1853, II, pp. 28–72.

[77] Just as the Bacon brothers were lodged with Whitgift in Trinity: see Lisa Jardine and Alan Stewart, Hostage to Fortune: The Troubled Life of Francis Bacon 1561-1626, London, 1998, p. 35, n. 34.

service, we may presume that Howard paid Baker, since we have evidence, albeit from a slightly later period, that other such patrician pupils did similarly with their tutors.[78] It looks certain that Baker entrenched his charge in the Catholicism that Bishop White had inaugurated.[79] Howard would not have taken examinations for his BA, since that was one of the privileges attaching to the college. On the 21 June 1566,[80] he supplicated MA. The examination itself was probably an oral discussion of set texts, although we do not know whether the examiners at King's demanded accurate pronunciation of Greek as was, it seems, the practice at Merton, Oxford.[81]

A grace from 1563 has been preserved from the university dealing with Howard.[82] This might suggest that we date his admission to

---

[78] *A History of the University of Cambridge. Volume II: 1546–1750*, ed. Victor Morgan, Cambridge, 2004, p. 325.

[79] Baker: ?1524–?1601; educated at Eton and then King's; vice-chancellor 1561–2; it was in Baker's lodgings that the Queen stayed in 1564, when we know Howard was present: *DNB* sub nomine; H. C. Porter, *Reformation and Reaction in Tudor Cambridge*, Cambridge, 1958, ad indicem.

[80] Not, perhaps, as the *DNB* maintains, 1564. The *ODNB* is more circumspect and silent on the issue.

[81] We are told that inceptors should 'locum aliquem ex Aristotele allegantes Graeco sermone eundem enuncient', *Registrum annalium collegii Mertonensis, 1521–1567*, ed. J. Fletcher, Oxford, 1974, p. 260. There is an official statement preserved on the issue: 'Non modo Aristoteles tum Academiae tum collegiorum lectionibus sua lingua legatur sed caeteri etiam quos quivis suis in scientiis profitentur non ex translationibus sed scriptorum ipsorum lingua quantum commode fieri possit' (Lamb, *Documents*, p. 309). The final rider makes me unsure how much reliance to place on it. I presume that pronunciation is, somehow, however being tested, a controversial issue: Erasmus's *De recta pronuntiatione* (1528) was reprinted 17 times in the sixteenth century. On balance, it seems that the provision of Greek within Cambridge in the 1560s and 1570s is likely to have been rather poor. There was the regius professorship but, without a college lecturer, it would take particular fame on the part of a visiting professor (e.g., Gabriel Harvey or Alberico Gentili: see Gabriel Harvey, *Rhetor*, London: Henry Bynneman, 1574, sigs A1[r–v]) to encourage attendance. King's College, however, is the only college to have a separate account for a college lecturer in Greek in 1546, although, according to the Peter Jones, current librarian of King's, we do not have the records to check whether this continues into the period of Howard's residency. On this topic in a European context, see now Luca Bianchi, *Studi sull'Aristotelesimo del rinascimento*, Padua, 2003, pp. 180–3.

[82] *Grace Book* Δ, *Containing the Records of the University of Cambridge for the years 1542–1589*, ed. J. Venn, Cambridge, 1910, p. 195, transcribing f. 86[r] of the grace book: 'Conceditur ... domino Hen. Howard ut studium trium annorum in hac academia in dialecticis philosophicis grecis latinisque literis sufficiat ei ad incipiendum in artibus sic ut eius admissio stet pro completis gradu et forma in iisdem ita tamen ut disputet in proximis comitiis et convivetur et admittetur vel cum ceremoniis vel sine eisdem pro suo arbitratu.' The graces divide into degree supplications and 'ordinary executive business of the university' (ibid., p. v). Graces cannot be made to bear much interpretative weight, but they were sufficiently flexible a medium to allow even straightforward confessional polemic (e.g., Lamb, *Documents*, p. 100).

1560.[83] The phrasing is significant: some measure of autonomy is granted him by the request for freedom from certain formal requirements 'at his own judgement' (*pro suo arbitratu*): words found in very few such graces. This may explain the otherwise mystifying absence of Howard from most of the college record books for the years of his supposed residency. Howard, however, was a noble, so we should not be too surprised by this.[84] In the *ordo senioritatis* for the MA degree supplications, Henry Howard was placed first.[85] The list was not necessarily ordered by merit.[86] As the name suggests, it was primarily based on seniority, but merit considerations seem to have played a part, especially in first few rankings. Howard's age (28) would have marked him out as very much one of the oldest masters, especially as the governing body of the university (particularly in the days before the centralizing Elizabethan statutes revision in 1570) was a relatively grey-haired body.[87] One wonders, furthermore, if the marginal ascription 'dominus' to Howard's name had a part to play, so that even if we could prove that any of his fellow masters were indeed senior, it would not necessarily mean that his first-place position demonstrated particular intellectual achievement.[88] The very fact of his commitment to an academic life, if only for a few years, should be taken properly into account.[89]

We have no exact notion of what Howard learnt at King's.[90] Although the early and strong tutorial focus there means that the importance of extra-curricular studies at King's in the development of humanism in

---

[83] The issue is not as clear as this, however. Venn (John Venn and J. A. Venn, *Alumni Cantabrigienses, a biographical list of all known students, graduates and holders of office at the University of Cambridge, from the earliest times to 1751*, 4 vols (1922–27)) gives Howard's matriculation date as Michaelmas 1564. But we know (see below) that he was present as a fellow-commoner at the visit of Queen Elizabeth which took place on 4 August 1564 and the days following – in other words, before the start of Michaelmas term.

[84] Howard's brother, the Duke of Norfolk, received a degree only by incorporation from Kings and so we are unable to compare like with like, as such degrees are not backed up by rankings.

[85] *Grace Book* Δ, p. 196.

[86] Peck, 'Mentality', p. 312 n. 11, assumes without argument a merit-based system by her use of the word 'ranked'. For considerations to the contrary, see *Grace Book* Δ, pp. viii–x.

[87] See BL Lansdowne MS 15 for a list or the ages of resident regent and non-regent masters for the year 1572: the age range is from 21 to 28.

[88] The word 'dominus' is, as noted above, not present for the Duke of Norfolk: it seems to be simply a Latin version of the courtesy title 'Lord' which was always used of Howard until his ennoblement in 1604.

[89] I am confining myself here to what can be said with certainty; perhaps due weight should be accorded to the seventeenth-century biography (p. 000), which asserts Howard was at Cambridge 'a long time'.

[90] See, however, L. Jardine, 'Humanism and the Arts Course in Sixteenth-Century Cambridge', *History of Education*, 4, 1975, pp. 16–31. It is much to be regretted that Victor Morgan did not choose to spend more time on the intellectual aspects of Cambridge University in his recent work.

Cambridge should not be underestimated, we may assume that there was some similarity in curriculum between King's and other colleges.[91] Howard would have arrived at King's competent in the ancient languages, and perhaps Italian, though there was private tuition for this language on offer. Certainly, he would have been imbued with the patterns of humanist exegesis and reading habits (which were also memory aids) which were the chief feature of a 'grammatical' education. Above all, it was an education in form rather than content. This was only partially changed by the other arts of the trivium and, in addition, we should be sensitive to the fact that changes in the informal instruction may have been in part due to a desire to meet the needs of a an increasingly well-born student body.[92] The diet of disputations at which Howard would have had to participate was a steady one. The 1549 statutes enjoined that they should take place on Thursdays, Fridays and Sundays for, respectively, mathematics, dialectic and natural philosophy.[93] In addition, there were college stipulations, such as those for Trinity College from 1570, which enjoin that there be three weekly disputations in the chapel: Monday at nine for philosophy, Wednesday either in philosophy or theology also at nine, and Friday in theology only at eleven o'clock.[94] Since 1549 the Visitors had been, in theory, required to attend these disputations; this presumably reflects the popular understanding of the new university course as useful and justifiable on wider socio-political grounds than previously, and so there was greater incentive to perform well. Howard needed little incentive to achieve, though circumstances, as we shall see, regularly frustrated his attempts.

[91] One of the interesting and very rare examples of manuscript collation in sixteenth-century England hails from King's: Robert Aldridge (fellow at King's, and previously provost at Eton) collated two Seneca manuscripts held in the library at King's and sent on the results to Erasmus to assist in the preparation for the latter's 1529 edition of the Roman philosopher (see Desiderius Erasmus, *Opus epistolarum*, ed. P. S. Allen, 12 vols, Oxford, 1906–1958, VI (eds P. S. Allen and H. M. Allen), 1926, epistle 1766, pp. 433–46, at 434).

[92] *A History of the University of Cambridge. Volume II: 1546–1750*, ed. Victor Morgan, Cambridge, 2004, pp. 131–9. This phenomenon should not, in the absence of precise evidence, be retrojected too far back into the sixteenth century, though there is more evidence for it in the early seventeenth century.

[93] Lamb, *Documents*, p. 128. They were to last from one o'clock to three o'clock in the afternoon. The respondent had to fix an account of these theses to be defended to the doors of the public schools. These were later printed, although none survives from the 1560s. The Trinity College Statutes, however, inform us that if the topic was one of rhetoric or dialectic, then 'proponantur omnino sine ulla praefatione' (Mullinger, *University of Cambridge from the Royal Injunctions of 1535 to the Accession of Charles the First*, Cambridge, 1884, p. 617).

[94] Trinity College Statutes, 1560, Statute 18 (Latin text at Mullinger, *University of Cambridge*, p. 615). The statute goes on to say that they may be cancelled for fast days and the period of Lent. The same question could not be disputed more than once in any given year, unless the topic was serious, which suggests that some more frivolous topics were admitted. All were expected to partake, with the exception of doctors of theology.

Chapter 2

'TANTA ASSIDUITAS'
A SCHOLARLY LIFE AT TRINITY HALL

KING'S did not hold Howard long, despite its deserved reputation for humanist studies. Instead, at some point between 1566 and 1569, he migrated to the more conservative Trinity Hall. This was not an uncommon practice, at least, for example, at the level of the fellowship. Gabriel Harvey moved between Pembroke and Trinity Hall. Trinity Hall, one of a clutch of colleges founded in the earlier part of the fourteenth century, was famed as a 'nursery for civilians'.[1] Civil law, useful in most 'international' careers of business and diplomacy, was probably the biggest draw of this college for Howard. It was equally famous for its religious conservatism: Stephen Gardiner, after all, had been master, and the current master, Henry Hervey, was of similarly traditionalist leanings. This conservatism could have found expression in a number of ways. The Statutes of 1549 laid down a number of public requirements in matters religious by the colleges. Each could have been broken, depending on the degree of publicity sought.[2] Howard was likely to have been for the three years after his graduation a regent master (presumably at Trinity Hall): that is the inference to be drawn from the grace of 7 July 1569 asking that 'Hen. Hawarde possit

---

[1] The phrase comes from Charles Crawley, *Trinity Hall*, Cambridge, 1976, title for chapter three. The college was founded by Bishop Bateman of Norwich, as Howard was fondly to recall in a polemical context a few years later: *A Defense of the Ecclesiasticall Regiment in Englande*, London: Bynneman, 1574, p. 98.

[2] Mullinger, *University of Cambridge*, pp. 112–13: 'Some of the ancient ceremonies, such as public processions at exequiae and other occasions, were forbidden; and the form of worship at the university church and in the college chapels was brought into conformity with the new liturgy.'

regere et non regere ad placitum'.³ This does not mean that he ceased to be in residence. There are lists of resident non-regent masters, after all.⁴ Most of the letters that he sends to Cecil in the period after 1569, however, were written from locations other than Cambridge, although the transcript of a disputation on the early church suggests that he had not entirely severed links with his old university.⁵ The statutes of 1570 had taken power away from the regent masters and placed it squarely with the heads of house.⁶ Howard can have felt little optimism about convincing a Cambridge increasingly zealous in matters religious to elect him to such a position. Indeed, it is now that we have the first reference to gossip about Howard's Catholicism: a letter to Cecil mentions a previous letter concerned with 'suspitione religionis'; merely because Trinity Hall seemed a safe retreat, that was no guarantee of it remaining so. As far as the confessional orientation of the college is concerned, we should not be misled by the well-known traditionalism of its provost, Philip Baker, who held that post from 1558–69 and who was vice-chancellor in 1561–2. Howard would have had to deal with the other fellows, whose inclinations can be gauged by a letter of 1565 to Cecil laying charges of Popery and laziness at their head of house.⁷

---

3 *Grace Book* Δ, p. 241. Although not identified in the index as Howard, I assume the reference to be to him. For 'Howard' spelt 'Hawarde' see the reference to the Duke of Norfolk as 'Hawarde' at p. 182. The scribe is the same throughout the book. It was not usual to stop being a regent master after three years, and so Howard's request to continue shows, at least minimally, a sympathy for the academic life.

4 See BL Lansdowne MS 15.

5 That disputation happened in 1573. Frustratingly, Crawley, *Trinity Hall*, pp. 62–3, gives no evidence for his assertion that Howard was 'in residence here at times between 1569 and 1573'. Howard is not one of the 170 signatories to the letter complaining to Cecil of the new Statutes (Cooper, *Annals*, pp. 254–64): an argument ex silentio cannot, however, be pressed. One piece of evidence which suggests (perhaps rather weakly) that Crawley may be correct is a letter from Howard to Hatton, which says that the time of his first coming to court was clouded by a 'plight', presumably Norfolk (BL Additional MS 15841, f. 43ᵛ). This would date his coming to court to about 1571 or later.

6 Exhaustive and not unintelligent discussion of this in *A History of the University of Cambridge. Volume II: 1546–1750*, ed. Victor Morgan, Cambridge, 2004, pp. 63–98.

7 Letter concerning suspicion of Howard's religion: BL Cotton MS, Titus C vi f. 11ᵛ; and fellows' letter on the topic of Baker: BL Lansdowne MS 8, f. 159, and again in 1567 (BL Harleian Ms. 7031 f. 2ᵛ–3ʳ) and in 1569 (BL Harleian MS 7031 f. 5ʳ⁻ᵛ, where there is the interesting charge that he gives financial aid to 'Louvanistes'). One wonders whether Howard was one of the 'superstitouslie minded' (BL Harleian MS 7031 f. 2ᵛ) people whom he 'meynteyneth at his howse' or at least one of the 'ordinairie gests' who were the most 'suspected Papists in all the Countrie'. According to the charges laid at his feet, Howard would have been in the company of a man who possessed 'masse bookes, with other blasphemous books used in the time of Poperie' and to whose table came a steady nighttime flow of Catholic visitors. The fellows won the day: despite representation to the

Lord Henry Howard: An Elizabethan Life

It is quite clear that he did not become a fellow of the college.[8] His world was that of the regent and non-regent master. Graduate tuition of undergraduate students has a long tradition, though it is an open question whether the creation of chairs, in the style of the University of Paris, helped or hindered the assimilation of new ideas. Certainly, regency was a very convenient and cheap form of undergraduate instruction from the colleges' perspective. Originally, the distinction between a regent and non-regent master was simply that one taught and the other had taught but no longer did so.[9] Those who were no longer regent were allowed back into the governing body and regency after a solemn ceremony.[10] Regency required at least one lecture in the schools for a year after inception.[11] This was the position at the close of the Middle Ages. This period was gradually extended. By 1566, the period of regency tended to be more like three years, although it was increased to five by the statues of 1572.[12] Regent masters were particularly numerous, according to one source in the 1560s.[13] This was in part due to the power conferred on them by the Elizabethan Statues of 1559, which gave them the ability to elect the vice-chancellor. It is not certain to what extent Cambridge followed Oxford practice in electing three masters per subject, although it seems likely that informal arrangements would vary.[14]

Chancellor, Baker fled in 1569. One interesting detail: the mundum books have no record of Howard having 'signed in' for meals; did he eat with Baker? I should mention here a problem in the dating of the original comment from Titus C vi. Nearly every holograph letter in this manuscript has a neat date written upon the top right-hand corner of the relevant folio. In other words, the dating was done when the manuscript was compiled, or at least a previously bound section thereof. The hand that writes in these dates must have been writing after the 1590s, by which time we can safely say that the hand is not that of Howard on paleographical grounds. Sometimes this date has been copied from either the date in the main body of the letter itself or from the endorsement. The former is naturally reliable, although the latter may be the result of an ignorant secretary (this is the account given for Walsingham's office by John Bossy in his *Under the Molehill: An Elizabethan Spy Story*, London, 2001, pp. 157–64, with my review in *Notes and Queries*, 49, 2002, 178–9). I work on the assumption that the dating was the result of one of Cotton's secretariat, who was perhaps no more knowledgeable about the early period of Howard's life than we are.

[8] *Warren's Book*, ed. A. W. W. Dale, Cambridge, 1911, pp. 142ff for a list of fellows.
[9] Mullinger, *University of Cambridge*, p. 140.
[10] Ibid., p. 142.
[11] See statute 134: 'De juramentis a magistris in inceptionibus et solemnibus praestandis' (cited from Lamb, *Documents*, I, p. 381).
[12] The Statutes of 1549 had increased its length to three years: Lamb, *Documents*, p. 141.
[13] See the anonymous complaint from 1571 that the younger sort 'doth daily increase more and more' and they became 'not only younger but more youthful and intractable at this day, then they were wont to be in times past', cited from Porter, *Reformation and Reaction*, pp. 108–9.
[14] The faculty of law did not elect regent masters.

A Scholarly Life at Trinity Hall

Howard played little part, it seems, in the administrative life of Trinity Hall or, indeed, the university. One would not expect him to take the role of university preacher, which by confessional nature would have been uncongenial.[15] The other tasks were perhaps unsuited to both a noble and one whose profile in the university was still relatively low. The one task that he undertook (and of which we have record) is his assumption of the role of 'examiner of questionists' or 'posers'. These were men who examined those supplicating for degrees and had a role to play in the assessment of rank.[16] Most of the famous names of late Elizabethan Cambridge appear in the registers as posers: Dering, Hawford and the rest. Even Whitgift had done duty in 1558/9.[17] This suggests that it was something of a crucial stepping stone for those interested in a life within the university.[18] The first reference to their existence in Cambridge comes in 1504, but we have no clear understanding of their duties.[19] One grace from 1582 lays down their responsibilities; but, frustratingly, it seems as much concerned with the potential that such a position opened up for academic fraud in the shape of back-handers for allowing given students to do well: examiners 'shall take … no money or any rewarde … neyther shall they …' and so it continues.[20]

The correspondence with Michael Hickes gives no detailed information on the question 'what did he teach?' (though a reference to his 'semihorae curriculum' at least tells us that lectures did not have to last very long and we know that he took part in the exercises that attended legal knowledge).[21]

---

[15] Indeed, none of those who officially graced Great St Mary's in the 1560s (*pace Grace Book* Δ, pp. 572–4) hailed from Trinity Hall, a famously conservative college in religious matters.

[16] Peck ('Mentality', p. 312 n. 11) calls these 'Readers', which has the wrong connotations today.

[17] *Grace Book* Δ, p. 131.

[18] Caius eventually asks for a total absence from his duties to attend to his negotia.

[19] *Grace Book* I, ed. J. Venn, Cambridge, 1908, p. 34. Various rituals of initiation are recorded, including 'Salting' (BL Additional MS 52585, ff. 44ᵛ–53, William Goldsmith's account of one such occasion with Latin verse from Trinity College in ?1603; Mullinger, *University of Cambridge*, pp. 400–1 (citing *British Magazine*, 32, 1847, p. 361 and pp. 508–28), though the late medieval custom of the appointment of a 'lord of misrule' was specifically forbidden (Cooper, *Annals*, I, p. 112).

[20] *Grace Book* Δ, p. ibid.

[21] BL Lansdowne MS 109, f. 55. Since lectures took place between the hours of nine and twelve, and were supposed to be an hour long, the reference may be humorous. I refer here to 'ordinary' lectures (those given by regent masters), not the 'cursory' lectures of bachelors stantes in quadrigesima. At some point private study took over the role of afternoon lectures, but practice in this transitional period would doubtless vary from college to college and person to person depending on the resources, in terms of personnel and finances, available. On Hickes, see Alan Smith, *Servant of the Cecils – The Life of Sir Michael Hickes*, London, 1977. It was not uncommon to be introduced to at least the *Institutes* of Justinian as a preliminary introduction to civil law during the arts course.

The obvious answer is that he taught some version of the arts curriculum.[22] The four-year introductory arts course aimed at a systematic treatment of the body of human knowledge, though it became less about a body of knowledge by the time of the humanist changes to it and rather more about the techniques of cognition and expression that were propaideutic to further substantive study.[23] The course consisted for the most part of the trivium, namely grammar, rhetoric and logic.[24] This was the bastard son of the late antique and medieval attempts to classify knowledge. The course had stabilized by the end of the thirteenth century through various routes and divagations that do not concern us here. This relatively stable entity consisted of the foundational trivium (grammar, rhetoric and dialectic) and the quadrivium (number theory, geometry, astronomy and music), together with the fields of metaphysics, natural philosophy and moral and political philosophy (the quadrivium had, for the most part, been abandoned by the time of Howard's education). It was a distinctive feature of the late medieval period that these branches of knowledge were taught from set books rather than

---

[22] That is the implication of the reference to 'Rhetoricke Reader' in the laudatory seventeenth-century biography in BL Additional MS 6298, f. 285. Reader, of course, means nothing more than someone that gives lectures: here, a regent master. Howard would also have had exposure to studies in civil law, given that Trinity Hall had so few students (see further on the interconnected nature of the arts faculty and the law faculty, D. R. Leader, *A History of the University of Cambridge*, vol. I, Cambridge, 1988, p. 195).

[23] See, still, P. O. Kristeller, 'The Modern System of the Arts', in his *Renaissance Thought II: Papers on Humanism and the Arts*, New York, 1965, pp. 163–227.

[24] See Lamb, *Documents*, I, p. 459: 'Primus annus rhetoricam docebit; secundus et tertius dialecticam; quartus adjungat philosophiam.' This is taken from the 1570 statutes. It is not likely (as L. Jardine, 'Dialectic Teaching in Sixteenth-Century Cambridge', *Studies in the Renaissance*, 21, 1974, p. 43, assumes) that this represents the decade before 1570, nor that it was an accurate description of Cambridge 1570, as far as philosophy goes. That, I suggest, is the conclusion we should draw from the letter to Cecil, complaining about the relegation of philosophy to the fourth year, and the introduction of theology in the first: Cooper, *Annals*, II, pp. 254–64. The substance of the complaints is the deleterious effect on students that this change would have. I therefore assume that there was considerable teaching of philosophy in the earlier years both pre- and post-1570. I cannot agree that Richard Holdsworth's 1620s teaching programme (reproduced in Jardine, 'Dialectic Teaching', pp. 47–9) is old-fashioned. For one thing, it includes Lucretius, and the natural philosophy texts are not specified, thereby not allowing us a glimpse of what sort of Aristotelianism they offered; we simply cannot say. A further modification to Jardine's article relates to the study of rhetoric: while the library lists upon which she bases her study do indeed suggest a prevalence of works on dialectic, it should be remembered that there is a built-in asymmetry in the argument to the extent that editions of Classical authors, especially the poets, orators and historians, usually came with a commentary and that commentary was far more indebted to rhetoric than dialectic, partially because the ancient commentaries upon which their epigones were similarly orientated. Therefore, for every work of dialectic one should oppose every edition of a Classical text to achieve a more balanced picture than Jardine's article would suggest.

being construed as simply a set of problems. The choice of such books was sometimes contentious, and usually fixed in statute form, though there could be considerable variation in what additional material was brought to bear or explain these readings (or *lectiones*). To the extent that the trivium could be said to have some conceptual unity, its aim was to explore problems related to the interpretation of texts (including grammar in the modern sense), meaning, class logic, argumentative manoeuvres and (at usually a rather lower priority level) verbal expression. The humanist curricular revolution emphasized this last element under the name of eloquence.

We are fortunate in having the reading material of one student from Howard's own college, King's, from 1545, only a few years before Howard's own attendance, and just four years before the statute revision of 1549. Already we see similarities with those 1549 statutes. This student possessed a copy of Philipp Melanchthon's work on humanist dialectic, an epitome of the work of Rudolph Agricola, another key figure in humanist dialectic, a work that is most likely to be the *Paedagogia* of Petrus Mosellanus, a manual of scholastic logic, and three works that would aid in the task of composition (a *Progymnasmata*, an edition of some of Erasmus's proverbs and his *Colloquia*). This gives us an indication that the nature of the instruction that this student, at least, received was predominantly dialectical and, to a lesser extent, rhetorical. The absence of philosophy, natural, moral or metaphysical, is very noticeable in this list. It was a fashion at this period to engage in discourse analysis and discourse production, and these were the skills that the trivium, in its humanist garb, inculcated. The influence of this highly dialectical education was to leave a lasting mark on Howard's works.

The existence of Howard's philosophy manuscripts suggests the strong possibility that he taught natural philosophy for the arts course as well.[25] The question of the evidence for civil law is more complicated because it is likely that he was 'learning' civil law at Trinity, having perhaps been introduced to an introductory text such as Justinian's *Institutes* while at King's by someone like Baker. There is evidence of his considerable knowledge of the law in his 1590 tract the 'Dutiful Defence', but it is unfortunate that there is not more influence of civil law argumentation in his 1574 tract against the Presbyterians, a time when we can connect him much more closely to the university environment. He cannot, however, fail to have been influenced by the civilians of Trinity Hall.[26] The master of that college,

---

[25] Though there is some doubt about a *very* close connection between his university activity and the manuscript.

[26] See also his letter of 7 April 1569, where he describes himself as having been part of an 'exercitatio' between 'legum & iudicum formulas': BL Cotton MS, Titus C vi f. 10^r.

John Cowell, unfortunately spends less time describing Howard's legal studies as much time on paying him the following notable compliment:[27]

> You passed your adolescence in that truly regal College and a fertile breeding ground for the humanities in such a manner that everyone gave you praise for the hallmarks of lightly-worn seriousness, for your innocence and moderation (a thing not uncommonly said about nobles in those days); your industry and capacity for hard work were also templates for all. You were often to be found in disputations, praelections, perorations, even though you had scarcely left your boyhood. Your great diligence in these matters was, however, very far from preciosity: not only did it not diminish your repute (as so often happens with others), but increased it daily by such a degree so that to assemble every man of every order it was sufficient to say: Today Howard comes forth into the arena.[28]

Certainly, Howard is unlikely to have learnt his civil law anywhere else. Cambridge in the 1560s offered rather limited opportunities for teaching in this subject, however.[29] Despite the relationship between equity and the civil law, apparent similarities in legal reasoning do not construct a demand. The number of students graduating with legal qualifications remained small in the period and, indeed, some of the fellows of Trinity Hall itself did not pos-

---

[27] One should, however, note the date: the work was written when Howard was in a position to dole out cash and favours, even if he very rarely did.

[28] John Cowell, *Institutiones iuris anglicani*, Cambridge: John Legate, 1605, sig. A3: 'Olim adolescentia tua in Collegio illo vere Regali et seminario bonarum literarum foecundissimo sic transacta est ut gravitatis multa urbanitate conditae, innocentiae, temperantiae summam laudem (nobilibus in illa aetate non raro denegatam) omnes uno consensu ascriberent; industriam etiam et diligentiam solertissimi omnium sibi imitandam proponerent. In disputationibus, praelectionibus, perorationibus, cum iam ex ephebis vix excessisses, frequens fuisti; in quibus tamen tanta assiduitas longissime a fastidio abfuit, existimationem tuam (quod plerumque fit in aliis) non modo non minuit, sed sic auxit quotidie ut ad omnes omnium ordinum convocandos satis esset dixisse: Howardus hodie prodit in arenam.'

[29] The historiographical issues are complex: for a brief overview, see Jonathan Woolfson, *Padua and the Tudors: English Students in Italy 1485–1603*, pp. 52–63. More detailed material on the effect of the break with Rome is in John Barton, 'The Faculty of Law', in *HUO*, III, pp. 257–62. The persistence of *mos italicus* material in Cambridge libraries of the period is shown by A. Wijffels, 'Law Book in Cambridge Libraries, 1500–1640', *Transactions of the Cambridge Bibliographical Society*, 10, 1993, pp. 359–412 (one should not push too far, however, with the bartolist survivalism argument, since books tend to have a long shelf-life). See the annotations of Gabriel Harvey on civil law material in L. Jardine and W. Sherman, 'Pragmatic Readers: Knowledge Transactions and Scholarly Services in Late Elizabethan England', in *Religion, Culture and Society in Early Modern Britain: Essays in Honour of Patrick Collinson*, eds A. Fletcher and P. Roberts, Cambridge, 1994, 113–24. See also Chapter Seven.

sess the degree. The study of civil law at this point in Cambridge was probably heavily influenced by the works of Andrea Alciato and, given Howard's later seeming insistence on the limited scope of the religious jurisdiction of the papacy, we should bear in mind that the Cambridge reforms of civil law teaching removed theological discussion from its remit.[30]

The library at Trinity Hall doubtless saw much of Howard in his years here. Located in a 'small upper room next to the chapel', it had yet to see its great age of benefaction and was perhaps a rather sparse affair, compared to some others.[31] With this speculation, we have come to the end of the tasks that were the lot of a college man in the period, curricular and administrative. The picture is equally murky when we come to look at what kind of private profile Howard was attempting to cultivate through the medium of his correspondence.[32] The content is predictable. Much of it consists in begging of one sort or another, though they are simultaneously examples of polished humanist rhetoric. The humanist letter, with its enabling fiction of being a communication between absent friends, allowed considerable latitude in what counted as a friend. While Howard's letters possess some similarities to the humanist letter between equals, there are situations in which the fiction of equality wears thin. In these scenarios, one either writes something panegyric, or one has an uneasy tension.[33] Cecil's patronage of Howard during his period of regency and therafter created a difficult relationship. Howard may thank his patron for 'divinum istud beneficium', and, continuing the language of gratitude, Howard has seen Cecil's 'clear image of duty, on which I am in the habit sometime of nourishing my eyes and soul' ('expressa pietatis effigies qua pascere nonnumquam oculos atque animam soleo').[34] Finally, he signs off with the hope that Cecil will

---

[30] See Mullinger, *University of Cambridge*, p. 126.

[31] Crawley, *Trinity Hall*, p. 62. Soon after Howard left, Gabriel Harvey, Matthew Parker, John Cowell and William Barlow all made substantial testamentary dispositions. It is not clear when the beautiful old library was constructed, though there is an outside possibility that it had already been built by the time of Howard's regency, though I incline to a later date (see further R. Wills and J. W. Clark, *The Architectural History of the University of Cambridge and of the Colleges of Cambridge and Eton*, Cambridge, with a new introduction by D. Watkin, Cambridge, 1988, III, pp. 412 and 415).

[32] On this topic in the Renaissance, see now in *Self-Presentation and Social Identification: The Rhetoric and Pragmatics of Letter Writing in Early Modern Times*, eds T. Van Houdt, J. Papy and G. Tournoy, Leuven, 2002.

[33] The only person (other than Cecil) to whom we have several letters of Howard is Michael Hickes, a man who was much more his equal (BL MS Lansdowne 109, ff. 55–57). These betray none of the humanist rhetoric between friends: you only plead equality when you're not equal.

[34] BL Cotton MS, Titus C vi f. 9ʳ.

consult him as often as he does himself.[35] Here, the connection between the academic context and the rhetoric of political counsel is close.[36] The language accounts for the references to Cecil as a Nestor figure.[37] Whether Cecil saw the connection as being so obvious is unknown: he had the advantage of a court perspective which, as yet, Howard did not.[38] Certainly, the connection is adumbrated in Ascham's *Scholemaster*, but there is sufficient scene-setting and distancing through different narrative frames in that text to make us rather wary of its verisimilitude.[39] It does not seem enough, in other words, to simply assert the connection between scholarship and politics as having been a valuable commodity to be bought and sold according to the rules of patronage that obtained.[40] One index of this is the opening Greek tag in a Latin letter written to Cecil:

ὡς ἂν ὑμεῖς ἀποδέξησῃ καὶ πρὸ ἕκαστον ἐχητ'εὐνοίας, ὁ λέγων ἔδοξε ὁ φρονεῖν. [41]

---

[35] The expression used is 'facultas consulendi': ibid.

[36] On the importance of the language of advice and the asymmetric duties of courtiers and princeps in this period, see John Guy, 'The Rhetoric of Counsel', in *Tudor Political Culture*, ed. Dale Hoak, Cambridge, 1995, pp. 292–311. In brief, Guy proposes two 'languages' of counsel, one feudal–baronial, the other humanist–Classical; naturally, one may quibble with any taxonomy, and a third species, godly and prophetic, has been proposed cogently by A. N. Mclaren, 'Delineating the Elizabethan Body Politic: Knox, Aylmer and the Definition of Counsel 1558–1588', *History of Political Thought*, 17, 1996, pp. 224–52. Howard's advice at this period can fairly be contained in the second category.

[37] 'Tua (mihi crede) fuit amicitia in qua salutis sua spem omnem et melioris fortunae expectationem cum gravissimis terroribus impenderet dux meus collocavit semperque me praesente Agamemnonem illum apud Homerum imitatus, ad recuperandam illustrissimae principis gratiam, Nestorem unum ['magis' – sic supplevi] quam decem Aiaces aestimavit', BL Cotton MS, Caligula C.iii f. 98ʳ (1571 letter to Cecil from Audley End); BL Cotton MS, Titus C vi f. 11ʳ (1571 letter to Cecil from Trinity Hall) and f. 34ʳ (letter to Cecil from unknown location). In the patronage context, see e.g. Joachim Du Bellay's sonnet (published in 1558) to Ronsard: 'Cependant que tu dis ta Cassandre divine, / Les louanges de roi, et l'héritier d'Hector/ Et ce Montmorency, notre français Nestor', Du Bellay, *Les Regrets*, ed. S. de Sasy, Paris, 1967, p. 81.

[38] The beginning of another letter (BL Cotton MS, Titus C vi f. 10ᵛ) quotes Demosthenes as a prelude to Howard's pleasure at Cecil having replied to his letter.

[39] *The Scholemaster*, London: John Daye, 1570, sig. B1ʳ (a passage dealing with Cecil's desire for learned discourse with those at his table).

[40] This seems to be the fault of the otherwise excellent book of Stephen Alford, *The Early Elizabethan Polity: William Cecil and the British Succession Crisis 1558–1569*, Cambridge, 1998, esp. pp. 9–42. The commodification of scholarship is a problem, not a stage in a political career.

[41] Demosthenes, *Orationes*. 18. 277: a translation of the current OCT gives a slightly different sense: 'the orator's reputation for wisdom depends upon your acceptance and your discriminating favour'.

A Scholarly Life at Trinity Hall

The concern with the dangers of appearing a 'mere' speaker, who achieves power by untrustworthy words, is even clearer when the context of this quotation from Demosthenes's *De corona* is addressed. It is an appeal rooted in Howard's slightly anomalous position as an aristocrat who is also a scholar.[42] These anxieties stem from exclusion, something which will resurface when we discuss a later work, *Regina fortunata*. Howard often makes reference in these letters to his sense of intruding into Cecil's time, and though this is obviously a matter of epistolary politeness, there is additional point in that Howard, despite his nobility, has a delicate relationship with Cecil and a limited experience of court life.[43]

We should remark upon another of Howard's connections. As we have mentioned, Howard was closely connected to Philip Baker, and, doubtless, regretted his being deposed. There is, however, a letter to Cecil in which Howard suggests the Bishop of Rochester as a replacement.[44] Howard had no history (nor would have a future) of promoting the interests of Protestants, unless they belonged to his family or served some other purpose. Edmund Gest, first Protestant bishop of that see, perhaps had earlier dealings with Howard about which we are ignorant.[45] The evidence of Gest's library is inconclusive.[46] He was a Protestant of the middle sort and, as such, perhaps presented a more favourable candidate to Howard (and, indeed, to Cecil) than the alternatives.

Howard's time at Trinity Hall is most interesting to later scholars because it is there that he penned what is the earliest tract on natural phi-

---

[42] Demosthenes, *Orationes*. 18. 276.

[43] See e.g. BL Cotton MS, Titux C vi f. 9ʳ: 'Cum nemo pene vel mediocris spei atque opinionis in nostra versetur Academia qui non aliquam (suae voluntatis significandae gratia) ad te scribendi occasionem arripuerit, verebar equidem ne in animi ingrati atque illberalis suspicionem [sc. me inducerem.].'

[44] Ibid, f. 11ʳ: 'nec alium quenquam novi qui statutis non repugnantibus cooptari possit solum Roffensem excipio episcopum qui gravioribus implicatus rebus Academiae negotiis interesse nequit nec semper abesse domenihea [sic] permittant leges.'

[45] Edmund Gest (spelt variously Gheast, Guest) was born in 1517 and died in 1577. He was educated at Cambridge, and was a fellow of King's (whence he was repelled into Marian exile); after return, he became Bishop of Rochester and then in 1571 Shrewsbury (see *Fasti Ecclesiae Anglicanae*, III.iii.15; III.iii.51; III.vi.1).

[46] The books are more or less purely theological in character, with nothing from the arts course remaining (no Aristotle, no literature). The evidence, however, is purely those books which happen to survive from Salisbury Cathedral library; therefore, it may well be that the books from the earlier part of his career were dispersed during the period of his Marian exile. Information about Gest's library was kindly provided to me by the Rev. David Selwyn of Lampeter College, who is preparing an annotated catalogue for the *Libri pertinentes* series; he is of the opinion that Gest had rather little to do with his old college, though he did attend the 1564 festivities.

losophy in English.[47] We are still far from having an accurate idea of the detail of Aristotelianism in early modern Oxford and Cambridge. The untitled manuscript is an eclectic work: it evinces a concern to accommodate Aristotelian thought to the Scriptures and, more occasionally, to elements of Platonic and Stoic thought. It does so, however, to a lesser extent than does its source, a near contemporary Latin treatise by a Spanish humanist. This accommodation of the tradition of revealed religion and Platonism is compared with, and distinguished from, the superficially similar approach taken by John Doget's earlier Cambridge commentary on the *Phaedo*. Indeed, Bodley MS 616 marked the beginning of a new interest in philosophy in England after a period of stagnation. The *terminus post quem* for the 'philosophical revival' in late Tudor England may be somewhat earlier than has previously been thought. The manuscript is testimony to the swansong of the impact of a particular tradition of Platonic (and, less frequently, Ciceronian) influence on natural philosophy in England, which, with the increasing vigour of Aristotelian thought, soon disappeared or became the preserve of more idiosyncratic figures such as Everard Digby. Howard dedicated the manuscript to his sister, Katherine, on 6 August 1569. Katherine Berkeley was signed in its author's own rather square italic hand.[48] Her response is unrecorded, but if she read it all, it will have been an undemanding read, easy on the eye and for the most part untaxing to the mind. This immediate context of sibling affection explains much in the text:

> To repeat the sundrie opinions of the philosophers as touchinge the principle of things would be very tedious ... especially manie of them being broughte in by waie of confutacion, as Plato in sundrie places under the name of Socrates taketh pretie occasion to strike at Anaxagoras and other obscure philosophers, wherefore I will only alleadge the authoritie of Plato and Aristotle whose cleere knowledge hath discovered the smokie mist of wasted ignoraunce ...[49]

This is not going to be an exhaustive treatment, but rather a protreptic to philosophy.[50] The reader is expected to take her quest for knowledge fur-

---

[47] Readers seeking a more detailed study of this text are referred to my 'Humanism and Natural Philosophy in Renaissance Cambridge: Bodley Ms. 616', *History of Universities* (forthcoming).
[48] BLO Bodley MS 616, f. 12^v. See Alfred J. Fairbank and Bruce Dickins, *The Italic Hand in Tudor Cambridge*, London, 1962.
[49] BLO Bodley MS 616, f. 11^{r-v}.
[50] Starting from antiquity (Aristotle, *Protrepticus*, ed. I. Düring, Stockholm, 1965), such protreptics had been at pains to emphasize the connections between the various elements of philosophy and in particular how the study of a given branch would lead one to happiness or to God.

ther. One further aspect, and a departure from Howard's models, which deserves underscoring in Howard's account of the manuscript is the stress on the vernacular:

> What paynes have bynne taken in the discussinge of some though necessary unpleasant pointe; and making that place in our bare englishe tounge which lieth soe obscurely in the copiose latin I am contented rather to dissemble[51]
>
> That how many soever have employed their endeavour in beautifienge our Englishe tounge either with the arte of Logike or the precepts of Rhetorike wherein a feeble braine may make a reasonable showe: yet hath attempted the wadinge in dark and obscure points of naturall philosophy, least with too hasty adventure as an unskillful pilot might make a folish shipwracke.[52]

Howard is more or less correct. Although Bodley MS 616 is clearly not part of the programme of translation of technical, often medical, literature from Latin into English that started in the 1530s, we cannot dismiss the 'question of language'.[53] Natural philosophy in English was indeed a bold departure, although we should not exclude the possibility that his sister's Latin was not sufficiently supple to allow her to read

---

[51] BLO, Bodley MS 616, f. 2ᵛ. The reference to 'copiose' Latin hardly suggests the language of Howard's sources, e.g. Javelli, Contarini or even Fox Morzillo; indeed, Contarini even says that he will use harsh words for difficult concepts (Gasparo Contarini, *De elementis*, in idem, *Opera*, Paris: Sebastian Nivelle, 1569, sig. A1ʳ). The Erasmian notion of copia (Desiderius Erasmus, *De duplici copia rerum et verborum*, Paris, 1512; last edition in his life, Basel: Froben, 1534: see Terence Cave, *The Cornucopian Text: Problems of Writing in the French Renaissance*, Oxford, 1979 and, more precisely, A. Locatelli, 'The Land of "Plenty": Erasmus' *De copia* and English Renaissance Rhetoric', in *Silenos: Erasmus in Elizabethan Literature*, ed. C. Corti, Pisa, 1995, pp. 41–57; see further my commentary ad loc.) is further discussed in Chapter Six of my dissertation, pp. 255–60. Although Howard's fondness for doublets and pithy sayings throughout the text, the style of the prose is normally not very elaborate.

[52] BLO Bodley MS 616, f. 1ʳ.

[53] Roger Ascham (in *The Schoolmaster*, ed. L. Ryan, New York, 1967, p. 149) praises the Italian exemplar of Felice Figliucci (on whom see now the article in *DBI* sub nomine). Girolamo Cardano's *De subtilitate* had been translated into French six years after it appeared in Latin (1556) and, only seven years after the publication of *De occultis naturae miraculis* by Levinus Lemnius (1505–1568), a French version of the work appeared. These were, however, discursive treatments of philosophical issues, and hence less close to the example of Howard than Figliucci (I do not posit direct influence between the two). A few years later John Woolton (by this time having left All Souls for an episcopal position in Exeter) produced a work on the soul, also in English: *A Treatise of the Immortalities of the Soule*, London: John Sheppard, 1576.

such a text.[54] The preface, in addition to running through *exempla* of learned women from ancient times, also mounts a defence of music by emphasizing its connections with philosophy. This may derive from his sister's, and his own, musical interests; and the relevance of the discussion of music itself as preparatory to the main body of the work is made explicit at one point by Howard when he writes:

> howe in bannishinge all idle and ungodly affections yt [i.e., music] prepareth the minde and maketh yt ready to embrace the heavenly precepts of wisdome.[55]

The preface also underlines that it is not a printed work, but rather a manuscript publication. If, one asks, Howard's work is such a useful piece of discourse, why hide it away in a single manuscript rather than publish it more widely? The underlying reason may be squarely placed at the feet of the hoary 'stigma of print' thesis.[56] The stated reason, however, adverts to a long tradition of philosophical pedagogy:

> If it be objected that such a pece of worke wherin a common profitt doeth consist ought rather to be communicatyd wyth many then directyd unto one speciall frend, I awnswer that many persones both in witt, learninge and experience excellent; if so noble presidents may be as Aristotle to his sonne Nicomachus; Tully to his frend Brutus; Isocrates to Nicocles and to stray no lenger in forren examples even in our tyme after the like sorte was that most excellent worke of the County of Castiglione called the Courtier first only directed to the Marquess of Pescara.[57]

---

[54] This would contradict, however, the claims made for her by the family manuscript, as we have seen in Chapter One. I have not been able to trace an earlier text of natural philosophy in English. Regardless of any given sixteenth-century woman's linguistic abilities, there was a tradition which associated women with the transmission and facilitation of Latin into vernacular: see M. P. Hannay, *Silent But For The Word: Tudor Women as Patrons, Translators and Writers of Religious Works*, Kent: OH, 1985 and S. Broomhall, *Women and the Book Trade in Sixteenth-Century France*, Aldershot, 2002.

[55] BLO Bodley MS 616. f. 8^v. I note in passing that this praise of music is couched in the language of rhetorical affect, rather than relying on a Platonic notion of music as linking men's minds and celestial influence through similarly proportioned elements (for which see D. P. Walker, *Spiritual and Demonic Magic: From Ficino to Campanella*, London, 1958, pp. 14–24). This is (slight) evidence for the notion that the Renaissance encouraged a move away from considering music as part of the quadrivium and a move toward viewing it as part of the expressive arts of the trivium.

[56] See the classic article by Harry Saunders, 'The Stigma of Print: A Note of the Social Bases of Tudor Poetry', *Essays in Criticism*, I, 1951, pp. 139–64. This thesis came under attack by Steve May, 'Tudor Aristocrats and the Mythical Stigma of Print', *Renaissance Papers*, 10, 1980, pp. 11–18, but all his examples are rather later than 1569, and so I think the thesis can be resurrected at least for the earlier Tudor period.

[57] Bodley MS 616, Oxford, f. 3^r.

Of course, this is tendentious since the Classical examples were hardly capable of being 'published' in the way that Elizabethan books were, but Howard's reasons, as already stated, are as much to do with a disinclination to appear in print and a positive evaluation of the capacity for scribal intimacy that manuscript publication possessed.[58] Finally, it is worth noting that the date of composition marks a turning point in Howard's career. It was around this time that saw him go to court in a bid to put the precepts found in Castiglione's work to more practical use than he had been able to do in a small and rather poor scholarly foundation.[59] Lady Katherine was as much witnessing a pledge of future worth on the part of her teacher as she was learning the elements of Aristotle's *Physics*.[60]

If our earlier evidence for humanist natural philosophy at King's (a late fifteenth-century manuscript by John Doget) derives from a college-based coterie of humanist influences, our next source shows how pervasive humanist sloganeering had become fifty years later. The 1535 injunctions mark a second convenient entry point for our inquiry into the position of natural philosophy in early modern Cambridge, though they too have to be seen against earlier statutory requirements.[61] They appear to consolidate the taste for the humanism for which Doget and others were the advance guard. There was some degree of freedom (perhaps greater as the sixteenth century wore on, with the rise of the fellow-commoner, the growth of the

---

[58] See Cathy Shrank, 'These Few Scribbled Rules: Representing Scribal Intimacy in Early Modern Print', *Huntington Literary Quarterly*, 67, 2004, pp. 295–314.

[59] See Chapter One for these dates.

[60] One further aspect about the preface that we should notice is the inclusion of verse (f. 12). What is most interesting about these lines is precisely their irrelevance to the text: they deal with the topic of how others' envy can degrade all good things: a prefatory topos in certain speeches (see, e.g., Hermogenes, 95.19–20 (Rabe)), but seemingly far from relevance here. Strictly speaking, the phrase about Aristotle's *Physics* is slightly misleading, because, like all other compendia and textbooks of the *Physics* in the Renaissance, there is considerable departure from the format and texture of that work.

[61] For discussion of the effect of these, see Mark H. Curtis, *Oxford and Cambridge in Transition: 1558–1642*, Oxford, 1959, pp. 23–4; note also Curtis's dispiriting, if accurate, comments at p. 92, that '[a] Cambridge bachelor followed much the same plan. He continued the study of philosophy which he had begun as an undergraduate, possibly pushing on from moral philosophy to natural philosophy and metaphysics', to which he appends the following footnote: 'The Elizabethan statutes are sketchy on all these points'. For the earlier period, see D. R. Leader, 'Philosophy in Oxford and Cambridge in the Fifteenth Century', *History of Universities*, 4, 1984, pp. 25–46. Though he had not space to subject his material to analysis, Leader amassed a considerable volume of material, to which we should add the work on Porphyry of Roger Whelpdale (fellow of Balliol College, Provost of Queen's College, Oxford, and Bishop of Carlisle 1420–3); BL MS Royal 12 B. XIX, ff. 36–45 and BL Harley MS 2178, ff. 14–23. See my article in *History of Universities* for a discussion of John Doget and his work (BL Additional MS 10344).

tutorial method of teaching and the increasing provision and affordability of textbooks) as to what a given student would have been taught.[62] The interests of a tutor will have been relevant – in Howard's case, probably, the notoriously Catholic provost, Philip Baker; we should also make allowance for the impact of the Regius Professor of Greek, Nicholas Carr.[63] Howard makes no reference to his additional extra-curricular studies while he was at King's, and there is no evidence for them. It makes sense, therefore, especially in attempting to reconstruct a context for a philosophy textbook such as Bodley MS 616, to have recourse, at least to begin with, to statutes.[64] This

---

[62] Some of the peculiarities in Howard's text may be explained by precisely this absence of direct link with a teaching scenario if we accept the arguments of Paul Saenger in *L'Histoire de l'édition française*, eds H.-J. Martin, R. Chartier and J.-P. Vivet, Paris, 1989, I, pp. 136–7. He suggests that the practice of private reading allowed the construction of an intimate intellectual sphere in which highly unorthodox opinions might be toyed with. A similar view is expressed in the English context by Mordechai Feingold, who notes that the more that university tutorials were dependent on the private reading of the student, the greater variety of opinion was potentially generated: *HUO*, IV, pp. 216–18.

[63] On whom see now *DNB* sub nomine. One should not tie influence too closely to the college structure. Consider the example of Richard Stanihurst and Edmund Campion. Stanihurst is explicit about Campion's role as a mentor in his commentary on the *Isagoge* (a work that Stanihurst compiled while still in his teens). This might be put down to prefatory politeness did we not know that Campion's only venture into formal philosophy was in the same field, albeit that Campion's manuscript actually post-dates Stanihurst's work (*Harmonia*, London: Wolf, 1570). Stanihurst was, however, at University College, Campion at St John's.

[64] We know that, from the *De modo audiendo textus Aristotelis*, the university had set out the following programme for ordinary lectures. There were 'ordinary' and 'extraordinary' lectures. The division between the two in the latter Middle Ages is 'a most involved subject' (M. B. Hackett, *Original Statutes of the University of Cambridge: The Text and its History*, Cambridge, 1970, p. 133, where see his further comments) but, at least for the Cambridge arts faculty, the former were the regular morning lectures read out by the regent masters. One had to read lectures on *dies legibiles* rather than on *dies disputabiles*: the particular disposition of these days across the week varied. This tradition appears to have continued into the sixteenth century, since one regularly finds that particular days are marked out for disputations).

First Year:	Winter: Porphyry, *Isagoge*; Aristotle, *Praedicamenta*
	Lent: Aristotle, *Peri hermeneias*, Gilbert of Poitiers, *Sex principia*
	Summer: Aristotle, *Topica*
Second Year:	Winter: *Elenchi*
	Lent: *Analytica Priora*
	Summer: *Analytica Posteriora*
Third Year:	Winter: *Physica*
	Lent: *Physica*
	Summer: *De generatione* or *De anima* or *De coelo* or *Meteorica* or *Ethica*
Fourth Year:	Winter: *Physica* or *Metaphysica*
	Lent: *Physica* or *Metaphysica*
	Summer: as in third year (Hackett, *Original Statutes*, p. 299).

evidence cannot be pressed too far. One can posit influence of a text prior to its existence in the statutes. For example, Howard's knowledge of and, to some extent, sympathy with Platonic natural philosophy was echoed in the statutes of 1570 – one year after the work in question. These record that the philosophy lecturer is to lecture, in addition to Aristotle, on Pliny the Elder or Plato; the lecturer in mathematics may also, if he is to discuss cosmography, use Plato as his base text.[65] In other words, the works of Plato which are prescribed fall broadly within the field of natural philosophy. This was certainly a departure from the supremacy of the *Physics* and the other *libri naturales* of Aristotle in the late medieval statutes. The only recent printed commentary (by Sebastian Fox Morzillo) on Plato was on the *Timaeus* and this fact may have influenced the choice.[66] Certainly several dons (the word is used loosely as a way of including both fellows and regent masters) involved in the teaching of the arts course possessed copies of this commentary. Furthermore, as mentioned before, we know that Howard was taught by Nicholas Carr, famed for his commentaries on Plato. It looks like we can begin to uncover a fresh, if briefly flourishing, Platonic impetus in early modern Cambridge. This one example shows how important is the presence of additional material to provide the context within which the teaching of university base texts, as specified in statutes, took place. In the case of Cambridge, at least for the 1530s to to 1560s, unfortunately, such additional evidence is rather sparse.

Howard's sister was promised at the end of Bodley MS 616 a second work, dealing with the natural phenomena of rain and hail, the 'sweetest pointes' of philosophy. This never materialized, as far as we can see. Still, her brother's attempt to naturalize continental learning in a domestic patronage setting is a notable contribution to the evolving discourse of English humanism.[67] First, it represents an innovative attempt to translate the idioms of the textbooks and the compendia of Aristotelian scientific thought into English. Secondly, its account of the scope of natural philosophy and its relation to theology is not without interest. Thirdly, the syn-

---

[65] Lamb, *Documents*, I, p. 457.
[66] Sebastian Fox Morzillo, *In Platonis Timaeum seu de universo commentarii*, Basel: Oporin, 1554. The Cambridge book lists (see Appendix I of my *History of Universities* article) contain four copies of Morzillo, which bolsters, to some degree, the suggestion made.
[67] See the argument of Arno Seifert, 'Der Humanismus an den Artistenfakultäten des katholischen Deutschland', in *Humanismus im Bildungswegen des 15. und 16. Jahrhunderts*, ed. W. Reinhard, Weinheim, 1996, pp. 133–54, who suggests that the growth in compendia and the associated decline in lemmatic commentaries resulted in less reading of the text itself.

cretic impulse, evident already in Fox Morzillo, is extended to include that mid-Tudor favourite, Cicero. How learned is Howard? It is hard to answer this question, given the absence of comparators in natural philosophy in England (though we have an exact, and seemingly more learned, contemporary in Nicholas Stanihurst). He was clearly aware of other approaches to the text that he jettisons in favour of the easy comprehensibility of Fox Morzillo. Of the ancient commentators, he had read both Simplicius and Themistius; of modern commentators, Vimercati, Javelli, Contarini and D'Etaples.[68] The particularly English fondness for Cicero renders that author a touchstone for Howard of philosophical knowledge.

The end of Howard's period in Cambridge cannot be dated precisely, though the years 1569 to 1571 look like a plausible terminating point; furthermore, the composition of his presentation manuscript of natural philosophy coincides with a more certain bid for court power.[69] It is within this same context that we should interpret Howard's first venture into print, which also comes in 1570.[70] This took the shape of a long pastoral elegy for Nicholas Carr, the Regius Professor of Greek at Cambridge. Carr had translated some orations of Demosthenes that were published posthumously, and verses from grieving colleagues were appended thereto to make a commemorative volume. Such collections, of course, are as much about the development of a collective image of the university and its role in the republic of letters as they are reflections on the nature of the particular relationship between the poet and the dead man. Careerism within Cambridge should not be pressed too far as a motivation, however. We should be alive to the possibility that there were simply no further opportunities at Cambridge. The list of fellows for Trinity Hall shows no deaths for 1569 and the end of the triennium of regency may mean that Howard was forced to look elsewhere. Further teaching (including private tuition) could doubtless be found but this appears not to have been the pattern Howard chose, perhaps because he considered such an occupation beneath him. Howard had to make his own way in the world, and the options were limited. The pattern of betrothal, fol-

---

[68] For more detailed proof of these claims, see my article 'Humanism and Natural Philosophy'.
[69] By 1569, Howard could not be considered sufficiently important an associate of Mary to make it likely that Don Guerau de Spes, the strongly anti-Elizabethan Spanish ambassador, would have taken time to engage with him specifically; consequently, it is unsurprising that there is no evidence for such a meeting in July of that year when De Spes made considerable efforts to check support for Mary after the flash-point of the Alva ship disaster (see below).
[70] See Appendix I for a transcription and commentary.

lowed by trainee diplomatic service abroad, was a widespread though not universal one.[71] It is possible, furthermore, that his ambitions did not confine themselves to the secular sphere, if one piece of evidence is to be believed. 1570 saw the death of Thomas Young, Archbishop of York, which naturally left open the question of who should accede to this influential see.[72] William Camden suggests that Henry Howard was jockeying himself for the position.[73] Some caution is advised in assessing this evidence. Howard was perhaps simply a convenient Catholic bogey-man. The implied reader of the *Annals* could assess the merits of Elizabeth's decision in selecting an apposite candidate to remedy the ills of the recently quelled rebellion of the northern earls all the more easily with the Earl of Northampton as a foil. After all, the *Annals* were published for the first time in 1615, safely after Howard's death in the previous year. The evidence would, however, explain in greater depth why Howard wrote his defence of, inter alia, the English episcopal hierarchy four years later but such nakedly end-based reasoning is best avoided. Equally, the increase in numbers and public position of those of Puritan and Presbyterian sympathies at Cambridge and elsewhere cannot have escaped Howard's notice. This makes Howard's bid at public profile through the poem for Carr all the more intelligible.

The elegy demonstrates both his close conformity to the genre and style of these poems and also their social function.[74] The genre in question is an epicedion, a sort of funeral lament, though as so often with such specific

---

[71] Stone, *The Crisis of the Aristocracy*, p. 196: 'By this means lengthy cohabitation was effectively postponed, and the young man prevented from getting trapped into an unsuitable marriage abroad': Duncan-Jones, *Sir Philip Sidney*, p. 46, is correct to see these expectations operative for Sidney, but one may point to the example of Anthony Bacon as closer to Howard's case. Bacon's stint with Sir Amias Paulet in Paris would probably have been too long to have kept any economically attractive bride out of the market-place.

[72] Thomas Young (1507–1568). York was an area replete with conservative religious sentiment: D. M. Palliser, *Tudor York*, London, 1979, p. 244.

[73] William Camden suggests so: 'And Henry Howard (who had aspired to the Archbishopricke of York) was upon suspicion committed to the custody of the Archbishop of Canterbury', *The Historie of the Moste Renowned and Victorious Princesse Elizabeth*, London: Benjamin Fisher, 1630, Bk 2, sig. Cc4^v. In any case, to be a bishop meant that you had to be ordained first, and Howard was not.

[74] For a transcription of the poem with brief commentary, see Appendix I. For a recent conspectus on Carr's life and works, see Michael Crawford's entry on him in *DNB*. I have not been able to locate any evidence from Cambidge that compares with that provided for, e.g., Sweden (S. Lindroth, *Uppsala Universitet, 1477–1977*, Uppsala, 1976, pp. 181–90), which suggests that the writing of funerary exequies formed part of rhetorical instruction, though the sheer quantity of such verse suggests as much.

labels for poems, there is a degree of terminological confusion.[75] The engagement with the genre is not only crucial for understanding the poem,

---

[75] J. W. Binns, *Intellectual Culture in Elizabethan England*, Leeds, 1990, p. 60, gives a classification based on Wills's *Poematum liber*, London, 1573, sigs D4^r–D5^r: *epicedium* combines praise of the departed's life with commiseration spoken over the corpse at burial; *monodia* is rather like an epicedium although was spoken to the accompaniment of a musical instrument; the *elegia* was a lament *pluribus versibus* (Binns glosses this to mean longer than an epigram, but many *epicedia* are long; perhaps length combined with the elegiac metre explains the category as far as Wills is concerned); *naenia* sung at the funeral pyre, but Wills has reservations about this method of disposing with a corpse since pyres are not Christian ways of dealing with the dead; *epitaphium* a brief and epigrammatic inscription for the tomb; *threnus* originally sung for the fall of a city (cf. *Iliad* 24); but cf. in general the close but slightly different taxonomy in Scaliger the Elder, *Poetices libri VII*, 1581, I.50, p. 129 [= Scaliger, *Poetices*, ed. Deitz, I, pp. 412–16], who, for instance, says that the word 'elegy' was also used originally of funeral poems. Furthermore, in another place [(Scaliger, *Poetices libri VII*, 1581, III.122, p. 425 [= Scaliger, *Poetices*, ed. Deitz, III, p. 191]) Scaliger gives the main opposition as being between *epitaphium* and *epicedium* (the first is for those who have been buried, the second for those that await burial). An alternative taxonomy is suggested by the German poet (and son-in-law of Melanchthon) Georgius Sabinus (1508–1560), who has the following definition (Sabinus, 'De prosodia' in Johannes Ravisius Textor, *Epitheta*, Geneva, 1640, p. 134) 'epicedion, id est, carmen quod in laudem defuncti ante cadaveris sepulturam cani solet, ut 'Extinctum nymphae crudeli funere Daphnin flebant', alio modo dicitur naenia vel monodia'. I do not have much faith in the stability of these generic definitions, unlike Binns, who claims that the 'titles of the collections in which they were assembled often show knowledge of these generic distinctions' (Binns, *Intellectual Culture*, p. 61). Indeed, his lists (pp. 475–81) of works which contain one or other of these words in their titles serves to undo his thesis. Furthermore, I wish to heavily underscore Scaliger's insight that genres are shared expressions or shared orientations toward feelings or events: one can have an epicedion, after all, in the middle of an elogium (that, at any rate, is Scaliger the Elder's comment on the generic status of the famous apostrophe to Nisus and Euryalus in book nine of the *Aeneid*: 'est autem quasi epicedion, non solum elogium', Scaliger, *Poetices libri VII*, 1581, III.40, p. 312 [= Scaliger, *Poetices*, ed. Deitz, II, p. 400). It is noteworthy that the word 'elegia' in England only exists as a title in books from 1621 onwards, thereby suggesting that in the 1620s some measure of agreement on what to call a poem on someone's death was emerging, doubtless under the influence of the growing dominance of the use of the English word 'elegy'. Certainly, one author, writing at the end of the sixteenth century, considers that elegy means love-elegy: so Don Cameron Allen, *Francis Meres' Treatise on 'Poetrie'*, Chicago, 1933, p. 79 (where Meres cites Surrey, Wyatt, Brian, Dyer, Spenser, Shakespeare, George Gascoigne, Page, Thomas Churchyard and Nicholas Breton). Several poems are called epicedia in the sixteenth century (fewer as the next century wears on), and this does seem to have had some autonomous life, beyond the classifications of the rhetoricians. For some general comments about the *Poetics* and the 'genre poetry' craze see Daniel Javitch, 'The Assimilation of Aristotle's *Poetics* in Sixteenth-Century Italy', in *Cambridge History of Literary Criticism, 3: Renaissance Criticism*, ed. G. Norton, Cambridge, 1999, pp. 53–65, and idem, 'On the Rise of Genre-Specific Poetics in the Sixteenth Century', in *Making Sense of Aristotle: Essays in Poetics*, eds O. Andersen and J. Haarberg, London, 2001, pp. 127–44.

as with most Renaissance literature, but also explicit.[76] Any such poem was supposed to have a threefold structure of praise, grief and consolation.[77] Howard clearly signals these stages in his poem, and indeed the transition between the praise and grief section turns on the word 'dolor'. This self-consciousness, hardly unexpected in a collection authored by a dead professor's university associates, continues throughout the poem. The well-developed Renaissance taste for structural elaboration and 'amplificatio' of discourse by various forms of digression is clearly exemplified.[78] One may see the funeral elegy in Tudor England as increasingly a genre in which the poet relates not so much to his grief and to the deceased as to his own poetic practice.[79] Howard's is certainly one of the

---

[76] For Renaissance genre theory in general, see Alastair Fowler, *Kinds of Literature*, Cambridge: MA, 1982; and *Renaissance Genres*, ed. B. Lewalski, Cambridge 1986. Alastair Fowler, 'The Formation of Genres in the Renaissance and After', *New Literary History*, 34, 2003, pp. 185–200, argues that genres are formed not so much out of genres but out of 'complexes' of particular metaphors and images (though the story is obviously different when dealing with mature genres, as is the case with Howard here, where the genre as genre has become part of the raw material for the production of a particular piece of persuasive discourse).

[77] Strictly speaking this is the threefold *dispositio* of the *loci* (each of which may well have been headed in Howard's mind by the same words) that have been gathered through *inventio*. In the first instance see O. B. Hardison, *The Enduring Monument: A Study of the Idea of Praise in Renaissance Literary Theory and Practice*, Chapel Hill: NC, 1962. The most detailed work, however, on the NeoLatin funeral poem known to me comes from Sweden: Annika Ström, *Lachrymae Catharinae. Five Collections of Funeral Poetry from 1628*, Stockholm, 1994 (Catherina Tidemanni was the wife of a theology professor at Uppsala); its bibliography is valuable. See also Walther Ludwig, 'Die Epikedien des Lotichius für Stilbar, Micyllus und Melanchthon', in *Lotichius und die Römische Elegie*, ed. Ulrike Auhagen, Tübingen, 2001, pp. 153–84 (this article suffers from an overemphasis on imitation at the expense of invention and disposition).

[78] See, e.g., Georgius Sabinus, 'De carminibus ad veterum imitationem componendis', in idem, *Poemata*, Leipzig: Iohannes Steinman, 1581, p. 513.

[79] This is the argument of the subtle and sensitive study of Dennis Kay, *Melodious Tears: The Funeral Elegy from Spenser to Milton*, Oxford, 1990. Regrettably, Kay does not deal with Neo-Latin material in any depth, and Leonard W. Grant, *Neo-Latin Literature and Pastoral*, Chapel Hill: NC, 1965, is a bald survey. Cf. G. W. Pigman III, *Grief and Renaissance Elegy*, Cambridge, 1985, who suggests a narrative of decreasing reluctance to engage in these public acts of grief as the sixteenth century wears on, and the work of Stephen Guy-Bray, *Homoerotic Space: The Poetics of Loss in Renaissance Literature*, Toronto, 2002, which detects an increasing tendency to eliminate homoerotic desire from the genre/discourse: the presuppositions and preoccupations of both books ill serve the milieu of the Carr collection, and, unless one expands the definition of 'homoerotic' so far that it ceases to describe much more than the warm emotional energies present in already existing social relations solely between men, there is little to be got out of the Guy-Bray thesis.

very first of these poems to be written by an Englishman, and he is, as we shall see, alive to at least some of the more self-conscious aspects of this genre.[80]

Scaliger, in his work on poetics, notes that an epitaph will differ according to whether the poem mourns a recently dead person or is an 'anniversarie'.[81] He then, however, gives an example from one of his own 'epicedia' as well as from one of his 'epitaphia'.[82] The parts that the poet must cover are 'praise, demonstration of loss, grief, consolation and exhortation'. The praise should not just be of the dead person, but of the death itself, and the demonstration of one's loss must move from a gentle to harsher style of narration, in which 'immoratio' and 'amplificatio' are appropriate figures to augment the desire for that which has been lost. From here, one is to go straight to the expression of grief. After this one needs to build up to the finale of the consolation.[83]

Howard's approach to poetry is fundamentally rhetorical. There was of course a theoretical tradition which separated poetry and rhetoric, but there were two other traditions which sought to eliminate the differences between the two. One was the Aristotelian notion, derived from the *Poetics*, of *imitatio*, not really developed in England until Sir Philip Sidney and the publication of his *Defence*; the other was that of humanist rhetoric, which viewed both media as simply different sorts of persuasive discourse.[84] The interlacing of words that Howard engages in, the composition of the smaller units and their relation to the distich, is not particularly successful or elaborate, and he is almost incapable of thinking in units larger than the line, or, sometimes, the distich. This lends a wooden quality to the poem. He is, however, scrupulous in avoiding rough caesurae in the pentameter and he avoids ending a pentameter on a present participle or anything

---

[80] Grant, *Neo-Latin Literature*, p. 328, makes Giles Fletcher the first so to have done, but that was on the occasion of the death of Edmund Bonner (1500–1569; supported anti-papal measures under Henry VIII but refused further doctrinal reform under Edward and Elizabeth, for which he spent the last ten years of his life in prison: see now the entry on him in the *ODNB*) in 1569, roughly contemporary with Howard's effort.

[81] Scaliger, *Poetices libri VII*, 1581, III.122, p. 426 [=Scaliger, *Poetices*, ed. Deitz, III, p. 193]: 'est igitur aut recens aut anniversarium'.

[82] Ibid., 'ut nos in Epicedio regio'.

[83] Ibid., pp. 426–7.

[84] See Erasmus, *Opus epistolarum*, I, epistle 283. The total assimilation of rhetorical 'elocutio' to poetry within poetic theory was achieved by the widely diffused *Poetics* of Scaliger: I have not thought it useful to dwell upon the poem's *elocutio*.

other than a disyllable.[85] He appears to share the Renaissance (and especially Ovidian) distaste for hiatus and elision.[86]

The self-consciousness that attends the work is signalled by Howard early on. In the face of his grief, he asks 'Why should I recount changed forms in a varied structure? ('quid repetam vario mutatas ordine formas?') This is surely a reference to the careful interlacing, or 'sampling', of themes and stock patterns, and phrases, that constitute poetic success in the period.[87] The very fact that it is modelled after the words 'prisca huc quid repeto?' in the anonymous *Epicedion Drusi* (where the phrase suggests the pointlessness of his poetic activity) only contributes to this sense of self-conscious intertexuality.[88] The poem starts with a general truth or 'propositio' contained in the first line, 'proved' through an exemplum.[89] The next couplet contains an 'objectio' which is also expanded through an exemplum. The couplet after that introduces the figure of the author and, through the figure of question, raises the emotional temperature. These last two lines are the first two lines of an eight-line extended comparison (an 'allegoria' in the language of the handbooks) which compares human life to a ship on the open main. The comparison is regularly viewed as one of the best ways of amplifying a text.

The transition from praise to grief is explicitly marked by the usage of

---

[85] For one account of this common Renaissance stylistic prejudice, see Georgius Sabinus, 'De carminibus ad veterum imitationem artificiose componendis', in his *Poemata*, Leipzig: Iohannes Steinman, 1581, pp. 486–514 at 511–12: 'in Pentametro versu tempestivae caesurae esse debent, vitanda est in medio, continuation carminis dura & hiulca … in Pentametro sunt vitanda Participia. Eodem in loco rarissime usurpandae sunt voces, duabus syllabis longiores.' Note the contrast between the relative metrical articulacy of English neo-Latin verse in Howard's time and that of earlier times: F. Cairns, 'The Metrical and Stylistic Competence of Latin Poetry in the Second Half of the Fifteenth Century', in *Homo Sapiens, Homo Humanus*, ed. G. Taurigi, Florence, 1990, pp. 33–40.

[86] Sabinus, p. 493.

[87] The phrase may be described as a strategy for deflating the sense of unreality that attends the pastoral scenario, something picked up in the series of questions and answers in lines 37–43. The phrasing also suggests the equally programmatic opening of Ovid, *Metamorphoses*, I.1.

[88] The parallel is certain. In addition to the general similarity of the phrase and the fact that both poems are epicedia, there is the even more significant question of structure: both phrases occur after an initial exordial section of traditional or sententious character.

[89] For the idea that poems are constructed in this way (by a proposition in an elegiac distich, followed by considerable expansion of that *propositio*), see Erasmus, *Commentarius in Ov.*, ASD, I.i., pp. 147–50 and Marc-Antoine Muret, *Opera omnia*, ed. D. Ruhnken, 4 vols, Leiden, 1794, I, p. 793. The high quantity of sententious material in this and other Renaissance elegies is a by-product of their authors' desire to emphasize the public status of the emotions confessed.

the words 'laudes' and 'dolor' in close succession at the appropriate juncture (lines 44–6), or, to put the point more historically, there are formal features which structure the *dispositio* of the *loci* in accordance with the threefold pattern into which, generally, the *dispositio* should fall (so the change from the exordial material to the laus is signalled by the rhetorical question 'fallor?'). Indeed, further accordance with generic expectations follows: what Scaliger refers to as the need to move from a smoother to a rougher style of narration of one's loss is followed by Howard between lines 42 and 88.[90] The shorter phrases, and the more dramatic content of lines 76–82, in particular, mark a sort of emotional high point to the poem. The passage is undergirded by a series of references to Vergil's *Aeneid*, whereby the image of the lecturing Carr that appears to Howard's mind is compared to that of the vanishing Creusa, Aeneas's wife, one of the most pathetic moments in that poem.[91]

The final section of the work, the consolation, starts at line 89. It is marked as a consolation by Howard's usage, in the final couplet (line 101), of the word 'solatur'.[92] The consolation that it offers is conventional enough. Consolations are typically directed toward other people, but the writing of them usually took on a self-therapeutic character. Howard consoles himself, in explicitly Christian fashion, with the hope that the passage of time will unite the two men once again.[93] The social act that such a

---

[90] The phrase 'is followed by' does not imply that genres are more literary rules than grids of situational and representational expectation.

[91] Line 78: 'more discedit fugientis more Creusae'; see Vergil, *Aeneid*, II. 768–791. The reader may compare numerous verbal echoes between such two passages as (the most sustained piece of imitation in the poem):
quaerenti et tectis urbis sine fine ruenti   771
infelix simulacrum atque ipsius umbra Creusae
uisa **mihi ante oculos** et nota maior **imago**.   =line 75
obstipui, steteruntque comae et **uox faucibus haesit**. < line 78 and =line 79
tum sic adfari et curas his demere dictis …   775
haec ubi dicta dedit, lacrimantem et multa uolentem 790
dicere deseruit, **tenuisque recessit in auras**.   < line 81

[92] The consolation is the least well-developed section of this poem, as with other such poems; we are reminded that (Hardison, *The Enduring Monument*, p. 114) 'praise is the essential element of the form. If consolation were the most important element, funeral elegy would be deliberative and not epideictic, since consolatio was generally classified in the former category'. One might comment that it would be hard (without the tripartite structure) to distinguish between *loci* of praise and consolation, since they naturally share common ground.

[93] For a similar final couplet, see Petrus Lotichius, *Poemata*, Leipzig: Iohannes Steinmann, 1576 (though available in earlier printings), sig. F7ᵛ 'sic tranquilla tibi requies, spesque inscia luctus | Iamque vale: manes subsequar ipse tuos'.

poem embodies was clearly not just one of praise for a dead tutor and colleague. It is as much about staking a claim in the social order.[94] This is not to suggest a poetic insincerity added on to a real relation, but rather that the very relationship itself had these elements of social function, which the poem as much reflected as created.

To reiterate, Howard's work contributed to the increasing reflexivity of the genre of the pastoral elegy and perhaps suggests that the university milieu was already experimenting with this form of self-consciousness rather earlier than was being done in the vernacular tradition. Furthermore, the investment in the scholarly life that the poem suggests was simultaneously a clear development of the taste for humanist learning that Howard had developed ever since his days of private tuition and a probable step toward the axis of educational elitism with possibilities for public service that was a marked feature of Cecil's understanding of the humanist endeavour. One should not simply, in a reductivist move familiar from recent secondary literature, over-emphasize the careerist view of humanism. A parallel may be drawn with the history of the scientific revolution. Recent scholarship has argued that it is important that we understand the social construction of the scientist in this period: in other words, that he is believed only because of his social status and because of the time and resources that he can deploy in the service of the new experimental knowledge; but there are intellectual criteria that determine one's social circle just as much as the other way round. Similarly, humanism is both constitutive of a higher standard of discourse for what counts as quality of persuasion in particular contexts *and* informed by the requirement to gain a particular result or career position. Howard's confused and marginal position on both sides of this axis was to remain both a political and an intellectual articulation of his career over the next three decades.

---

[94] The fact that Howard's poem comes first in the book reminds us of the socially graded positioning of sonnets within sonnet sequences (Howard is the highest ranking noble in the collection): A. F. Marotti, 'Love is not Love: Elizabethan Sonnet Sequences and the Social Order', *English Literary History*, 49, 1982, pp. 296–328.

Chapter 3

'BEWARE OF TO MUCH ARTE'
BETWEEN CAMBRIDGE AND AUDLEY END

A SCHOLARLY life was, even then, not necessarily a well-remunerated one. Howard's financial situation was always precarious. His loyalty to some members of his clan was not reciprocated with lavish annuities by the rest of them. It is worth noting that Howard is mentioned as one of the beneficiaries of the *reversionary* interest of various lands of his brother after the life-interest of very many others had been extinguished (including Thomas Bromley, Lord Burghley (as William Cecil became in 1571), the Earl of Sussex, the Earl of Leicester, Sir Christopher Hatton, Francis Walsingham, Sir Walter Mildmay and several others).[1] Still, coupled with the allowance from his sister, he seems, with borrowing, to have kept his head above water financially.[2] The same could not always be said of his political reputation, as the upshot from the Ridolfi affair demonstrates.

International events did not feature prominently in Henry Howard's first thirty years. The power that his brother possessed in abundance was local and inherited, not traded and international.[3] Continental alliances did not seem necessary and were potentially dangerous. Furthermore, too illustrious a union might upset the Franco-Spanish balance that was the principal cause of the peace that obtained between England and Spain.[4] Howard's insular political focus at this stage, however continental his intellectual formation,

---

[1] TNA: PRO, CPR, 24 Eliz. 1, part xii, 2017.
[2] For his borrowings, see, e.g., p. 121.
[3] For the connections between Thomas Howard's power and the counties in which he had his seat, see D. MacCulloch, *Suffolk and the Tudors. Politics and Religion in an English County 1500–1600*, Oxford, 1988, ch. 2.
[4] The change in historiographical habit from explaining the antecedents of the Armada to explaining the reasons for the Anglo-Spanish peace of the earlier part of Elizabeth's reign is given canonical expression by M. J. Rodriguez-Salgado, 'Paz ruidosa, guerra sorda', in *La*

was not unusual. It is noteworthy that, according to the testimony of Lawrence Bannister (the family lawyer), when a marriage between himself and Mary, Queen of Scots, was originally proposed, he wanted no part of it, and suggested that Mary would do better to marry his brother, Henry.[5] Mary's party was distinctly unimpressed, retorting (so Bannister tells us) that the brother was an unknown. However, Howard's involvement (albeit by implication) in the Ridolfi affair was a good schooling in how not to organize a plot, as well as providing an insight into the poised geo-politics at stake.

Roberto Ridolfi was a man in the wrong place at the wrong time. The year of 1568 had seen a number of events that, taken together, created a definite deterioration in the relations between Spain and England. Philip II had broken off contact with John Man, England's last ambassador at the Spanish court.[6] Then there was the famous act of aggression of the destruction of the fleet of an English merchant, Hawkins, by Spanish ships.[7] Increasing the fraught atmosphere was the sudden arrival of Mary, Queen of Scots, who had fled Scotland, and was now under house arrest in the Midlands. Into this atmosphere came Ridolfi, a financier from Florence who bankrolled Mary, Queen of Scots, and the Duke of Norfolk. He was also, by his own admission (to Fenelon, the French ambassador), a man with a papal mission to restore Catholicism in England.[8] He had been in England since 1562, and since 1566 had been handling the monies sent by Pius V to sustain English Catholics. He had transferred some monies to the

---

monarquia de Felipe II a debate, ed. L. Ribot Garcia, Madrid, 2000, pp. 63–119, esp. 63–70; this essay also notes, however, that the Ridolfi plot is the major exception to her thesis. An important earlier work in this vein is Pauline Croft, 'Trading with the Enemy, 1585–1604', *Historical Journal*, 32, 1989, pp. 281–303, to whose references on the anxiety felt by the business community by the disruption in Anglo-Spanish trade relations, add [I.B.], *The Merchants Avizo*, London: Richard Whittaker, 1604, sig. A3ʳ; and see, more generally, *England Spain and the Gran Armada, 1585–1604*, eds S. Adams and M. J. Rodriguez-Salgado, Edinburgh, 1991.

[5] William Murdin, *A Collection of State Papers Relating to Affairs in the Reign of Elizabeth from the Years 1571 to 1596*, London: William Bowyer, 1759, p. 134. The reliability of Bannister's testimony (under threat of torture) is unclear. However, the rumour was to resurface years later (see p. 58 of this chapter): perhaps Howard had kept the tale alive himself. Note that Mary (1542–1587) was daughter of James V of Scotland, himself son of James IV of Scotland and Margaret Tudor, daughter of Henry VII.

[6] G. M. Bell, 'John Man: The Last Elizabethan Resident Ambassador in Spain', *Sixteenth-Century Journal*, 2, 1976, pp. 75–93.

[7] J. A. Williamson, *Hawkins of Plymouth*, London, 1969, pp. 100–56. See Harry Kelsey, *Sir John Hawkins: Queen Elizabeth's Slave Trader*, New Haven, 2003.

[8] The traditional account is Conyers Read, *Lord Burghley and Queen Elizabeth*, London, 1960, pp. 38–50, which quotes generously from Cecil's own unpublished version of events at TNA: PRO SP 12/85/11. See also C. Roth, 'Roberto Ridolfi e la sua congiura', *Rivista storica degli archivi toscani*, 2, 1930, pp. 119–32 (a transcription of Ridolfi's own account);

Lord Henry Howard: An Elizabethan Life

Bishop of Ross as well as making loans to Lumley and Arundel.[9] He was arrested in September 1569 and turned over to Walsingham for questioning. He was released, either because he had been 'turned' or simply because he managed to convince Walsingham of his legitimacy.[10]

The plan of Cecil and Elizabeth at this point was to strain the Franco-Spanish power axis as much as possible. After all, England might align itself (and its queen) with France in order to further France's desire for power in Western Europe; this was the great obstacle to Spain's hopes of approach to England.[11] It is against this background that the seriousness of later events becomes clear. In April 1571, two men were arrested at Dover on charges of carrying prohibited books.[12] One of them, Charles Bailly, eventually revealed (under a mixture of the rack and threats of disfigurement) that he was carrying letters in cipher addressed, to among others, two English noblemen who were termed 30 and 40. After renewed pressure, the Bishop of Ross claimed that '30' and '40' were, respectively, the Queen of Scots and the Spanish ambassador. One presumes that suspicions at this point were aroused since

---

Williams, *Thomas Howard*, London, 1964; Francis Edwards, *The Marvellous Chance, Thomas Howard, Fourth Duke of Norfolk, and the Ridolfi Plot, 1570–1572*, London, 1968; Geoffrey Parker, 'The Place of Tudor England in the Messianic Vision of Philip II of Spain', *Transactions of the Royal Historical Society*, 12, 2002, pp. 167–221, esp. pp. 215–21. One reason why Ridolfi survived suspicion so long can be ascribed to recent military decisions in the Netherlands: the importance of Antwerp as a centre for Anglo-Dutch trade had been weakened by the decision of Elizabeth and Cecil to retain a fleet of ships loaded with gold and silver, destined for the Duke Alva, the Spanish Governor of the Netherlands, and owned by the Duke's Genoese merchants (on Alva, see W. S. Maltby, *Alba: A Biography of Fernando Alvarez de Toledo, Third Duke of Alba*, Berkeley, 1982). Without it, the progress of the Spanish war in the Netherlands was delayed. Reaction was swift: English sailors off Zeeland were imprisoned and trade embargos placed upon the Merchant Adventurers (G. D. Ramsay, *The Queen's Merchants and the Revolt of the Netherlands*, 2 vols, Manchester, 1986, II, pp. 154–7). Consequently, some of Cecil's Protestant friends in the business world encouraged the opening up of other trade links (e.g. Emden or Hamburg) which required refinancing from an influx of welcomed Italian financiers like Ridolfi. In summer of 1569, the Spanish crew were released, just as Cecil and Leicester were bribed to accept the financing services of the Italians.

9 For the financial details, see F. Edwards, *The Dangerous Queen*, London, 1964, pp. 298–30, and the new material uncovered by Parker, 'The Place of Tudor England', p. 192 n. 51.

10 For the turncoat theory, see Parker, 'The Place of Tudor England', pp. 192–3.

11 There was no necessary connection between Mary and Spain, since she 'was brought up at the French court and closely related to the French royal family' (Parker, 'The Place of Tudor England', p. 188).

12 There were also some letters of more directly seditious contents but these were kept from Burghley's eyes by Lord Cobham, Warden of the Cinque Ports, a position, as rumour-mongers were to prove under Howard's tenure of the post thirty-five years later, that was far from the uncontroversial sinecure that a bare description of its duties might suggest: see [Sparke] *A Historicall Narration*, pp. 57–8.

these two figures were hardly threats to the extent that one might have presumed them to be hostile and in any case, issues of legal jurisdiction prevented them from being questioned too heavily. Who these nobleman really were now possessed the Privy Council and Parliament. Such concerns would not, however, deflect the queen from making another of her lavish progresses round the country. August saw her prevail upon the generous hospitality of the Duke of Norfolk at his house near Walden, Essex. Unluckily for Norfolk, a suspicious Welsh draper, to whom Norfolk's secretary, Higford (sometimes, Hickford), had entrusted the conveyance of a package, found that the package contained a cipher which he delivered, doubtless anxious to save his own welshing skin, to Cecil. Higford was examined and revealed the existence of a key to the code. In a detail not calculated to soothe concerns over national security, he told his interrogators that the key was situated hard by a map of England that hung in Howard House. This looked bad for Norfolk, who was translated to the Tower on 8 September. After further torture of Norfolk's secretaries, the full details of a plot came out.[13] Unsurprisingly, Henry Howard soon wrote to Cecil. More surprising is its content: a request for a greater pension.[14] Either Howard was completely unaware that this was not the moment to push his luck, or he was engaging in double-bluff. The letter

---

[13] I use the words 'a plot' *sous rasure*, as it were, since there were various revisions made to these testimonies: see Edwards, *The Marvellous Chance*, ch. 5. I do not accept the theory that 'Thomas Howard and Mary were unjustly convicted ... The real plot was contrived by Cecil to get rid of a rival and a threat to his master plan for the new England' (Francis Edwards, 'Sir Robert Cecil, Edward Squier and the Poisoned Pommel', in *Recusant History*, 25, 2001, pp. 377–414, at 378); such an interpretation rests on a rather crude understanding of what consitutes a 'plot' (when does antipathy and secret communication end and treason begin?). In any case, there was after the machination of the Spanish in Ireland clearly some degree of international support for anti-Elizabethan feeling, which would legitimately transform the 'antipathy' into a 'plot', regardless of the interior ambivalences, if such they were, of Norfolk and the rest of his party.

[14] One should note, however, the comment of Joy Rowe ('The Lopped Tree: The Re-formation of the Suffolk Catholic Community', in *England's Long Reformation 1500–1800*, ed. N. Tyacke, London, 1998, pp. 167–93 at 170) – which has particular resonance for Howard – that '[a]lthough many of the Suffolk gentry had been clients of the 4th Duke of Norfolk, his disgrace in November 1569 did not greatly disturb the relationships which were the stuff of everyday life. Sir Thomas Cornwallis of Brome in Hartismere deanery, prominent among the conservative group [and associate of Howard], was summoned to appear before the Privy Council at Windsor in October 1569 "for matter of religion" ... He was able to exploit his long acquaintance with the Queen in her earlier years and his old friendship with Sir William Cecil to clear himself of the charge of disaffection ... Like many of his fellow Catholics in the 1560s, he was still prepared to temporize over the issue ... Cornwallis's stance, although equivocal, marked the end of a period of indecision for the Catholic gentry of East Anglia ... From the time that Sir Thomas Cornwallis returned to the county in June 1570, the influence of the religiously conservative gentry of Norfolk and Suffolk was limited to the exploitation of personal links to achieve very restricted successes in local affairs ...'.

mentions that, of course, his brother would help him out were he in a position to do so and finishes with the peculiar comment 'to be sure, I am voyde of any certayne place of abidinge'.[15] The letter was penned from Audley End, but the tone may suggest that Howard felt his tenancy there was unsafe – his actions suggest a reason to hide, but one tantalisingly absent from our other sources. Moreover, the records show that a servant of the Duke of Norfolk, Lawrence Bannister, was also tortured. From him we learn, as mentioned above, that it was Henry Howard and not his brother Thomas who was originally destined for marriage with Mary.[16] Anxiety over his position presumably accounts for the otherwise contentless letters of the next couple of months, one a new year's good wish from all at Audley End sent to Burghley by Howard on the 29 December 1572 and the other a 'get well soon' greeting dated 20 January 1573.[17]

Meanwhile, the pope and the king of Spain were involved in a plot to dethrone Elizabeth and make Mary queen of England. Norfolk said that he knew of these and had been approached but nothing more. John Leslie was subject to an examination and confessed all. His testimony served to provide the all-important evidence which enabled Norfolk to be brought to trial, as happened on 16 January 1572. He was beheaded on 2 June 1572. The Spanish ambassador, Guerau de Spes, was sent packing. The consequences for Norfolk's younger brother were less severe, if still grave for a man with no party. He was likely to have been resident at Howard House, and a man so intelligent and with so acute an eye for intrigue cannot have failed to scent that something was afoot. It is doubtful whether he took any active role in the plot, not even the removal of the key to the code from its original resting place. Suffice it to say that sufficient suspicion attended Henry Howard to have him placed under arrest. A letter dated 26 April 1572 from Lambeth states that Howard is under surveillance at Lambeth Palace, which is not to his liking.[18] He claims that he would prefer imprisonment at the Fleet.[19] This state of affairs probably changed soon, though he had not moved by July 2, when Matthew Parker writes a meagre five lines to Burghley asking liberty for Howard.[20] Perhaps, with the execution of his

---

[15] BL Cotton MS, Titus C vi f. 13ᵛ.
[16] See above (the claim is also asserted by W. Addison, *Audley End*, London, 1953, p. 25).
[17] BL Cotton MS, Titus C vi f. 18ᵛ.
[18] *CSPD, 1547–80*, p. 441.
[19] Given the less salubrious (although more open) conditions of the Fleet, one would have thought that Howard's claim is a mere figure of speech.
[20] Parker's biographer dramatically over-interprets this note, when he says that it evinces the archbishop's love of order and lawfulness: V. J. K. Brook, *The Life of Archbishop Parker*, Oxford, 1962, p. 296 (with further references).

brother a month earlier, any chance of uncovering any further evidence against Howard were judged slim. That aside, one suspects little love lost between the reform-minded archbishop and Howard, even if he had taken of late a somewhat resigned attitude toward his position, although the withdrawn noble of uncertain loyalties was at least an ally in scholarship, even if Howard did not share Parker's enthusiasms for Anglo-Saxon.[21]

He was soon allowed his freedom, however. Burghley was presumably the motive force behind this. Doubtless the architect of the Elizabethan polity saw the potential usefulness of Howard. Equally, he will have had doubts about the young man's loyalty. His indiscretions could not be put down, like those of the Earl of Oxford, to an erratic and impulsive personality. Howard seems to have been living in the mid-1570s in Audley End, close to the court if need be, and Burghley sent him to meet Oxford on his disembarcation at Dover from his travels on the continent. Howard engaged in correspondence with Burghley to ascertain 'whether he knew that my Lord her husband would go to Court … My Lord Howard sent me word that as yet he could not tell'.[22] The queen, too, has, according to Howard, harboured suspicions unjustly against him.[23] Whether these are really ways of talking about his relationship with Cecil we cannot be sure, since the queen remains tight-lipped on this, as on almost every other issue.[24] What he continued to do was teach and write, both activities that depended upon reading.

Reading, and the closely allied task of writing, has long been viewed as central to the cultivation of the public profile of the humanist. Certainly, Henry Howard was a reader and a writer throughout his life.[25] For most of

---

[21] Trinity Hall was a college to which Parker made several gifts and bequests: a silver-gilt standing cup and cover in 1569 and a tankard in 1571: Crawley, *Trinity Hall*, p. 45. It is possible that Howard was actually staying at his brother's house in Lambeth, since there is a reference in Matthew Parker's will to 'my house and land, lying and being in Lambeth, known by the name of the Duke of Norfolk's house', or, a little later on 'Duke's House' (so John Strype, *Life of Matthew Parker, Archbishop of Canterbury*, London, 1711, p. 474).

[22] HMC Hatfield House, II, pp. 131–2.

[23] E.g. BL Cotton MS, Caligula C iii f. 98ᵛ: 'Deum immortalem testor me ne cogitatione quidem vel levissimam Maiestatis suae offensionem lacessivit nec esse cur suspicere.'

[24] [Elizabeth Tudor's] *Collected Works*, ed. Leah S. Marcus et al., New York, 2000, provide not one reference to Henry Howard.

[25] On the centrality of reading and writing to humanist intellectual activity, see A. T. Grafton, *Defenders of the Text: The Traditions of Scholarship in an Age of Science: 1450–1800*, Cambridge: MA, 1994. See now the beautifully cautious and wryly elegant work of Daniel Wakelin, *Humanism, Reading and English Literature, 1430–1530*, Oxford, 2007.

Elizabeth's reign, political power simultaneously attracted and eluded him. Such influence as he wielded took the guise of elegantly written letters, orations and treatises.[26] Perhaps, indeed, it was precisely his distance from the mechanisms of administrative power and his self-conscious presentation of himself as a scholar and humanist, albeit without the most secure of philological foundations, that caused the rumours of mistrust to swirl about him. Howard's capacity for pursuing his own self-interest and a certain bitterness in his personality cannot have helped; such explanations, however, do not fall within the province of intellectual history.[27] To those whom he had alienated or whose ideological agenda he found distasteful, he was a flatterer, but flattery has a long-running connection with argument and persuasion. Howard was, above all, a humanist rhetor.[28] Howard's own, often farouche, persuasive efforts are heavily – if at times in ways which it is evidentially difficult to spell out – dependent on his reading. This fact embraces a methodological amalgam of more and less rigorous notions of what counts as the standard of proof in history. Such modulation, however, may be unavoidable given the evidential limitations from which the history of reading in the Renaissance suffers. Much must be inferred about the actual practice and mental modulations involved in book reading in the Renaissance. We must simply accept their own pronouncements at face value that ideas are based on reading, partly as a result of the intensively 'grammatical' and 'readerly' educational drill to which Elizabethan schoolboys were subjected. This was their education in grammar – a subject with, it would appear, a rather shadowy existence in the universities, despite statute assertions to the contrary, and one for the most part taught beforehand: it was, after all, intimately linked to tuition in reading. It is particularly problematic that the dividing line between grammar and rhetoric is not an exact one, for the tuition of grammar involved an element of composition, inculcating principles of elegance, variation and appropriate construction of thought. Grammatical exegesis of this sort brought with it a set of cognitive habits but did not, with the right pupil, take the place of knowledge. The trivium, after all, was propaideumatic to

---

[26] And, of course, verbal counsel, opportunities for which under the female monarch were perhaps more significant than they had been under her father (since there were fewer opportunities for courtly credit to be won in traditional areas from which Elizabeth was excluded).

[27] The increased receptivity to the 'rhetorical' notion of character distinguishes Peck, 'Mentality', from the earlier Peck, *Northampton*.

[28] What is left out of this picture is Howard's devotional sensibility, but that is partly because it is harder to reconstruct from an evidential point of view.

what in a twentieth-century lexicon would be called 'facts'. One should be a little wary of reducing knowledge to the disciplinary strictures of grammar, rhetoric and dialectic. What, then, we are witnessing in the slow institutionalization of the humanist educational programme is the gradual creation of a culture peculiarly and pleasurably attentive to the philological basis of proof and persuasion. Grammar, given that it was an education in proper discourse, was by the same token an introduction on the one hand to the social functions of that discourse (correct social and linguistic criteria, the notion of the civil conversation) and on the other to the higher disciplines of the arts course.

While it is sometimes possible to discern quite 'personal' enthusiasms in reading, we should, therefore, exercise much caution before pouncing on any given annotation or collection of *sententiae* in a commonplace book as being evidence for or against a particular position.[29] We are fortunate in having a comment from Howard himself that bears upon the topic, a comment that faces, Janus-like, in both directions of this 'humanist culture vs. individual response' debate. 'Bookes are livelie Ideas of the authors minds that compilid them': so he wrote in one of his series of aphorisms that date, probably, from the 1580s.[30] The phrase 'livelie Ideas' demands a little philology.[31] The word 'idea' was a modern one in English at the time that Howard wrote: the *OED*'s first citation comes from 1531.[32] Howard in 1569 knew of the Platonic meaning of this word when he glosses it as synonymous with εἶδος in his manuscript on natural philosophy.[33] The Platonic meaning, strictly speaking, is a metaphysical exemplar for all of the

---

[29] The reader will detect a similarity with the stance taken by Fred Schurink, 'Like a hand in the margine of a booke: William Blount's Marginalia and the Politics of Sidney's *Arcadia*', *Review of English Studies*, 2008, 59, pp. 1–24. For some, of course, humanist pedagogy has been seen as an authoritarian discourse (e.g., Richard Halpern, *The Poetics of Primitive Accumulation: English Renaissance Culture and the Genealogy of Capital*, Ithaca: NY, 1991, pp. 31–4), but we should not underestimate the opportunities for the adoption of a variety of 'subject positions' in rhetoric (though the notion that the pathway to all knowledge about the world consists in the exegesis of a set number of books must have certain consequences for a culture).

[30] Henry Howard, aphorism (this title is my own), BL Cotton MS, Titus C vi f. 292[v]. This dating is suggested by two factors: the contents of each section of this manuscript volume appear to follow a roughly chronological order; and, secondly, the hand used can be plausibly assigned to the middle of Howard's career.

[31] The seminal work is *Idea*, eds M. Fattori and L. Bianchi, Rome, 1990, upon which depends R. Ariew, *Descartes and the Last Scholastics*, Ithaca: NY, 1999, pp. 58–76; see also, with some caution, Erwin Panofsky, *Idea: A Concept in Art Theory*, London, 1968.

[32] *OED* s.v.

[33] BLO Bodley MS 616, f. 14[r] with my commentary ad loc. There is no accentuation of Greek vowels or dipthongs in Howard's tract.

instances that form the extension of that concept.³⁴ There is also, however, the meaning of 'image', which, though it has affinities with the Platonic meaning, appears to be a separate subset. The *locus classicus* for this meaning of idea in Classical Latin literature occurs in one of Seneca's letters.³⁵ Seneca's words make it sound as if the idea is some sort of mental representation of the artificial work. The visual analogy makes it possible to imagine that we are simply talking about a mental image, rather than a 'rough draft'; but Seneca's explicit avowal that it can apply to what one has placed in one's mind in some internal operation makes possible the application of the notion to non-visual fields of practice. It is in this sense that Sir Philip Sidney uses the word in his *Defence*:

> Neither let this be jestingly conceived, because the works of the one be essential, the other in imitation or fiction; for any understanding knoweth the skill of each articifer standeth in that idea or fore-conceit of the work, and in the work itself.³⁶

Howard's sense is subtly different: his words make it clear that the book is not the artist's image of an object in the world but rather a representation of the self.³⁷ This difference is readily explicable. Sidney's usage of the

---

[34] Plato applies the theory of forms to both naturally occurring and artificial objects: see Republic 596B; 597C; and Cratylus 389B–C.

[35] Seneca, *Epistulae morales*, 65.4 (cited from Seneca, *Opera*, 4 vols, Leiden: Elzevir, 1649, II, p. 168): 'An non putas inter caussas facti operis numerandum, quo remoto factum non esset? His quin tam Plato adiucit, exemplar, quam ipse ideam vocat: hoc est enim ad quod respiciens artifex, id quod destinabat, efficit. Nihil autem ad rem pertinet, utrum foris habeat exemplar, ad quod referat oculos: an intus, quod sibi ipse concepit et posuit. Haec exemplaria rerum omnium Deus intra se habet, numerosque universorum quae agenda sunt, & modos mente complexus est'; for a Senecan distinction between the Greek *eidos* and the Latin *idea*, *Epistulae morales*, 58.17–18). The word is excessively rare in Classical Latin. Into medieval Latin would creep an adjectival formation, *idealis*, first testified in Martianus Cappella: see *A Glossary of Later Latin to 600 AD*, ed. A. Souter, Oxford, 1949 s. v. 'idealis'. Panofksy argues for the wide diffusion of this letter of Seneca. We should also note Scaliger the Elder's usage of the word, *Poetices libri VII* [Heidelberg]: Petrus Santandareus, 1581, III, i [= Julius Caesar Scaliger, *Poetices libri septem. Sieben Bücher über die Dichtkunst*, ed. L. Deitz, 5 vols, Stuttgart, 1992–2003, II, p. 80]: 'Sicut igitur est idea picturae Socrates, sic Troia Homericae Iliados'.

[36] Sir Philip Sidney, 'A Defence of Poetry', in *English Renaissance Literary Criticism*, ed. B. Vickers, Oxford, 1999, p. 344.

[37] The degree to which the word is at this stage in its history being pulled about in different directions may be seen from Sidney's contemporaneous usage of the word. It was the Platonic sense that won out, after an initial flirtation with the artistic sense, in Thomas Elyot, *Dictionary*, London: Thomas Berthelet, 1538, sig. K3ᵛ s.v. 'Idea', whose definition is repeated almost word for word in Thomas Thomas, *Dictionarium linguae latinae et anglicae*, Cambridge: Thomas, 1587, sig. Dd 8ᵛ (s.v. 'Idea'): 'The figure conceived in imagina-

Between Cambridge and Audley End

word is the usage of someone interested in the creation of an artefact. Howard's interest in the presentation of his own self and that of others suggests that he views 'books' as revelations of character, or, as Renaissance rhetoricians would have termed it, *ethos*.[38] *Ethos* was a persuasive mode of rhetoric (along with *logos* and *pathos*); it afforded the orator the opportunity to project an image of himself for his audience which would anchor their perceptions of what he had to say.[39] Howard sees works, or strictly speaking, 'bookes' as part of a continuum of persuasive discourse; Sidney's usage of the word idea shows he is inclined to a more 'artefactual' account of the creative process.

We should tarry too over the word 'lively'. It might be thought to introduce the notion of verisimilitude, which was the standard term of praise in Renaissance portraiture: representations are always said to be 'ad vitam'. It is more likely, however, that the word has the meaning 'affecting the senses', since the mental content presumed by the phrase 'authors minds' has not yet been the object of the adorning devices of rhetoric. The semantic field for 'lively' in this period of Elizabethan English is fairly wide. In addition to the root meaning of 'possessing life' (OED μ 1), there is another sense, closer to that of Howard. Here the lively is opposed to some less enlivening form of representation or instruction (OED μ c).[40] Therefore, if we accept that 'lively' has this sensory connotation, we may interpret Howard's comment to mean: a book is a rhetorically pleasing representation of its writer's mind. In other words, unlike the passage of Sidney which we quoted earlier, Howard's ideas are representations of a particular human being's mind. This is, in turn, part of a long rhetorical tradition about the identity of the man and the style.[41] In particular, we are aware of the authors' minds that 'compilid' them. The words

---

tion, as it weare a substance perpetuall, beeing as a patterne of all other sort or kinde: as of one seale proceedeth many printes, so of one Idea of man proceedeth many thousands of men'. The novelty of the word in Elyot's time is proved by the fact that he gives it a full definition, whereas for most other words he confines himself to a couple of translations. Howard uses the word again in one of his Latin works (BL Egerton MS 944, f. 46ᵛ: 'formam quondam et ideam, mente animoque'), but the highly copious style of that work in general, and the particular context of doublets within which the word is found rather disbars us from making any precise comments on its meaning.

[38] It follows, as we shall see, that Howard is acutely conscious of the social implications of writing and publishing.

[39] W. Süss, *Ethos. Studien zur älteren griechischen Rhetorik*, Berlin, 1910, continues to be justly cited by students of ancient literature.

[40] E.g., John Dee, *Mathematical Preface*, 5: 'They which will are not liable to atteine to this without lively instruction' (cited by the *OED* CD ROM).

[41] See the famous account of Maecenas' effeminate style in Seneca, *Epistulae morales*, 133 or Cicero's description of a particular discouse as 'virilis' (*De oratore*, I. 231).

Lord Henry Howard: An Elizabethan Life

strongly indicate Howard's view of the writing process as rooted in the gathering together of other men's flowers.[42] This was a common notion of composition in the Renaissance. Howard varies the metaphor, though keeping the essential point, in describing the task of composition later on: 'setting the smalle pieces of sweet wood together in a worke of markantree'.[43]

We now turn to the evidence for Howard's own raw material for these elaborate works of marquetry, his engagement with reading. After all, there has been a flurry of work in recent years on Renaissance reading practices.[44] One influential account has been what we may refer to here as the

---

[42] The meaning given in Elyot's 1538 *Dictionary* (at sig. D5ʳ) for 'compilo' is simply 'to extort'. Thomas Thomas 1587 *Dictionarium* (at sig. M7ᵛ) repeats Elyot's definition verbatim and then adds 'to gather or heape together in one'. I can find no late fifteenth-century nor early sixteenth-century usage of the English word compile in this 'combinatory' sense, so it would appear that Thomas is explaining current Anglo-Latin usage. A good parallel to the present passage is found in Sir Philip Sidney ('A Defence of Poetry', p. 368) where he uses the word to describe the process by which axioms of grammar or logic are turned into verse-form for mnemonic purposes. There is an earlier medieval usage of the word *compilatio* (see, e.g., M. B. Parkes, 'The Influence of the Concepts of *Ordinatio* and *Compilatio* on the Development of the Book', in *Medieval Learning and Literature: Essays Presented to Richard William Hunt*, eds J. J. G. Alexander and M. T. Gibson, Oxford, 1976, pp. 115–41, esp. pp. 128–9), but I see no obvious lines of descent there, though for the early period a case is made out for a progressively more positive sense of the word for the late medieval period by N. Hathaway, '*Compilatio*: From Plagiarism to Composition', *Viator*, 20, 1989, pp. 19–44. This emphasis on structural elegance and the interlacing of small units in a pleasing form will be seen as the best way of viewing the literary goals of his epicedion and his prose encomium of Elizabeth.

[43] Henry Howard, 'Dutiful Defence, BL Additional MS 24652, f. 8ᵛ. Howard is describing the composition of the 'Dutiful Defence'. The image also appears in Seneca, *Epistulae morales*, 65 (with Scarpat ad loc.); Basil, *De utilitate*, cap. 4 and see more generally, E. MacPhail, 'The Mosaic of Speech: A Classical Topos in Renaissance Aesthetics', *JWCI*, 66, 2003, pp. 249–63. I thank Jill Kraye for this last reference.

[44] To limit myself to some of the more recent examples: Kevin Sharpe, *Reading Revolutions in Early Modern England*, Yale, 2001; Lisa Jardine and Anthony Grafton, 'Studied for Action: How Gabriel Harvey read his Livy', *Past and Present*, 129, 1990, pp. 30–78; Mack, *Elizabethan Rhetoric*; W. Sherman, *John Dee: The Politics of Reading and Writing in the English Renaissance*, Amherst, 1995. For a recent argument that marginalia afford us privileged access to their author's mind, and that this encouraged some increased sense of self in the period, see Craig Kallendorf, 'Marginalia and the Rise of Early Modern Subjectivity', in *On Renaissance Commentaries*, ed. M. Pade, Hildesheim, 2005, pp. 110–29 (Kallendorf's article suffers from a possible conceptual fault and one which may undermine the seemingly historical argument he wishes to make: rhetoric is fundamentally about reader response, and hence it was only natural that with the growth of rhetorical instruction, especially those forms of rhetoric which emphasized affective response, that there should be a renewed emphasis on the responses of the characters and readers both within and beyond the text. The point turns upon the antecedent one of the relationship between the didactic and the affective).

'transactional' model. This phrase simply means that reading in the English Renaissance was an activity that had its roots in a essentially 'productive' view of discourse that would in turn furnish the mind with material to amplify problems concerning the rights and wrongs of human action, these rights and wrongs being on occasion capable of being tied to particular political scenarios.[45] One might also note in passing that, with the exception of John Dee, no one annotates as heavily (or as opinionatedly) as Gabriel Harvey, thereby reducing his value as an exemplar. I find it hard to agree that

> [t]o be sure, Harvey was a particularly well[-]equipped reader, but the care with which he used and created marginal glosses helps to establish their importance – I'd like to say the centrality – of the margins in the latter half of the sixteenth century.[46]

To repeat, what is going on, most of the time, is not detritus of an ego's engagement with the text, but rather an increasingly secure culture of grammatically sensitive 'argufying'. For the most part, Howard's annotations mimic the mechanics of this culture (underlining the central arguments, noting *sententiae* and so on) and sometimes they are simply indexing *avant la lettre*: underlining the central arguments, putting in headings in the margins and so on. Sometimes he goes further, and uses the works in a more obviously propaideumatic fashion: the starting point for discourse creation. This 'productive' emphasis in Northern Humanism provides one explanation of why it is so hard to say anything about rhetorical or dialectical education, and their influence, on the basis of marginalia, though one might have thought that they would be a good starting point.[47] Despite the arguments offered by a number of scholars for the importance, both theoretical and practical, of 'commonplaces' as an approach to the study of how Renaissance men actually read and then wrote texts, such an

---

[45] Jardine and Grafton, 'Studied for Action'. One might back up this statement by noting that the standard exercises for rhetorical composition took as their starting points typically moral or sententious material, which the student was then left to amplify: see, for a convenient synthesis of some sixteenth-century English evidence, Mack, *Elizabethan Rhetoric*, pp. 32–6. For a slightly different view of transactional reading (deriving explicitly from Grafton and Jardine), see Stewart, *Close Readers*, pp. 148–60.

[46] William W. E. Slights, *Managing Readers: Printed Marginalia in English Renaissance Books*, Michigan, 2001, p. 93.

[47] On the connection between humanist education in England and the ability to speak and write, see W. Boutcher, 'Vernacular Humanism in the Sixteenth Century', in *The Cambridge Companion to Renaissance Humanism*, ed. Jill Kraye, Cambridge, 1996, ch. 13.

approach stands in need of some qualification.[48] That is in part a problem of evidence. While printed commonplace books tend to have fairly precise and detailed instructions about how the Renaissance schoolboy should go about compiling such works, few commonplace books that survive seem to conform to these prescriptions. Of course, the exercise of marking *sententiae* and extraction of commonplaces is crucial to the creation of the reading culture, even if that is not always the focus of particular texts.[49] Howard's reading, as expected perhaps, shows us both some of this general culture and on occasion some more personal elements. This, admittedly somewhat deflationary, claim nonetheless best answers the evidence.

The history of reading, then, can be a sparse territory. The natural rejoinder to this rather dyspeptic view is that it is impossible to understand the history of reading without utilizing the actions of writers, i.e., other texts. Indeed, this is the historical answer. After all, for the humanist-educated student with his commonplace books, it is hard to distinguish between the two levels at the theoretical level. Still, if the recovery of reading presents with another 'writer', it is just as important to distinguish, with some degree of historical plausibility, the different senses that such a formulation may bear. After all, if all 'engagements' are 'writings', then we have expanded the concept of writing further even than the humanist sloganeers. And let us remember that notions of the closely allied tasks of reading and writings are, for the most part, just that: slogans. So perhaps, at least as a first step, what scholarship should be doing is attempting to do justice to the

---

[48] See A. Moss, *Printed Commonplace Books in the Renaissance*, Oxford, 1997, passim; Max Thomas, 'Reading and Writing the Renaissance Commonplace Book: A Question of Authorship?', in *The Construction of Authorship: Textual Appropriation in Law and Literature*, eds Martha Woodmansee and Peter Jaszi, Durham: NC, 1994, pp. 401–15, esp. 412; and K. Meerhof, *Entre Logique et literature: Autour de Melanchthon*, Paris, 2001, p. 72: 'Enfin le lieu commun est, bien entendeu, le lieu ou se rencontre lecture et écriture'; for recent attempt to meld the commonplace with various accounts of intertextuality, see Paul Dyck, 'Reading and Writing the Commonplace: Literary Culture Then and Now', *(Re)soundings*, 1.1, www.millersv.edu/resound/xvol1/iss/cbpface.html, consulted 10/05/04. For some English examples of noting *sententiae* in a commonplace book (with the intent of using these phrases at some later point in writing) see Thomas Blundeville, *The True Order and Method of Wryting and Reading Hystories*, London, 1574, sigs H2^v–4^r; Francis Bacon, *The Advancement of Learning*, ed. M. Kiernan, Oxford, 2000, p. 118. I have already mentioned Edward VI's notebooks in Chapter One.

[49] There is a sizeable bibliography on the topic of the marking and utilization of 'sententiae': see, e.g., George K. Hunter, 'The Marking of *Sententiae* in Elizabethan Plays, Poems and Romances', *The Library*, series V, 6, 1951, pp. 151–88; Charles George Smith, *Shakespeare's Proverb Lore: His Use of Leonard Culman and Pubilius Syrus*, Cambridge: MA, 1963; E. McCuthcheon, *Great House Sententiae*, Claremont, 1977; and Bruno Basile, 'Tasso e le "Sententiae" di Stobeo', *Filologia e critica*, 7, 1981, pp. 34–41.

internal consistency and variety offered by annotations, before attempting to accommodate them into labelled forms of discourse such as 'scholastic', 'humanist' or 'legal'. These internal modulations will naturally vary between the different sorts of text that one finds annotated. For example, it is noteworthy that texts which are (or may be seen as being) of an expository or philosophical character lend themselves to more ordered forms of annotation.[50] That is because the connections between schoolroom or university practice and the reading experience will be closer. One may contrast the less ordered and less obviously coherent forms of annotation that one finds in literary or purely polemical texts.[51] Similarly, free-wheeling annotation may be found in the highly idiosyncratic or the egotistical.[52]

Howard left annotations in a number of books, three of which are dealt with here: *Il libro del cortegiano* by Baldassare Castiglione, a scientific work by the Italian philosopher Alessandro Piccolomini, *Il libro della sfera del mondo*, and the 1585 edition of Seneca's works by the Franco-Italian humanist Marc-Antoine Muret.[53] Castiglione, born in Mantua on 6 December 1478, studied at Milan, though we cannot be sure what he learned there. Following the main chance, with the imminent collapse of Sforza hegemony, in 1499 he returned to Mantua in the service of Francesco Gonzaga. After a varied diplomatic career for the Gonzagas at the papal court, he died on 17 January 1529. His famous 'Book of the Courtier' (to call it by its English title) was first published in 1528 in Venice, and was soon reprinted and translated throughout sixteenth-century Europe.[54] Howard

---

[50] Consider Pasquale Arfé, 'The Annotations of Nicolaus Cusanus and Giovanni Andrea Bussi on the *Asclepius*', *JWCI*, 62, 1999, pp. 25–59 (where the recuperation is best served by attending to the thematic complexity of the annotation) or, in a different fashion, where there is an attempt to weld reading to a particularly specific sixteenth-century theoretical system, Peter Mack, 'Ramus Reading: The Commentaries on Cicero's Consular Orations and Vergil's *Eclogues* and *Georgics*', *JWCI*, 61, 1998, pp. 111–41.

[51] If I had a taste for sloganeering: Everything has its past, but that does not mean that everything can have a history. We may have to content ourselves that most forms of reading don't have histories.

[52] E.g., John Dee or Gabriel Harvey.

[53] There is also his edition of the Sybilline Oracles, in the possession of Nicholas Barker: see further Nicolas Barker, 'The Books of Henry Howard, Earl of Northampton', *Bodleian Library Record*, 13, 1990, pp. 376–8, and more generally on the fortunes of Howard's library Linda Levy Peck, 'Uncovering the Arundel Library at the Royal Society: Changing Meanings of Science and the Fate of the Norfolk Donation', *Notes and Records of the Royal Society*, 52, 1998, pp. 3–26.

[54] For a stimulating, if at times unreliable, synthesis, see P. Burke, *The Fortunes of the Courtier*, Cambridge, 1996. A sensitive account on the English side is to be found at A. Bryson, *From Courtesy to Civility: Changing Codes of Conduct in Early Modern England*, Oxford, 1998, pp. 199–203.

Lord Henry Howard: An Elizabethan Life

was far from the only Englishman to have taken interest in the work. Sir Thomas Hoby had translated the work in 1561 (and it was to be reprinted several times, starting in 1577).

Howard's annotations date from early in his career, on both paleographical and circumstantial grounds.[55] It is trite that annotation habits will provide something of a context for a text. Howard takes this further and provides on the frontispiece of the work a few key phrases that orientate the reader.

> Antiquitus quo proprius aberat ab ortu ac divina
> progenie hic melius ea fortasse quae erant vera cernebat[56]
> Cicero tusc disput pag 73

> Semper dignitatis iniqu   μισω σωφ[ιστην]οστις
> quus iudex est, qui aut   ουκ [αυτωι] σοφος[57]
> invidet aut favet[58]

>   μετα [.]ολθ παν
> gravius est spoliari   των γλυκ[.]
> fortunis quam non augere
> dignitate[59]

>   Perdonnando troppo a chi falla
>   si fa iniuria a chi non falla[60]
>   Ma non hebbe piacere, che
>   Fosse uguale al mio dolore[61]

In addition he writes down the right-hand side of the frontispiece the tag: 'quando havranno fine i miei guai / vedrem luce la nube semper i rai', after which he signs his name.[62] These phrases allow the reader to

---

[55] See Chapter Two for some of these reasons.
[56] The quotation is from Cicero, *Tusculan Disputations*, I.XII.26 'Because antiquity was less far removed from the origin and the divine stem, was perhaps better able to discern truth'.
[57] The quotation is a Euripides fragment (*fr.* 905 Nauck): 'I hate a sophist that is not wise for himself'. Howard is most likely to have read it in Cicero (*Epistolae ad familiares*, 13.15.2); for other, less likely, sources (which Howard would have to have read in Greek) see *Tragicorum graecorum fragmenta*, V/2, ed. R. Kannicht, Göttingen, 2002, p. 913. The square brackets indicate paleographical uncertainty.
[58] The quotation is from Cicero, *Pro Plancio*, III.7: 'The envious or biased man will always be a poor judge of rank'.
[59] The quotation is from Cicero, *Pro Plancio*, IX.22: 'it is a more serious thing to be stripped of one's fortunes than not increase in rank'.
[60] The quotation is from *Il cortegiano*, I.23: 'To forgive too readily the man at fault does injury to the man who does not err.'
[61] 'His pleasure was not equal to my pain'.
[62] I have been unable to identify the source for this couplet (with its peculiar compression in the second line).

understand much of what follows in the annotations: an anti-courtly emphasis on 'true' nobility, the degree to which a person's speech must be taken seriously, and a rather personal obsession with envy, bitterness and the whirligig of time. They also take us beyond the notion of Renaissance reading, wearily familiar from the secondary literature, as simply a quarry for snippets. Howard is presenting his reading of the text as a whole: it is a way of making the text his 'own' (Howard's desire to personalize and individualize the reading experience will resurface again in this Chapter).

Howard's comments can be grouped thematically.[63] For example, the arts interest him. He gives handwritten headings for those sections that deal with 'MUSICA' 'PITTURA', 'STATUARIA' and 'PROSPETTIVA'.[64] Again, as an indexer, he writes 'eccellentissimi pittori' by the names of Michelangelo and Raphael.[65] This has been seen as evidence of Howard's own taste, but it is almost impossible that he can have physically seen any of these paintings.[66] He also notes the affective theory of beauty, namely that what produces a pleasurable response counts as beautiful

---

[63] The physical format of the book places some bounds on interpretation. Howard's attention to the text takes one of three forms: underlining, marginalia, other additions. The first category is self-explanatory, the second must be subdivided into further parts: Howard's original comments, and those marginalia which simply reproduce or rewrite what has he has read in the parajacent text. The third category consists of decorative additions that have no very clear connection with the text because of their position, such as the frontispiece. The edition which Howard is using is the 1541 Aldine edition of the work: all references are to pagination from this edition (B. Castiglione, *Il libro del cortegiano*, Venice: Aldus Manutius, 1541 (in private possession of Dr Bent Juel-Jensen, to whose kindness in making the work available to me I am much indebted – since Dr Juel-Jensen's death, the location of the book has become uncertain)). Throughout these next four paragraphs, I have assumed a working knowledge of the book. In interpreting Howard's attentions to the text, I give significantly more weight to the first subdivision of the second category.

[64] Ibid., sigs F3^v, F4^v, F5^v.

[65] Sig. F6^r.

[66] Howard had not travelled abroad at this point, and, indeed, perhaps never did, and there were no opportunities to see these works in England. It is possible that he knew these works through engravings or prints (see, for Raphael, Lisa Pon, *Raphael, Dürer and Marcantonio Raimondi: Copying and the Italian Renaissance Print*, New Haven, 2004, and Malcolm Bull, *The Mirror of the Gods: Classical Mythology in Renaissance Art*, London, 2005, pp. 345–7, on the diffusion of Raphael's 'Judgment of Paris'; and for Michelangelo see *Fortuna di Michelangelo nell'incisione: catalogo della mostra*, ed. Mario Rotili with the assistance of Maria Catelli Isola and Elio Galasso, Benevento, 1964 and, above all, A. Wells-Cole, *Art and Decoration in Elizabethan and Jacobean England: The Influence of Continental Prints 1558–1625*, New Haven, 2004).

and not the other way around.[67] Is it too simplistic to see in Howard's underlining of the passage of the desirability of musical education a reference to his own lute-playing lessons?[68] Certainly, almost every word in the two short pages on music is underlined. The only other shortish passage with underlining as heavy (together with marginal graphics) comes early in the second book, where the interlocutor praises the contemporary arts in comparison with those of the ancient world.[69]

He takes particular interest in those passages of *Il cortegiano* which deal with the relationship between speech and writing. This is one of the areas where Castiglione marks a distinct change of emphasis from the tradition of works of the 'social' or 'adminstrative' virtues, and where he is most in debt to rhetoric. By the words 'la scrittura non è altro che una forma di parlare', his marginalium rewrites these words and again a few lines later with the words 'le parole scritte simile alle dette'.[70] This conjunction is marked again by Howard in the paragone of Homer and Vergil.[71] The creation of a single vernacular for all modes of discourse was obviously of interest to Howard in the late 1560s when he experimented with the creation of a scientific English in his manuscript on natural philosophy. In the light of this, we should perhaps see as significant the fact that by Castiglione's words on the ancient Greek language and its many dialects ('un sol nome chiamavono lingua Greca'), Howard writes: 'lingua Athenese di tutte le Grece più elegante.'[72] In a similar vein to the discussion about imitation, Howard emphasizes that one should maintain just the one style (at seeming odds with some other statements in dialogue).[73]

---

[67] Castiglione, *Il libro del cortegiano*, sig. F6^v: Howard writes 'non è bella quella che è bella ma bella è quella che piace.' Howard has adapted a famous scholastic tag ('pulchrum est quod visum placet') originally from Thomas Aquinas (Summa, I, iq5 a 4 ad 1), but which itself had been the object of considerable adaptation before Howard (for the idea that it is a proverb which can be found in ancient texts see Marc-Antoine Muret, *Variae lectiones*, Paris: Guillaume Rovillé, 1594 (but many editions brought out in the 1560s onwards), IV.4, sigs I1^v–I2^v; in deleting the reference to sight, Howard makes the reference capable of greater application across diverse fields of discursive production.

[68] Ibid., sig. F2^v, he puts a floral symbol in the margin and underlines the words. See further Chapter One on Howard's and his sister's early taste for music.

[69] Ibid., sig. G3^v.

[70] Castiglione, *Il libro del cortegiano*, sig. D3^v. Throughout these next four paragraphs, I have assumed a working knowledge of the book.

[71] Ibid., sig. D5^r.

[72] Ibid, sig. D8^v.

[73] Ibid., sig. D4^v: 'Bisogna imitare una che al con[se]ntimento di tutti sia più eccellenti [presumably a slip for 'eccellente']'. For some Renaissance perceptions of the diversity of English pronunciation and usage see the oft-quoted words of George Puttenham, who, among other chauvinist precepts, enjoins his readers not to stray further linguistically

Il cortegiano's largely positive account of the plasticity of personality nonetheless depends, as later anti-courtly literature was to insist, on a measure of deception.[74] Given his background and subsequent suspicions, it comes as no surprise that Howard underlines the words in Castiglione's discussion of sprezzatura 'cioè, di nascondere l'arte' and nearly every other reference to deception and lies in the book, a theme which we will pick up in a moment.[75] These comments allow us, however, to do nothing more than speculate on certain plausible biographical details. I am also concerned to say something about the nature of Howard's reading activity. There are different levels of 'response' to a text, from the merely 'organizational' to the more 'expansive'. It was characteristic of humanist philology to seek out 'loci communes' in a Classical text as a means of better understanding the tone, thought or context of a particular passage. Certainly, Howard does note 'sources' in the fashion of the by then established philological commentary.[76] His consistent usage of Cicero, however, goes beyond this level. If we may characterize two lower levels of engagement with the text, the first editorial, and the second expository, this rather represents a third 'level' of reading and may be described as a frame or context through which the initial text is viewed. The frame chosen comes chiefly from Cicero's rhetorical and moral works, as one would expect, given the subject matter of the dialogue, and deals with the question of the sincerity or seriousness of one's utterances.[77] Later readers have not primarily

---

than that speech practised in 'London and the shires lying around London within lx miles, and not much above' (George Puttenham, *The Arte of Englishe Poesie*, London: Richard Field, 1589, p. 121) and for related material on English dialects, see Adam Fox, *Oral and Literate Culture in England 1500–1700*, Oxford, 2000, pp. 64–72 (most of his material post-dating the likely date of these annotations).

[74] On this reaction see Bryson, *From Courtesy*, together with the comments of John Gillingham, 'From Civilitas to Courtesy: Codes of Manners in Medieval and Early Modern England', *Transactions of the Royal Historical Society*, 12, 2002, pp. 267–89 (Gillingham is especially good in his attack upon the work of D. Knox, 'Erasmus *De civilitate* and the Religious Origins of Civility in Protestant Europe', *Archiv für Reformationsgeschichte*, 86, 1995, pp. 7–55). See now the theory that there are connections with Cicero's concept of 'dissimulatio' (J. Richards, 'Assumed Simplicity and the Critique of Nobility: Or, How Castiglione read Cicero', *Renaissance Quarterly*, 53, 2001, pp. 212–32). Richards does not show direct influence, rather homology between the concepts; furthermore, she strains the text to include a notion that there is a latent critique of aristocratic accomplishment).

[75] Castiglione, *Il libro del cortegiano*, sig. D1^v.

[76] E.g., at sig. I5^v Howard notes the source for Castiglione's comments on the difficulties of friendship between morally bad men: Cicero, *De amicitia*, 'malorum non amicitia coniuratio potius dicendo'.

[77] Burke mentions this, but does not develop it or give precise references either to Howard's annotations or to Cicero. Richards ('Assumed Simplicity') makes much, without precise reference, of the supposed debt to Cicero's rhetorical thought.

thought of *Il cortegiano* as a work of philosophy, but this is clearly how Howard views the work.[78] Soon after the opening lines of the second book, the narrator is asked to give his speech in response to that of the Count; he reluctantly does so, saying 'perchè in vero tutti da natura siamo pronti più a biasmare gli errori, che a laudar le cose ben fatte, e par che per una certa innata malignità.'[79] This is Howard's adored topic of envy and backbiting (which, of course, he underlines). Then the speaker continues with a discussion of the societal value of the moral virtue prudence:

> e non solamente ponga cura d'aver in sé parti e condizioni eccellenti, ma il tenor delle vita sua ordini con tal disposizione, che 'l tutto corrisponde a queste parti.[80]

Howard's marginalium is a little enigmatic: 'Cicero. De fin.' Without a more precise reference it is hard to see what he is getting at, but at least it establishes a philosophical lineage for the dialogue. Possibly there is a Stoic reference, as with his underlined passage a few lines later:

> tutte [sc. le virtù] talmente tra sè concatanate, che vanno ad un fine e ad ogni effetto tutte possono concurrer e servire.[81]

The interest in moral education Castiglione writes of the morally 'auto-corrective' instinct of the young and their ability, unlike brute beasts, to rein in their natural appetites. Howard fills the margin with a lengthy quote from the most widely disseminated of Cicero's ethical treatises in Renaissance England, the *De officiis*.[82]

Rhetoric had long been open to the charge that it involved people in a lack of sincerity. There are several passages in *Il cortegiano* that deal with the issue and the allied one of the 'seriousness' of one's conversation. The section on 'dissimulatione', which we might rather term 'irony', is the sec-

---

[78] Howard's response may not have been untypical. It is important not to underestimate (as does Peter Burke in his recent monograph) the extent to which large chunks of *Il cortegiano* derive from moral philosophy: see the following paragraph for some examples.

[79] Castiglione, *Il cortegiano*, sig. G6^r.

[80] Ibid.

[81] Ibid. Baldassare Castiglione, *Il libro del cortegiano*, ed. Ettore Bonara, Milan, 1972 notes ad loc. that the probable source is 'Cicerone De off. iii'.

[82] *Il cortegiano*, sig. H4^{r-v}. The Cicero passage (*De officiis*, I.136) runs: 'obiurgationes etiam incidunt necessariae in quibus utendum est fortasse quae vobis continuatio et verborum gravitate – moderate ac considerate porro' and comes from a section of the work (I.133–138) in which Cicero discusses the conversational style.

tion most heavily marked by Howard.[83] The word itself is underlined followed by the words 'fanno le viste di piangere estimar bugiardi e sciocchi adulatori'.[84] Howard then goes to what he has seen as the intellectual source of the work, Cicero's *De oratore*. By the words 'Pero accio che non paia che in compagnia', he quotes Cicero to emphasize the natural status of the imitative instinct, thereby rendering it less morally problematic.[85] On a similar front, Howard counters one of the interlocutors' comments that 'nelle facetie non esser arte'.[86] In 'facetie' there can indeed be a sort of art, since he notes that there are two sorts of such verbal jest: Howard implies that the speaker has failed to understand this distinction.[87] The following lines of Castiglione elicit a response from Howard that suggests he is emphasizing the importance of conversational context and the ease with which one's words may be twisted.[88] Still, such 'thematic' or 'biographical' reading is of limited value. It is more interesting to note that, though Howard's usage of *sententiae* from the works of Cicero is clear, it is by way of the establishment of a context or frame: Howard may well have marked sententiae in his commonplace book, or in his memory, and then he has 'compilid' them as a means of emphasizing the roots in Classical moral philosophy of the tradition of Renaissance 'public' or 'social' ethics, to which *Il libro del cortegiano* was simply the most well-diffused heir (along, in a rather different fashion, with Nicolò Machiavelli's *Il principe*).

The next book we consider is Howard's copy of the complete works of

---

[83] One should note that *dissimulatio* had a place in the long and not dishonorable position in the tradition of Renaissance 'public' ethics: see, e.g., Giovanni Pontano, 'De prudentia', in idem, *Opera omnia*, 3 vols, Venice: Aldus Manutius, 1518, I. sig. Ccii^{r-v}.
[84] *Il libro del cortegiano*, sig. K5^v.
[85] Sig. K6^v. The quotation from Cicero in full is 'Sed cum illo in genere perpetuae festivitatis ars non desideretur (natura enim fingit homines et creat imitatores et narratores facetos adiuvante et vultu et voce et ipso genere sermonis) tum vero in hoc altero dicacitatis quid habet ars loci, cum ante illud facete dictum emissum haerere debeat, quam cogitari potuisse videatur?' (*De oratore*, II.219). It is the passage in brackets that Howard quotes.
[86] Sig. K6^v.
[87] Cicero, *De oratore*, II.218: 'Et enim cum duo genera sint facetiarum, alterum aequabiliter in omni sermone fusum alterum peracutum et breve.' By 'facetie', Howard did not mean amusing little stories in the style of Poggio Bracciolini's famous collection (widely diffused in the original and translations: see, e.g., Poggio Bracciolini, *Les facecies de Poge*, eds F. Duval and S. Hériche-Pradeau, Geneva, 2003), but something closer to carefully crafted pointed sayings. We know this since Howard uses the word as the title for a series of his aphorisms (BL Cotton MS, Titus C vi, f. 279).
[88] Sig. K6^v: 'maledictio autem nihil habet propositi praeter contumeliam; quae si petulantius iactatur, convicium, si facetius, urbanitas nominatur.' Cicero, *Pro Caelio*, 6 and 'Quod facete dicatur id alias in re alias in verbo habere facetias', Ep. 5º (Howard's reference is again incorrect – the correct reference is Cicero, *De oratore*, II.248).

Seneca, edited by Marc-Antoine Muret.[89] We should note in passing that the question of through what filter Howard read this text is in no way to be answered by adverting to Muret's commentary. The annotations dwell upon the text itself rather than on the preface, notes or similar animadversionary material: content over context here at least. What then is the content in which he seems interested? How can we discern internal distinctions? The markings in the text are of three sorts: underlinings, marginal sigla and marginal comments. The two varieties of marginal sigla employed are N and the floral symbol. Again, in reconstructing the reading process, the following assumption has been made, which seems unproblematic but should be made explicit for methodological reasons. The greater the number of annotatory marks on a given passage, the greater the significance to the reader. A response to a possible caveat: naturally, the extraction of 'points' for the purpose of improving one's own style seems to account for some percentage of the annotations, but the fact that a thought is expressed in singularly witty and sententious fashion does not exclude the possibility of its autonomous significance.

The annotations are informative about Howard's own attitudes toward the gift-giving rhetoric of the time. I have commented on the rather jejune methodology that simply looks at annotations in the light of the author's 'interests', as if the explanandum was a personality and not historical change in the field of reading and writing. It is, however, clear that for the most part annotation habits are themselves insufficiently rich to say anything other than: this must have interested the annotator. If Howard was indeed a figure resistant in some sense to the offers of reciprocal advancement of patronage, then it becomes clear why he might have underlined such a passage as 'dignus est decipi qui de recipiendo cogitavit, cum daret'.[90] The peculiar status of the gift is also noticed: 'ista enim perierunt, cum darentur', along with the psychological corollary of this status: 'nihil carius aestimamus quam beneficium, quando petimus; nihil vilius cum

---

[89] There are no indications of previous ownership in the book so we may assume a purchase date soon after that of publication: in any case, certainly roughly contemporary with the poems in discussion. We await a suitably well-rounded monograph on Muret's engagement with the Classical past.

[90] Seneca, *Opera omnia*, ed. Marc-Antoine Muret [Heidelberg]: Hieronymus Commelinus, 1594, sig. A1^r. [= *De beneficiis*, I.1]: 'He is worthy to be deceived, who thinks about receiving when he is giving'. Howard was not the only figure from the English Renaissance who was struck by these words: a translation of the phrase is found in William Baldwin, *A Treatise of Morrall Philosophie*, edited with additional material by Thomas Palfreyman, London: Thomas Snodham, 1605, sig. M3^v.

accepimus'.[91] A concern with how one behaves to one's social inferiors is pronounced, and there are lengthy underlinings of those passages dealing with how one may be 'too grateful' toward those with whom one has gift-giving dealings.[92] The sensitivity to the slights of others that we have suggested earlier on as a key element in the self-presentation of Howard is confirmed by the underlining of nearly every occurrence of the word 'iniuria'. He seems most concerned with those passages which affirm that acts of kindness slip from the memory whereas as insults never do: 'beneficia excidunt, haerent iniuriae'; 'maiorem iniuriam'; 'nam cum ita natura comparatum sit, ut altius iniuriae, quam merita descendant, & illo cito defluunt, has tenax memoria custodiat'.[93] Since his annotations become quite scarce after *De beneficiis*, it is quite hard to generalize from them about what model of reading they suggest: one can simply say that he was interested in this or in that passage.

Lord Henry Howard wrote a series of annotations on the text of Alessandro Piccolomini's work of astronomy, *La sfera del mondo*.[94] The annotations are mostly in Latin in the hand that he uses for both Latin and English writing from the late 1570s until the 1590s. There are some annotations that are in the hand he normally reserves for English writing. They demonstrate a close reading of the text, though there is nothing that he disagrees with – his marginal annotations take the form of expansions and summaries, with a suggestion that he had some interest in the practical mensural aspects of the natural philosophy that Piccolomini outlines. As

---

[91] Seneca, *Opera omnia*, sig. A1ʳ [= *De beneficiis*, 1.1]; *Epistulae morales* 31.28: 'we value nothing more highly than a beneficiu when we seek it, and nothing more lowly on receiving it'.
[92] Almost the entirety of *De ben.* VI.25 is underlined, and there is one of Howard's rare marginal notes, emphasizing the content: 'nimis grati': D4ᵛ.
[93] *Epistulae morales* 31; ibid; ibid; A1ʳ [= *De beneficiis*, I.1].
[94] *La sfera del mondo*, Venice: Giovanni Guarisco, 1579. Currently held in the Royal Society Library, shelfmark AI22. Alessandro Piccolomini (1508–1578) was a member of the Intronati and the Infiammati and a significant figure in the intellectual life of mid-century Italy. The Infiammati have been seen as effecting a change in the orientation of humanist studies in Italy from the rhetorical to the more scientific: Francesco Bruni, 'Sperone Speroni e la Academia degli Infiammati', *Filologia e letteratura*, Naples, 1967, pp. 27–71 – a piece which shows evidence pitting the literary Speroni against the more intellectually catholic Piccolomini. For further information see Florindo Vincent Cerreta, *Alessandro Piccolomini: letterato a filosofo senese del cinquecento*, Siena, 1960; Isabelle Pantin, 'Alessandro Piccolomini en France: La question de la langue scientifique et l'évolution du genre du traité de la sphère', in *La réception des écrits italiens en France à la Renaissance*, ed. Alfredo Perifano, Paris, 2000, pp. 9–28 (worthless); Nick Kanas, 'Alessandro Piccolomini and the First Printed Star Atlas (1540)', *Imago Mundi*, 58, 2006, pp. 70–7. The book deserves a more extended treatment that I can provide it with here.

with the earlier work on Castiglione, we can see a number of different levels of engagement with the text. Howard is an attentive, respectful reader and is keen to correct typographical errors.[95] One can, however, see a certain pattern emerge from Howard's 'higher level' engagement. Much of what he underlines is, of course, purely explanatory.[96] His approach to the structure of the texts emphasized the more aphoristic and epigrammatic points in the text. This is precisely what appealed to him in Fox Morzillo's axiomatic approach to natural philosophy.[97] Not only does he underline such passages, he sometimes goes to the trouble of writing out a Latin maxim to 'cover' or 'explain' the content of the Italian text. During Piccolomini's discussion of the celestial spheres, there is a discussion of the different senses of vaccuum (both sublunary and interspherical) and their own relation to the hoary topic of motion in a void.[98] At this point Howard writes in the margin of Piccolomini's interspherical condensability: 'otherwise there would exist void, which nature abhors'.[99] Now, strictly speaking, this is not quite the point of the passage, but Howard is keen to slot the work, through these maxims, into what he already knows of basic Aristotelian science. Howard does this repeatedly, sometimes closer to and sometimes farther away from the point. For one extended example, in a discussion of oblique horizons (as opposed to horizons which cut the equinoctial at right angles and where the pole is elevated upon the horizon), Howard's marginalium ('for no proportion

---

[95] E.g., ibid., sig. A5[v], Howard corrects 'non che dio trovare in essere altra dimensione, che le tre dette, per il lungo, per il largo, & per il profondo' by striking through the 'o' in the second preposition; and at sig. C3[v] he writes 'contatto' for 'contratto' in 'Ma dire forse alcuno, che un cosi fatto contatto, o toccamento non può quivi veramente trovarsi'.

[96] Ibid., A6[r–v]: 'L'angolo piano adunque si produce da quello inchinamento che fanno due linee l'una verso l'altra, quando si toccano per il transver /so, & non per il diritto; cioe non congiunendosi per il lungo. Et alcuni vogliono che così fatto angolo sia quella apritura che fanno le due dette linee nel lor contatto, ò ver toccamento. Et altri stimano che sia piu tosto quello spatio, che per il toccamento di dette due linee s'interchiude tra quelle il più vicino al contatto, che esser possa. E l'una e l'altra di queste opinoni intesa come s'ha da intendere, potria salvarsi; & più la seconda; poscia che <u>denotando l'apritura piutosto qualita, che quantita, & essendo l'angolo, quantita, pare che piu tosto a quello s'accomodi</u>'.

[97] See Chapter Two for Howard's use of Fox Morzillo.

[98] Piccolomini, *Il sfera del mondo*, sig. C3[r–v]: 'Habbiamo da notare ancora intorno all' ordine & sito delle dette Sfere, che le non sono continuate tra di loro, quantunque si tocchino l'una l'altra senz' alcun mezo. Percioche quando fusse questo, bi/sognarebbe , che solo un movimento di <u>tutto fusse, & che insime di un sol movimento si movessero tutte</u>. Se gia noi non volessemo dire, che le fusse rare fattibili, & condensabili: cosa che alla perfezione delle cosi fatti corpi non ben conviene. Non son dunque continui, o ver continuati questi orbi, ma son contingui.'

[99] Ibid.: 'Alioqui vacuum esset quod natura detestatur'.

of magnitude can exist between heaven and earth') seems again to miss the main thrust of the rather unAristotelian passage for the sake of a handy Aristotelian tag (rather like the 'no proportion can exist between the finite and the infinite').[100]

Sometimes these brief expansions are, if not insightful, then at least helpful, and indications of an ordered and careful approach to the text, such as some comments on angles and spheres.[101] In Piccolomini's discussion of rectilinear and circular motion, Howard's marginalium makes the idea in the text more explicit. Piccolomini is discussing those that think the stars move rectilinearly: 'dovrebbono dire questi tali in che modo le stelle, partire da noi che le ci sono, & nascoste, possim poi ritornare al luogo, dove di nuovo le vengan fuso.'[102] Howard writes 'nisi perficiant circulum'. Sometimes, this fleshing out of the argument takes Howard a little further, such as his exemplification.[103] In that chapter of *Il libro della sfera* that Piccolomini devotes to a discussion of the four cardinal points, there is a passage which Howard decides to accurately sum up by way of an

---

[100] Ibid., sig. H4ʳ: 'Solo volo per aggiungere per hora questio in tal materia, che qualunque si trova superficie della terra, se ben non può à punto vedere la metà del cielo, si come avverrebbe, quando nel centro del Mondo si ritrovasse: nondimeno per essere il semidiametro della terra quasi insensibile rispetto all grandezza del cielo, si può convenevolmente dire, che stando nella superficie della terrra, se ne vegga ancora, la metà. Ma si portrebbe bene per imaginatione considerare, che elevandosi un huomo per l'aria a volo, , potesse alzarsi nell'elemento dell'aria tanto, che non solo la meta del cielo discoprirebbe, & discernerebbe a punto; ma parte ancora meggiore alquanto della meta con la vista discoprirebbe; nè accascaria che per far questo si levassi fino alla Sfera del fuoco; come per lineari geometrichi demostrationi potrei provar facilmente …' By this Howard writes: 'quia nulla est magnitudinis proportio inter coelum et terram.' This habit of extracting a philosophical-sounding aphorism or axiom can be seen earlier on in his annotations to *Il libro del cortegiano*, sig. P5ᵛ, where Howard writes he glosses the text with the phrase 'substantia non suscipit magis aut minus' in relation to discussion of the nature (or substance) of man: for further Renaissance discussions of the metaphysical undergirding of gender distinctions see Maclean, *The Renaissance Notion of Woman*.

[101] *La sfera del mondo*, sig. A8ʳ: 'Et perche in qual si voglia figura piana rettilinea, sempre tanti sono li lati, quanti sono gli angoli, di qui e, che non solo possan le figure prendere il nome dal numero de i lati, ma del numero degli angoli ancora.' By this Howard notes 'due denominationes res una'; and sig. C3ᵛ: 'quia idem est unius finis et alterius principium' is Howard's rather clearer way of putting the point made by Piccolomini thus: 'A chi cosi argomentasse si dee rispondere, che quelli due punti non sono veramente due, ma sono un sol punto; il quale ha potentia di terminare quelle due linee, si come d'ogni linea diremo il medesimo, ogna volta che in due parte si dividesse, dividendosi ella sempre in un punto & quivi causando due punti dopo la divisione'.

[102] Ibid., sig. D5ᵛ.

[103] 'Exemplum' has connotations both from rhetoric and natural philosophy.

example.[104] Throughout Howard's reading of the work, we see a careful reader, attentive to the verbal means by which the argument is developed.

Annotations, then, tell us something about the humanist culture of exegesis, though occasionally they are a useful guide to a given individual's interests and preoccupations. *Quot homines, tot marginalia*. Although they are often evidence for the creation of the common humanist culture of philologically sensitive, argument-marshalling reading, it is hard to fit them into any notion of pre-determined grids, whether derived from rhetoric or dialectic. Where annotations seem to have an internal coherence, that is in part due to the coherent or ordered nature of the text whose parasites they are. Even then, they may fall prey to the crude and speculative literalism of biography. The historian of reading often seems a man whose reach exceeds his grasp.

***

Consider the following passage:

> That irregular and willfull Tyrant Custome, whose bare word is holden and embraced as a Law, constraineth me, though much against my will, to salute the Reader with a breefe Epistle. For first I was never apt by Nature, to crave acquaintance of a private person, without urgent cause, much lesse at randome of a multitude, which neither can be visible in one certain place at any time, as the Civil Lawes set downe, nor saluted otherwise than in a generality.[105]

And again:

> For mine owne part I am taught by Sappho, that no note of Musicke, and by Crassus, that no vaine of Rhetoricke contenteth all mens eares, that listen or apply their senses to the sound of harmony.[106]

---

[104] Ibid., sig. K2ᵛ: 'Bene intesa adunque la distintione di questi quattro punti principali, dico che nella Sfera retta dove si trovan quelli, l'Orizonte de i quali, passa per li poli del Mondo & hanno il loro Zenith nell'Equinottiale, accasca che chiasceduna di queste quarte del Zodiaco, che io ho detto contenersi tra I detti punti principali, ha il suo nascimento uguale a se stesso; in guisa che nasce seco una quarta parimente dell' Equinottiale.' Howard writes: 'Exempli gratia, si solstitium sit in Horizonte et inde ascendat ad meridianum necesse est ut punctum aequinoctii quod prius sub terram deprimebatur ascendat in Horizontem ut ita quarta pars Aequinoctialis ascendat cum quarta parte Zodiaci.'

[105] Henry Howard, *A Defensative Against the Poyson of Supposed Prophecies*, London: John Charlewood, 1583, sig. A7ᵛ.

[106] Howard, *A Defensative*, sig. A7ᵛ. Of course, Howard's work is a highly elaborate piece of work and it may be for this very reason that the next major work to appear in English

Howard's desire to emphasize the 'personal' nature of the literary act is probably connected with his aristocratic desire not to appear to need to curry favour through the undignified medium of print. Howard's next comparison is telling in that it conjures up the social context of this debate.[107] The Latin works that we have so far considered represent a taste for abundance, not for overloaded imagistic complexity. There are signs, however, that as he got older Howard engaged in a more clotted style. There are several passages of very extended comparisons and strained images in his 1583 *Defensative* which show an increased taste for the contorted. The following phrases come from a ten-page collection of phrases that Howard terms 'Sententiae' in one of his notebooks:

> Use your wisedome and finesse agaynst such a cunninge spider as spinneth thredes undiscernably fine and the end of the web onley to nourish and extricate the purest poysons that by their suttlety runne soonest to the harte.[108]
>
> To discourage profferes of affection and devotion is the next waie to cutte the verie windpipe of advertisement.[109]
>
> Beware of to much arte in raisinge suche a miste as maie wette your self to the skinne havinge no other purpose than to seduce others.[110]

Howard's style never had much of the simple about it, but it is fair to say that these phrases and other passages in his *Defensative* mark a more involved style than anything found in the earlier Latin letters or the 1574 *Defense*. Perhaps, however, Howard did not wish to be understood too readily. While the traditions of humanist rhetoric placed an emphasis on clarity and communicability, there were other traditions. We are fortunate in having evidence from Howard's hand that connects social standing and intelligibility:

---

refuting astrology opens its preface with an attack on overblown rhetorical treatments of the topic: John Chamber, *A Discourse against Judicial Astrologie*, London: John Harison, 1601, pp. 1–3. Chamber's work, however, makes no conceptual advances on that of Howard, and we are reminded that the plain style speaking for truth, as opposed to the rhetorical style speaking of fantasy, has a long history still alive in the early seventeenth-century: Brian Vickers, 'The Myth of Francis Bacon's Anti-Humanism', in *Humanism and Early Modern Philosophy*, eds Jill Kraye and M. W. F. Stone, London, pp. 135–58.

[107] Howard, *A Defensative*, sig. A7ᵛ: 'For either the Worke it self deserveth praise, in which case, dainty wine is rather called into question by those that haunte the Taverne …'.
[108] BL Cotton MS, Titus C vi, f. 292ʳ.
[109] Ibid., f. 281ʳ.
[110] Ibid., f. 281ᵛ.

Some to satisfie others are contente to disgrace themselves eg Paulus Vergerius translated Arrianus in a base rude and unworthie style that he mighte be the better understoode by sigismond the emperor who understood no grammer and could not iudge of eloquence.[111]

For Howard, as for anyone trained in Renaissance rhetoric, discourse was an audience-directed persuasive act, but the ability to write with elaboration and elegance has implications other than the purely aesthetic. The events of the next few years were to provide him with ample opportunity to deploy this compact of social and intellectual superiority.

---

[111] Ibid., f. 281ᵛ–282ʳ. This aspect of Vergerio's translation early on became a topos: see the information collated by Philip A. Stadter, 'Arrianus, Flavius' in *Catalogus Translationum et Commentariorum*, eds F. E. Cranz and P. O. Kristeller, Washington DC, 1960, III, pp. 1–20.

Chapter 4

'THE SKILL OF PHILENUS'
TEACHER, POLEMICIST, PAPIST

In casis that have equalle natures reasones proportiones and partes wherby to worke we must iudge equally onlesse we take upon us the skill of Philenus that tooke upone him to distinguish one egge and another.

Henry Howard, aphorism.[1]

LETTERS, along with printed media, were one of the few forms of political 'action at a distance' available to the Elizabethan intriguer. Forged letters, buried letters, letters in code and letters sewn into doublets: all are familiar to the historian of early modern espionage, charge and counter-charge.[2]

---

[1] BL Cotton MS, Titus C vi f. 281ʳ. The reference to Philenus would appear to be to a gastronomic expert, member of the Roman Academy and friend of the fifteenth-century humanist Bartolomeo Sacchi (1421–1481), il Platina. It is seemingly derived from his *De honesta voluptate*, a culinary work first published in 1480 or some later sylloge or compend of this work (see for the diffusion of this work M. E. Milham, 'The Manuscripts of Platina's *De honesta voluptate* and its source', *Scriptorium*, 26, 1972, pp. 127–9, and eadem, 'The Latin Editions of Platina's *De honesta voluptate*', *Gutenburg Jahrbuch*, 52, 1976, pp. 57–63). There is an edition with commentary: Platina, *On Right Pleasure and Good Health*, ed. M. E. Milham, Tempe, 1998, and for a reference to Philenus 'Archigallus' in a recipe for a spring pie see p. 365 – examination, however, of the apparatus criticus for this passage, and the discussion of stemmatically separative errors at pp. 71–2, make it clear that the Philenus reference (and other less clear references to this person) was found only in the manuscript tradition and not in the printed editions of *De honesta voluptate*, and it is for this reason that I suggest the reference is derived from some intermediary source. Incidentally, no reference to Philenus is made at all in the section on eggs. One might also think of Erasmus, *Adagia*, I.V.10, 'Non tam ovum ovo simile', and the similar idea used by Montaigne at the beginning of *Essais*, III. i, 'De l'experience' (Michel de Montaigne, *Les Essais*, ed. F. Strowski, Hildesheim, 1981, 3 vols., II, pp. 360–61).

[2] Forged letters: BL Stowe MS 1083, ff. 17–20 (Throckmorton denies the italic hand in an incriminating letter to be his); buried letters: *Calendar of Letters and State Papers Relating to English Affairs Preserved Principally in the Archives of Simancas*, ed. M. A. S. Hume, London, 1892, p. 634 (Mendoza to Philip II on a story of how some of Mary's letters were found buried in a garden); letters in code: Bossy, *Under The Molehill* (hereafter *UTM*), passim; letters sewn into doublets: *Calendar of State Papers Relating to Scotland and Mary, Queen of Scots 1547–1603*, V, ed. William K. Boyd, Edinburgh, 1907, p. 90. See the entertaining skit of the Spanish ambassador Gondomar by Thomas Middleton ('letters conveyed in rolls, tobacco balls'): Thomas Middleton, *A Game of Chess*, IV.2.44.

It was very often upon the interpretation of letters that Howard's numerous troubles with the ruling authority turned, as evidenced by a slew of interrogatories or notes preparatory thereto. Unfortunately, these letters, sometimes denied to be authentic, sometimes lost, occasionally illegible, remain our best source for the political twists and turns with which Howard, often peripherally (perhaps because of his rank and the protection it afforded him in Elizabeth's eyes), is time and again associated in this period. It was the real limits to his desire to conform in matters of religion, together with the particularly low regard in which some members of the Walsingham camp appear to have held Howard, that account for the absence of hard evidence of his treasonous intent.

To the extent that one may describe a coherent pattern of behaviour, given the constraints of our documents, one may begin to see him as less atypical and less duplicitous in his actions than his enemies, and later biographers, have suggested. Howard, it will be argued, was not so very different from other courtiers in the way he attempted to build up political power bases among potentially conflicting groups at court and, perhaps, with a nod to his relations with the Spanish and French ambassadors, beyond it. What marked him out as different was, first, his – near public – lukewarm sentiments towards the Elizabethan settlement.[3] A second distinction between him figures such as Burghley-sponsored moderates Sir James Croft and Sir Christopher Hatton (both of whom had, for a while, warm relations with the Spanish ambassador) resides in his distance, for most of the 1570s, from the particularities of court life and the responsibilities of any public office or service. After all, the desire to engage in the rituals of courtly persuasion, while not in fact being at court, perhaps explains, together with the smaller number of people who would have accepted his suit, some of Howard's odder political decisions.[4] A third distinction is the taint of moral danger, his 'vyle nature', that appears to have so excited the ire of such divergent persons as William Herle and Francis Bacon's mother, who warned her son about Howard's circle.[5] Such an inter-

---

[3] See, for some gossip on Howard's supposed religious duplicity that found its way outside the immediate circle of the court or Walsingham, the poem at BLO Malone MS 23 f. 1^r and the tasteless story of his behaviour at the Queen's death bed: *The Diary of Sir John Manningham, of the Middle Temple, and of Bradbourne, Kent, Barrister at Law, 1602-3*, ed. J. Bruce, Westminster, 1868, pp. 170–1, though both these texts derive from a later period.

[4] I count among these decisions his decision to ally himself with Oxford and with Mendoza long after it became clear (at least to others) that these men were liabilities.

[5] This was clear in her suspicion of Philip II's ex-secretary and sodomite on the run, Antonio Perez (who is one of Howard's associates during his sojurn in England): see G. Unguerer, *A Spaniard in Elizabethan England: The Correspondence of Antonio Perez' Exile*, London, 1988, ad indicem, sub nomine 'Bacon'. One should remark that Lady Bacon saw sodomy everywhere.

pretation does not emerge, Minerva-like, fully formed from the evidence; or, to the extent that it does, it leaves its progenitor with a considerable forensic headache. It rests rather – to return to the theme with which we began – upon a welter of documents, the very circumstances of composition of which are often in dispute. The reader will soon appreciate that any reconstruction of *wie es eigentlich gewesen ist* in this culture of suspicion and mistrust, and on the slenderest of documentary evidence, requires more the skill of Philenus than of Ranke, and even then one may have to content oneself with clearly defined statements of ignorance.[6] Indeed, the phrasing of Howard's aphorism ('tooke upon him') suggests that this skill may have proved illusory. Furthermore, attempts to pin down Elizabethan religious identities in particular are notoriously difficult, since they are the product of contested vocabularies, yearly shifts of emphasis and public rhetorical acts that maintain a healthy distance from our concepts of sincerity, as Howard's next work shows.

Sometime in the summer of 1573, Howard wrote a long letter to his 'patron', Lord Burghley, informing him of contemporary religious controversies.[7] That letter showed its writer capable of dealing with the topic and perhaps functioned as a spur to Burghley, persuading him that Howard was an appropriate person to pen a biting but scholarly tract against certain religious fanatics who were endangering the good order of the kingdom.[8] Upon the accession of Mary Tudor to the throne in 1553, many Protestants went into voluntary exile. Their favoured destinations were Geneva, Zurich and Strasbourg. In these continental strongholds of reformed doctrine, they imbibed theological ideas and experienced modes of political and ecclesiological organization that some had high hopes would be replicated in England, following the death of Mary and the accession of Elizabeth.

---

[6] Howard's movements and preoccupations throughout most of the 1570s are unclear, owing to paucity of evidence. The phrase 'culture of suspicion and mistrust' should not suggest that England, even in the 1580s, was a police state. The contrast with France and Spain, where the prince had stronger revenue-raising powers and his own army, is clear.

[7] BL Cotton MS, Titus C vi, ff. 19^r–22^v. A later hand has inserted '11 July' beneath Howard's own later ascription of the year 1573. We know that the disputation, a transcription of which he appends, was a 'set piece': Howard writes (f. 19^r) that he thought it would not be unpleasant for Burghley 'somewhat to understande of our Commencement dealings' and this is a reference to the university festival of Commencement. The first Tuesday of July was designated Commencement Day for all faculties by the Edwardine statutes of 1549, a ruling which was afterwards embodied in the Elizabethan statutes of 1559 and 1570 (see Hackett, *Original Statutes*, p. 127).

[8] Given the emphasis on the political threat that these persons represent, one notes Howard's comment (BL Cotton MS, Titus C vi, f. 19^v) that the Presbyterians' concerns have 'rather sprung up of late uppon […]ancy and desire of innovation'.

Lord Henry Howard: An Elizabethan Life

The pace of change proved frustratingly slow, however, and it became increasingly clear throughout the 1560s that London was not going to be modelled after Geneva. Too many popish trappings in vestment and prayerbook remained. In 1566 some of these concerns came to a head in another eruption of the long-discussed 'vestments controversy'. Then Thomas Cartwright's Lady Margaret theology lectures, delivered in 1570 at Cambridge, found a ready audience among the zealous students of that city, but it was the publication in 1572 of John Field and Thomas Wilcox's *An Admonition to Parliament*, with its overstatements and offensive tone, that showed how wide the gap between the two wings of the Protestant faithful had become.

The fanatics (called variously at the time 'Puritans', 'Precisians' and 'Apostles', and since referred to as Presbyterians) were enthusiastic preachers of the Gospel, with scant regard for the traditional structures of church authority (proponents of which are referred to in the secondary literature as Conformists[9]) and anxious to erect their own system in its stead, albeit that their self-presentation is one of return and renewal. The Presbyterian challenge to the ecclesiological status quo (in particular, the proper scope of church and secular jurisdiction) consisted in an appeal to the authority of the primitive church from which the Elizabethan settlement appeared some way distant. A battle, then, between two groups.[10] Though Burghley's response to Howard's letter is unrecorded, the following year a work indeed appeared, albeit anonymously, attacking those Presbyterians who would deprive justice of its 'lawfull iurisdiction and authoritie': *A Defense of the Ecclesiasticall*

---

[9] E.g., Peter Lake, *Anglicans or Puritans? English Conformist Thought from Whitgift to Hooker*, London, 1988.

[10] Terminology for the different groups involved is contentious. This is chiefly because the words are not labels for outsiders *ab initio*, but ways of characterizing one's own: see P. Collinson, 'Concerning the name "Puritan"', *Journal of Ecclesiastical History*, 41, 1980, p. 485, and Christopher Hill, 'The Definition of a Puritan', in his *Society and Puritanism in Prerevolutionary England*, London, 1964, pp. 15–30. One notes especially the relevance of chronology: Henry Howard's fellow jurist in the Gunpowder Plot, Lord Coke, saw terminological disputes as irrelevant until the hardening of confessional heart that occurred sometimes in the early 1570s: see Henry Howard, *A True and Perfect Relation of the Whole Proceedings against the Late Most Barbarous Traitors*, London, 1605, sig. H2^r, and see a number of discussions in the 1571 Parliament recorded in Hartley, *Proceedings*, I, pp. 204–8. Bibliographical details and a bare comparison with relevant polemical kith and kin (including earlier ones such as the Vestments controversy and later ones such as the Martin Marprelate pamphlets) may be found in Peter Milward, *Religious Controversies of the Elizabethan Age: a Survey of Printed Sources*, London, 1977.

Regiment of England.[11] The emphasis throughout Howard's letter is on the intellectual incapacity of the radicals and on the danger to the state which they represent. Howard has clearly understood, or at least so represents to Burghley, that the Admonition Controversy consisted in a move from a liturgical dispute (the Vestments Controversy) to a governmental or political one.[12]

The *longue durée* of the history of the Christian Church (and not just the 'Reformation') is filled with impassioned cries for spiritual renewal.[13]

---

[11] [Henry Howard], *A Defense of the Ecclesiasticall Regiment in England*, London: Bynneman, 1574, p. 132. (STC10393: exact date of publication not known since Stationers' Company registers are missing for this year). The copy I have used bears the Royal Library stamp (BL shelfmark 697 a 25). The work is anonymous and the first reference I have found to the authorship of the tract is from 1583 in John Dee's library catalogue: see Julian Roberts and Andrew G. Watson, *John Dee's Library Catalogue*, London, 1990, index, sub nomine 'Howard, Henry'. A frontispiece annotation in the copy in the Cambridge University Library (shelfmark: Syn 8.57.11³) identifies the work as Howard's, but the hand is not datable (though it does refer to Howard as the 'L. H. Howard', which at least suggests a *terminus ante quem* of 1604, when the title Earl of Northampton was conferred upon him). The book receives a notice from J. Strype, *Life of Matthew Parker*, London, 1845, pp. 463–4, but no indication of authorship; the work's topic is, however, 'very aptly treated of'. As we have seen, Howard wrote letters on the religious difficulties to Burghley and perhaps the work was written at the Lord Treasurer's request, though there is no mention of it in the surviving letters between the two men. The book was published by the same publisher that Whitgift had used for his own contributions to the Admonition literature. Whitgift and Howard knew each other perhaps from Cambridge and, perhaps, it was Whitgift who suggested the work's composition. I am reluctant to imagine it was a topic immediately congenial to Howard, unless it was part of his attempt to make himself a member of the episcopacy (about which doubts are to be raised). A more detailed study of this work may be found in D. C. Andersson, 'Dialectic and the Church: Ecclesiology, Experience and the Limits of Argument in the Presbyterian Controversy', *Renaissance and Reformation* (forthcoming).

[12] For a recent argument that the significance of the Vestments Controversy may have been overstated in the context of the country as a whole within the 1560s, see B. Usher, 'Edward Brocklesby: "The First Put Out of his Living for the Surplice"', in *From Cranmer to Davidson: A Church of England Miscellany*, ed. S. Taylor, Woodbridge, 1999, pp. 47–67.

[13] Many had urged the abandonment of unnecessary or unscriptural ceremonies: e.g., John Wyclif (*Tracts and Treatises of John de Wycliffe*, ed. R. Vaughan, London, 1845, p. 251) and Johannes Oecolampadius (*In Hieremiam commentariorum libri tres*, Strassburg: Apiarius, 1530, sig. B4ᵛ: 'qui caerimoniarum multitudine lucem Evangelii obscurant'). Bernard J. Verkamp (*The Indifferent Mean: Adiaphorism in the English Reformation to 1557*, Athens: OH, 1977, p. 10) suggests that Jean Gerson is to be numbered among these people, with his negative emphasis on canon law. Perhaps, but the evidence he affords does not back this up. Gerson explains the nature of ecclesiastical power and its relation to charity but does not suggest abrogation of ceremonies; he simply notes the difficulties that what later scholars might term an adiaphoristic division has caused the Church: Jean Gerson, *Liber de vita spirituali animae*, in *Oeuvres*, ed. Mgr. P. Glorieux, Paris, 1962, p. 143–4, where he emphasizes that the distinction between 'de eis quae spiritualia proprie dicuntur et quae solum attributive' is an 'adinventio autem spiritualitatis' which has caused 'turbationes plures quam scribi

Such cries should not be particularized into silence; rather, they deserve to be seen as variations on a theme.[14] For present purposes, one might designate that theme as a Pauline 'Kampf zwischen Glaube und Gesetz'.[15] Very often these pleas for renewal have taken the shape of a call to live in accordance with the ways of Jesus and the first disciples.[16] Whatever else such a claim may be, it is certainly an *historical* claim.[17] Or, put less tendentiously, it is a claim about the past. One needs to know how, as a matter of fact, those men and women described from the Gospel actually lived, which involves the understanding the Bible and other early documents. Accordingly, and perhaps merely subordinately, there are issues of *interpretation*. Nothing delighted humanists more than issues of textual interpretation, often from a position with no explicit confessional or theological *parti pris*. It was then only a matter of time before the 'Puritans', as part of

potest'). Only after the assimilation of the *artes sermocinales* to religious debate, however, does the element of Biblical interpretation come to the fore (this, at least, is what I hope to prove in this Chapter): for one recent interpretation of the impact of these *artes* in the context of the Reformation, see F. de Michelis Pintacuda, *Tra Erasmo e Lutero*, Rome, 2001, esp. pp. 13–39. In addition, the upward mobility of the Holy Spirit within the history of Christian theology (from esoteric and minor enthusiasm of the philosophical Greek fathers to all-inspiring force of Western Christianity) cannot be forgotten (see the – slightly eccentric – study of J. F. Nuttall, *The Holy Spirit in Puritan Faith and Experience*, ed. Peter Lake, Princeton, 1992), though one should equally note the gradual decline of the Holy Spirit as having a role in hermeneutics in the seventeenth century with the rise of 'rational religion' (see, for example, Andreas Wissowatius, *Religio rationalis*, ed. Z. Ogonowski, Wolfenbüttel, 1982, pp. 30–1).

[14] There is a strong cases for the *Annales* language used in my opening paragraph, if one agrees with Michel Houellebecq, *Les éléments particuliers*, Paris, 2001, p. 10 that '[l]es mutations métaphysiques sont rares dans l'histoire de l'humanité. Par example, on peut citer l'apparition du christianisme. Dès lors qu'une apparition métaphysique s'est produite, elle se développe sans rencontrer du résistance jusqu'à ses conséquences ultimes.'

[15] Martin Heidegger, *Phänomenologie des religiösen Lebens*, Gesammtausgabe, LX, ed. M. Jung, Frankfurt am Main, 1995, p. 158. The context is a reading of tensions in Paul's Corinthian epistles.

[16] Indeed, that seems to be the message of the very first call for renewal, though a non-polemical one: see *The Gospel of Thomas*, ed. M. Meyer, San Francisco, 1992. For one vigorous early modern formulation, see Samuel Przypkowski, *Dissertatio de pace et concordia ecclesiae*, ed. M. Brozek, Warsaw, 1981, pp. 68–9 at p. 69: 'Quae curiositas quam infeliciter orbi cesserit, credamus conquerenti Hilario, qui felices Galliae episcopos praedicat, quod aliam nec excudisset nec recepisset nec omnino cognovissent confessionem quam veteram illam atque simplicissimam, quae ab aetate Apostolorum apud omnes Ecclesias recepta fuerat!' (in the context of attacking the over-elaborate Trinitarian doctrine). For a view of the relations between philology and history in the context of the early stages of the Reformation, see Pintacuda, *Tra Erasmo e Lutero*, pp. 177–82.

[17] For a brief overview of the developing connection between religious legitimation and historical truth (or its fabrication), see H. Küng, *The Catholic Church: A Short History*, London, 2001. For the sixteenth century, see the classic study of Pontien Polman, *L'élément historique dans la controverse religieuse du 16ème siècle*, Gembloux, 1932.

their ongoing struggle against elements hostile to the Reformed church, viewed the issues of reform through a lens of Renaissance philology and dialectic to make more persuasive arguments.[18] Influential too was a tradition of evangelical sensibility that found the practice of biblical interpretation (a protreptic to the practice of preaching) more congenial a means of settling theological debate than the modes of medieval scholastic theology.[19] The combination of these two elements, the textual and the historical, resulted in the sort of religious polemic which we find so superabundantly in the sixteenth century, and which, more precisely, we will study in relation to Howard's contribution to the pamphlet that later historiography has termed the 'Presbyterian Crisis'. England's enthusiastic vernacularization of Renaissance dialectic also left its mark on the Presbyterian controversy of the 1570s, since, naturally enough, argument was felt to be necessary for the legitimation of religious authority. The techniques of argument hugged closely those of the university disputation, since the participants in the dispute were themselves heavily involved in academic life.

Dialectic, in both its humanist and scholastic forms, taught the art of proper reasoning through which, it was supposed, one might better arrive at the truth, though in some more rhetorical versions of dialectic, its skills were much closer to *in utramque partem* reasoning and, accordingly, closer to the goals of rhetorical ability.[20] One can certainly see what might be called a strong dialectical inheritance in Howard's work, and his pointing out of argumentative errors recalls the manoeuvres used by the participants in the disputation of one year earlier. This was only to be expected: the participants were all fellows at Cambridge colleges and, at least some of the time, it was these failures of dialectic reasoning that would abolish faith in the arguments of their opponents. There are limits to which this 'dialec-

---

[18] I use the word 'Reformed' in the narrow sense of the Calvinist consensus of mid-century Europe, against which Elizabeth's settlement of religion (largely the work of the anonymous authors of the 1558 tract Device for Alteration of Religion) was to prove ever more Quixotic. By using the phrase 'only a matter of time', I do not want to suggest that we cannot pinpoint some very historically precise factors which shaped the humanist reading of the Bible among Protestants: see, e.g., the Prophesyings.

[19] On the transformation of the educational institutions which were fitted to create a preaching ministry (and of the increased popularity of such a career toward the end of Elizabeth's reign, after a false dawn at the end of Mary's reign) see Rosemary O'Day, *The English Clergy: The Emergence and Consolidation of a Profession 1558–1629*, Leicester, 1979.

[20] For one such rhetorical version hailing from England, see Thomas Wilson, *The Rule of Reason*, London: Richard Grafton, 1551, sig. B1^r: 'Logique is an art to reason probably on both partes'. For an English account which emphasizes the scholastic inheritance of semantics over this insistence on probable reasoning, see Stanihurst, *Harmonia*.

tical' approach to Howard's works is subject, for these tools themselves were not always adequate to dealing with the issues in dispute between the parties. This was for two reasons – firstly, the difference between the parties were ones of religious outlook which were simply ill served by being characterized in the dialectical tools available to them; and, secondly, much of the dispute was couched in the language of scriptural hermeneutics which allowed (and, after the enthusiasms of humanist exegesis, often demanded) a broader (let us say, for the time being, a philological) approach to the resolution of issues of the meanings of words. Howard's decision to write a more rhetorical work, albeit that his dialectic was already a highly rhetorical one, and his decision to cast it in the invective and polemical mode, were evidence of an awareness that some of the issues in dispute were best settled through means other than the *ars dialectica*.

Our *point d'appui* for this enquiry is the disputation that Howard's letter to Burghley introduces.[21] It would appear to be dependent on the previous publications in the *Admonition* Controversy rather than being a wholly independent treatment of the same theme.[22] Accordingly, its value as a source for 'pure' disputational argumentative procedure is more limited; it is for this reason that its range of what counts as an argument is rather broader than one would have imagined from looking, for example, at the slighter later work of Robert Sanderson.[23] What this disputation allows us to see is the recasting of issues in dispute into the forms of scholastic argument that would allow the participants to exercise their skills in dialectic upon the propositions and words involved. A few examples will suffice. At one point Dr Hawford notes that: 'ministers should not involve themselves in secular matters, ergo, neither should the prince involve himself in ecclesiastical ones'.[24] This brings the very clear rebuke from Dr Redman that 'the antecedent proposition is simply not the case, though the argument also does not follow'.[25] Though the dialectical procedure is not explicit in this instance, the reformulation of arguments into this very bald form does make it easier to spot the logical errors. Or again,

---

[21] This is transcribed with commentary as Documentary Appendix III in Andersson, 'Studies'.
[22] Consider, for example, the fact that it quotes some of the very same non-theological passages as Thomas Cartwright's *A Replye Made to an Answere Made of Doctor Whitegifte*, London, [1573].
[23] For this reference, see Documentary Appendix III in Andersson, 'Studies'.
[24] BL Cotton MS, Titus C vi f. 21ʳ: 'Ministri non debent sese implicare secularibus ergo nec princeps se rebus eclesiasticis immiscere.'
[25] Ibid.: 'antecedens proposition non est simpliciter vera, quamvis non consequatur argumentum'.

Teacher, Polemicist, Papist

Redman cleverly uses the classic dialectical technique of 'distinctio' in a discussion of the different notions of 'the people' from whom consent must be sought in some matters.[26] This is precisely the sort of semantic subtlety, transmitted through the techniques of dialectic, which the late medieval sciences of words had developed to a high degree.

It should be observed, however, that while these techniques of conceptual and semantic disambiguation are useful for dealing with some sorts of question, they are rather poor at dealing with issues of textual interpretation; and it was upon precisely such issues that much of the *Admonition* Controversy turned. For example, to the extent that the disputation is able to discuss one key piece of evidence for congregational election, it is noteworthy that it must abandon the procedures of syllogistic reasoning and *distinctio* and so on. That piece of evidence is the proper translation of the word χειροτονια, and here the requirement is one of hermeneutics rather than of dialectic.[27] Howard, of all the participants in the debate, realizes the importance of a different medium to deal with the different issues thrown up. His is a work of invective as well as one of hermeneutics – his use of dialectic is conditioned by his overall rhetorical purpose, something which it is very hard to say of Whitgift, and, of course, of the disputation.

As the later printing history of the dispute demonstrated, the punctilious fugue and counter-fugue between the two groups had little natural end point.[28] Howard, now out of the academic environment, seeks to close down the argument, since too detailed a treatment would frustrate his aim and could not be achieved 'without some tediousnesse'.[29] *A Defence* strives at a cumulative effect of arguments, indignation and the construction of ethos, together with jokes and ironic asides. To this 'rhetorical' end, much is grist to his mill, not only the etymological biblical exegesis. Howard uses a rich diet of argumentative techniques, itself typical of the humanist *declamatio*.[30] Consider the playful tone of the following passage:

---

[26] Ibid: 'Valet regula in his quae spectant ad omnes quasi ad singulos non ubi ad omnes quasi ad universos et inter quos singulorum consensus requiritur'. Disambiguation (which is both a rhetorical and a dialectical technique) is one of the main ways in which the dialecticians suggested that a 'question' be treated, it was a crucial part of the 'methodos': see, e.g., Wilson, *Rule of Reason*, sigs E4ᵛ–6ᵛ.
[27] See Andersson, 'Dialectic and the Church'.
[28] For this later printing history, see Milward, *Religious Controversies*.
[29] Howard, *A Defense*, p. 51.
[30] For the coexistence of different argumentative registers within a single text, see Chapter Seven.

> Many other texts of scripture to like effect might be alleaged, if decision of this question rather stoode upon heapes of places, than force of arguments, or were sooner ended by multitude of allegations than certentie of matter.[31]

'Heape' is an obvious reference to the dialectical phenomenon of the 'sorites' and, to emphasize the dialectical register, Howard uses the word in conjunction with 'places', in other words the loci of topic logic, just as (perhaps) 'decision' carries overtones of one of the two main areas of dialectic, 'judicium', the other one being invention.[32] However, in fact these words have been evacuated of proper dialectical meaning to produce a rhetorical effect. After all, 'places' is in fact a pun since the schoolroom connotation is clearly secondary to the basic sense of 'scriptural passage'; Howard has suggested that his opponents are prolix and not compelling, whereas his discourse is one more reliant on less flimsy forms of logic, an suggestion to which the final two parallel phrases, lengthier in syllables than the pair to which they in apposition, make an abundant contribution.[33] Howard frequently points out his logical reasoning to the audience: all part of ethos.[34] One good example is his use of the *reductio ad absurdum* technique.[35]

Neither Howard (playfully) nor Whitgift (more earnestly) is the first to emphasize his superior skills in dialectic in the context of Reformed ecclesiology.

> There be many fonde people which have much dispraised all temporall lawes & civil lawes, thinking it mete that al common weales should onlye have the gospel, and none other lawe at all.

---

[31] Howard, *A Defense*, p. 24.

[32] Classical Latin sources for the *sorites*: Horace, *Epistles*, 2.1.47; Cicero, *Academica*, II.49; Persius, 6.80; and, used punningly or playfully, Horace, *Odes*, 2.2.24 (see R. G. M. Nisbet and Margaret Hubbard, *A Commentary on Horace Odes II*, Oxford, 1978, pp. 30–1).

[33] For another example from the same chapter which uses (in an even vaguer way) the language of dialectic, see Howard, *A Defense*, p. 22: 'These places being, as in deed they are more evident than that maye bee shyfted off wyth Sophisticall interpretations, I fynde no grounde sufficiente to exclude such persons from the ministerie, as eyther have been seduced upon ignorance, or faynted by infirmitie.'

[34] So, for example, he uses an a fortiori argument at p. 14: 'Wherefore, if the greater bee not prohibited, the lesse maye bee permitted'; again at pp. 134–5; and p. 139: 'must we humble our hearts which is the greater, and not bende our knees which is the lesser?' Another good example is found at p. 58: 'The argument is proved by a Topicke place of their owne. For if it be lawfull for them to teach ab authoritate negative, there were no Metropolitanes among the Iewes beyng Gods chosen people, Ergo there ought to be none among the Christians, it shall be much more lawfull for us affirmatively to reason thus: There was a difference in the legal priests in honour, ergo there should be among the Christians.'

[35] Howard, *A Defense*, p. 149.

Teacher, Polemicist, Papist

This seemingly conformist statement comes not from Richard Hooker or John Jewel or John Whitgift. It is found, rather, in the popular handbook of vernacular dialectic, *The Rule of Reason*, by Thomas Wilson. The ecclesiological comment inaugurates his lengthy digression to illustrate the logical term 'distinctio'.[36] The role of 'reason' in the sense of arguments from dialectic is in dispute. Cartwright wishes to erect a church on an intuitive appeal to community (or Church).[37] That is the function of edification. Cartwright is pure, his opponent would say, emotional excess: 'The ende of M Cartwrightes meditation is that we be enflamed.'[38] The distinction that Wilson is keen for his readers to understand is the difference between reforming a polity and reforming a church, and only the most tyro of logicians could fail to grasp his point. That, however, is not the point. The threat is that there is a new way of interpreting the Bible that, even if it does not run quite counter to the norms of dialectical argument, at least supplements them. After all, one of the key logical problems that the two sides have is *what is the negative scope of a positive injunction?*[39] What is not forbidden does not equal what is licit, says one side. Consider the dilemma of holy days. Howard is keen to show that there is express scriptural commandment for some such days.[40] One can understand Howard's point that, logically, his opponent's argument that holy days detract from the celebration of the word is a poor one: 'By this pretie Logicke, we may conclude that the binding of the Levies to serve God morning and evening was a mean to make them idle all the days besides.'[41] This is not a problem that dialectic is particularly adept at getting to the bottom of. Certainly, the error can be pointed out, but that is hardly the point. Rudolph Agricola's chapter on opposites would be no help, and indeed, the problem is not one that can be solved by the application of dialectical principles, but rather through context, the exploration of

---

[36] Wilson, *Rule of Reason*, sig. D8ᵛ.
[37] In other words, we should see the dispute as a central one about rival religious phenomenologies which have a number of side effects, including political.
[38] Howard, *A Defense*, p. 133. The context is what should be the right attitude at prayer, and so the word 'meditation' strictly speaking, I think, refers only to prayer. But as a rhetorical ploy, it seems very clear to me that this is Howard's tactic (with 'meditation' meaning the entire work of Cartwright) to suggest an overly emotional approach to his construction of certain actions in the church community.
[39] This logical aporia has already been emphasized by Lake, *Anglicans or Puritans?*
[40] Howard, *A Defense*, p. 149.
[41] Howard, *A Defense*, p. 151.

background assumptions (or, put more grandly, religious phenomenology) and philology.[42]

Attending to the structure of the work would have made it very clear to Howard's readers that it was going to be different in nature from its immediate predecessors in the dispute. Howard's introduction to the work is an attempt to site the point for point scholarly polemic in a rhetorical context.[43] That rhetorical context is the construction or, rather, demolition of character of Cartwright. He uses, in other words, the persuasive technique of ethos. He explains that Cartwright is motivated by envy and that his own appeal to unity in the Church should nonetheless be seen against his culminating prefatory marker of rhetorical genre: that of Cicero's invectives against Verres. The invective genre, a sort of capacious omnium-gatherum mode with close connections to that favoured humanist genre, the half-serious declamation, served Howard well.

Earlier studies of the Presbyterian crisis have emphasized the radical nature of the ecclesiology involved. However, the range of issues that were thrown up (ceremonies, orders, scriptural interpretation, the role of preaching) was sufficiently diverse that it makes more sense to view these works as responses to renewed religious sentiment, anxious to justify itself with philology, dialectic and history. Only later can we speak of solidification into a programme for building a particular sort of Church. In any case, the definition of church was precisely one of the points at issue. Was it a political institution? Bricks and mortar? Or something else? It is enough, for present purposes, to say that some of the dispute revolved around the issue of hierarchy in the visible church. Henry Howard's tract makes, naturally enough, several references to the Church. The longest passage, enlivened by a simile, is tellingly political and hierarchical in its implications:

> The Church is very fitly compared by S Hilary to a ship tossing upon the sea, in respect of her endlesse trouble and vexation: but as it is not lawfull for every Mariner to play the pylote, or guide the helme, when stormes and pirries come, no more is it fitte for every Minister to reach at an Archbishops dignitie ... The same Churche is called by Solomon in his sonets, acies ordinata, a ranke or armye set in order: but what order I beseche you can there be, where there is no difference between the Captayne, Peticaptayne and the Generall?[44]

---

[42] R. Agricola, *De inventione dialectica*, ed. L. Mundt, Tübingen, 1992, 1. 26.46–49. Whitgift is more keen on demonstrating his arguments' debt to formal argumentative procedures: even including arguments from law (see W. iii. 336: 'Further, you must learn that an argument a facto ad jus is commonly of small force ...').

[43] Sig. A1–2; alternatively pp. 1–3.

[44] Howard, *A Defense*, pp. 89–90.

Ecclesial language tends toward the metaphorical and the associative.[45] The range of metaphors is drastically reduced in Howard to that of Hilary's ship or the well-ordered State, thereby indicating the stamp of his own preoccupations. These were already clearly signalled in the letter to Burghley in a passage where Howard discussed the principal *quaestio* of the Commencement disputation: '1. the election of ministers is of necessity a matter to be dealt with by the people and 2. The "procuratio" of religion is a matter that applies to the civil magistrate.'[46] The people, retorts Howard, can have no claim or interest in the election of ministers, unless the church be made a 'playne democratia'.[47] We have seen then the importance of Howard's choice of polemical invective, and seen further confirmation of his understanding of the governmental and political account of what was once a purely liturgical affair. This significance of this excursus into two broader contexts (rhetorical mode and political implications) can be put like this: Howard's awareness of a wider audience which he has to persuade encourages him to diminish the dialectical arguments and the 'philological' ones which both Cartwright and Whitgift made.

There are other differences between Howard and his fellow participants, such as over the concept of edification (see Appendix II of the current work), but however interesting Howard's experiential ambivalences and the deliberately broadened rhetorical approach to arguments culled from dialectic in this work may be, they were qualities which passed unnoticed. Richard Bancroft owned a copy of the book, but not only is the work unannotated but by the time that the future archbishop came to write his own attack on the Puritan wing within the Elizabethan Church, *Dangerous Positions*, the terms of debate had changed fundamentally; divine law

---

[45] For one outstanding recent philological study, see F. Ledegant, *Mysterium Ecclesiae: Beelden voor de Kerk in de Leden bij Origines*, Leuven, 2001. On religious language in general and its pull toward the metaphorical and inductive, see Battista Mondin, *Il problema del linguagio teologico dalle origini ad oggi*, Brescia, 1971; and, within the Renaissance, see the seminal work of Charles Trinkaus, *In Our Image and Likeness: Humanity and Divinity in Italian Renaissance Thought*, 2 vols, Chicago, 1970, I, pp. 62–3. For examples from Renaissance England see B. M. Kroll, *Henry Peacham's 'The Garden of Eloquence' (1593): historische-kritische Einleitung mit einer Kommentar*, Frankfurt am Main, 1996, pp. 21–2, and Thomas Swynnerton, *A Reformation Rhetoric*, ed. R. Rex, Cambridge, 1999, pp. 176–9. See also the section on the 'Ausdruck des Lebensgefühls und der Weltbeziehung' in the context of twentieth-century practical divinity in *Das Problem der Sprache in Theologie und Kirche*, ed. W. Schneemelcher, Berlin, 1959, pp. 89–111.

[46] BL Cotton MS, Titus C vi f. 19ᵛ: '1 electio ministrorum necessario ad plebem referendam esse 2 procuratio religionis spectat ad civilem magistratum'.

[47] Ibid. He continues that 'it hath ever been a principle in well governed states that multitudinis iudicio paucissima committenda'.

rather than the primitive church was now said to sanction the Elizabethan ecclesiology. The English Reformation moved fast.[48]

This speed was in part the working out of certain religious ideas, but it was also, obviously, a response to political events. The consequences for Howard and for England that flowed from, for example, the Ridolfi affair need to be filled in. There was a feeling among the Protestant movers and shakers that not enough was being done to combat the threat of Mary in the years 1572–4.[49] Mary, after all, could coherently be seen as the only genuine threat to domestic unity. She was rendered all the more threatening after 30 May 1574 when the pro-Guisard Henri III (1551–89) succeeded Charles IX (1550–74) to the throne of France, though Henri's intentions were not yet clear. Howard's involvement with the Scottish queen in the years 1573–4 appears evanescent but persistent.[50] Much of his dealing with her ambassador, John Leslie, the Bishop of Ross, revolved around shared contacts, and perhaps shared interests, in books and the book trade; this made it all the harder to distinguish politically dangerous intent from religiously conservative concerns. The first report of Howard's connection with Mary, since the Ridolfi affair, came in 1575 from one Henry Cockyn, though it seems clear that Howard was in contact with Leslie from at least the end of 1572. The mini-drama of Cockyn and his books needs, however,

---

[48] Richard Bancroft's copy of Howard's book is identified by his bookplate; the copy is currently housed in Lambeth Palace Library (Shelfmark 1574.04). William Lambarde also owned a copy (in the Huntington Library: see bibliography for details) of the work, but I have not been able to read the few Latin comments he makes in the margin.

[49] See T. Hartley, *Proceedings of the Parliaments of Elizabeth*, I, passim. A secret plan was also being hatched, according to Leo Hicks, *An Elizabethan Problem: Some Aspects of the Careers of Two Exile Adventurers*, London, 1964, p. 95, by Burghley and Walsingham in this year to send Sir Henry Killigrew to Edinburgh with the purpose of negotiating with the Earl of Morton and the Earl of Mar that Mary be handed over to them on condition that she be put to death. It seems impossible that Elizabeth would have agreed to this. Consider the comment of Burghley himself in his (anonymous) *Salutem in Christo: Good Men and Evil Delight In Contraries*, London: [Richard Grafton?], 1571, sig. A4[r–v].

[50] To the references and bibliography in Conyers Read, *Mr Secretary Walsingham and the Policy of Queen Elizabeth*, 3 vols, Oxford, 1925, II. pp. 348–50, add Hicks, *An Elizabethan Problem*, pp. 99–103. Howard provides a reference himself to his knowledge of a man who may be one Henry Cockyn, of whom more later (Howard actually calls him a 'bookbinder' in a letter to the Queen six years later: BL Cotton MS, Titus C vi f. 7[r]). It was Cockyn with the 'servant to a stationer dwelling at the sign of the Olifant in Fleete Streete' who passed the autograph version of John Leslie's (aka the bishop of Ross) account of the Ridolfi affair to Howard, in whose study it was subsequently found: Edwards, *The Marvellous Chance*, London, 1968, p. 51 n.1; I have not been able to trace this shop west of Fleet Street. For the account itself, see BL Additional MS 48027, ff. 45–70, where we learn that it was found in Howard's study by Ivy Bridge Lane.

Teacher, Polemicist, Papist

to be set against the larger, and possibly more dangerous, picture of goings-on in another noble household.

Early in 1572, Queen Elizabeth had persuaded George Talbot, sixth Earl of Shrewsbury, to get to the bottom of any Marian intriguing in his household.[51] Two young boys (one of whom was called John Steward) in the earl's household came forward to accuse the Welsh arriviste Thomas Morgan.[52] On 27 February 1572, some letters purportedly belonging to Mary were found hidden under a stone. Morgan was sent to the tower but the affair blew over. Until, that is, further dubious letters were found in the possession of another man in the Earl's employ. Talbot had sent off his schoolmaster, Alexander Hamilton, with packets of letters for Mary. This was, at any rate, the testimony of the eight-year-old go-between whom the two nobles employed. Burghley and Walsingham (though it is quite unclear what the division of labour and responsibility was between the two men) acquired information linking these persons with other Marian sympathizers and, for a while, it looked as if an important node in this dangerous network was a young bookbinder and bookseller from St Pauls.[53]

---

[51] So Hicks, *An Elizabethan Problem*, pp. 98–9, upon whose account I chiefly rely in this paragraph.

[52] For Morgan's career, see Hicks, *An Elizabethan Problem*, pp. 1–6 and 80–103. Morgan had become, upon Cecil's recommendation (see the letter from Cecil to Shrewsbury 15 May 1569 printed in Lodge, *Illustrations of British History*, London, 1838, p. 473) secretary to the earl at the same time that his seat had been designated the location for Mary's house arrest. He performed services for Mary, or so his latter testimony suggests, for which he was imprisoned in the Tower.

[53] On St Paul's and the book trade see now Peter Blayney, *The Bookshops in Paul's Cross Churchyard*, Cambridge, 1990 (strictly speaking, there is an issue over the extent to which Fleet Street, where we know Cockyn worked from, may be counted as part of St Paul's – this in turn is related to the issue of the extent to which bookbinders had their own separate binderies, independent of, and perhaps serving more than one, 'stationer' in the sense of printer/publisher). More detail on the Essex-born Cockyn (apprenticed to George Bucke from 1565 onwards; fined for not attending Quarterday celebrations in 1577, by which time he disappears from documentary sight) may be culled from Edward Arber, *A Transcript of the Registers of the Company of Stationers of London, 1554–1640 AD*, 5 vols, London [and Birmingham], 1875–1894, I, p. 255; II, 28; II, p. 306; and II, p. 845. Since he was apprenticed in February 1565 for eight years (though it is worth bearing in mind that there was an ordinance, perhaps later altered, that no apprenticeship should terminate before the apprentice had reached 24 years old: W. W. Gregg, *A Companion to Arber*, Oxford, 1967, p. 2), we may assume he now functioned independently; and indeed the publishing output of his master, George Bucke, appears to have dried up by 1565: see *A Short Title Catalogue of Books Printed in England, Scotland and Ireland and of English Books Printed Abroad, 1475–1640*, III, ed. Katherine Pantzer, London, 1991, p. 31. His one venture into print was an improving Classical miscellany, John Bishop's *Beautiful Blossoms*, London, 1576, thereby suggesting that his chief source of revenue was from bookselling, bookbinding and as a copyist (as we discover) rather than as a printer (albeit

Henry Cockyn, a young man only recently out of his apprenticeship, married to a woman with a taste for Juan Luis Vives, was hauled before Burghley for questioning on 16 January 1575, when the treasurer put together some 'memoranda' for his examination.[54] Among the numerous allegations made in this document, it was said that he 'receaved divers letters from the Bishop of Ross and others' and that 'he receaved letter by a boy who cam out of Flaunders this last sommar, who lay at on Wilsons house in St Catherines at which tyme he had sent to the Queen of Scotts by a servant of the Erle of Shrewsbury to which Morgan the Erle of Shrewsbury's man was privy.' He was intimate, it was further alleged, with servants of the Bishop of Ross and one 'Nichola', a servant of the French ambassador; 'he [sc. Cockyn] hath much conference with D. Astlow D Good Mr Morgan and the Lord Harry'. No sooner was the ink dry on Howard's 1574 defence of the English ecclesiastical settlement, it would seem, than he was engaging in cautious dealings with dangerous contacts.[55] By the time that Cockyn answers the questions of 20 January in a document dated 21 January, there is no mention of Howard at all. We do not know why Howard dropped out of Burghley's investigatory purview between 16 and 20 January. In his answers to the questions of 20 January, Cockyn admits to knowing the bishop of Ross's entire household but only because the bishop used him for the purpose of buying books.[56] These answers were not, it would appear, sufficient to grant Cockyn his freedom, for he was questioned again on 5 February.[57] In the second of these ques-

      that the various occupations merge in this period: for one recent and elegant contribution to the secondary literature on this topic, see David Pearson, *English Bookbinding Styles: A Handbook 1450–1800*, London, 2003, pp. 164–77, esp. 166).

[54] That is the date of TNA: PRO SP 53/10/78. There is an extensive but sometimes abbreviated and inaccurate transcription of these documents in *Calendar of State Papers Relating to Scotland and Mary, Queen of Scots 1547–1603*, V, ed. William K. Boyd, Edinburgh, 1907, passim. Previous accounts do not appear to have used the documents directly.

[55] For bibliographical details of this work, see Chapter Four p. 85n. 11. Interestingly, a document dated four days later (TNA: PRO SP 53/10/81), also in Burghley's hand, consisting purely of a list of questions to be put to Cockyn, omits any mention of Howard, though it repeats most of the other charges. Perhaps the former document was information given to him by his spies (such as Herle), who had a particular dislike of Howard. The sheer brutality and ignorance of many of the adolescent toughs upon whom Walsingham relied has received fresh emphasis from M. Honan, *Christopher Marlowe*, London, 2005.

[56] Note the book choice: TNA: PRO SP 53/10/81: 'Robinson came to me from the Bisshop for the workes of St Thomas More which bookes I had not.'

[57] There are two sets of interrogatories: TNA: PRO SP 53/10/82: '2. Howe he grewe fyrst to be acquaynted with the B. of Rosse. 3 whether he ever served the B of Rosse and howe longe and by whome he was recommended unto him' and, in another hand, TNA: PRO SP 53/10/84.

Teacher, Polemicist, Papist

tionings on that day, he was asked 'whear upon grewe thacquayntance with his Lord Henry, and what he [...] he hath had unto him and the cawses'.[58] These examinations were conducted by Walsingham, since it is his hand that completes this last list of interrogatories.[59] Burghley played no further role in the questioning of Cockyn and it is perhaps noteworthy that it is only when Walsingham takes over that Howard begins to feature in the questioning again.[60]

A further set of interrogatories, apparently lost, was put to Cockyn, which he answered in his next examination on 16 February 1575. In these lost interrogatories the charge against Howard must have been more serious, involving dealings with Mary.[61] Four days later, on 20 February 1575, Cockyn penned a 'confession', a fascinating document which fleshes out considerably the soured relations between Mary's ambassador and Howard.[62] Cockyn relates that in December 1573 the bishop of Ross, then in lodging with the Bishop of Winchester, called for him to undertake binding work on some medical books.[63] They fell into conversation, and the bishop asked what the *communis opinio* of him was. On hearing Cockyn's reply that there were those who felt his dealings had been dishonourable, he said: 'it is tould me that sume men are so sore bent agaynst me that they have vowed to kil me before I depart the realme, and namely the Lord Henrie'. Cockyn had talked with Howard at the Charterhouse and assured the bishop that Howard was 'evill affected towards him, but not in the mynd wither to kill hurt him'. The bishop then said that he intended to placate his ill-wishers before leaving England. Cockyn continues

> the Bishop used D Good to pacifie my Lord of Southampton: and the Bishop had of purpose made a little treatise to send to Lord Henrie before his departure, intituled (as I remember) 'An Apologie or Defence of the

---

[58] TNA: PRO SP 53/10/84.
[59] The majority of the document is in the hand of Sir Thomas Randolph.
[60] We should bear in mind that it is from the period 1573 to 1577 that we have evidence of the warmest relations between Burghley and Howard (as seen in the dealings with Oxford and the possible commissioning of both the *Defence* – for which see Chapter Five – the defence of female rule: on which see (with caution) Anna Christine Caney, 'Let He Who Objects Produce Sound Evidence: Henry Howard and the Sixteenth Century [sic] Gynecocracy Debate', unpublished MA dissertation, Florida State University, 2005).
[61] TNA: PRO SP 53/10/87: 'To the ixth he sayeth he knows the Lord henry and in ... and he sayeth he was with him att the charter howse abowwt Easter for the sellinge unto him of divers prayer books and for no other cawse and knoweth nothinge of any ... with the scottish queene'.
[62] TNA: PRO SP 53/10/89.
[63] Robert Horne was the bishop of Winchester at this time, and his seat was Farnham Castle.

Bishop of Rosse touchynge his honest and friendly part always keped toward the honourable Lord the late Duke of Northfolke'. But the Bishop was advised by D Good (as I thinke) not to send it before he was out of the realme, for fear lest the said Lord Henrie should showe the same to some of the Queenes Majestys counsel, whereby he might be stayed and not suffered to departe the realme.[64]

When the 'Apologie' was eventually sent by Leslie through Cockyn to Howard at Audley End, it came with a message: that Mary was most desirous of retrieving a 'letter of contract' and a ring which she had sent to Howard's brother. Cockyn relates that Howard replied that the contract was burnt but the ring had been mislaid.[65] He goes on to say that Howard and Mary exchanged letters, though their contents were nothing but well-wishings. In other words, seen through the prism of Cockyn's testimony, the relations between Howard and Mary were simply cousinly and affectionate.

This confession evidently did not provide enough in the way of evidence against Howard for Walsingham and his associates, who, as we have seen, had taken over the interrogations from Burghley. That is the conclusion forced upon us by a letter from Cockyn to Walsingham, answering the charge that Cockyn had 'seemed to afraid to discover anie thing that might touche greate personages.'[66] Who might such 'great personages' be? Cockyn carries on with the name of Henry Howard: 'At first I was afraid to discover that which I knew bothe of the Lord Henry and the Lady Cobham who were the personages I stood in doubte of.'[67] The letter provides no further information on either figure. At this point, perhaps frustrated by the lack of hard evidence against those nobles, to whose ranks he was never freely admitted, Walsingham writes – in almost hectoring terms – to the Queen.[68] He clearly wants permission to move against more high-ranking figures.[69] In a second letter, dated 26 February, his tone is almost threatening.[70] There is no doubt that while Burghley continued to correspond on friendly terms

---

[64] TNA: PRO SP 53/10/89.
[65] Ibid.
[66] TNA: PRO SP 53/10/90.
[67] Ibid.
[68] TNA: PRO SP 53/10/91 and TNA: PRO SP 53/10/92.
[69] TNA: PRO SP 53/10/91: 'I do not doubt but that your majestie shalbe able to discover a great number of the corrupt members of your estate, especiallie such as remayne most dangerously about your person.'
[70] TNA: PRO SP 53/10/92: 'Touchinge the matter it self, your Majesties delaye in resolvinge doth not only make me voyd of all hope to do anye good therein … but also quite discourage me to deale in like cawses, seeyinge myne and other your poore faythfull servants care for your safetie frutelesse.'

with Howard during this period, Walsingham, or at least his spies, were considerably less well disposed towards him.[71] Whatever else had happened to incriminate Howard, it was certainly not enough to have him committed to the Tower, since the published Acts of the Privy Council again do not contain any reference to him.[72] Read in full, however, it is quite clear that Walsingham did not share the details of his suspicions even as they related to Cockyn with the other members of the Council.[73] The need to deal carefully with a noble, especially one with connections to Burghley, probably explains Howard's archival elusiveness. In addition to bringing out something of the Walsingham–Burghley tensions through the Cockyn episode, we also learn of the importance of the manuscript medium as a way of changing what one has said. The Bishop of Ross required Cockyn to produce another redaction of his 'Discourse of Proceedings', one more suited for Henry Howard to read. Cockyn was then instructed to bind this second redaction with the 'Apologie' and deliver only this edited account to Howard, and even this second redaction 'must be holpen in some places to, or els the the Lord Henrie will skarse like well of it'.[74]

Whatever Howard may have thought of the book shows, again, the difficulty of pinning down Howard's precise loyalties, and the importance of the book trade (which encompasses both printed and manuscript works) as a public emblem and cipher of the more private circulations of ideas and commitments for those on the ideological margins of the Elizabethan political establishment. More importantly, the episode with Cockyn under-

[71] For one instance of the tension between the different networks of Walsingham and of Burghley, see the comments of the ever-vile William Herle warning the Lord Treasurer of the 'hollow' friendship of some of those whom he chose to keep about him: BL Harleian MS 6991, ff. 111^r–112^r.

[72] *Acts of the Privy Council 1571-5*, ed. J. R. Dasent, London, 1890–1964, p. 336. The council was held at Richmond on 6 February 1574 (the last one having been a fortnight earlier).

[73] BL Harleian MS 6991, f. 112^r 'A letter to Mr Secretarie Walsingham and the solicitour general and Mr Randolph Master of the Posts to examine one Cicking, a bokebinder in Powles Churchyard lately committed to the Tower *upon such matter as Mr Secretarie Walsingham was privey of*' (italics mine). I consider it plausible, until better evidence comes along, to believe that the letter dated 3 February 1574 (BL Harleian MS 6991, f. 114^r) is a copy of the letter to which the act refers.

[74] TNA: PRO SP 53/10/103. These passages are underlined in the original document. It is this edited version (and the editing, Cockyn says, was in fact done by Dr James Good) of the bishop of Ross's with the 'Apologie' that was found in Henry Howard's lodgings in Ivy Bridge Lane when they were later searched, extracts of which remain extant today, though the original appears to have been lost. Good himself later denied this editorial role, and indeed the advice not to send the work too early to Howard (presumably because it would imply a greater knowledge of the workings of the Howard–Leslie axis than he wished to own up to): see BL Cotton MS, Caligula C v. f. 15^r.

scores a theme that resurfaces again and again in Howard's life: the power of rumour.[75] Certainly, St Paul's Churchyard was a particularly important node in the news network of the time, but given its populous and popular nature, together with possibilities of seditious books, information could quickly turn to rumour.[76] There were few means available to the inhabitant of Elizabethan London to confirm or deny a report about a person; in addition, given the absence of long-range communications, opinions were formed by rumours that could, Chinese-whisper-like, change in the telling. Howard's desire for court attendance can be seen as an attempt to control his 'reception'. His difficulty in controlling the various reports of his behaviour and actions that circulated can be seen in the often conflicting nature of the evidence which his biographer has to deal with.

On the margins, indeed, Howard would stay for some years to come, both ideologically and geographically. We know from Cockyn's testimony that Howard was at Audley End in early 1573; and this was to be his base out of London for most of the 1570s.[77] His movements for most of this decade are not clear, however. Little more certain, and the subject of recent scholarly attention, are his relations with Michel de Castelnau, Seigneur de Mauvissière, the French ambassador (1520–1592).[78] There was much the two men had in common: a faith that was personally devout but politically moderate, a cultivated taste for the products of humanist literature and a love of courtly life.[79] Castelnau was a more acceptable ambassador to Elizabeth than his Spanish counterpart Don Bernadino de Mendoza (1540–1604), whose response to the Anjou marriage plan would be sufficiently antiseptic that the two men were no longer speaking to each other at that stage (1581). Howard's contacts with Castelnau seem to have revolved around Mary. In late May 1583 a letter from Henri Fagot (a French spy in the pay of Walsingham) claims that Howard is, with Sir Edward Stafford (1552–1605), her chief agent, and is perpetually arriving at Salisbury Court at midnight.[80]

---

[75] See Hans-Joachim Neubauer, *The Rumour: A Cultural History*, tr. C. Brown, London, 1999.
[76] For some examples of contemporary 'newsmongering' at St Pauls, see Fox, *Oral and Literate Culture*, p. 347 n.18.
[77] TNA: PRO SP 10/53/103 for Cockyn's testimony that he was delivering books to Howard there.
[78] For recent accounts of Castelnau and his cultural circle, see John Bossy, *Giordano Bruno and the Embassy Affair*, London, 1996 (hereafter *GB*), and Bossy, *UTM*.
[79] For biographical details of Castelnau see *Memoires de Michel de Castelnau*, eds J. Le Labourer and C. Godefroy, Brussels, 1731, passim.
[80] BL Cotton MS, Caligula C vii, f. 211 (see Bossy's translation: *GB*, p. 200). Unbeknown to Bossy, there exists a further version of this letter located in The National Archives which I have not consulted but which Hicks, *An Elizabethan Problem*, p. 31 n. 89, refers to as being

Teacher, Polemicist, Papist

Both William Herle and Fagot inform upon Howard to Walsingham in 1583, but Herle is less to be trusted.[81] The gaps are a severe impediment to telling a smooth story, but it seems that there was a growing bond of allegiance between Howard and Castelnau right up to the events of 1583.

Castelnau writes that the Earl of Oxford informed him that, at their first meeting in June 1577, it was Henry Howard who had suggested that the Earl pay this visit to Salisbury Court, so presumably Castelnau and Howard had built up something approaching a relationship by this time.[82] After all, Cockyn mentions on several occasions in his testimony his role as a go-between, usually at one remove, for Mary, the French ambassador and various English persons. Again, surely Howard was influential in arranging the meeting, if not also present, between his nephew, Philip Howard, and the ambassador at the newly refurbished Surrey House which happened the following year.[83] Certainly, Howard was active in promoting the interests of his nephew in this year.[84]

The years immediately following Howard's retirement from court life saw Howard retire to Audley End to direct the attention of his nephews,

---

dated 23 April 1583. I have not been able to make sense of Hicks' reference ('MQS xl1 n. 61') and hence have not been able to locate it, though it apparently formed the basis of the transcription in the *Calendar of Letters and State Papers (Scotland)*, VI, p. 430. The date is perhaps a wrong endorsement; in either case, nothing turns on the dating for the present purposes.

[81] For instance, he thinks Howard is a priest and is enrolled as one of the pope's cardinals (BL London, Lansdowne MS 39, f. 191).

[82] See, most recently, Tiziana Provvidera, 'The Printer of Bruno's English Works', *Bruniana et Campanellana*, 1996, pp. 361–6 (deriving from a doctoral thesis).

[83] On 20 August 1578 the queen 'dined at my Lord of Surreys at Surrey House on Mushold Hill, where were the French Ambassadors also, a most rare and delicate dinner and banquet': see W. T. Besley, 'St. Leonard's Priory, Norwich', *Norfolk Archaeology*, 12, 1895, pp. 190–233 at 196–7.

[84] See 'Regina fortunata', BL Egerton MS 944 ff. 5ᵛ–6ʳ: 'Surreium enim (sic enim tua Celsitudo eum nuncupari voluit) multis de causis coniunctissimum deum immortalem testor nulla ratione esse chariorem quam quod ab ineunte aetate ad tenendum illum vitae cursum omnem suam operam studium et industriam quem reginae Elizabethae (omnium quae vel sunt vel fuerunt aliquando praestantissime maxime gratam vacillanti stirpi salutarem et Reipublicae fore opportunum, utilemque iudicavit: Non ignorat enim se suorum culpa et errore, non solum de spe magna sed re certa etiam, atque possessione de turbatum sola Maiestatis tuae gratia et liberalitate sustentari, sibi vero etsi omni suppeterent adiumentaque vel usu homines ingenio aut eloquentia consequitur, numquam verbis explicare poss[u then e written in]m, quantum tuae Celsitudinis benignitati et clementiae debeam quae me ad aliena calamitatis al[…] et proiectum scopulos inter fluctus procellasque consolata est, quaeque pietate erga miseros afflictosque semper fuit, non est passa, humiles abiectosque frutices (qui radicibus imis adhaeserunt) illius altae ac procerae arboris lapsu et ruina praegravari, ex cuius (dum floreret maxime) prosperitate, patulisque ramis, non dico fructum sed vix umbram essent consequti.'

though he maintained links with Cambridge University.[85] What stamp Howard left upon his nephew, Philip, during these years and how lasting an impression it was, we cannot say. It is worth recalling that in his youth Philip Howard was not the saintly devotee of the Church that later confessional historiography painted him and he found himself embroiled with Gabriel Harvey's sister, who lived at nearby Saffron Walden, about which Harvey wrote an angry pamphlet, *A noble mans sute to a cuntrie maide*.[86] One poignant vignette of familial affection is, however, preserved. Just before his death in the Tower twenty years later, the young man asked for either of his uncles to attend him, a request which was denied by the queen.[87] There was much that was congenial in the role of pedagogue to Howard, but the court was ever his lodestone and his interest in courtly life drew him into further difficulties, many of which focused around the Earl of Oxford. Like many of his clan, Henry Howard was the last person to allow personal dislike to get in the way of a useful friendship. Natural dislike between the two kinsmen was compounded by the perceived threat that Oxford posed to Howard's main chance of survival at Court, as he saw it in these years: Burghley.[88] There was, perhaps, in all of Howard's letters a mild untruth about how alone he was; after all, he would not wish to give too much solidity to the 'party within a party' of the 'Court Catholics' and

---

[85] A letter from Norfolk to his eldest son, Philip, makes it clear that Lord Burghley was Norfolk's original choice for adoptive father for his children, something that gave the dying duke 'no little comfort': BL Additional MS 15891 f. 189, reprinted, with slight inaccuracy, in *Memoirs of the Life and Times of Sir Christopher Hatton KG*, ed. H. Nicolas, London, 1847, p. 11. Since Norfolk had achieved this by 'earnest petition', we can presume that Burghley had agreed in principle, and then very quickly offloaded the responsibility onto Henry Howard.

[86] *The Letter Book of Gabriel Harvey AD 1573–1580*, ed. E. J. L. Scott, London, 1884, ad indicem. This detail has been missed by those scholars (see Chapter Six) who attempt to ground the bad blood between Howard and Harvey in relation to Howard's 1583 book on astrology upon an assumption about a feud based on the uses of astrology itself.

[87] *The Life of Philip Howard: Earl of Arundel Saint and Martyr Edited from the Original Mss by the Duke of Norfolk*, London p. 52.

[88] Howard's seeming refusal to have any dealings with Leicester in the late 1560s and 1570s suggests (in so far as it may not be ascribed to the possibly fortuitous destruction of letters to Leicester) that there was a clear division (in Howard's mind at least) between the two men, whether or not 'faction' is an appropriate term. The evidence for the 1569 'overthrow' of Cecil by the Leicester faction is not incapable of being impugned since it all comes from the French ambassadors who were very eager to report division at the English court to their master (Kervijn de Lettenhove, *Relations politiques*, Brussels, 1882–1900, V, p. 307; *Correspondence diplomatique de Bertrand de Salignac de La Mothe-Fenelon*, ed. A. Teulet, 1838–40, I, pp. 233–7 and 258–62: I am indebted for these bibliographical references to a transcript of lecture of a course of lectures of Simon Adams).

Teacher, Polemicist, Papist

focusing instead on their disunities.[89] Still, as we shall see, even if Howard had friends, he was to make many enemies, but their animus toward him strikes one as rather disproportionate to his position. Howard may not have been wealthy.[90] We see him currying favour with Burghley. We see Howard writing to Burghley from Audley End on 14 October 1572, thanking Cecil for his 'honorable and carefull dealing' (presumably in relation to the Ridolfi plot and his release from the Fleet).[91] By the end of 1573, we see Howard seeking in a more proactive fashion service at Burghley's hands. A letter dated 5 October records Howard's apologies in not being able to make it to Greenwich where he had hoped to meet Burghley, but he will be ready when his Lordship wishes to 'employee this carkase of mine in any kinde of service'.[92] Howard was clearly part of a circle sympathetic to the restoration of Mary. No sooner was the ink dry on his apologetic for the Elizabethan state church than he was, as we shall see, in communication with her and was immediately imprisoned at Walsingham's command in early 1575. Perhaps his improved position in the years between 1572 and 1574 led him to these confident dealings. In any case, they lead us to suspect once again the picture of indebted powerlessness that has usually been drawn.[93] Certainly, he was currently without a following, but his own family history had seen enough dramatic tergiversations at the hand of fortune to know that a new broom would sweep very clean indeed. After all, Elizabeth might die at any moment.[94] In which case, his poor carcase would be swept to unimagined heights of power and influence and wealth. Such, perhaps, was the hope of some of

---

[89] The identification of the shared concerns of the court Catholics: J. Bossy, 'English Catholics and the French Marriage, 1577–1581', *Recusant History*, 5, 1959, pp. 2–16.

[90] Howard was for these years mainly dependent on a small income provided for him by his sister Lady Katherine Berekeley: so Peck, *Northampton*, p. 10, citing 'John Smyth, *The Berkeley Manuscripts*, 3 vols, Gloucester, 1883, II, pp. 265–449'.

[91] BL Cotton MS, Titus C vi f. 17^r. The letter also mentions the 'good progresse in learninge' made by the 'Lord of Surry'. This is our first evidence of Philip Howard's use of the courtesy title.

[92] BL Cotton MS, Titus C vi f. 24. A very similar request on 28 May 1575: f. 25.

[93] See Howard's own desciption of the long years of disfavour: Henry Howard, *Dutifull Defence of Lawfull Regiment of Women*, BL Additional MS 24652, f. 8^r, 'this disgracefull time, wherein I lived many yeres without anye almes of [slip for 'or'?] comforte'.

[94] After all, she had almost died in 1562 from a bout of smallpox. Howard was not the only person to keep contact with the 'dangerous queen'. If Elizabeth did die, then the only bar to Mary's accession to the throne was express statutes to the contrary passed by Elizabeth, just as there had been statutes denying the succession of both Mary and Elizabeth Tudor. This perhaps explains the fact that, of all people, we find Leicester taking the waters with Mary at Buxton.

the seminary priests. Some time later, Thomas Norton, in the manuscript work *A Chayne of Treasons*, reported the notion that it was Henry Howard who was the English Catholics' first choice as an alternative king for Mary.[95] By this time Mary was undergoing her transformation from regent on the run to Ersatz Elizabeth.[96] The recently published *Treatise of Treasons*, written (perhaps) by John Leslie, Mary's chief ambassador, put forward a highly intelligent and knowledgeable view of the relationship between Elizabeth, Mary and her ministers.[97] The degree of knowledge makes one suspect that much of what is contained therein derives in some way from Howard, though there were clear disagreements, as the next chapter shall demonstrate, between Leslie and Howard. Howard and Leslie (for let us assume it was they) portray Elizabeth's advisers as frustrating the potential amity, born out of blood and common noble purpose, between the two women. It is no wonder, then, that this interpretation of the polity would generate frustration amid Elizabeth's most trusted servants. Their response, conscious or otherwise, was to blame the messengers of this alternative polity of female nobility with its alternative cadre of advisers. The hostility of Norton and Leicester to Howard was simply the more obvious interpretation of this response.[98] This alternative king for Mary was, said Norton, to have been Catholic, noble and a bachelor.[99] Norton clearly had it in for Howard; it is a presumption of the work that the treasonous one 'cannot be the late Duke of Norffe, but … one that survyved him or yet lyveth because the whole treatise was since the dukes deathe'.[100] Upon being pressed, one John Hart, seminary priest and guest of the tower, 'made no direct answer but gave commendation

---

[95] This material has already been covered in great detail by Hicks, *An Elizabethan Problem*, pp. 223–42. On Norton, see Michael Graves, *Thomas Norton*, Oxford, 1999.
[96] The next few sentences show that biography can sometimes show up very clearly how political history is always already the history of conflicting interpretations of present events.
[97] Anon., *A Treatise of Treasons*, Louvain: John Fowler, 1572. Elizabeth ordered all copies of this work banned. I have not investigated the question of the authorship of this work.
[98] Cecil, more calculated, attempted to weld such persons as Howard into his own power struggle.
[99] BL Additional MS 48029, 'Tho Nortons Chayne of Treasons' (this title is written in a later hand at 73^v), ff. 58–62, at f. 60^v. In fact there are two formulations of the bachelor stipulation: one, that he must be a bachelor; two, that he must be a bachelor or man unmarried. There is no clue to dating in this manuscript. It is clearly based on near contemporaneous interrogations, but when put together I cannot say.
[100] BL Additional MS 48029, 60^v. For more information, see Graves, *Thomas Norton*, to whose discussion of this material I am endebted.

to the Lord Henry Howard'.[101] It is not quite true, however, to say – as Father Hicks does – that 'these additional details are to be found only in this document'.[102] Certainly, the allegation does not find its way into the confession that Hart felt himself capable of signing in 1580.[103] On the other hand, he is clearly refusing to implicate Howard directly, and so we cannot expect him to have signed an article to that effect. Furthermore, there are indeed earlier traces of rumours about Howard as a potential husband for Mary.[104] Therefore, it is hard to follow Father Hicks in suggesting that the rumours were a government fabrication. They reflect rather the ember-like hopes of a range of Marian supporters, including the hopes of the man whom she would refer to as her 'brother'. The next twenty-five years, however, were to see the hopes of the Lord Henry Howard only intermittently realized at best.

---

[101] Ibid., 61ʳ. The passage continues: 'adding withall that Gregorie Martin called Martin a notable busie traitor sometime familiar with that Lord henrie and schole master to the dukes children did say at Rheims that he thought it wisdome that Lord Henrie to be where they were and owt of England or the like effect. Whether that Lord be the persone aspiring to that election or marriage I cannot say or think onely this I take for true that all the 5 requisite qualities aforesaid are congruent to his person besides the vith qualitie; that is the general favor of the Seminarians and busiest papistes in action.' For more gossip/information on Hart, see ibid., ff. 140v–141ʳ.
[102] Hicks, *An Elizabethan Problem*, p. 228.
[103] For this confession, see ibid., p. 225 n. 664.
[104] TNA: PRO SP 12/168 f. 30r; Bossy, GB, p. 200.

Chapter 5

'IN SOME SORT COMMUNICAT WITH DAUNGER' SURVIVAL, SUCCESS AND DEFEAT (1578–1582)

THE YEARS immediately following Henry Howard's anonymous publication (seemingly at Burghley's behest) of the *Defense of the Ecclesiaticall Regiment of England* in 1574 were not marked by any significant upturn in his fortunes. We have seen how Burghley may have remained warm toward Howard, despite the more hostile feelings of Walsingham and his spies. It is, however, unsurprising to discover that the letters from the period are still marked, where they are marked at all, from Audley End.[1] Neither Howard's immediate prospects at court nor the wider political scene were encouraging. Any chance of advancement for Howard within the English ecclesiastical hierarchy (if that had ever been congenial to him) was made much more remote by the death of Archbishop Parker and his replacement by the still more robustly Puritan temperament of Edmund Grindal in 1575.[2] Indeed, the most 'public' event at which Howard could attempt to reclaim favour was the scholarly dispu-

---

[1] BL Cotton MS, Titus C vi ff. 27–9. His previous place of abode, Howard House in Charterhouse Square, was either sold or rented (presumably by the Crown) to the Portuguese ambassadors until 1581, when it passed back (it is, again, uncertain how) to the Duke of Norfolk's eldest son, Philip Howard: see *The London Encyclopedia*, eds Ben Weinret and Christopher Hibbert, London, 1993, pp. 146–7, and Bruno Barber and Christopher Thomas, *The London Charterhouse*, Museum of London Archeology Service 10, London, 2002, pp. 81–2. This fact poses a problem for the dating of two of Howard's letters in the Cotton MS, Titus C vi volume. These letters follow a roughly sequential order; two, however, are written from Howard House and have dates suggested as 1575 and 1577. Either the dating is wrong, or Howard kept lodgings with the Portuguese.

[2] See the magisterial work of P. Collinson, *Edmund Grindal 1519–1583: The Struggle for a Reformed Church*, London, 1979.

Survival, Success and Defeat

tation held at Audley End before the queen in 1578, at which event large numbers from the University of Cambridge were present.[3] The frontispiece to one account of this event shows Elizabeth attended on her right side by three figures, presumably Sir Christopher Hatton, Burghley and Leicester.[4] Sir Philip Sidney, as Leicester's nephew and rising star in the courtly firmament, also gets a mention. There is very little to suggest to the innocent reader that any of the events took place at Audley End, or that any members of the Howard family were involved, though presumably Howard himself was present. The large presence of continental guests is notable.[5] Gabriel Harvey penned a long poem entitled 'De vultu Italiae', which is a praise of all things Italian.[6] The poem's central theme is the desire for and difficulty of transforming English manners into Italian, complimenting a stereotype of Leicester's own tastes. It is a literary progress as well, for its author appears to appropriate that canonical text of literary and social upward mobility, the *Eclogues*, in the context of his attempts to write in the approved way:

> tamen Italus esse
> Reginae videor; quid multis? me quoque dicunt
> Vatem pastores sed non ego credulus illis.[7]
> Ac mihi nescioquis de caelo spiritus alto
> Clamitat assidue (neque enim memorare pigebit
> Antiquum carmen, quod dictat Cynthius, aurem
> Vellens: o semper liceat meminisse monentis)[8]
> Plus aliis de te, quam tu tibi credere noli.
> Legi ego Petrarcham: placet & Boccaccius: & me
> Sylvius, & Dantes, & Castilionis amoenae

---

[3] Addison, *Audley End*, p. 21, says that '[w]e do not know how many members of the Howard family were present'. Primary source: Gabriel Harvey, *Gratulationum Valdinensium libri quatuor*, London: Henry Bynneman, 1578 (September).

[4] These are the main co-addressees of the opening poem by Harvey.

[5] E.g., Petrus Bizarus (Pietro Bizari, 1525–1583 on whom see *DBI* sub nomine and, for further evidence of his scholarly wanderings, Jason Harris, 'The Practice of Community: Humanist Friendship During the Dutch Revolt', *Texas Studies in Language and Literature*, 2005, pp. 299–325); Benedetto Varchi (the famous humanist and art theorist).

[6] Harvey, *Graulationum*, pp. 20–7.

[7] See Vergil, *Eclogues*, 9.33–4: 'me quoque dicunt | pastores sed ego non credulus illis'.

[8] See Vergil, *Eclogues*, 6.3–5: 'cum canerem reges et proelia, Cynthius aurem | vellit et admonuit 'pastorem Tityre pinguis | pascere oportet ovis, deductum dicere canem'. These are both central passages in the careerist reading of Vergil's poetry. For one modish account of careerism in Renaissance pastoral, see Richard Rambuss, *Spenser's Secret Career*, Cambridge, 1998.

Deliciae, miro multum affecere lepore.
Agnoscit nihil istorum mea Musa, nec ullam
Laureolam ingenii, nec linguae vendicat ullam.[9]

Any doubts that the reader might have had about Harvey's ability to become this new Italianate poet would be dispelled by the immediately following poem, which, Harvey tells us, was the composition of Pandolfo Strozzi, whom he happened to meet in his local ale-house in London, and which concludes with the words 'Let England bragg that the patrician Strozzi family has applauded Gabriel Harvey'.[10]

The event at Audley End, quite apart from the *arriviste* remodelling by Harvey of the *Eclogues*, is symbolic of the increasingly obvious tensions that existed between the sober traditionalist aristocracy (as they saw themselves) and the *novi homines* who were gaining the upper hand at court.[11] This, in addition to the tensions growing between Burghley and Walsingham, was the dominant axis of courtly faction in the 1570s and, indeed, throughout the period with which this chapter is concerned. Certainly, in the rival account of the Audley End event published by Thomas Churchyard, who had once lodged at Kenninghall with the Earl of Surrey and his children, this courtly careerism disappears in favour of a vision of a queen at one with the shires of her people, and, unlike Harvey's account, it at least mentions 'the Earl of Surry'.[12] These tensions worsened as the 1570s wore on until the failure of the conservative party in 1583, as we shall see later on, at a time when Howard was preoccupied by dynastic and international affairs.

---

[9] Translation: 'But the Queen thinks me Italian. What need for many words? The shepherds say that I too am a prophet, but I don't believe them. And for me too has some kind of spirit from the lofty sky made noise. And there'll be no shame in remembering that old poem, the one that Apollo intoned as he tweaked my ear: ah, always to remember the one that gives advice! When it comes to yourself, don't trust others more than you would yourself. I've read Petrarch, and I like Boccaccio, and Piccolomini too (= Enea Silvio Piccolomini, Pope Pius II) and the sweet pleasantries of the Courtier: I'm quite stunned by their delicate wit. My muse recognizes nothing of them, nor stakes a claim to any little laurel crown of talent or tongue.'

[10] Harvey, *Gratulationum*, p. 28.

[11] Terminology for these two groupings or alliances is historiographically loaded. Long ago, Conyers Read and Sir James Neale saw them as embryonic political parties, or 'factions', though more recent scholarship has emphasized the commonalities and fluidities that cut across such an analysis: Simon Adams, 'Favourites and Factions at the Elizabethan Court', in *Princes, Patronage and the Nobility: The Court at the Beginning of the Modern Age: c. 1450–1650*, eds R. G. Asche and A. M. Birke, Oxford, 1991, pp. 265–88.

[12] Thomas Churchyard, *A Discourse of the Queene's Majesties Entertainment in Norfolk and Suffolk*, London: Henry Bynneman, 1578, reference to Surrey at sig. B3^v. It may be an overstatement to call this a 'rival' account.

By contrast, in the years 1574–8 Howard was firmly anchored in the private sphere. This role was perhaps welcome, certainly necessary after his troubles by association with the Ridolfi affair and the more definite difficulties thrown up by the discovery of his involvement with Henry Cockyn and the bishop of Ross. It is unfortunate that we know so little of his movements during this period since, whatever pedagogic obligations he shouldered, we have evidence that he was not his nephews' sole tutor.[13] Howard still hoped for some advancement at the hands of Burghley, who clearly used him from time to time; and Howard felt able to drop by unannounced at Theobalds, the Lord Treasurer's pleasure house near Cheshunt, Hertfordshire.[14] He is recorded as having dined with Burghley in June 1576 and June 1577.[15] It would appear, however, that no consistent pattern of preferment or patronage was forthcoming, on the basis of the documents available to us. Given this uncertain position and his day to day distance from the court, there is a possibility that Howard began to make influential connections with other interest groups, in particular the conservative faction, or perhaps merely continued to cultivate them. These connections grew out of a long-standing association between such figures as Thomas Radcliffe, Earl of Sussex, and Lord Paget, who both shared a degree of enmity towards the new-found dominance at court of Leicester. Certainly one document from a few years later. Howard was caught up in what are known as the 'Oxford libels', a tortuous series of charges and counter-charges thrown up by a falling-out between the erstwhile friends the Earl of Oxford, Howard and Charles Arundell. Howard appears to have 'confessed' to having been reconciled to the Catholic Church in 1576, in May or thereabouts. There were, however, as a fresh document suggests, limits to Howard's desire to conform to the Elizabethan settlement. In a letter to Walsingham, Howard not only actively incriminates himself in past wrong-

---

[13] See BL Lansdowne MS 18, f. 11.
[14] Examples: a memorandum by Burghley: 'I sent for my son th cecil who was more than hundrid miles from London to come in post and mete him [Oxford] at Dover within ii howres after my Lord Howard and others, and thither carried my commaundment': HMC, Hatfield House: II, pp. 131–2. Sir Thomas Cecil in the same year asked his father to pass on his apologies to Howard for not having been able to entertain Howard in person: HMC, Hatfield House: II, pp. 205–6; this could appear, however, to be a snub.
[15] Conyers Read, 'Lord Burghley's Household Accounts', *Economic History Review*, 9, 1956, pp. 343–9 at 347 and 348. On the latter occasion Sir James Croft, another astute political moderate linked with Burghey, was present. It would appear that it was during this period of limited favour with Burghley that Howard received the commission to write his 'Dutiful Defence': see Chapter Seven.

doing in the shape of attending private mass, but also seems to make a plea for liberty of liturgical conscience:

> Trewe it is that restinge not well satisfied in point abowt the Sacrament I rather chose in some sorte to communicat wth daunger of the Lawe than altither to neglect that pipe whereby so great a strength maie be derived to me faith and so quite a discharge of a loden conscience.[16]

Reconciliation to the Catholic Church was perhaps more felonious than attending private mass, since the former touched on the polity rather than private zeal. There were most definite limits to Howard's conformity.[17]

It was roughly at this time that Howard appears also to have finished his polished, but poised, work in praise of Elizabeth, the 'Regina fortunata'.[18] Attention has already been drawn, in discussing Howard's letters to Burghley from his university days at Cambridge, to the fact that he had no permanent position at court (and indeed, was often not welcome there), and that, for all his nobility and evident talent, the increasing suspicion surrounding his religious views or practices, combined with the dominance of the Leicester grouping at court, gave much impetus to the epistolary commonplaces of not wishing to obtrude and not wanting to appear a 'mere' orator. Howard, for whatever reason, had not pursued an academic career (presumably as *infra dignitatem* for a noble) but, without a following, and 'employed' in effect as a private tutor during this period (1574–7?), he was hardly in a commanding position to present himself as a civic humanist counsellor. For the 'Regina fortunata' is closer to counsel than it

---

[16] Howard to Walsingham TNA: PRO SP 12/147/6. His numerous liturgical writings (e.g., BL Arundel MS 300) suggest that Howard was probably continually engaged in private masses. For a more detailed study of the information contained in these libels, see Nelson, *Monstrous Adversary*, passim, and Andersson, 'Studies', ch. 2.

[17] One is reminded of the vignette, preserved by John Manningham's diary, that Howard, at Elizabeth's deathbed, was sufficiently disgusted by the Anglican priest's liturgy to have exited the room (see reference cited earlier at p. 82 n. 3 above).

[18] 'Regina fortunata', BL Egerton MS 944. This would appear to be the work mentioned in one of the Oxford–Arundell–Howard libels from 1580 (TNA: PRO SP 12/151/46 f. 104), where Oxford is accused of '3 diswation, to my Lord harrye for setting furthe<r> a treatise callid Encomia Elizabethii and the reasons whiche he used profferinge my monye to diswade my Lord harrye from printinge of it'. This matches up with another of the letters in this warfare of libels, from Howard to the queen, where he accuses Oxford of more or less the same offence: BL Cotton MS, Titus C vi f. 6ᵛ. The dating of the work appears to be secure on the basis of internal evidence: Howard refers to a time period of eighteen years in which England has enjoyed the benefits of Elizabeth's rule (f. 2ʳ), thereby dating it to 1576.

is to praise.[19] This is not to say that there is not praise in the work, but the tone is delicately balanced. Its epideictic character was designed to raise emotion in its reader and to this end Howard slights the Stoics: 'nec Stoicorum placet insolentia, qui ut ipsi omnium sermone celebrentur laudarique sinunt neminem'.[20]

Much of the emotion in the work is not, however, so much directed to the creation of 'admiratio' at the queen (as the opening sentence suggests) as to pathos at his own situation.[21] Indeed, there is as much emphasis on Howard's difficulty in speaking and his own relation to the queen as there is on her achievements or virtues. In particular, Howard continually refers, via allusion or image, to Elizabeth as a figure at whom one cannot look, or whom one is punished for observing too closely. The opening itself starts with a reference to the queen as an immense light.[22] Howard at one point uses visual imagery to emphasize her virtues, and takes from Aesop the fable of the panther who was progressively emboldened to draw closer to the lion.[23]

A few pages later, Howard emphasizes, with further visual language, the difficulties of addressing the great.[24] His sense of his own distance from the

---

[19] It is very clear that its models are not the prescriptions of Menander Rhetor (for a brief analysis of his approach to epideictic orations of praise, see the Pseudo-Ciceronian *Rhetorica ad Herennium*, 3.10–3.15, and, in general, see *Menander Rhetor*, eds D. A. Russell and M. Winterbottom, Oxford, 1981).

[20] BL London Egerton MS 944, f. 25^v. For the hostility of the Stoics to praise and blame see, e.g., Marcus Aurelius, *Meditations*, IV.20.

[21] For the opening section dealing with admiration see BL Egerton MS 944, f. 2^r: 'Cogitanti mihi saepius de Maiestatis tuae laudibus (Regina serenissima) quae parvis Britannorum finibus latebrisque non contentae transcenderunt Alpes et universum pene terrarum orbem pervagatae sunt magnam sane et incredibilem movebat admirationem, sive hominum sive temporum nostrorum necligentia qui vel reticiendo sepeliri, vel dicendo observari tantae lucis ornamenta patiuntur.' One might compare the long preface to his 1590 defence of female rule in this regard.

[22] Ibid., f. 2^r: 'sive hominum sive temporum nostrorum necligentia qui vel reticiendo sepeliri, vel dicendo observari tantae lucis ornamenta patiuntur.'

[23] Ibid., ff. 3^v–4^r: 'ut verum fatear, etsi quoties mihi ante oculos non adumbrata, sed expressa, Maiestatis tuae virtus observatus quae non modo iuris communis aequabilitatem fortunae et dignitatis suae praestantia superavit, sed inveterato etiam sermoni hominum optimorum principum celebritati, noctem tenebrasque effudit, in ipsis dicendi initiis exalbescam, Panthera tamen apud Aesopum imitabor, quae leonem casu quodam fortuito, conspicata primum nervis artubusque omnibus contremuit secundo observabant diligentius, tandem vero confidenter est alloqutus.' The reference to the Panther does not appear to be a true Aesopian reference.

[24] Ibid., f. 8^v: 'sed quis ego sum, qui nec naturae beneficio ad dicendum informatus, nec artis ope et praesidiis, ad dicendum instructus et armatus, solem multis partibus ampliorem Universa terra, cuius etiam radii, tot [Linceum] et Argorum aciem sensumque perstrinxerunt, aspicere aut contueri ausim?'

centre of things is variously illustrated by, for example, the phrase that it is wise not to approach sleeping lions and, in an example which combines recklessness and the light/sun imagery, by a comparison with Daedalus.[25] In even more dramatic and violent mythological terms, Howard describes the dangers of approaching too closely to a female goddess, and at one point he appears to suggest that it would, using the language of the Actaeon and Diana myth, be easier for him to deal with the topic if he were at court (in a temple) rather than in the country (or, again, in the language of the myth, in the wood).[26] This suggestion, combined with the notion of Howard's possible intemperateness, is confirmed by the words which immediately follow:

> For it makes a great deal of difference not only with what intent and disposition one makes one's mortal offerings of prayer to an immortal deity, but also where and with what gesture and at what time: many have spoken clumsily on a topic that was [sc. otherwise] very pleasant by speaking out of turn.[27]

Howard then discusses the skill that monarchs have in interpreting their own fates, stars and obscure dreams, and the difficulty which others have in making such predictions.[28] It is hard not to read this as an expression of

---

[25] Ibid., f. 10^{r-v}: 'Immo in senatu consessuque sapientum spartanus ille senex audiatur, qui eminus aspici non prope salutari magistratus caveri non excitari leones dormientes timeri, non attingi principes debere iudicavit', and, for the Daedalus image, f. 10^v: 'Si praeceptis quispiam aut exemplis ab instituto cursu revocari velit, ex ipso salo, fluctibusque sapienter admonebit Daedalus, ne se suamque operam in rebus gravioribus, quae sustinere valeant interponat'.

[26] Ibid., f. 11^v: 'Quis nescit, viso et conspecto Baccho perisse Semelem, Minerva vero salutatam, revinxisse Aesculapium, nec tam funesto lugubri exitu, Actaeonem periturum suspicor, si caste magis quam cupide in templo, non in sylva Dianam conspexisset?' For the myth see Ovid, *Metamorphoses*, 3. 192–243. Dating is a slight issue here. John King, 'Representations of the Virgin', *Renaissance Quarterly*, 42, 1990, pp. 34–49 at 43, argues with good evidence that it was only after Elizabeth was confirmed in her childlessness that the Diana myth was used – i.e., after 1580. King's account, albeit that the image in Egerton 944 is connotational and not identificational, should accordingly be nuanced.

[27] BL Egerton MS 944, f. 11^v–12^r: 'Multum interesse enim, non qua mente voluntate studio, sed quo loco gestu, tempore humanae deo immortali efferantur praeces, et multis vehementer obfuit, de causa periucunda, intempestive disseruisse.'

[28] Ibid., f. 15^r–16^v: 'Quis physicos, aut qui astrorum cognitione antecellunt, et in multos annos siderum motus atque cursus persequuntur, celsiorem regum libertis, in celesti sphaera locum sedemque assignantes, a veritatis transitu deflexisse sponte, regibusque summis fallaciter imposuisse, iudicabit? Quid quod regum ortu, et occasu principum, stellatum saepe cursus et naturae perturbatur ordo, de optimatum caede et discordiis, Dii immortales saepe monent de clarissimorum crurium dissensione, praedicunt sacerdotes, impendentem iis qui rerum summa praesunt tempestatem, de caelo inflammata tecta, et

Howard's own difficulty in addressing the queen in the absence of the oxygen of court attendance. Later on in the oration, he is explicit about his distance from public office.[29] Howard understood clearly from the precepts of rhetoric that the ability to persuade was dependent upon the particularities of the situation – ignorance of those particularities meant a correspondingly weak basis for one's persuasive discourse.

It is clear that Howard was not in contact with the queen at this point, and perhaps remained in her disfavour, despite the signs of rehabilitation with Burghley (or continued goodwill, depending on how serious a breach occurred between the two men as a result of the Ridolfi affair) that we have seen. It is therefore obvious that he cannot simply rely on the epideictic commonplaces alone, since his purpose is as much ingratiation and exculpation of himself as straightforward panegyric of Elizabeth. It is for this reason that the work is rather different from other straightforwardly encomiastic pieces. One other fairly obvious reason for its difference from such works is that it was written to be read by a limited audience, perhaps only the queen herself. Howard was already more intimate with his addressee by virtue of rank, previous dealings and the costly elaborate 'intimacy' of the manuscript as a physical object. Conversely, his recent difficulties rendered him rather far from the source of political light. It is for this reason that Howard adopted a different mode of presentation, which was more akin to the more fluid tonal modulations of the humanist letter.

Our evidence for the next three years of Howard's life is again very slender, mostly consisting of a few letters to Burghley. The close connection with his family that was natural given his residence was strengthened when he was appointed in 1578 one of the auditors of his nephew Philip, the others appointed to this role being Sir Nicholas Lestrange, Sir Roger Townshend, Richard Cuttes, Robert Buxton and Henry Russell.[30] Until his

---

de labra mortalibus praesignificent, et astra τῶν ἀρίστων portendant calamitatem, stuporem prorsus nullum aut admirationem commovebit? Huc accedit quod multorum regum animis, extrinsecus ineicta quidem, sed divinitus inclusa est, praesensio quaedam atque praesagitio futurorum, unde prae ea vere queant quae deorum voluntate, suis eventura civibus, tam longe prosperunt. Non leviculus enim, aut ineptus poetarum princeps Homerus iudicandus est, qui tortuosa et obscura somnia (quae a diis plaerunque dormientibus obiiciuntur) interpretandi facultatem, non tyranno cuique aut signifero, sed regi principique Agamemnoni tribuendum putet, cum eodem plane modo, impendentem plebi suae famem, inter somniandum ex vaccarum macie, Aegiptorum princeps [Gen 40] Pharao, in scripturis praevideret. Raro colloquentes cum obscuris viris, deos immortales reperiemus.'

[29] Ibid. f. 26ᵛ: 'quanto a dignitate publica, absum et disiungor longius'.
[30] CUL The Buxton Manuscripts, 59/17: letter dated 25 November 1578.

confinement in 1580, Howard's prospects at court had begun to improve, and this welcome change in his fortunes came about through an unexpected piece of dynastic manufacture. At the battle of Alcantara on the southern tip of the Iberian peninsula on 25 August 1580, Philip II, inheritor of the sprawling and ambiguous legacy of his father, annexed the Portuguese throne. Its previous occupant had been Henrique o Casto, a childless cardinal. Rumours had been circulating that this had been Philip's intention two years earlier, thus rendering the attractions to the English queen of a marriage with a Frenchman all the more manifest. Furthermore, this time, perhaps, her heart was in it; but by the time that Philip had effected the Lusitanian coup, Elizabeth's will had been broken by her Council.[31] It was now that Henry Howard chose to wade into the controversy over this marriage. It was now that Howard penned a treatise in favour of Elizabeth's proposed marriage to François, Duke of Alençon.[32] There would be further attempts to resurrect the marriage; but Howard's response was characteristically measured. The background to this work on a much-debated subject is complex. Jean de Simier, Baron de Saint Marc, a trusted member of Anjou's household, was sent across the channel to discuss possibilities. He arrived on 5 January 1579 and was well received. Anjou's reasons for entering into the marriage were obvious. The Franco-Spanish carve-up of Western Europe in 1579 shows the pivotal role played by the Low Countries.[33] In August 1578, he had received the welcome alliance with William of Orange, but his attempt to press the fight further was going badly: desertions from his own troops, defections

---

[31] Her initial interest: *CSPS*, p. 680.

[32] 1554–1584; youngest son of Catherine de Medici. In 1574, he became Duke of Anjou, a term that had previously belonged to his brother, who took the Crown of Poland. It was his death that caused the League, in the face of childless Henri III, to reform, inaugurating the war of the three Henris. These following paragraphs, though enlivened on occasion by evidence culled from my own researches in the British Library, and except where they touch upon Henry Howard and his work, add nothing original to the picture already well painted by Bossy, 'English Catholics', pp. 2–16; Susan Doran, *Monarchy and Matrimony: The Courtships of Elizabeth I*, London, 1996; Blair Worden, *The Sound of Virtue: Sir Philip Sidney's Arcadia and Elizabethan Politics*, London 1998, esp. pp. 89–114; K. Barnes, 'John Stubbe: The French Ambassador's Account 1579', *Historical Journal*, 34, 1991, pp. 421–6; Mitchel Leimon, 'Sir Francis Walsingham and the Anjou Marriage Plan', unpublished PhD dissertation, Cambridge University, 1989 (this work has been influential in showing the self-interested nature of many of Burghley's actions, and provides good evidence for the difference in opinion and grouping between the Walsingham and Burghley camps); and W. MacCaffrey, *Queen Elizabeth and the Making of Policy, 1572–1588*, Princeton, 1981, pp. 243–66.

[33] Terminology is contentious, but I refer to the Low Countries when considered as a whole in this period, and Northern and Southern provinces where appropriate.

to Alexander Farnese, Prince of Parma, and a bullish Philip II rendered a match with England highly desirable. Anjou could not look to his brother for aid, since Henri had other concerns. The Northern Provinces remained firm under William of Orange, but for how much longer? And what of Navarre? Indeed, a clear sign of the shifting loyalties of what would become the 'United Provinces' was given on 6 January 1579, when the Union of Arras between Hainaut and Artois was declared: that union made it obvious that its allegiances lay with Spain, just as, on 23 January 1573, the Northern Provinces had formed the confessionally opposed Union of Utrecht.[34] A combination of religious duty to oppressed Protestants and fears about a too powerful Philip made Elizabeth receptive to the Frenchman's suit. Anjou himself, however, would have to come to court; he hesitated, perhaps remembering the Queen's previous inconstant behaviour toward him in the early 1570s.

On the one hand, there was a feeling that something should be done to help the Northern Provinces; on the other, a range of other considerations, often financial, pushed Elizabeth and her councillors in other directions.[35] Internal paranoia against Catholics began to increase. Accordingly, the potential dangers to the realm that a Catholic king would pose weighed heavily on the minds of many.[36] It is worth remembering that the first Jesuits had arrived on English shores only a year before. Resistance to the marriage did not, however, come only from the zealous. Howard's kinsman, Charles Arundell, a man of traditionalist religious sentiment, was unenthusiastic.[37] Catherine de Medici was also having doubts and, in mid-February, attempted to delay Anjou from following Simier to England. Elizabeth ceded some of the freedom that her coquettish behaviour had won her and from the end of March to early May she began to negotiate terms, together with the Privy Council, as an encouragement to the duke.

---

[34] The Union of Utrecht was not formally recognized as such until the end of the eighty years' war in 1648.

[35] Considerations of religious duty had not prevented Elizabeth promising her councillors in summer 1578 that she would send forces to the Northern Provinces and then promptly refusing to honour it. See now the excellent work of Paul E. J. Hammer, *Elizabeth's Wars: Society, Government and Military Reformation in Tudor England, 1558–1604*, London, 2003.

[36] For example, Fulke Greville, *The Prose Works of Fulke Greville*, Lord Brooke, ed. J. Gouws, Oxford, 1986, pp. 28–30 (to Sidney stressing the importance of maintaining the Baltics and Poland); Stafford E. Lehmberg, *Sir Walter Mildmay and Tudor Government*, Texas, 1964, pp. 157–9.

[37] TNA: PRO 31/3/27, f. 266. For the Arundells, see A. L. Rowse, *Tudor Cornwall: Portrait of a Society*, London, 1969, pp. 342–79.

After some persuasion by his wife, Henri III finally agreed to let his brother go to London on 21 August 1579.[38]

Religion proved a sticking point for Sir Walter Mildmay and for his close ally on the Privy Council, Sir Francis Walsingham. Additional 'pretexts' included the Queen being too old to bear children and, therefore, too old to marry. Pragmatic considerations prevailed in the minds of the supporters of the marriage, chief among whom were Thomas Radcliffe, third Earl of Sussex, and Burghley: if Elizabeth did not marry him, someone Spanish might.[39] This conflict between Walsingham and Burghley also explains the intervention of Henry Howard. Throughout the early and mid-1570s, Burghley was the key figure in Elizabeth's administration. Walsingham, however, was biding his time; he was building a network of spies and garnering support from the more enthusiastic Protestants. Perhaps Howard felt that if Walsingham were to gain ground at court, his ambitions for power would be dashed. If the marriage went ahead, then Burghley's influence at court would not, at least, diminish further, thereby allowing Howard the oxygen of court attendance that those ambitions required.[40]

Howard had to prove himself somehow. Unlike Leicester and Christopher Hatton, whose charm and affection for Elizabeth had won them increased influence in the 1570s, Howard's personality was less clearly suited to the task. His own position at court at this time was linked, albeit inversely, to that of Leicester. Elizabeth's quasi-law that Leicester should not marry proved too much of a strain for him, and he married Lettice Knollys (1540–1634), the widowed countess of Essex, secretly in late 1578. When the queen found out a year later, she was furious, and Leicester had to leave court. Who was responsible for informing Elizabeth? Henry Howard.[41] Together with his kinsman Arundell, he now risked the wrath of Leicester's loose-knit group of friends, clients, co-religionists and those of the Dudley blood.

---

[38] Howard often appears in archival records in this period in relation to his hospitality of the French, e.g., HMC, Hatfield House, II, 756 and 757 (Howard entertaining the Duc d'Anjou and acting as the chief go-between for Simier and the Queen); HMC, Hatfield House, II, 449 (Moine being entertained by Howard and Stafford).

[39] It may be right to go even further (as does Doran, *Monarchy and Matrimony*, p. 159, relying on Leimon, 'Sir Francis Walsingham') and suggest that Burghley was in effect motivated by self-interest. On Sussex, see S. Doran, 'Thomas Radcliffe, 3rd Earl of Sussex, ?1526–1583', unpublished PhD dissertation, London University, 1979.

[40] Susan Brigden, *New Worlds, Lost Worlds*, London, 2000, p. 271: 'The brilliant and unquiet Lord Henry Howard now dared to joke of his favour at court in the sacred terms of "the chosen" and "reprobation"'.

[41] References provided by Doran, *Monarchy and Matrimony*, p. 250 n. 41.

Survival, Success and Defeat

Howard had another reason for writing his response. Stubbs, author of the original tract against the marriage, was married to the sister of Thomas Cartwright, whom Howard had attacked in print six years earlier. One scholar claims that Burghley 'handed over' the main points of Stubbs's attack to some of his party in order to prepare 'counter-propaganda'.[42] However it happened, within a few months of Stubbs's polemic Howard had written his own response.[43] If the main arguments in Stubbs's work were the traditional ones about France, Catholicism and Elizabeth's age, the tone was unmistakably Puritan: apocalyptic and highly coloured imagery and perpetual references to the providential position of England as a second Israel.[44] Howard's work is self-consciously more measured, just as his earlier work against Presbyterianism had abandoned the more overwrought elements of Puritan rhetoric. It also pointedly contains a compli-

---

[42] Ibid., p. 168. Doran gives no evidence for this statement, and it is not in the other main accounts. It may be that she is referring to a manuscript source not mentioned nearby; alternatively, she is extrapolating from the evidence. If the latter, it seems wildly unlikely that Burghley would not have assumed Howard capable of mastering the brief himself.

[43] The exact date of composition is not certain. The work is known by various titles; it shall here be called 'An Answer'. All references are to the edition by Lloyd E. Berry, *John Stubbs' Gaping Gulf with Letters and Other Relevant Documents*, Charlottesville, 1968, pp. 153–94. Sir Simonds D'Ewes bound Howard's work with that of Stubbs and other related works in Harleian MS 180 ff. 75^r–147^v. It bears the date '1580', but that copy cannot be from the sixteenth century (as Berry thinks); it contains a reference to 'the Earle of Northampton' (f. 75^r), and so must have been written after 1603. Berry's edition is a good one, though he is a little misleading on textual matters. For example, he does not emphasize sufficiently that BL Additional MS 48027, though perhaps earlier than the other two manuscripts (for details of which see Berry, p. lix), makes considerably less sense: see, e.g., the impossible paradosis mentioned in Berry's apparatus criticus at pp. 170, 171 and 184. Accordingly, I would consider a more likely stemma to be A deriving from a lost exemplar x, which in turn was a copy of the archetype y. The two remaining extant manuscripts derive directly from y. Stubbs is not mentioned, perhaps because in late 1579, along with his bookseller, his hand had been cut off. One near-explicit reference to Stubbs's work in the main body of the text seems to be an instance of the rhetorical figure *confutatio*: 'And will then these jolly libellers that by their glorious glosses do seem to pretend a most faithful respect of Her Majesty and the realm, deprive them both of so precious and inestimable a jewel as the having of issue would apparently rebound to be and by the want therof intrude into the ugly and fearful *gulf* of all miserable calamities.' *Answer*, p. 164. In more general terms, there is in the very last section of the work a reference to having refuted the arguments of 'the libeler', p. 194.

[44] This would become a hoary theme; Alexandra Walsham, *Providence in Early Modern England*, Oxford, 1999, pp. 281–325, is a study of the English Jeremiad, enlarging on the sensitive study by Patrick Collinson, 'Biblical Rhetoric: The English Nation and National Sentiment in the Prophetic Mode', in *Religion and Culture in the English Renaissance*, eds C. McEachern and D. Shuger, Cambridge, 1997, pp. 27–45.

ment to Castelnau on the first page.[45] He explains that the multitude's distaste for the marriage is only to be expected given 'their weakness of judgment to discern of things beneficial for them'.[46] It is certain that Howard was involved with Castelnau at this time, and we will see his opinion on the marriage. Howard has only two arguments in favour of the Anjou liaison. The first is the danger of a royal marriage without issue, whence 'there consequently have followed infinite dangers and most perilous mutilations and alterations of the state'.[47] Some of Howard's examples suggest that the work was written with, among others, a French audience in view. The merits of lineal royal succession, he continues, can be seen by how successful the French were against the English when their issue was uninterrupted. This would not have been the most obvious argument to make to an English audience. Once again, however, the fact that it is a manuscript and not printed should bear some explanatory weight. Howard's humanist instincts allow him to criticize the unnamed pamphlets of those unnamed authors opposed to the marriage on the ground of lack of historical awareness: they 'make known their folly by neglecting the examples of past ages, whereby every wise man should learn to beware … Are they so ignorant they cannot or so obstinate they will not see the contention of Lancaster and York is like to be set on foot again?' This is another difference in the temper of Puritan and non-Puritan historiography.[48] The former, addicted to the prophetic, edificatory and apocalyptic mode, was loath to approve a cyclical view of history. By contrast, those who were unencumbered by providential history could much more easily look to patterns of behaviour inherent in the nature of man's engagement with society.[49] In similar vein,

---

[45] Howard, 'An Answer', p. 156: 'A gentleman of good note and credit about him and of a goodly wit and of great dexterity in managing of affairs'. Two points: note the wide remit of the phrase 'managing of affairs', unqualified by some such phrase as 'his nation's' or 'his'; secondly, there is no compliment in the work to any other politician, including Burghley or the remaining members of the Privy Council.

[46] Ibid.

[47] Ibid., p. 158. The argument is then fleshed out by exempla from Merovingian and English history.

[48] In essence, the issue may be reformulated as a difference in regard to the Bible. Stubbs's exempla tend to come not from recent history, but from the Old Testament. Howard drops the biblical element from his discussion entirely.

[49] It is usual to say that the 'cyclical' view of history derives ultimately from Polybius (see *Histories* 1.4.1–8 with Walbank ad loc.) and that its enthusiastic adoption by the Quattrocento humanists rests on the assumption of potential assimilation of the ancient world through *imitation*, and was probably diffused into England through the popularity of Machiavelli, whose *Discorsi* are another locus classicus for the theme: Machiavelli, *Discorsi*, 1.10, 1.39 et passim; G. Sasso, *Machiavelli e gli antichi*, 3 vols, Milan, 1988, I,

Howard must reinterpret the protestations of fealty to prince that are scattered throughout the anti-Anjou tracts as, characteristically, flattery.[50] To go further would be to admit that both sides are loyal to what the queen should do, not to Elizabeth herself.[51] Again, the accusation would be harder to make in print, since flattery is pre-eminently a courtly vice, and not an instrument of mass political theory.[52]

The second section of the work enters into 'particular consideration of those which remain throughout Christendom presented unto Her Majesty for convenient choices of marriage'.[53] Howard (with a glance at Leicester) alludes to the dire consequences to the realm of a British appointment, and moves on to the problems and prospects of foreign princes.[54] The queen must find an equal, for marriage is a form of 'amity' and in amity there is no inequality.[55] This strategy of argument recalls the one adopted in the earlier work, *The Treatise of Treasons*, with its view of the queen's ministers frustrating the natural concord between the two monarchs that derive from their similar experiences and positions.[56] As before this sympathy to Mary

---

pp. 3–65; A. Momigliano, *The Classical Foundations of Modern Historiography*, Berkeley, 1990, pp. 59–62 and 'Polybius' Reappearance in Western Europe', in his *Sesto contributo alla storia degli studi classici e del mondo antico*, I, Rome, 1980, p. 115; some French variations on the theme may be found in D. R. Kelley, 'Badouin's Conception of History', in *Renaissance Essays II*, ed. W. J. Connell, Woodbridge, 1988, pp. 307–29. One might add that Lucretius's conception of history could be read in this way (see *DRN* 5 and 6, especially 6.1030 to the end, where Lucretius paraphrases the plague scene in Thucydides, 2.47–55). In addition, the lines between humanist and prophetic are not drawn quite so sharply: is there not something prophetic about the closing pages of Machiavelli's *Il principe*?

[50] Howard, 'An Answer', p. 195.

[51] A pithy verse protest against the marriage is an example of this: 'Wee subjects trwe untill our queene, the forraine yoke defye', quoted in Doran, *Monarchy and Matrimony*, p. 157. For a first-rate account of how this political tension found cultural expression see the precise study of Marie Axton, *The Queen's Two Bodies: Drama and the Elizabethan Succession*, London, 1977.

[52] What about the beginning of p. 166? The most famous work of the controversy, Sir Philip Sidney's *Letter to Queen Elizabeth* (almost certainly sponsored by Leicester, Sidney's uncle), also circulated in manuscript, thereby making its arguments more palatable; for details of the manuscript and its subsequent reception see Woudhuysen, *Sir Philip Sidney*, pp. 151–3.

[53] Howard, 'An Answer', pp. 172–3.

[54] He does so with a tone that seems dangerously seditious: 'there is no strength for Her Majesty to expect by any alliance at home, considering the forces which her subjects possess are only derived from that estimation and credit which they enjoy under the favour of her Majesty', Howard, 'An Answer', p. 173. This sounds double-edged.

[55] Howard, 'An Answer', pp. 173–4. Stubbs, by contrast, had insisted on the inequality of the relation between man and woman, saying that Elizabeth, 'a weaker vessel', would naturally be drawn into the faith of her suitor: Stubbs, *Gulf*, p. 11.

[56] See Chapter One for brief discussion of this work.

suggests, though does not depend upon, a reception for the work in the circle of Castelnau, as when he gives an example of the results of a lack of amity in a relationship:

> The lamentable example of the most infortunate and poor afflicted Mary Queen of Scotland doth yield hereof an evident testimony. For who seeth not that the *only* cause of *all* her calamities hath proceeded from the discords ensuing that unhappy match between her and the Earl of Lennox, her subject in respect of his chiefest dignity, who, carried away with an overweening conceit of his own perfections, and too safely presuming upon the assured good opinon of her affection towards him, emboldened himself to the undertaking of practices far unfit to him to intermeddle withal … which in the end procured both ruin to himself and the misery of his princess.[57]

If Howard was in contact with Mary through Salisbury Court in 1580, and she had read the book, she would have been pleased with this rewrite of her history, though it was unlikely to persuade anyone else, including Elizabeth, however much she wanted evidence, not rumour, of her neighbour's guilt.[58] Indeed, at this stage, we know that Elizabeth was not opposed to doing a deal with Mary, since it represented a way of creating concord between her confessionally divergent subjects. The political analysis in Howard's work is couched in terms of utility to the broad interests of the nation (rather than individual conviction and conscience) and an emphasis on the similarity of the two queens (rather than the seeming religious gap); this was an analysis already familiar from *A Treatise of Treasons*.

My contention is that Howard wrote this work with a double purpose. Since we cannot be certain of the date of composition, it is not possible to say that he knew that the marriage plans were off. On the other hand, one commentator writes that '[the question] never really regained the intensity it had acquired in 1579'.[59] If this is true, Howard had, in effect, a double audience, English and French, Elizabeth and Castelnau, on the one hand professing

---

[57] Howard, 'An Answer', pp. 174–5. Italics mine.
[58] In addition, it is impossible that Simier and the ambassador would not have met, there by making a connection with Howard the more likely. The otherwise untrustworthy William Herle (BL Lansdowne MS 39, ff. 190–2) does mention that it was Howard who advised Simier 'to precede by the Papistes to establish his master here, and to purge religion of the blood of sundry of our greatest houses in England'. The last detail does not sound authentic, and indeed the first point may simply be a recognition of Howard's authorship of the tract.
[59] Worden, *Sound of Virtue*, p. 92. However, we find Burghley giving a banquet for the duke in 1581: Read, *Lord Burghley*, p. 258.

admiration for a once-loved but perhaps impossible suitor and, on the other, demonstrating his readiness to serve the French interests. And, at least in the mind of the French ambassador, those interests were no longer being identified with an inconstant Anjou, but with a far grander person, Mary.

Howard's career had not progressed smoothly. For all of his affectionate dealing with numerous courtly and diplomatic figures, Howard did not escape the indignity of debt. He seems to have given Burghley's name as surety. One of Howard's creditors, Rowland Rayleton, waited seven years for payment of £33 before writing off to Burghley requesting settlement of the sum.[60] In 1581, the Spanish ambassador began relations with the captive regent. As we shall see later on, Howard was clearly in contact with Mary, albeit secretively in this period. It was, perhaps, the ambassador's association with Mary that made Howard feel it was not impolitic to engage in what to later eyes looks almost like treasonous behaviour.[61] His motivation was, as before with his tract in favour of the Anjou marriage, and as later with his role as kingmaker to Mary's son, to secure a prominent position in a regime which would be more religiously acceptable to him. We note that Howard was passing information to Don Bernardino de Mendoza, but that his own influence at court by the end of 1582 had diminished, causing the Spanish ambassador to complain of the paucity of information flow by this point.[62] Only a couple of years earlier, however, various privy councillors had maintained much warmer relations with Mendoza.[63] The lines of battle that were clearly drawn by the mid-1580s

---

[60] *CSPD, Addenda, 1580–1625*, London, 1872, p. 27: 1580? (Rowland Rayleton was a resident of the City of London: see *Two Tudor Subsidy Rolls for the City of London, 1541 and 1582*, ed. R. G. Lang, 1993, London, p. 273). Other debts: BL Cotton MS, Titus C vi f. 4^v is a letter dated 29 October 1589 complaining that 'Sir Roger Townshende leaves me nothing at all' (this is probably the Sir Roger Townshend who had been a servant of Howard's brother, the Duke of Norfolk: see further *DNB* sub nomine); f. 44^v contains a similar complaint about another debtor, one Doulewes. Howard was presumably helped by a statute of 1572, which prescribed a maximum rate of interest: Stone, *Crisis*, p. 237. His debts would have been much worse had he owned any realty, for debts secured on which compound interest was available after 1571.

[61] For a discussion of what counted as treason, and the varying motives of those who accepted monies from Mendoza, see G. Parker, 'Treason and Plot in Elizabethan Diplomacy: The "Fame" of Edward Stafford Reconsidered', in his *Empire, War and Faith in Early Modern Europe*, London, 2003, pp. 70–95, esp. 90ff. Parker stresses that it was possible for given courtiers not to consider war between the two nations inevitable. A similar rehabilitation of the motives of those accepting pensions from the Spanish, including Howard, twenty years later is discussed by Somerset, *Unnatural Murder*, pp. 25–6.

[62] *CSPSp*, pp. 362–4.

[63] For the various dealings with Mendoza by such diverse figures as Burghley, Sir James Croft and Hatton, see *CSPSp*, s.vv.

between England and Spain should not be retrojected to 1580.[64] It should not be forgotten that Stafford had accepted a pension from Mendoza, and others were busy ensuring that they did not needlessly abandon relations with Mary. After all, many thought of her as the rightful heir in the event of Elizabeth's death.[65] Even the Earl of Leicester is known to have taken the waters at Buxton with the captive monarch.[66] Sir James Croft, whom we last saw dining at Theobalds with Howard and Burghley a few years earlier, received a pension from Philip II from 1579 onwards.[67] By reason of his near-public Catholicism, a history of intrigue (never quite proved) and an abrasive manner, Henry Howard had a more limited number of persons upon whose favour he could depend. He was, however, in essence playing the same game as everyone else, with more limited resources. The more zealous reformed wing would have nothing to do with him. It seems that Burghley and, at an earlier date, Sir Christopher Hatton were chief among Howard's contacts at court. One may guess that his motivation was not purely 'political': in addition, unlike Burghley or Hatton, but like Stafford, Howard needed the money. His behaviour was not traitorous, but in the struggle for place his options were fewer. He was simply someone who had to ally himself with men who, by a sequence of unfortunate events, were themselves either erratic in behaviour, such as the Earl of Oxford, or who rapidly became distant from favour, such as Mendoza, whose sometimes unusual notions of what was going on at court suggest that he too suffered from not being at the heart of things. Despite these limited options, or unfortunate choices, Howard survived, again. This was probably due to his rank (Elizabeth was famously reluctant to move against those of her own noble blood[68]) and to a piece of luck: Walsingham's increasing isolation at court and subsequent death, which strengthened – to the point of unassailability – Burghley's position. Howard continued, however, to sail very close to the wind.

---

[64] For the evidence, however, that many around Philip II had by the early 1580s come to see the conquest of England as the best means of securing an increasingly sprawling imperial amalgam, see G. Parker, 'David or Goliath? Philipp II and his World in the 1580s', in his *Empire, War and Faith in Early Modern Europe*, London, 2002, pp. 19–38, esp. 28.

[65] Patrick Collinson has insisted on this: see his *Elizabethan Essays*, London, 1994, pp. 48–55, and his 'The Elizabethan Exclusion Crisis and the Elizabethan Polity', *Proceedings of the British Academy*, 84, 1993, pp. 51–92.

[66] Patrick Collinson, *The English Captivity of Mary, Queen of Scots*, Sheffield, 1987, p. 20.

[67] Martin Philippson, *Ein Ministerium unter Philip II: Kardinale Granvalle am Spanische Hofe, 1579-1586*, Berlin, 1895, p. 56.

[68] As Jamie Canife reminds me, however, if Elizabeth had really been so distraught about her execution of Mary, Queen of Scots, she would not taken to wearing the dead queen's jewels herself.

Survival, Success and Defeat

Howard must have taken pleasure at his new-found security at court.[69] This security was not to last long. Howard's fall from favour was precipitate. From July to September 1580, he was with the Queen at Oatlands, a royal manor house in Weybridge, Surrey.[70] By New Year's Eve, he was under house arrest in the residence of Sir Thomas Bromley (1530–1587), York House, whither Howard seems to have gone directly after his stay with the Spanish ambassador, and where he remained in confinement until at least the end of July.[71] He was now under suspicion but there was no evidence of any specific wrongdoing. Howard was clearly a well-wisher of Mary, but perhaps nothing more.[72] The conflict at this point between Howard and officialdom is particularly contentious from the documentary perspective. It revolves around a very large number of 'libels' exchanged between the Earl of Oxford and, in particular, Arundell, but also Howard. They have recently been the subject of an extended scholarly treatment, in addition to a very clear précis of thirty years earlier.[73]

In essence, around Christmas 1580, Oxford broke ranks with his previous co-religionists Arundell and Howard, who in turn responded with a vast slew of accusations: atheism, sodomy, bestiality, conspiracy to murder, drunkenness, treason and amusing addenda such as the Bible was written only as an instrument of social control and that King Solomon had three

---

[69] Henri III even writes to Howard in grateful terms for all that he had done to further the match: *CSPF*, p. 252.

[70] He tells us as much: BL Cotton MS, Titus C vi f. 7ᵛ: 'After two monthes overblowen at Otlandes, I bade him welcome out of Spayne'. My guess is that the answer to Stubbs was written in this period.

[71] We have a letter from Howard to Burghley on 20 July 1581 (Cecil Papers 98/129). He was definitely free again in Highgate by the time that he wrote to Leicester on 27 October of the same year (TNA: PRO SP 12/150/51). This, then, is the context for Mendoza's request in 1581 to Philip II to keep an eye on all Englishmen trading in Spain and for the speculation that it was in essence a 'tip-off' from someone 'like Henry Howard': Alan Haynes, *The Elizabethan Secret Services*, Stroud, 2000, p. 98.

[72] It is important to distinguish the purely prudential in Howard's position from more deliberately pragmatic or conciliatory policies that some sixteenth-century rulers espoused in confessional matters: see, e.g., Jean-Louis Bourgeon, *Charles IX devant la Saint-Barthélemy*, Geneva, 1995, and Howard Louthan, *Johannis Crato and the Austrian Habsburgs: Reforming a Counter-Reform Court*, Princeton, 1994. Perhaps Elizabeth, at least in the 1560s and 1570s, should be included among this group.

[73] D. C. Peck, *Leicester's Commonwealth: The Copy of a Letter Written by a Master of Art at Cambridge (1584) and Related Documents*, Athens: OH, 1985, and Nelson, *Monstrous Adversary*. The latter book contains excellent transcriptions of most of the documents, and it is out of fear of wasted reduplication of labour, combined with Peck's judicious narrative based on these documents, that I have decided to abbreviate this section of the biography. The Earl of Oxford industry has responded with predictable levels of intemperateness to Nelson's work.

hundred concubines. Oxford was, however, merely a childish, egomaniacal distraction, albeit an inconvenient one, compared to the larger forces at court. He had forced out of Howard his confession of reconciliation to the Catholic Church, but that was not enough by itself to neuter Howard.

We have seen, at various levels, the political and cultural tensions between the conservative faction at court and those that grouped themselves around Leicester, with Burghley occupying an uncertain middle ground.[74] The French ambassador began to activate, or intensify, his relationships with the conservative contacts at court (Philip Howard, the Earl of Oxford, Charles Arundell, the Earl of Northumberland and Henry Howard). Far from this being, however, an open charm offensive to influence Elizabeth and the most powerful of her advisers, Castelnau clearly conducted these relationships in secret; and it was this very secrecy that led them to being viewed with suspicion when details emerged as a result of the rift between Oxford and his one-time friends at court. Mauvissière himself knew not to weaken his hand with the more religiously zealous by too much open association with the court Catholics. When Leicester was banished from court, the conservative faction may have felt that their time for power, at last, had come.

The case for the French marriage weakened, however, as time went on. Leicester returned to court, and Oxford's revelations of suspicious behaviour by Howard, Arundell and others served to further undermine their cause. These revelations did not, in the first instance, appear to have seriously influenced the queen's view of Howard and his co-religionists. Howard and Arundell received word of his imminent arrest and took shelter on Christmas Day with Don Bernardino Mendoza, the Spanish ambassador. There is no previous documentary trace of relations between the Spanish ambassador (who had arrived in London in 1578) and these men, but he saw in them, for a time, useful contacts with the court. How honestly they gave indication of their access to the Queen we do not know. Still, for a while, Howard seemed a useful contact to the ambassador.[75] It is after

---

[74] Talk of faction, naturally, underemphasizes the extent to which given figures attempted to smooth over potential rifts. Aside from the more obvious example of Burghley (who receives oddly favourable treatment in *Leicester's Commonwealth*), others were anxious not to burn their Marian bridges. It is usually thought that Howard was one of the sources of information for *Leicester's Commonwealth*, with Arundell or Persons the actual writers of the work. I have not investigated this issue, but see Federico Eguiluz, *Robert Persons: El Architraidor. Su vida y su obra*, Madrid, 1990.

[75] *CSPSp*, 1580–86, pp. 245–6. Though Howard appears to have accepted a pension from the Spanish for his services, the ambassador was to become more disillusioned with Howard as it became obvious how low his stock had fallen at court: see further Parker, 'Treason and Plot', pp. 70–95.

Howard and Arundell were arrested that the main body of the libels from Oxford, and defences from those accused, began to flow. The truth of these libels is hard to ascertain; Oxford's claims are often extreme and hard to maintain, though some of them appeared to have created particular difficulty for Howard, who, along with his allies, was in semi-retirement through 1582 and 1583. These years saw him continue his contacts with the French ambassador and intensify those with Mendoza. In 1583, a meeting was held between Charles Paget and the Earl of Northumberland at Petworth to discuss a French invasion of England. Soon afterwards, most of the figures were brought in and interrogated.

In dealing with Howard's involvement with the high politics of the 1580s, some introduction to the changing international landscape is necessary. The shaping of foreign policy in these years, following the uneasy peace of the latter 1570s, was driven partly by economic and dynastic factors and partly by the personality of Elizabeth herself.[76] The financially impoverished and bitterly divided England of 1555, a minor player on the international stage, could seem to many a distant prospect. A skilful use of propaganda had begun to generate the image of 'Good Queen Bess' that was to prove so lasting, despite the considerable frustration with the queen that would surface more strongly in the 1590s. In addition, by 1580, it is not too early to speak of a Protestant nation again, despite traditionalist practices in the dark corners. The noisier Presbyterians were driven out of the univerisites and the argument was won to the satisfaction of many. To the English diplomats stationed in Venice and Paris, there was little sign of immediate danger. The Catholic league was more or less defunct, its original ideological drive soon petering out. Elizabeth managed to keep the balance between France and Spain. England had not known significant failures of harvest for some years. The enclosure acts may have been unpopular, but despite growing vagrancy, credit difficulties and overcrowding in the cities, England was more prosperous than for any time in a generation. Mary kept an absentee court at Paris, but her royal person was safely confined in the wilds of the north, and foreign supporters could look to the

---

[76] Doran, *Monarchy and Matrimony*, p. 210, argues powerfully that there was in fact no room for Elizabeth's personal considerations in the web of policy, and, indeed, that '[h]ad her Council ever united behind any one of her suitors, she would have found great difficulty in rejecting his proposal'. The best evidence for this position is to recall that Mary Stuart's prompt deposition from power in 1567 was caused by her subjects' distaste for her new husband. Even if Elizabeth did not attend many meetings of the Privy Council, it does not follow that the Privy Councillors thereby could disregard the imagined and discussed state of mind of their monarch.

example of the Bishop of Ross and others to see what their just deserts would be. What could go wrong?

Everything, and quickly. The most important catalyst for events was France. Here events moved with a horrifying rapidity. The succession was in dispute. Legal arguments were not decisive in ascertaining whether the Catholic cardinal de Bourbon or the Protestant prince of Navarre, Henri (who would become Henri IV of France), should accede to the throne on the death of the current king, Henri III. The king chose to steer a dangerous course of confessional fluidity, attempting to persuade the Guisards, the mainstay of the now reformed Catholic League, that he would play along with their succession plans. He was seemingly brought to terms in 1584, agreeing to the succession of Bourbon. Only a few months later, however, thinking that the Guisards (who by this time) need only be killed to be destroyed, he plotted and achieved the cardinal's death. Far from quieting discontent, the king soon realized that popular outrage extended to academe, then as now, more potently connected with the state in France than in Italy or England. The Sorbonne declared France independent of her king. Suddenly, England's position in the Netherlands was made crucial. With a Catholic king now on the throne of France, how long before France and Spain joined forces to divide up the spoil of their Protestant neighbour? England could not risk antagonizing Philip II by openly giving military and financial aid to the Netherlanders' revolt. Accordingly, in the light of these events, the issue of Mary became ever more pressing both for the nation and for Howard.

Chapter 6

'SOMEWHAT CLOSELY CARRIED' RHETORIC AND ASTROLOGY

HOWARD spent the first half of 1583 (and probably much longer than that) writing his attack on prophecy and astrology. It is noteworthy that he chose to dedicate the work to Walsingham. Perhaps it was in relation to his examination (for unspecified reasons) earlier in the year.[1] Why did Howard write the *Defensative*?[2] One suggestion, deriving from a contemporary source, is that it was written in response to a work by Richard Harvey.[3] Harvey's marginalia-prone brother, Gabriel, wrote at the foot of one page of Howard's work the following note:

> Iwis it is not the Astrological Discourses, but a more secret marke, whereat he shooteth. *Latet anguis in herbis, et per me latebit, etiam adhuc.* Patience, the best remedy in such booteles conflicts; God give me, and my Frends, Caesars memory, to forget such injuries, offerid by another; and to remember

---

[1] See below, p. 146.
[2] Although the work was originally published in 1583, references are to the second edition, *A Defensative against the Poyson of Supposed Prophecies*, London: William Jaggard, 1620. I have compared the two texts carefully, and there is no material difference between them. The second edition is, however, considerably easier to read and more readily available. Howard's work found an unexpected *Nachleben* in Shakespeare's *Macbeth*, via Thomas Nashe's *Terrors of the Night*: see, most recently, K. Duncan-Jones, 'Christ's Teares: Nashe's Forsaken Extremities', *Review of English Studies*, 49, 1998, pp. 167–80, at n. 29.
[3] Richard Harvey, *An Astrological Discourse upon the Conjunction of Saturne & Jupiter*, London: Bynneman, 1583 (the conjunction was that of these two slow-moving and important planets in the fiery trigon). Harvey's book was published, according to the stationers register, in January of that year: for further details, see Virginia F. Stern, *Gabriel Harvey: His Life, Marginalia and Library*, Oxford, 1979, pp. 70–4, at 70. For a full bibliography on Harvey and his annotations, see Nicholas Popper, 'The English Polydaedali: How Gabriel Harvey Read Late Tudor London', *JHI*, 2005, pp. 351–81, at 381 n. 1.

especially such requisites, as especially concern, and apperteine owrselves. An Ostridges stomack can digest harder iron, then this. *Qui seipsos confirmant, alios abunde confutant. Dabit Deus his quoque finem*.[4]

The amount of work that went into Howard's book, though, militates against any proximate cause in the same year of its publication.[5] It had obviously been long in the making; and it simply represents Howard's first venture into print to which he put his name, on a subject in which he was intellectually interested, but one that also possessed certain contemporary resonances.

Certainly, there was one very immediate such political resonance, for he told Walsingham (who was to become the work's dedicatee) that Leicester had induced Oxford to accuse Howard of enquiring into the future of the monarchy via astrology. This accusation took place in the context of the 1581 Oxford–Arundell libels.[6] Howard notes that the queen did have some concern about the interpretation of a prophecy, a matter which caused trouble for both Howard and Arundell.[7] Howard had to apologize to Leicester, however, for this implication, so there may yet be something in the notion of the queen's dislike of a pro-Howard political prophecy. It would, after all, explain the heavy emphasis on the astrological threat to the body politic which is an unusual feature of the work.

Whatever the immediate motivation, the work was published in the summer of 1583.[8] If Howard had indeed written it to exculpate himself, he would have found his subsequent imprisonment perplexing. Our most immediate evidence for any supposed heresy in the work comes, moreover, from an unreliable source. William Herle always gave the dimmest possible view of Lord Henry Howard's dealings. Although he was himself briefly imprisoned for his (very minor) role in the Ridolfi affair, his interest was advancement, not ideological consistency.[9] He writes a note to Burghley in November 1583, reporting the opinion of 'some learned man' that Howard's work on astrology contained 'sundrie heresies' and 'spyces withal

---

[4]   Stern, *Harvey*, p. 72.
[5]   Howard's book was published in the Stationers Register in July of 1583, which would have given Howard about six months, if it had indeed been a response to Richard Harvey's work, to write this his longest, most ornate and reference-laden book.
[6]   For details of which, see p. 000.
[7]   The letter to Walsingham: TNA: PRO 12/155/44; the examination of Howard and Arundell about the prophecy: TNA: PRO 12/155/47 and TNA: PRO 12/155/48.
[8]   For one summary, see John Strype, *The History of Edmund Grindal*, London, 1710, p. 157.
[9]   For more details on Herle, see *DNB* sub nomine and see now Robyn Adam, 'Both Diligent and Secret: The Intelligence Letters of William Herle', unpublished PhD dissertation, University of London, 2004.

of treason'.[10] There follows a qualification: these heresies are 'somewhat closely carried'. A second letter, written on the following day, suggests that the *Defensative* be remitted to the official censor to weed out its presumed heresies.[11] As we have seen, moreover, there is evidence that Howard was imprisoned for his work, so it looks (the argument might run) as though the work was indeed heretical. This informs us of the degree of control and sophistication shown by the Elizabethan police state in the circulation of ideas and the book trade.

Perhaps. An argument, however, is only as strong as its weakest link and, on examination, the argument stumbles from one shaky stepping stone to another. Firstly, the phrase '*somewhat* closely carried [italics mine]' suggests that there was nothing very manifest about the work's presumed heterodoxy.[12] We should therefore be alive to the possibility that Herle had invented, or at least magnified the importance of, the anonymous learned man. Furthermore, as will be apparent by the end of this chapter, it is hard to see what, short of discussion of the queen's horoscope, counted as heretical in astrology in Elizabethan England. There was little, *grosso modo*, in the way of party lines or schools when it came to astrological thought in the early to mid-Elizabethan period. Again, due weight should be given to the bias not only of Herle but also of this 'official censor', who was none other than Thomas Norton, a figure with a history of antipathy to Howard. Finally, what we know of press censorship in Elizabethan England makes it clear that it was only the more flagrant breaches of decorum or political duty that would, other factors being absent, cause writers to have their books censored, let alone be thrown in prison.[13] Indeed, it should be noted that, whatever may have happened to Howard himself, his book itself appears to have been uncensored.[14] Therefore, let us work from the idea, based on this evidence – or rather lack of evidence – that the work contained *nothing* heretical: the publication of the *Defensative* simply allowed the ruling authorities to haul Howard in on a pretext, since he was under close surveillance at this period for his dealings with Castelnau.

---

[10] BL MS Lansdowne MS 39, f. 139ʳ. John Bossy considers that the learned man is Bruno (see Bossy, *GB*, p. 30). The notion that Bruno could have mastered sufficient English in the short time he was there to be able to sift through Howard's book is not plausible.
[11] See Bossy, *GB*, p. 100 n. 5, for documentation.
[12] Note, too, the sexual implications of the word 'close': see Stewart, *Close Readers*.
[13] Susan Cyndia Clegg, *Press Censorship in Elizabethan England*, Cambridge, 1997.
[14] Contrast the insensitive and oafish recall of the Howard-sponsored first edition of Byrd's *Gradualia* twenty years later: see David C. Price, *Patrons and Musicians of the English Renaissance*, Cambridge, 1981, ad indicem, sub nomine 'Howard'.

We know that elsewhere in sixteenth-century Europe astrology in various guises was sometimes taught as part of the curriculum in natural philosophy. This seems particularly to have been the case in Italy. There were versions of astrology that seeped into the works of such textbook authors as Cornelius Valerius and Philipp Melanchthon, both of whom we know were used by tutors in Elizabethan Cambridge. Henry Howard was in residence at Cambridge University for perhaps as long as nine years, that is, from 1560 to 1569, and maintained contacts there until at least 1573.[15] It is natural to suppose, therefore, that, when he came to compose a learned work such as the *Defensative*, albeit in the vernacular, he would draw on the academic enquiry with which he was so intimate. It is noteworthy, however, that none of the sources mentioned in the margins of his book was published in England.

Furthermore, we should be careful before rushing to believe that either Oxford or Cambridge was replete with enthusiasm for astrological studies, despite the picture of a flourishing interest in occult and scientific studies that has recently been drawn by a wide-ranging and influential article by Mordechai Feingold.[16] We should, perhaps, be (slightly) more cautious. At the very least, one should note that for the period up to the 1570s firm evidence of interest in science and, especially, occult pursuits, is hard to find.

---

[15] For these dates, see Chapter One.

[16] This picture was influentially made by Mordechai Feingold, 'The Occult Tradition at English Universities', in *Occult and Scientific Mentalities in the Renaissance*, ed. Brian Vickers, London, 1984, pp. 73–94, and developed in his *Mathematicians Apprenticeship Science, Universities and Society in England, 1540–1660*, Cambridge, 1984. Feingold's evidence is accepted uncritically by R. S. Dunn, 'The Status of Astrology in Elizabethan England', unpublished PhD dissertation, University of Cambridge, 1994. For the persistence of the 'School of Night' thesis, see the accurate demolition by Stephen Clucas, 'Thomas Harriot and the Field of Knowledge in the English Renaissance', in *Thomas Harriot: An Elizabethan Man of Science*, ed. R. Fox, Aldershot, 2002, pp. 93–106, esp. pp. 94–101. Further and now outdated works which concentrate more on the popular dissemination of astrological ideas include Don Cameron Allen, *The Star-Crossed Renaissance*, Durham: NC, 1941, and the introduction to John Melton, *Astrologaster: or the Figure-Caster*, ed. Hugh G. Dick, Los Angeles, 1975. For earlier English practice see Sophie Page, 'Richard Trewythian and the Uses of Astrology in Late Medieval England', *JWCI*, 64, 2001, pp. 193–228. I do not discount the importance, long recognized in the secondary literature, of the growth of mathematical practice in London as opposed to the universities: for the most up-to-date bibliography, see Popper, 'The English Polydaedali', p. 367 n. 40. Again, chronology is important, for there was a fellow of Gonville and Caius, Edward Wright, who was interested in aspects of practical mensuration and, most famously, navigation; but he was there from only 1586 onwards (on Wright, see E. G. R. Taylor, *Mathematical Practitioners of Tudor and Stuart England*, Cambridge, 1954, pp. 181–2). The late Elizabethan picture is different from that of the 1570s.

To be fair, it is in the nature of the more occult sciences to be difficult to trace since their practitioners are unlikely to have been open about their interests. Still, the idea must be examined critically. The first figure that Feingold uses to bolster his thesis is John Dee, who is by any estimate a most untypical figure.[17] As regards Robert Fludd, we are on surer ground, but we are talking about a completely different milieu – the Oxford of the 1590s and, later, the continent. As for Sir John Cheke and Sir Thomas Smith, whom Feingold calls Dee's 'patrons', it is hard to know how much of his occult enthusiasms it is permissible to project on to them.[18] Again, Feingold's claim that 'for the rest of his life, Harvey devoted much time to the mathematical sciences as well as to the occult sciences' may be an overstatement. Mathematical and astrological works are easily the least significant works among his books, though that is not to say that he did not annotate these interestingly too.[19] When we read further that 'Harvey's relationship with Smith almost certainly contributed to these interests', one notes the hesitant formulation of that 'almost' and the vagueness of the word 'relationship'. John Caius, with (if Harvey is to be believed) his manuscript of secret transcriptions of conjurations, is a good example of a prominent university figure involved in magic, and Feingold rightly gives him due prominence; but he is the exception rather than the rule (and, in any case, when one actually looks at the manuscript one discovers that it is in fact a seventeenth-century copy which purports to have been copied from Caius's original).[20] The very fact that these conjurations were secret should also give us pause.

There are other figures, some of whom Feingold mentions, such as Christopher Heydon and Thomas Hood. Chronology is crucial here, though, for Heydon's defence of astrology was published twenty years after he graduated in the early years of the following century, and Hood's unpublished manuscript on astrology dates from 1595.[21] Any attempts to tie Howard into a tradition existent in 1560 look rather implausible. The fiery St John's Puritan William Fulke is another figure used to bolster the

---

[17] Feingold, 'Occult Tradition', p. 80.
[18] Feingold, 'Occult Tradition', p. 87.
[19] Popper, 'The English Polydaedali: How Gabriel Harvey Read late Tudor London', pp. 351–81.
[20] BL Additional MS 36674.
[21] Christopher Heydon, *Defence of Judicial Astrologie*, Cambridge: John Legat, 1603 (all the more relevant, too, that it was Thomas Bredon, another figure from outside the university environment – he was in fact a vicar – who collaborated with Heydon on his work); Thomas Hood's treatise on astrology may be found in BL Additional MSS 71494 and 71495.

notion about occult and astrological knowledge in the universities.[22] Feingold notes that in 1560 Fulke had published an attack on astrology (the *Anti-prognosticon*), but then goes on to suggest that after his return to Cambridge in 1563 he 'allowed himself to come under the influence of NeoPlatonic elements in scientific thought'. Feingold is here relying on earlier scholarship that does not have the precision or depth of his own. NeoPlatonism in 1560 was far from having any necessary connection with occult studies, though one could better understand that connection when looked at from the perspective of, say, the 1620s. One figure that Feingold omits is William Gilbert, who does seem to have engaged in, for example, observations of comets while he was at St John's as early as 1569.[23]

These doubts centre particularly around Cambridge; there is perhaps slightly surer evidence for Oxford. Feingold is correct to emphasize Richard Forster and William Camden.[24] Howard's connections, of course, were with Cambridge and the picture is not at all clear here. Feingold cites the example of Henry Spelman and his astrological studies.[25] The references, however, are misleading. By far the greater part of the volume Feingold cites is given over, in fact, to an account of the common law and recent cases in Norfolk.[26] There is, by contrast, only the briefest section on astrology: six folios on the properties of the planets (hardly recondite material, and which appears to derive from the Italian writer Guido Bonatti); five pages of diagrams plotting character traits; an astrological poem; and a very short discussion of domification.[27]

The picture of Elizabethan astrology and the occult is, then, rather more sparsely populated than the one drawn by Feingold. I do not wish to discuss the wide diffusion of basic astrological principles that one finds in poetry and the almanacs.[28] The absence of much sophistication in the university environment is, rather, the point to underscore. Consider, for exam-

---

[22] Feingold, 'Occult Tradition', p. 83, relying on R. Braukham, 'Science and Religion in the Writings of Dr William Fulke', *British Journal for the History of Science*, 1975, pp. 17–31.
[23] S. Kelly, *The De mundo of William Gilbert*, Amsterdam, 1965, p. 17.
[24] For Camden, see BL Cotton MS, Julius F XI, ff. 70–1.
[25] Feingold, 'Occult Tradition', pp. 93–4 and n. 66.
[26] BL Harleian MS 6360, ff. 32–133.
[27] Domification tract: ibid., ff. 16^r–21^v; the short poem: f. 2^r. An edition of the domification material would be a worthwhile service to scholarship.
[28] See, for example, the work of B. Capp, *Astrology and the Popular Press: English Almanacs 1500–1800*, London, 1979. For other general works on astrology (not belonging to the genre of intellectual history as such, but rather to the field of cultural or social history) in early modern England, see Patrick Curry, *Prophecy and Power: Astrology in Early Modern England*, Cambridge, 1989, and, most recently, if somewhat tangentially, the highly successful Lauren Kassell, *Medicine and Magic in Elizabethan England*, Oxford, 2005.

ple, some short tables by Richard Forster, a mid-century medic and fellow of All Souls.[29] The Forster manuscript was presented to Jane, elder daughter of Henry Fitzalan, twelfth earl of Arundel. Forster created these tables by slight alteration of previously existing ones, already printed.[30] These tables existed for many latitudes and it was but basic mathematics to move the latitudes around so that the fixed stars position at different hours and minutes in different constellations of the zodiac could be calculated. Forster's sidereal tables are constructed for the latitude and longitude of 51.34, a point too far south of Oxford for them to be of any use to Forster himself, and therefore perhaps of use to the Lady Lumley in one of her estates in Buckinghamshire. Forster clearly suggests that Lumley (or someone in her circle) will be employing them for the purposes of judicial astrology.[31] Since, however, Forster later revised this work and published it, the engagement with astrological thought (if any) was carried on among the houses of the nobles rather than the university environment – since its origin was that of the noble patronage context.[32]

So while it is difficult to see Oxford and Cambridge as centres of astrological learning, let alone the wider gamut of occult practices which are the focus of Howard's attack, there were perhaps other nodes of scientific and occult interest. One such network existed around the household of the Earl of Northumberland. It is in great houses like this that astrological influence should be looked for and not in the compulsorily orthodox atmosphere of the universities. The increasing sophistication of the theoretical undergirding of the 'practical' scientific interests of practitioners in the city of London should also be given its due weight.[33] It is noteworthy that when, in 1595, William Covell, a doctor of theology, published his attack on astrology in Cambridge, he explicitly addressed it to Oxford, Cambridge and the Inns of Court, the three 'daughters of England'. Moreover, his source throughout this

---

[29] BL MS Royal 12 E II, ff. 1–27ᵛ.
[30] E.g., BL Additional MS 34,603 ff. 2–17ᵛ, and Oronce Finé, *The Rules and Ryghte Ample Documents Touching the Use and Practise of the Common Almanackes which are Named Ephemerides*, tr. Humfrey Baker, London: Thomas Marshe, 1555 (and reprinted in 1570).
[31] BL MS Royal 12 E II f. 2ᵛ: 'quia utilitatem maximam ad iudicialem Astrologiam a[dquaes]esissse animadverti' (I owe the emendation within the square brackets to Jill Kraye). Whether they were in fact so used, it is not possible to say.
[32] R. Forster, *Ephemerides meteographicae*, London: John Kyngston, 1575.
[33] See Stephen Pumfrey, 'Science and Patronage in Early Modern England 1570–1625', *History of Science*, 2004, pp. 137–88, with very voluminous bibliography on patronage, though much of the key material he treats dates from after the date of the publication of the *Defensative*. Pumfrey's article perhaps over-emphasizes the extent to which social context provides a grid to determine intellectual content.

treatise is not any of the Latin works with which he might have been familiar from the university milieu, but rather Howard's vernacular *Defensative*.[34]

We should be clear about the distinction between producers and consumers of astrological/occult and scientific material. As the reign of Elizabeth drew to a close, scientific knowledge was as much about being involved in certain groups and practices as it was about a series of 'discoveries' among its producers. It is the great houses where we see the coherent collection of both practice and knowledge and in the various practically focused intellectual groupings of scientific interest in London (such as Humphrey Gilbert's Academy, Gresham College, or, most famously, Sir Francis Bacon's intellectual programme in the *Advancement of Learning*) that we find scientific and, to an extent, occult and astrological interest.[35] It is not in the universities of the 1560s and 1570s. With this historical restriction in mind, we turn to see the broad basis of Howard's critique. It is crucial to understand the overall structure and organization of the *Defensative*, since this is part of the formal aspect of the text, as important for a proper understanding of the past as the purposes, both stated and to be inferred, for which the *Defensative* was written. This, in other words, is simply to say that we should read the most rhetorical of Howard's works, rhetorically.

Howard lists the sorts of people who will not like his work:

> The first sort, setting downe their iudgement touching any matter, looke not in the subiect, but the Writer that discourseth thereupon, and that with such a partiall and preiudicate conceite, as Battus shalbe sooner crowned with Lawrell, if he bear their Livery, than Homer with an ivy garland, if he write not in their honour. If the person whom they like not for particular offence, be found to flourish in discourse, they charge him with too much abounding in his words (though Cicero preferre a wit, from which we may detract, before that whereunto we shall be faine to adde), if he gather and conclude his reasons in a narrow roome, they touch him with obscurity accoording to their manner, which as one writes, *Nec brevia valent intellegere, nec prolixa amant legere* ...[36]

The second sort accuses writers of theft, and as proof against this charge Howard has attempted to give accurate citations for the authorities he uses.[37] In this paranoid preface, Howard reuses what was obviously a

---

[34] W. Covell, *Polimanteia*, Cambridge: John Legate, 1595.
[35] For Humphrey Gilbert's clarion call, see BL Lansdowne MS 98, ff. 2–9; for Gresham, see *Sir Thomas Gresham and Gresham College Studies in the Intellectual History of London in the Sixteenth and Seventeenth Centuries*, ed. F. Ames-Lewis, Aldershot, 1999.
[36] *Defensative*, sig. A4^r.
[37] Ibid., sig. A4^v.

favourite quotation from Cicero (for he wrote it years earlier on the frontispiece to his edition of *Il cortegiano*): 'It is a rule in Cicero, that of all men those are most unfitte to iudge, *Qui aut invident aut favent*.'[38] He continues that, though he will abide by the judgement of those who know better in each of the disciplines on which his discourse touches (philosophy, civil law and divinity), those who criticize must be wary that they do so with good reasons.[39] The rhetorical imprint of what will count as proof comes to the fore in Howard's statement that the best way of dealing with these criticisms will be 'to oppose one cause against another, *ut & causa cum causa certet*', since Howard's Latin tag derives (almost certainly) from one of Cicero's speeches.[40] This is less a patient examination of a topic than a gladiatorial display. The centrality of the rhetorical and polemical approach cannot be doubted and, indeed, to look at the work in isolation from this context and to regard it merely as a contribution to the Renaissance critique of astrology strips the work of much that is significant and interesting about it.

The main body of the *Defensative* opens with a tale which derives from Homer's *Odyssey* (or, perhaps more likely, some Renaissance mythological compendium or similar work) about those perverse humans (such as Odysseus's companion Gryllus) who prefer not to use their reason.[41] This exordium sets up the main theme of Howard's work, aiming his critique less at the intellectual failures of astrology as a system than the reasons why such a flawed system has been successful. Characteristically, Howard interprets this failure as an absence of gratitude toward God. Not only do humans do wrong in not exercising their reason, since that is part of their inheritance from God (with whom we share this faculty of thought), but such wrongdoing is readily understood 'as it falleth out by dayly proofe among our selves, that nothing slippeth out of memory, then the print of benefits received from our friendes'.[42] This theme of gratitude will resurface as a means of linking the duties of the subject to the duties of the godly. For in a later chapter he

---

[38] Ibid., sig. A5ʳ. See p. 000 for its occurrence in his *Il cortegiano* annotations.
[39] *Defensative*, sig. A5ʳ.
[40] Ibid., sig. A5ᵛ. The quotation derives from Cicero, *Pro Caelio*, 22.
[41] The most famous such work is Giovanbattista Gelli, *Circe*, Florence: Lorenzo Torrentino, 1549. There was an English translation: *Circes of G B Gello, Florentyne, translated out of Italyon into Englishe, by H Iden, B. L.*, London: J. Cawoode, 1557. It should be pointed out that starting one's discourse with a fabula was entirely in keeping with that basic manual of Renaissance prose amplification, the Progymnasmata of Aphthonius. Behind Gelli is Plutarch's entertaining dialogue (usually called Gryllus): Plutarch, *Bruta animalia ratione utantur*, Cologne, 1522. This work of Plutarch has a greater fortuna than is sometimes realized and a study of its reception is required.
[42] *Defensative*, sig. B3ᵛ.

notes that it is precisely the psychology of the ungrateful person which accounts for both the seeking after secret knowledge and the danger in such persons attempting to second guess the fortunes of kings.[43]

His own description of the 'method' that he will employ in the work (which seems to mean nothing more than order) is: he will give reasons why men believe these practices (which boil down to a religious justification – that men will seek after knowledge that God has in fact not vouchsafed them – and a social criterion – namely that men are desirous of being deceived); next he will disprove the basis of these practices; then he will give reasons why these false prophets are not to be suffered 'in a godly Common-wealth'; and, finally, he will launch a full attack on prophecies which have seduced the vulgar sort.[44] It is quite clear that Howard's emphasis is on the political danger that these persons pose, though of course he must also refute the practices of which he complains. This is, again, wholly in accord with the early modern rhetorical notion that a number of elements, including considerations of character, go toward making a proof persuasive.[45] Interestingly, Howard draws a parallel, doubtless mindful of his 1574 attack on the Presbyterians, between the political danger of the prophets and astrologers on the one hand, and that of those who discuss the early church for the purpose of subverting 'just authoritie' on the other.[46]

Previously to Howard there were three main strands of critique of astrology in Renaissance England, as on the continent: the godly, the legal/political and the philosophical/technical.[47] Howard's achievement in the *Defensative* is to weave these strands, for the first time in English, into a

---

[43] Ibid., sigs F3ʳ–F4ʳ.
[44] Ibid., sig. B4ᵛ. For the idea that it is man's lack of faith in God that spawns these practices, see sig. C3ʳ. For the description of men (where the social criterion of their 'vulgar' state comes out clearly) as simply being too given over to credulity see sig. D2ʳ.
[45] See, conveniently, R. W. Serjeantson, 'Testimony and Proof in Early Modern England', *Studies in the History and Philosophy of Science*, 30, 1999, pp. 195–236.
[46] *Defensative*, sig. G2ʳ⁻ᵛ.
[47] For the godly critique, see the material below on Calvin, though one should take due note (from a different religious standpoint) of the blistering attack on astrology penned by Savonarola, which has some parallels with that of Calvin: Girolamo Savonarola, *Contro gli astrologi*, ed. C. Pompeo Faracovi, Rome, 2000; for the legal/political critique, which subdivides into the danger posed by astrology to the common good and danger to the monarch, see the various laws passed against astrology (see the convenient conspectus in Dunn, 'Status', Appendices). The *locus classicus* for the philosophical critique is, of course, Pico and such figures as Thomas Erastus, the Swiss medic (whom Howard cites: *Defensative*, sig. Q4ᵛ). One should also point out that Erastus wrote an explicit defence of Savonarola: *Defensio libelli Hieronymi Savonarolae in astrologiam divinatricem adversus Christophorum Stathmionem* [Paris]: Jean Le Preux, 1569 – this then the most likely direct route for the 'godly' critique then in Howard.

coherent persuasive whole.[48] The closest contemporary example that he had in front of him is probably the work of Thomas Erastus, who used the fluent and easily modulating humanist genre of epistolography to attack astrological theory and practice, and thereby showed Howard a way of dealing with a range of different modes of critique but with a unifying tone, genre and style.[49] Although Howard was in the end to choose a slightly different means to effect his aim (one, as we shall see, more indebted to the copious style and to the epideictic mode), it was plausibly Erastus who functioned as the closest model.[50] Howard draws on what we might term the 'godly' critique of man's disposition to believe in astrology in his earlier chapters. The most widely diffused example of this critique in the Northern Renaissance, prior to Howard, was probably that of Jean Calvin.[51] Howard's themes are very close to those of Calvin: God's purposes are fundamentally unknowable and those sometimes grant to the wicked their desires, or so it seems, just as he sometimes allows the good to go unrewarded.[52] This emphasis on the unknowability of God's purposes and the difficulty of using the terrestrial analogies of influence for the way that the superlunary world affects the sublunary one surfaces in less godly aspects of the critique: it is this sceptical attitude to the expansion of certain (accepted within most brands of Aristotelianism) ways of discussing natural causation to inappropriate spheres that forms the cornerstone of Howard's attack.[53] This attack, however, is corroborated (and perhaps

[48] I am not aware of an earlier published attack on astrology in England that so clearly does this.
[49] Thomas Erastus, *De astrologia diviniatrice epistole*, Basel: Grynaeus, 1580 (the work was published close enough in time to the date of the *Defensative* to also make it plausible as a source).
[50] One should be clear that Howard's work, unlike Erastus's, is not aimed, being a vernacular work, at an international scholarly audience.
[51] Jean Calvin, *Advertissement contre l'astrologie qu'on appelle judiciare, et autres curiosités qui règnent aujourdhuis dans le monde*, ed. O. Millet, Geneva, 1985 (first published 1549; there was a Latin translation, *Admonitio adversus astrologiam quam judiciariam vocant*, by François Hotman, then secretary of Calvin). An English translation (*An Admonition against Astrology Judicial and Other Curiosities that Rayne in the World*) was put together by the noted Puritan Godfrey Gilby and published in London without a date. See, in general, *Divination et controverse réligeuse en France au XVIe siècle*, ed. N. Cazauran, Paris, 2002. Much of Howard's emphasis on how little man does or ought to know can be paralleled in Calvin.
[52] *Defensative*, sig. D2ᵛ. Howard continues: 'That whensoever we crave any thing of God, with zealous prayer and sincere repentaunce for our sinnes, which is both fit for us to receive, and for him to give, Aut dabit, aut quod novit esse utilius: eyther he will grant the same which we require, or what he knows by providence to bee more profitable.'
[53] It leads to the position outlined in N. Jardine, 'Scepticism in Renaissance Astronomy: A Preliminary Study' in *Scepticism From the Renaissance to the Enlightenment*, eds R. H. Popkin and C. B. Schmitt, Wiesbaden, 1987, pp. 84–102.

inspired) in Howard's work not only by an emphasis on the innate folly of the crowd, but also by drawing on a particular historiographical tradition. It is a consistent feature of the surviving writings of Tacitus and of Thucydides's *History of the Peloponesian War* that the reader is presented with the participants' occlusion from or uncertainty about the true causes of events.[54] This is a novel feature of Howard's critique; it certainly does not feature in any of the attacks on astrology published in the previous couple of decades or so, and may be linked to the rise in popularity of, in particular, Tacitus in the latter years of the sixteenth century.[55]

Time and again the works of Tacitus and Thucydides are drawn upon to function as a historical analogue to the theological and epistemological limits on knowledge that were more familiar to any reader of Renaissance polemics directed against the science of the stars. Sometimes, it is simply a matter of Howard's using the texts of both authors to prove points rather removed from this delimitation of human knowledge and aspiration.[56] At others, he uses Tacitus to bolster a more fundamental point, such as the replacement of the true causes of historical events with mysterious ones.[57] 'For though we be forewarned of those dangers and mishaps which are

---

[54] See Thucydides, *History of the Peloponnesian War*, II. 3; 6; 13; 17; 47; 54 (tr. Rex Warner, London, 1954, pp. 125, 128, 132, 135, 152, 156), for some examples from just one book of man's inability to interpret signs or predict the future or the uselessness of human skill in the face of unexpected events.

[55] For a recent conspectus on the turn toward Tacitus in England, see Blair Worden, 'Court Centred Politics and the Use of Roman Historians, 1590–1620', in *Culture and Politics in Early Stuart England*, eds K. Sharpe and P. Lake, Basingstoke, 1994, pp. 21–43, esp. 25 and n. 19.

[56] E.g. *Defensative*, sig. D3ᵛ: 'as Tacitus supposeth the first, *in adulationem praesentis potentiae*' [= Lactantius, *Divinae institutiones*, I.15 – Jill Kraye pointed out this reference – and cf. Quintillian, *Institutio oratoria*, XII.10.13: ' postea vero quam triumvirali proscriptione consumptus est, passim qui oderant, qui invidebant, qui aemulabantur, adulatores etiam praesentis potentiae non responsurum invaserunt'] in discussing foolish men; sig. D3ᵛ: 'And againe saith Tacitus, *uti mos est vulgi fortuita ad culpam trahunt* [=*Annales*, IV.64]'; sig. E1ᵛ: 'Much after the same sort, one Arantius a Roman was said to speak upon his death bed, *more vatum* [*Annales*, VI]'; sig. E3ʳ: '*Nunquam enim temeritas &c* [the marginalium reads *Annales* III but this seemingly derives from Cicero, *Pro Marcello*, 7]. 'For never temerity is coupled with true wisedome, nor chance called into Cownsell touching matters of great moment'; sig. F2ʳ: an example of Tacitus doubting the miraculous explanation of bubbles in the Euphrates (see *Annales*, XV); sig. F3ʳ, for men's propensity to believe the worst: '*unde nulla innocentia cura, sed vitae impunitatis* [the marginalium reads *Histories*, III, but this derives in fact from *Histories*, I.72].

[57] E.g., *Defensative*, sig. F1ʳ: 'Cerealis, as we read in Tacitus [*Annales*, XIV], was wont to impute all overthwartes ... to <u>Destiny</u>'; ibid.: 'it was no rare or dainty practice with Tiberius, to wrest the smallest opportunity ... to the course of private benefit'; ibid.: 'Were not Sibylline oracles abused in the vilest manner, howsoever some esteemed them as Registers of the Commonwealth, and Kalendars of <u>destiny</u>?' (emphasis mine).

decreed by destiny; yet can we not eschew the trappe'.[58] A central point about the accepting the political status quo is that, according to the Roman historian, 'Ignoramus enim quid conducat nobis in vita nostra'.[59] No other ancient historian is relied on as heavily as Tacitus (Sallust, for example, is not mentioned at all). His use of Thucydides is more sparing than that of Tacitus, but more focused on the issue of the internal inconsistency of prophets and the more general difficulty in knowing what is the relation between an event and its cause, which is perhaps one of the most signal themes of Thucydides' work.[60]

> Thus may we take our leave of all contingents, and of fortune their Soveraigne: which having none other vassailes, over whom to raigne and exercise her tyranny, then such as are not otherwise at all, then (in conceit) must rest content with that precinct and liberty which a wise man in Thucidides affordeth her: *Quid enim fortuna aliud est, quam verae causae ignoratio?*[61]

It is this history of man's inability to discern the course of historical events that Howard produces which sets the context for what one might refer to as the more philosophical element of Howard's attack on astrology. In many ways, this is the least interesting aspect of the *Defensative*. Certainly, the attack at this point is at its least original: all of the arguments (from twins, from secondary causes and so on) had been put together in different formats in earlier, often more technical, works.[62] Howard rarely dwells long on a philosophical point before putting it in either a religious or political context:

> [T]hough some people think some things are merely contingently related, they are in fact determined in the providence of God: 'Hee guideth all things, not by that golden chaine of causes, linked one within another in such a manner as they cannot slip, whereof the Stoyke dreame: but by the rule of order, which directeth our attempts to the scope of his owne pleasure.[63]

---

[58] *Defensative*, sig. G4ʳ: A translation of 'Quae enim satis sunt, etiam praesignificata non vitantur.'

[59] Ibid., sig. F4ᵛ, which Howard translates as 'For we know not what is fittest for us in our life'. This appears not to be an authentic reference to Tacitus, though, just as significantly, Howard thought it was.

[60] E.g. *Defensative*, sig. F1ʳ: 'Thucidides reporteth the Prophets of his time, *Cantasse varia & inter se differentia*'.

[61] Sig. G3ʳ. I have not traced the Latin translation of Thucydides that is the source of this tag.

[62] For the development of the critique of astrology in the Renaissance see Steven vanden Broeke, *The Limits of Influence: Pico, Louvain and the Crisis of Renaissance Astrology*, Leiden, 2003.

[63] *Defensative*, sig. G3ᵛ.

All of this comes in what is broadly the introduction to Howard's more detailed discussion of each of the forms of irrational practice which he attacks; it sets out the basic nature of his critique (of which there are two main elements, one theological, or better, godly, and the other politico-cum-historical). It is only within this context, as well as the account of why men behave in this way, that we receive 'philosophical' or logical arguments which Howard has culled from earlier authors. The highly wrought style of the work is another useful indication that it departs from the tradition of the philosophical treatise and is, again, an invitation to read it rhetorically.

Historians are properly allergic to the use of the word 'rationalism' in writing about practices and belief structures of the past which appear to discount the supernatural and the marvellous. It has been shown time and again that the supposedly rational account relies on, or is put in the service of, an agenda with a variety of belief presuppositions often as 'irrational', at least by modern lights, as the objects of its attack. To begin with such retrojected abstractions as 'rationalism' is in any case a rather poor way to engage with, and make sense of, the large body of Renaissance material in which 'reason' – or 'ratio' and its various cognates, Latin and vernacular – are put forward to defend or attack a given position taken by one's opponent. The word opponent is justly employed, for these works often arise from particular disputes. To put it another way, we are to view the appeal to reason in works from the Renaissance which seemingly decry irrational or superstitious practice as one of a number of ways in which an author makes persuasive arguments within the context of a particular rhetorical, often polemical, purpose. These arguments were sometimes be taken from *logos*, sometimes from *pathos* and sometimes from *ethos*, just as Aristotle had long ago noted, and his Renaissance inheritors continued to affirm.[64] Ratio, then, or *logos*, simply indicates a mode of rhetorical proof (admittedly, often with strong connections to the stricter procedures of logic – one way in which the human mind's cognitive capacities provide the rhetorician with material).

Howard, naturally, makes reason central to his argument in the *Defensative*: for, as we have seen, the work is introduced by the fable of Circe and Gryllus. Reason is the capacity to engage in the sorts of argumentative procedure that distinguish men from beasts. After the general description of the reasons why men engage in astrology and like practices, and after the contextualization of the godly and then the historical and hence political critique of human knowledge, Howard moves on to provide

---

[64] See Aristotle, *Rhetoric*, I.2, 1356a 2–4.

more detailed arguments by which to refute the internal coherence of each of the various forms of 'prophecy'.[65] The introduction to this second section of the work takes the form of a praise of human reason and then proceeds to a discussion of the theory of sense-perception. The connection between these two commonplace lines of argument is interesting: Howard cites St Augustine (from a passage that I have not traced) that although

> reason is a gift conferred, not uppon this man or that, but upon kinde of men in Genere; yet our owne experience, which is the surest guide, instructeth us that neither all men, nor any man ... hath either grace or gift to prophecie.[66]

Howard uses Augustine precisely because it is rather hard to find the connection between a general encomium of reason and the more technical point that follows. This forms the prelude to an argument (or rather tag) taken from Aristotle's *De anima*: *Nihil est in intellectu quod non fuerit prius in sensu*.[67] Howard's version in fact makes reference to the notion of the common sense, in other words, the faculty which combines the sense impressions.[68] It should be pointed out that this does not make Howard an 'empiricist' for two reasons: firstly, he allows the possibility of innate ordering devices (the common sense) in the human soul and, secondly, he allows the implantation by God (in approving a passage translated from Aristotle, so he says) of 'formes and figures of all outward things in our understanding'.[69] Howard describes how the active intellect possesses certain 'beames' by which it 'gives a cleere light to the passive understanding'. This does not, however, extend to insights based around future sense impressions since the future 'was never lodged in the common sence, nor transported by the fantasie'.[70] This psychological account of the impossibility of prophecy is immediately tempered by the notion that, of course, divinely inspired prophecies are in fact possible, for providence can get around this distinc-

---

[65] *Defensative*, sig. H1^r.
[66] *Defensative*, sig. H2^r.
[67] Howard's formulation is in fact in English: sig. H2^r: 'Philosophy doth teach that nothing is in Intellectu, which hath not first been drawne from common sence.' The phrase is Aristotelian rather than actually found in Aristotle: see P. Cranefield, 'On the Origin of the Phrase, "Nihil est in intellectu quod non prius fuerit in sensu"', *Journal of the History of Medicine and Allied Sciences*, 25, 1970, pp. 36–47 (I thank Jill Kraye for this reference).
[68] For the Aristotelian background, see K. D. Park, 'The Organic Soul', in the *Cambridge History of Renaissance Philosophy*, eds Q. Skinner, E. Kessler and C. B. Schmitt, Cambridge, 1988, pp. 464–84, at 470–1.
[69] *Defensative*, sig. H2^r.
[70] Ibid.

tion for it is through providence that God can see all things simultaneously; therefore only through God's 'extraordinary grace and favour', operating outside of the notion of an art or science with rules based on the disciplines of the arts curriculum, can any knowledge of future events become viable.[71] This account allows him to draw on the Stoics, who held planted the 'pallace of τὰς προνοίας above the Moone'. Thus Howard can make the connection between the delimiting of sublunary causation, which was long associated with the critique of astrology, and forms of prophecy, which in fact takes up the remainder of his works.

However indebted to the traditions of astrological critique of Pico and others, it was rather the instruction in the trivial arts of rhetoric and dialectic which allowed the broader polemical thrust of Howard's *Defensative*.[72] Indeed, it was his own, perhaps original, interest in the histories of Tacitus and Thucydides that provided Howard with much that was distinctive and effective in the work. This broader focus was the result not only of the larger audience (including his own English political enemies) whom Howard hoped to persuade, but also due to the absence, at least in Cambridge, of any very well-documented tradition of occult and astrological interest, let alone instruction, upon which Howard could draw. One may contrast (and here we return to the issue of rhetoric and to the scope, degree and quality of 'technical' astrological knowledge in the universities with which we began) Howard's broadly conceived 'historical' and 'political' and 'philosphical' critique of astrology with the 'technical' defences launched by, most obviously, John Harvey, whose defence of his brother Richard's earlier work is couched in the internalist reasonings that would have been familiar to any true believer.[73] The question of whether or not to defend or attack astrology from 'within' or 'without' can be seen as one of the ongoing debates surrounding astrologers in the wake of Pico's demolition of the discipline.[74] Once again, we see both the importance of the more porous aspects of the Renaissance arts curriculum in shaping Howard's critique as well as the ways in which that curriculum, especially rhetoric, allowed its students a wider platform upon which to argue and to persuade than was

---

[71] The reference to grace should be lingered over. It is important to understand that much that looked like the foretelling of the future was, for the Christian, in fact dependent on the operation of unearned grace: see Augustine, *De natura et gratia*.

[72] The standard edition is Giovanni Pico della Mirandola, *Disputationes adversus astrologiam divinatricem*, ed. E. Garin, 2 vols, Florence, 1946–1952.

[73] John Harvey, *An Astrologicall Addition or Supplement to be annexed to the late Discourse upon the Great Conjunction of Saturne, and Jupiter*, London: Richard Watkins, 1583, passim.

[74] See, especially, Broecke, *The Limits of Influence*.

available to the student of syllogistic logic alone, or to the writers of the more 'philosphical' treatises upon which the *Defensative* depends.

One good example of this deals with the question of the legitimation that its history brings to a disputed discipline. The myth of historical origins, and hence legitimate authority, of astrology among the Chaldees had been popular among the discipline's practitioners. Howard subjected it to the sort of historical enquiry that humanists were accustomed to bringing to the past.[75] Just as Howard chose a broad-based attack on the Presbyterians, so here, too, he engages in arguments culled from the well-stocked storehouse of his humanist education, across all of the disciplines, united by the *artes sermocinales*, to achieve his conjoint intellectual and political purpose. This was helped, however, by his isolation from the more cutting-edge technical aspects of the debate both in London and across the continent. Howard was soon, however, to experience isolation of a much more direct and personal character.

---

[75] This point is well-made and backed up (with contrasting references to the Harveys) by Dunn, 'Status', p. 69. Behind Howard here is Pico: see Anthony Grafton, *Joseph Scaliger: A Study in the History of the Classical Tradition. I: Textual Criticism and Exegesis*, Oxford, 1983, pp. 217–22.

Chapter 7

'NO TERMINATION BUT *IN VOCATIVO*' FAILURE, VOTARY AND CIVILIAN

> If you call to minde how longe and like a *non proficit* I have declined this noun *tempus per omnes casus et per omnia tempora* either you must deeme me as I must esteeme myself as a verie bad grammarian that can make no termination but *in vocativo*.[1]

NO TERMINATION but *in vocativo*. The vocative is the case-ending of the Latin noun used to denote a relationship of address. Howard's learned phrasing does not attempt to conceal the unpalatable truth: his politics can only be the rhetorical politics of address. We have seen that Howard's *Defensative* was dedicated to Walsingham; but dedications do not a loyalist make. If Howard hoped to escape further arrest by means of his penmanship, he was wrong, as his encounter with Henry Carey was to prove. Carey was a busy man.[2] He had consistently held the queen's favour, and she rewarded him with abundant duties. He was the chief commissioner in a range of anti-Catholic (or 'treasonous') trials in the latter part of the 1580s and was often involved in the execution of Catholics.[3] He was, however, no zealot. He had shown himself in favour of the marriage between Elizabeth and the Duc d'Anjou; still, on 11 December 1583, Henry Carey was engaged in an interrogation, for Howard once again was in trouble.[4] To

---

[1] Henry Howard to Sir Philip Sidney, DUL Howard MS 5, f. 40^v.
[2] Henry Carey, ?1524–1596. His mother, sister to Anne Boleyn, ensured early prominence at court. Elizabeth made him Lord Hunsdon in 1558/9, granting him some lands in Kent in the process.
[3] Including that of Philip Howard, Earl of Arundel.
[4] The date is that which another hand has written on to a crossed-out draft of Howard's examination contained at BL Cotton MS, Caligula C vii, ff. 349^r–350^r, at 349^r. There is a transcription of this document in *CSPSc*, Edinburgh, 1910, VI, pp. 675–6.

enable a better view of this examination, we need to consider the reasons, or suspicions, that led to Howard's arrest a month earlier. 'Gunpowder, treason and plot': only gunpowder was missing from this trinity on 5 November 1583. Whose treason, however? And who were the real plotters? Sir Thomas Leighton banged on the door of Henry Howard's residence and promptly arrested him.[5] This was the culmination of several months' surveillance of Castelnau and the interception of his correspondence with Mary. The evidence was not firm, but merely suspicious. Francis Walsingham was told that on 29 April 1583 that Lord Howard had visited Salisbury Court for a midnight meeting with Castelnau.[6] The writer of this letter was Henri Fagot, whose reliability as to this rendezvous, and the information that subsequently passed between the two men, may be disputed.[7] The letter reports that Howard had heard of a Scot being kept within Salisbury Court for fear of imprisonment since the Scot had been found in the home of an Irishman who was subsequently put in prison.[8] The absence of names means that, if names were ever mentioned to Fagot, he did not catch or recognize them (or their pronunciation – Fagot is clearly not English). This letter was the follow-up (perhaps there were others) to an earlier one in which Fagot explained that the chief agents of Mary were Throckmorton and Howard.[9] This is the first evidence from Fagot of Howard's suspect contacts with the French ambassador. If they had not been suspicious, why were they conducted at midnight?

Howard's dealings with the ambassador and, through him, with Mary, must long have been suspected. The whiff of disloyalty that attended his

---

[5] On the identity of the arresting office, see Bossy, *UTM*, p. 80–1 n. 49, and see the same note for the (slight) uncertainty over the dating of Howard's arrest.
[6] BL Cotton MS, Caligula, C vii f. 214.
[7] On the issue of the identity of Fagot, see Bossy, *GB*; Bossy, *UTM* (with my review of the latter).
[8] Bossy, *GB*, p. 191 n. 3 thinks that the reference may be to one M. Huton, who is referred to later on in the correspondence.
[9] BL Cotton MS, Caligula, C vii f. 211. Transcription available in Bossy, *GB*, pp. 197–9 (where Bossy also gives details of other copies and two earlier transcriptions). The dating of this letter is controversial (see Jill Kraye's review of Bossy, *GB*, in *The Heythrop Journal*, 33, 1992, pp. 324–7), and I only wish to add one detail. Bossy argues that since BL Cotton MS, Caligua C vii f. 214ᵛ contains the phrase 'Henry [Howard], a Roman Catholic and Papist', it introduces Howard since it gives this additional information. However, Bossy's translation is mildly tendentious. The manuscript has 'Henry Catholic romain et Papiste' without the intervening indefinite article. I suggest that without this article the four words after 'Henry' move away from being a new piece of information presented to the reader, and become something more in the way of a titular epexegesis: 'Henry, [sc. being] Roman Catholic and Papist'. Given Fagot's peculiar French, however, arguments like this cannot give much comfort either way.

name was well-known and, sometime in early July 1583, Howard was brought in for questioning.[10] We do not know why, but this generalized suspicion is important. There would, however, soon come into the arena fresh evidence of Howard's treasonous intents, though it looks like there was, until the final capture of letters, at least as much suspicion circling round Arundell.[11] A little later William Shelley was sent for (along with Courcelles and one Lymbeck) and was arrested.[12] The next entry in the office diary gives the instruction 'to pass the lord henry howards letter'.[13] On the following page of the diary (I have not been able to confirm if this was written on a subsequent date) there is an entry reading 'for the examination of W Shelley and the L H Howard'.[14] This was presumably the first stage in putting together the information that was needed for the full examination of Howard on 10 December. Which letter this might be, we cannot say. As we have seen, there are assorted references to Howard in the correspondence passed between Castelnau and Mary (and that found its way into Walsingham's hands) and some of this information came after the time of this, Howard's first 1583 questioning.[15] One letter (dated by Bossy 24 August) requests the ambassador to keep him informed of the negotiations at Sheffield, when all others are not.[16] She also sends with the letter a ring, a replacement for an earlier gift which had got lost, a ring whose existence was to cause distinct difficulties for Howard at his next interroga-

---

[10] BL Harleian MS 6035, f. 20^v. Bossy (*UTM*, p. 67) also has this reference but has missed (or, more probably, decided not to deal with) the other references to Howard that this manuscript contains (though he does use it elsewhere (e.g. *UTM*, p. 81). The manuscript is a sort of 'office diary' of Walsingham. Bossy's explanation of why Howard was arrested is that one Feron passed on to Walsingham the fact that Howard had been corresponding with Mary. This does not seem quite enough, since there are no letters outstanding for this period.

[11] The name of Arundell is first in a list of points arising out of a letter recorded by Walsingham's office diary some time early in November (BL Harleian MS 6035, f. 37^v). The letters were couriered by one George More, though it is worthy of note that when More was brought in for questioning, so too was (ibid., f. 49^r) his brother Edward.

[12] BL Harleian MS 6035, ff. 40^r and 42^{r-v}. Shelley was later brought to Walsingham's house in Seething Lane (f. 44^r).

[13] Ibid., f. 43^r.

[14] Ibid., f. 44^r. Presumably, Shelley was examined again, since there is a further entry for 5 January 1584 that Shelley is to be examined. I should say that this is not the last reference to Howard in Walsingham's diary there is one further, rather enigmatic entry. At f. 54^v, the diary has two columns of names to which memos are to be sent; Howard's name heads the list of 'private' memos (there was another list of 'public' memos) which confirms Howard's suspicious but not evidentially corroborated role in the story.

[15] I am much endebted to Bossy's extremely valuable tabular chronology of these letters and their copies (Bossy, *UTM*, pp. 180–6).

[16] BL Harleian MS 1582, f. 320.

tion.[17] William Herle then stuck the knife in. He wrote a letter dated 15 November 1583 in which he attacked Howard directly, saying that he was a priest and that he was 'in the secret register of the popes cardynalls.'[18] Walsingham is unlikely to have believed so far-fetched a tale and the rest of Herle's letter contains not fresh information but rather a filter on things already known.

> Ytt is he that advised Simiers to procede by the papistes to establish his Monsieur here, and to purge religion by the blood of sondry of our gretest houses in England, and that he should stand stoutly to have the article of freedom for religion granted, for that her Majestie he sayd was nott resolved of whatt religion yett to be of, A voyce that savoured of his own Blasphemy, and vyle nature.[19]

The only new piece of information is that Howard foresees the execution of such nobles as Dudley as the price to pay for the projected revolution. Even this does not change the picture of Howard that we have. He presumably recognized that in any coup or change of monarch's confession, blood would flow through acts of confessional heroism that he himself found uncongenial. There is clearly animus against Howard; perhaps Herle was angered that he had not managed to entrap Howard through his machinations ten years earlier in the Ridolfi affair.[20] A few days later, Herle informed Burghley (perhaps having got nowhere with Walsingham) of a conversation he had had with a gentleman who recommended that Howard's work on judicial astrology be sent to the censor 'for that the said booke is consefed by some of good iudgement to conteyne sundrie heresies and spyces withall of treason, though somewhat closelie carryed as the

---

[17] Ibid. At this stage in the chronology, perhaps I should include Howard and Castelnau's attendance at dinner (12 June 1583) with Sir Edward Stafford (so Bossy, *UTM*, pp. 71–2, citing as evidence 'HMC Hatfield, iii, 3; Cecil Papers, 162, f. 105 [sic]'). The manuscript is not signed, not in Howard's hand, and does not otherwise identify Howard; therefore, though I am inclined to accept Bossy's identification, I relegate such acceptance to a footnote.

[18] BL Lansdowne MS 39, f. 190ᵛ.

[19] Ibid., transcription from Bossy, *GB*, pp. 202–3. Howard's backing of freedom of conscience (along with his support of Anjou) were hardly state secrets.

[20] For a good example of Herle's feelings towards Howard, see BL Cotton MS, Caligula C vii f. 206ʳ (a letter from Herle to Burghley dated [in a later hand] 23 November 1584; for the correct date of 23 November 1583, see Bossy, *GB*, p. 206): 'I am glad to knowe unto mi selfe, in respect of publyck securitye to our gracious soveraine that she is furnisshed with matter of her self to convynce the L H Howard criminalye, when pleaseth to extend it. His sprite otherwise is within no compasse of quiett dutye, and his owne side saye of that travailling mynde of his that aut non capiendus aut non relaxandus.'

author imagynes'.[21] Apart from anything else, it is hard to see what in the book would be controversial. In any case, Herle's first tirade against Howard was written several days *after* Howard (along with Throckmorton) had been arrested: Herle would not want to be seen to be doubting the validity of the arrest.

The reason for the arrest of 5 November and the subsequent examinations was the discovery of an incriminating letter of Castelnau's to Mary about Throckmorton.[22] It is rather unclear, however, why this letter should trigger the arrest of Howard. Indeed, in the 'official' account of the conspiracy, it is Throckmorton who gets the spotlight.[23] He was certainly the most illustrious of the contacts disclosed by the Castelnau–Mary correspondence, but he did not possess any lands (and, most especially, any seaports) into or across which the Catholic armies working for the 'Enterprise of England' could pass.[24] I suggest that his detention was driven by paranoia surrounding the slender evidence of the evident goodwill between himself and Mary. The queen was reluctant to authorize any heavier or more violent form of interrogation on her noble kinsman Howard. Walsingham, too, as he looked over the correspondence with Howard, may have come to more benign conclusions about him. It is interesting in this context to note that Walsingham ordered an inquiry into the assets of both Lord Paget and Arundell, but not those of Howard.[25]

---

[21] BL Lansdowne MS 39, f. 193^r. Bossy's suggestion that 'some of good iudgement' refers to Bruno seems highly unlikely: firstly, the letter reports what Herle has heard from one man 'as well qualifyied in state causes as devynitie' (which could hardly be Bruno, whose interest in political theory was minimal, and, though an ex-Dominican, his writings deal only tangenially with God in the traditional theological sense); and, secondly, the reference to 'some of good iudgment' seems to be the reported speech of the principal informant as the syntax ('for that the work ...') makes clear. The fact of Herle's authorship and evident bias against Howard also must be taken into account.

[22] Letter of 5 November 1583: TNA: PRO SP 53/12/62 (this is a copy made by Thomas Phelippes). A transcription is available in *CSPSc 1581–3*, p. 654. For more details, see Bossy, *UTM*, pp. 79–80, and see ibid., pp. 80–1, for convincing speculation on who provided the tip-off for this information.

[23] [Q. Z.], *A Discoverie of the Treasons Practiced and Attempted against the Queenes Maiestie by Francis Throckmorton*, [London], [1584].

[24] It was, after all, the list of favourable havens in England with which Throckmorton was found that was considered most dangerous to the government authorities. On the changing travel routes between Rome and England, see the excellent article by Bossy, 'Rome and the Elizabethan Catholics', pp. 135–49 at 135.

[25] BL Harleian MS 6035, f. 48^r: 'Charles Arundells goodes The L Pagetts goodes'. The same note recurs at f. 57^r (sometime early in 1584). I do not know whether this is merely an enquiry or also something like a seizure order. Howard is not mentioned in this regard, but less weight should be placed on this detail since he obviously had rather less in the way of assets than the other two.

But if Elizabeth (and Walsingham?) were perhaps convinced of Howard's lack of treasonous intent, others found his ostentatious private religious beliefs a step too far in the direction of tolerance. Sometime after his interrogation in December, he appears to have been moved. A letter dated 19 December 1583 informs us that Howard was in the house of Sir Ralph Sadler (1507–1587), Chancellor of the Duchy of Lancaster at this time and Privy Councillor. Sir Henry Neville (d. 1593) writes to Sir Nathaniel Bacon that Mary

> hathe greate frinds. Yow here how the Erle of Arondel is comendid to attend & Northumberland comitid to Mr Leyton but they wil do wel inoughe. My Lady of Arundel very moche detectid of Papistri. My Lord Hary is at Mr Sadlers whom I hope wil after a whil kis the Towr. He deservs it well. He prays dayly as lowd as he can crye, 'Ave Marya, Ave Marya'. I think to the Scots Quen he means ther wil som more matter fawl owt.[26]

Nothing more felonious ever did 'fawl owt', and Sadler's hopes came to nothing, though the mechanics of Howard's eventual release are a little unclear. Howard was not comfortable at Sadler's house. There was soon to be a written complement to his loud Marian invocations, various manuscript devotional and pentitential writings, which we will discuss shortly. Howard was also soliciting help, however, from less celestial directions: letters survive to several figures in which Howard pleads for assistance, for, as he wrote, letters are 'the onlie meanes now lefte to bewaile my miserie'.[27] He wrote to Walsingham, Sir Christopher Hatton and Burghley.[28] An appeal to Sir Philip Sidney, contained in a letter dated 27 August 1584, was perhaps more surprising given the strength of Sidney's opposition to the Anjou marriage project, evident in the *New Arcadia*.[29] Howard's perpetual sense

---

[26] *The Papers of Nathaniel Bacon of Stiffkey*, eds A. Hassell Smith and Gillian Baker, Norwich, 1983, II, p. 269. Sadler was acting as 'keeper' to Mary, Queen of Scots. Quite why Walsingham thought it prudent to place Howard and Mary in proximity is another mystery.

[27] DUL Howard MS 5, f. 40.

[28] BL Cotton MS, Titus C vi ff. 32, 33, 35.

[29] DUL Howard MS 5, f. 40. John Bossy has written an unpublished article on this letter ('Henry Howard and Philip Sidney 1583–4') which he kindly let me see. My interpretation differs slightly from Bossy's, in that I do not consider it obvious that (as he believes) 'Sidney was … aware that the queen got on with Howard a great deal better than she did with himself'. Furthermore, there is no evidence for the claim that 'Walsingham … continued to find political benefit in Howard's influence over loyal Catholics' – to believe so is simply to replicate Howard's own fantasies, and in any case, the court Catholics were in 1584 a spent force, with many symphathizers having gone into Parisian exile. I am not also certain about the identification of Howard with the Clinias of Sidney's *Arcadia* (*The Countess of Pembroke's Arcadia (The New Arcadia)*, ed. Victor Skretkowtcz, Oxford, 1988),

of not being close to the centre of the information flows on which so depended the ebb and flow of political power surfaces again in the letter, and we learn that, presumably in the early part of 1584, Howard's 'deskes and coffes have bene broken uppe my papers serched'.[30] We also learn that he was still ordinarily resident, confinement aside, in Howard House, where

> out of my closette as shall be deposed if need by the other of vie or six some persone not so iust nor honest as the rest and more regardinge his owne benefitte then the queenes affaires hath conveied a boxe of perles that costs me 45 pounds with a black tablette and a pointe diamond worthe 18 pound which wear the greatest of my poor substance.

Most significantly, however, the letter shows that Howard was contemplating going to Paris to join the rump of the failed palace revolution revanchists.[31] The move from Sadler's house to that of John Dannett (presumably related to the evangelical historiographer Thomas Dannett), from where Howard wrote the letter to Sidney, at least implied a bettering of conditions; although he referred with particular distaste in one letter to the 'venomous' jailor, he was in fact given (in keeping with the often generous provisions of Elizabethan house arrest) a space of three miles within which to roam (indicating that this was an isolated country retreat).[32]

The letter to Sidney is found today in a collection of devotional writings, some of which, in inspiration if not composition, may date from his confinements with Sadler and Dannett. Despite (considerable) difficulties of internal chronology that attend Howard's biography in the 1580s, a large trawl of his notebooks derives (at least in part) from this period and just beyond. Although they have been described as commonplace books, they are not notes from reading arranged topically (in the special dialectical sense of that word).[33] They are rather a series of rough drafts of works,

---

partially because of how to read Sidney's comment that Clinias had been 'an actor in Tragedies' (p. 285). Finally, Bossy's interpretation depends upon Howard in August 1584 being well-informed of Sidney's Parisian activities as ambassador to Henri III in July 1584 'perhaps via Stafford's mother, the queen's Mistress of the Robes': this is unproven.

[30] DUL Howard MS 5, f. 40^r.
[31] DUL Howard MS 5, f. 40^v: Howard asks for 'libertie to seeke my chaunce abroade'.
[32] DUL Howard MS 5, f. 40. There was a John Dannett of Dannett Hall near Leicester.
[33] See A. Moss, *Printed Commonplace Books and the Structuring of Renaissance Thought*, Oxford, 1996, and now A. E. Vine, 'Francis Bacon's Composition Books', *Transactions of the Cambridge Bibliographical Society*, 13 (2008), forthcoming. The question of dating these manuscripts is complex. Howard's own library was regularly dispersed and his 'coffers broke into' by various state-organized raids (as he mentions, for example, in the

most of which were never finished by Howard. He planned, for example, a work on alchemy, though to judge from the notes in DUL Howard MS 1 it would have belonged to that well-established Renaissance genre the praise (or blame) of a discipline. Law, medicine and astrology were favoured examples, though the wilder shores of the genre could encompass such works as Cornelius Agrippa's *De incertitudine et vanitate scientarum*. Now the status of a given discipline as art or science was a Renaissance commonplace, and it is unsurprising to find Howard opening his notes with a section on alchemy's *incertitudo*.[34] It is difficult to provide his comments with a great deal of intellectual context, or at least of such a specific character as to be able to speak with greater precision about the style of alchemy involved. One may contrast even so basic a fifteenth-century work as George Ripley's *Compound of Alchemy*, which was published for the first time soon after the date of these notes in 1591.[35] There are parallels, albeit that we must speak carefully, given that we do not have the finished product, with Howard's treatment of astrology, though at an even greater distance from the arts course disciplines.

At one stage further removed are Howard's 'offices' or idiosyncratic liturgical and psalmic compilations.[36] Partly these are the result of traditional manipulation of liturgical material, in ways which had not altered significantly from the Middle Ages, as recent scholarship confirms.[37] Partly,

---

beginning of his 1590 tract on female rulership). Since we have no notes for any of his pre-1583 works, we can assume that one of these instances of thuggery deprived Howard of those notebooks. Therefore, it makes sense to assume that these date from a period from 1584. There is so little overlap between the astrological material contained in DUL 3, ff. 1–5 and the material in the *Defensative* that they are best considered as separate works. We have no reason to place faith in sequential dating for the manuscripts; the first manuscript contains two entirely different works composed at different times (probably) and (certainly) on different papers.

[34] DUL Howard MS 1, ff. 1 and 25–31. For the art/science distinction, see, for example, Robert Sanderson, *Logicae artis compendium*, ed. E. J. Ashworth, Bologna, 1985, pp. xxxvi–vii.
[35] *George Ripley's Compound of Alchemy*, ed. Stanton J. Linden, Aldershot, 2001.
[36] These are currently the object of study by Professor John Bossy, and, in the interests of an unwillingness to engage in scholarly reduplication of labour, I should register a worry about the word 'academic': there were certainly masses composed by 'in-house' composers at the colleges of Oxford and Cambridge (the intellectual and ludically mathematical content of which one recent scholar has emphasized: Roger Bray, 'Music and the Quadrivium in Early Tudor England', *Music and Letters*, 76, 1995, pp. 1–18), but the extent of this practice is difficult to determine.
[37] See *The Divine Office in the Latin Middle Ages. Methodology, Source Studies, Regional Developments, Hagiography*, eds Margot Elisbeth Fassler and Rebecca A. Balzer, Oxford, 2000, is an excellent recent collection of essays which, taken together, functions as a guide to the sorts of traditional variation of liturgical material.

however, they are in debt to the practice of the humanist commonplace and, furthermore, the practice of excerpting commonplaces from scripture was not novel to Howard. Mark Greengrass cites the Spondheim Abbot Johannes Trithemius's *In Praise of Scribes* as evidence that 'copying and extracting from the Bible was a means of internalizing the Scriptures, to enlighten the heart'.[38] Howard explicitly commends this practice.[39] There was, in addition, the particularly Protestant (or evangelical) practice of versification of the psalms, such as those produced by the French poet Clement Marot, a practice which, it has been shown, found a ready English audience.[40] For Howard, there was another, much more personal antecedent: his father, the Earl of Surrey, had produced paraphrases of several psalms. What distinguishes (at least parts of) Howard's texts, however, is their combination of scriptural commonplacing with the liturgical (or quasi-liturgical) round. There are four such manuscripts, two of which seem to be closely related to each other. Arundel 300 and Additional 78414, it would appear, have a *terminus ante quem* of March 1589.[41]

Howard is explicit in a prefatory epistle to Burghley about his fondness for the Pius V breviary.[42] He does not mention Thomas Cranmer's efforts at all. We know (because Howard cites it at one point) that the breviary that Howard used to model his offices was the *Officium B Mariae virginis, nuper reformatum Pii V pontificis maximi editum*, which was published initially in Rome in 1568 and then subsequently in, for example, Antwerp. Howard draws the 'Conditor caeli et terrae, Rex regum et dominus dominantum qui me de nihilo fecisti' prayer (usually found in confessional and penitential contexts) of MS Arundel 300 (f. 11^r) from this breviary and, furthermore, the structure of his office also mimics that of this breviary: certain introductory 'psalms', some responsions and antiphons, 3 *lectiones* (which are in fact scriptural commonplace collections), a hymn, a prayer and finally a litany.[43] The addressee, as ever, may have been determinative of tone and

---

[38] Mark Greengrass, 'Informal Networks in French Protestantism', in *Society and Culture in the Huguenot World, 1559–1685*, eds Raymond A. Mentzer and Andrew Spicer, Cambridge, 2007, pp. 78–96, at 80.
[39] BL Additional MS 78414, f. 42.
[40] See, for example, M. A. Screech, *Clement Marot. A Renaissance Poet Discovers the Gospel*, Leiden, 1994.
[41] BL Arundel MS 300; BL Additional MS 78414; BL Cotton MS, Titus C vi and Durham University Library, Special Collections, Howard MS 4.
[42] BL Additional MS 78414, f. 52.
[43] Howard cites 'pag. 301' of this breviary. I have not been able to locate the precise edition (on the basis of this pagination), but it is found, e.g., in the 'Preces' section of *Officium B. Mariae virginis nuper reformatum et Pii V editum*, Antwerp: Plantin, 1575, p. 325.

content. The material to Burghley is less clearly political than that of the Durham collection, which has comments on the suffering of the Church[44] that inevitably recall the *Super flumina Babylonis* motet of Byrd, of whose 1605 *Gradualia* Howard was the dedicatee.[45] We know that Byrd had already been interrogated in 1583, along with Howard.[46] Perhaps the Durham material was destined for a more confirmed Catholic dedicatee, or was perhaps purely private.

The sensuous appeal of the language of the Old Testament, and above all of the Psalms, received new emphasis in the practices of post-Tridentine spirituality. It is noteworthy that some of the editions of the Pius V office, in their prefatory material, were given illustrated borders with images of the various body parts of Christ, but with the pierced heart taking pride of place, to stress the imaginative identification possible consequent on the reading of Scripture.[47] This appeal was not confined to the Catholic tradition, as the famous injunction on the reading of Holy Scripture found in the 1547 edition of the Homilies testifies.[48] It is therefore noteworthy that the means by which Howard puts together many of his prayers are not simply topical associations, but that they move by conjoint association of image and idea. For example, his 'lectio' (which takes the place of a single Biblical passage in the Pius V model) consists in the weaving together of separate passages from the Bible linked by the image of the stone.[49] This technique is found throughout the collections, and is best viewed in relation to various 'pictorial' rhetorical figures that Howard would have studied while at Cambridge.[50]

The dependence on the Pius V breviary and its liturgical orientation is found elsewhere. The hymns, for example, derive from this material (such

---

[44] DUL, f. 70: 'Deploratur calamitas qua vera Christi Ecclesia affligitur.'

[45] Although the gradualia is a setting of the church year, there are only sporadic hints of particular festivals that attach to Howard's devotional offices.

[46] See John Bossy, 'William Byrd Investigated, 1583–4', *Annual Byrd Newsletter*, pp. 5–7, in *Early Music Review*, 2002.

[47] *Officium B.*, p. 4.

[48] 'A fruitful exhortation to the reading and knowledge of the Holy Scripture' in *The Book of Homilies*, 1547: 'These books ought therefore to be much in our hands, in our eyes, in our ears, in our mouths but most of all in our hearts.'

[49] BL Additional MS 78414, f. 106: 'Ecce ego mittam in fundamentis sion lapidem probatum angularem pretiosum pono in Sion lapidem offensionis et pretium scandali et omnis qui credunt ineum non confunditur. Lapidem reprobaverunt aedificantis factus est a caput anguli. A domino factumest istud et est mirabile in oculis nostris. Qui ceciderit super lapidem istum confringetur super qumvero ceciderit conteret eum'. This is a conflation of Isaiah 28.16, Romans 9.13, Psalm 117.23 and Matthew 22.24.

[50] For example, 'allegoria', sustained metaphor.

as 'lucis creator optime').[51] One may view similarly Howard's use of images in one of the collections. At certain points throughout his office for the holy trinity, an artist was commissioned by Howard to produce illustrations to accompany the text. These illustrations are for the most part shared with the Pius V breviary. Both books have an adoration of the Magi, an annunciation, a baptism of Jesus and something drawn from the story of the Pentecost.[52] Where Howard has departed from his immediate models is in his selection of two Old Testament images which commence the visual material – one of David (author of the Psalms, and hence a comment on the work itself) and another of the Burning Bush.

These centos are interesting for a number of reasons. Firstly, we customarily look to Westminster Abbey, with its long and elaborate tradition of choral music under Elizabeth, to explain the liturgical ceremonialism of the Stuart church.[53] However persuasive such an argument may be, Howard's centos, unless so untypical of the liturgical interests of various religious conservatives, may be taken for evidence of a more widely diffused taste for the elaborate in late Elizabethan England than has hitherto been thought. This suggestion, in turn, leads to a nuancing of the scope of the roots of the Laudian revolution. Secondly, and relatedly, the fact that the devotional manuscripts were sent, or at least look as though they were sent, to important Protestant figures provides another clue to the cultural space which Howard seeks both to exploit and to enlarge to provide a religious middle ground. Thirdly, they contribute significantly to our understanding of how the psalms were mined and transformed by rhetorical techniques.

**

Howard appears to have remained under some mild form of state oversight throughout 1584 and on into 1585. The venue appears to have changed, however; it looks like he moved at some point to Redgrave Hall, home to Sir Nathaniel Bacon. Anthony Bacon had left to travel in France a few years

---

[51] Found in *Hymni per totum annum*, sig. A1ʳ (usually bound with the Pius V breviary, as in the 1575 Antwerp OBMV breviary).

[52] BL Additional MS 78414, f. 70ʳ; f. 87ʳ; f. 116ʳ; 146ᵛ; 165ʳ; 199ᵛ. Parallels in the 1575 Plantin Office (see n. 43) at p. 32 (annunciation); p. 101 (adoration of the Magi); p. 306 (Pentecost). The images do not, however, derive from the editions of the Antwerp breviary which I have seen (which were done by Petrus Vander Borcht).

[53] The most recent survey of music at Westminster Abbey in the early modern period is Stanford Lehmberg, 'The Musicians of Westminster Abbey, 1540–1640', in *Westminster Abbey Reformed 1540-1640*, eds C. S. Knighton and Richard Mortimer, Aldershot, 2002, pp. 94–113.

earlier, and Nathaniel Bacon was no obvious friend to Howard. We have a long letter from him complaining of his health (dated 1 June 1585), expressing concern about his nephew and pleading to be back in London, and by implication, court:

> My illustrious Lord, given your good judgment, I have no need to recount any further the *fons et origo* of my recent troubles. It has already been been the object of well-trodden rumour [around the walkways of (the bookshops of) St. Pauls?]. Your Lordship knows that I am not to be caught amongst those who would bear arms against the state but amongst honourable men, not in clandestine concourse, but in the open... Your Lordship knows too that I was hurriedly taken from my peaceful path into this captivity, with the crowd watching, and with practically a twisted neck, from which same condition I suffer still. I remember reading in Cicero's *Pro Roscio* of a man who by the votes of the most fair-minded judges was vindicated and absolved from every suspicion of murdering his father. He had done this by the tranquil peaceful life he had led with honesty and restraint for two years, cut off from the banter of the courts and without even glimpsing or greeting Rome.[54]

Despite Howard's frequent references to his 'deep disgrace' in this period, it would appear that Burghley did not wholly abandon him. In a later letter (also written from Redgrave Hall, dated 19 July 1585) Howard praises the great man's 'enclination' and 'favore'.[55] Perhaps this was in relation to a change of location. For all that, the reality was that his fortunes had not been at a lower ebb. His last major work of the Elizabethan period, and the last with any significant intellectual content, was long in the making. It appears that he first put pen to paper in 1581, to judge by one reference in its prefatory letter to Elizabeth. The immediate circumstances of composition are difficult to pin down because of the problems involved with the length of time of composition – at one point, Howard says that a member

---

[54] BL Cotton MS, Titus C vi f. 35ʳ: 'Non est necesse (vir Ornatissime) ut apud tuam prudentiam, recentis mali fontem et originem, iam diu in Paulinis ambulachris tritam atque pervagatam repetam paulo altius. Novit T. D. me non inter perduelles, sed honestos non in clandestino coetu, sed in foro … deprehensum esse atque a tranquillo cursu et itinere nihil suspicantem mali, quasi contorto collo idque spectante multitudine in hanc custodiam festinanter arreptum esse, et eiusdem adhuc morbi laborare contagione. Memini quemdam apud Ciceronem Roscium ipsis iudicum aequissimorum suffragiis ab omni parricidii suspicione prorsus fuisse vindicatum atque absolutum quod quietam et tranquillam vitam ab omni forensi strepitu seiunctam per biennium (ne conspecta aut salutata quidem Roma) probe modesteque peregisset.'

[55] BL Cotton MS, Titus C vi f. 37ʳ.

of the Privy Council approached him with a request that some such work be written.[56] This, apparently, had been thirteen years prior to the date of its presentation: in other words, some time in 1577. He goes on, however, to suggest that he did not in fact start composition since some other 'far more dangerous conflict' was occupying his time.[57] It must be a matter of speculation which of Howard's conflicts this must have been, but the most likely answer is that this refers to his difficulties with the Earl of Oxford. This came to a head in 1581, and so we may perhaps assign a date of initial composition to some time in late 1581, with a further interruption following the disclosure of his involvement with some of the participants in the Throckmorton plot; this interruption Howard refers to, in his almost obsessively common language of seagoing and shipwreck, as the decision to 'cast anchor in a quiet harbour'.[58] These were evidently dark times for Howard. The rhetorical figure of *paradiastole*, which he used to look back on these years, aptly characterized the sense of how incapable this 1590s Elizabethan loyalist was of understanding that he had been thought a traitor: 'Integrity was then accounted flattery, respect to conscience corruption, plain dealing, fraud'.[59] He claims to have withdrawn again from public life and resided often in a room in Greenwich, on terms provided by his kinsman Lord Admiral Howard.[60]

He was, moreover, now more isolated than ever before. The man closest to his own position, confessionally and politically, Charles Arundell, had fled to Paris to become one of a group of Catholic exiles.[61] Howard remained in England, but was subject to continuing suspicion. A particularly grievous example of Elizabethan state surveillance is recorded by him. According to Howard, his study, with its desks and coffers, was six times 'broken up, [his] papers rifled and sundry books of notes conveyed away'.[62] In an apparently miraculous example of providence, the 'Dutiful Defence' manuscript was once stolen from him, but mysteriously returned. Howard gave no dates for these instances of bully-boy surveillance, but one possible explanation is that

[56] BL Lansdowne 813 f. 2^r.
[57] Ibid., f. 3^v.
[58] Ibid., f. 4^v.
[59] Howard, 'Dutiful Defence', f. 3^v. For the figure, which here has a strongly Tacitean flavour, see now the instances given by Quentin Skinner, *Reason and Rhetoric in the Philosophy of Thomas Hobbes*, Cambridge, 1996, pp. 163–4.
[60] Howard, 'Dutiful Defence', f. 5^v; BL Cotton MS, Titus C vi f. 28.
[61] For Arundell and others of this influential group of expatriates, see now Katy Gibbons, 'The Experience of Exile and English Catholics: Paris in the 1580s', unpublished PhD dissertation, 2004, The University of York.
[62] Lansdowne, f. 7^r.

they occurred in the immediate aftermath of the unravelling of the Babington plot. The tide in the affairs of men had not yet turned.

Changes in the wider European political scene make it easier to understand the paranoia that attended the 'discovery' of the Babington 'plot'. Above all, the meddling by Elizabeth in the affairs of the Netherlands was the fire in which the new political culture of the remainder of her reign and the early years of James' was forged. As the 1580s progressed, England could with some reason see itself as an increasingly isolated bulwark of the true faith. The earlier accommodations between Catholics and Protestants in France had buckled under the weight of an ever more aggressive Catholic league. The fall of Antwerp to Parma's troops on 17 August 1585 was a symbolically important failure of Protestant Flanders to rebel from Spanish control; from England's perspective, this presaged the end of political or diplomatic solutions to the Netherlands, with the prospect of any Anglo-French union looking ever more remote, especially after Anjou's death in 1584 and Henri III's decision to annul the various earlier concessions made to Protestants. The treaty of Joinville (December 1584) made provision for Spanish aid, military and financial, to be given to France. Financial concerns, and an unwillingness to replicate the disastrous wars in Calais of her father, made Elizabeth hesitate, but the Northern Provinces could no longer be regarded as safe following the brutal assassination of William of Orange. The issue of Mary Stuart was not going away, and every piece of news from Ireland reminded the court that it was as difficult of English subjugation as it was attractive to Spanish geopoliticking. War, financially ruinous and militarily uncertain, began in 1585 to feel inevitable.

The Spanish ambassador, Mendoza, had been in contact with John Ballard, a seminary priest, who had informed the disgraced Spanish ambassador there was a sufficient groundswell of Marian feeling in England to hope for a change of ruler. The signing of the extraordinary document the Bonds of Association (which envisaged the creation of a brutal police state should Elizabeth be assassinated) in 1584 intensified this feeling. On 6 July 1586, Anthony Babington wrote a long 'encrypted' letter to Mary, Queen of Scots, asking for information on how best to proceed with some fairly obviously treasonous activities.[63] Mary replied with a letter that found its way into the hands of Thomas Phelippes. Phelippes in turn forged a letter requesting Babington for the names of the plot's participants. Following various interrogations of Mary, Babington and others,

---

[63] The standard account is C. Read, *Mr Secretary Walsingham and the Policy of Queen Elizabeth*, Oxford, 3 vols, 1925, III. 1–70, but see Haynes, *Invisible Power*.

Mary was executed (against Elizabeth's wishes) on 8 February 1587.[64] The tentacles of Babington's purported (for it was in large part the result of careful machinations by Walsingham's agents) plot spread far and wide. Mendoza had written to Philip II with the (scarcely credible, given Howard's limited financial resources) report that Howard stood ready to summon troops to put at the service of the purported rebellion.[65] As hard to stomach as the picture of Howard the military figure may be, we are to believe that he proffered his services to the queen to assist at sea against the oncoming Spanish Armada.[66] It is difficult to imagine that Howard thought his offer would have been taken seriously, given his utter absence of military experience, and indeed, it was refused, though he claims 'to have worn the steppes of every councillor' with his pleading. If not by the sail, then Howard would, once more, attempt to gain favour by the pen.

Whereas the devotional works depend (in large part) on other traditions than the academic ones of the curriculum Howard learnt at Cambridge, Howard's 1590 tract in defence of female rule (purportedly a response to the reformer John Knox's intemperate book written against Mary Tudor) appears at first sight rather closer to the university environment. It is a substantial work, informative for its conceptions of evidence and argument. The large number of presentation copies deriving from this point in Howard's life suggests how seriously Howard took the need to redeem himself through the written word, harking back once again, despite his now complete lack of influence, to the role of the humanist adviser. Sir John Stanhope, Thomas Heneage, Burghley and the Earl of Essex all received Howard's lengthy work, as well as the queen.[67] By the time that Howard came to write his manuscript, the topic had a recent history, fraught with manoeuvre and countermanoeuvre.[68] Earlier studies of

---

[64] Drafts of some Latin elegiacs composed by Howard in Mary's memory survive: BL Cotton MS, Titus C vi.

[65] *CSPSp*, 604. This stands at odds too with BL Cotton MS, Titus C vi f. 138.

[66] BL Cotton MS, Titus C vi f. 38^r: a letter requesting 'a sending to the sea', wherein Howard 'crave no charge but as a private gentleman wold learn to serve'; he particularly requested to be attached to either the ship of his nephew or Charles Howard, Lord Admiral.

[67] See Bibliography for information on these copies.

[68] The most important works are: John Knox, *The First Blast of the Trumpet against the Monstrous Regiment of Women*, Geneva: n.p., 1558; John Aylmer, *An Harborowe for Faithfull and Trewe Subjects*, London: Day, 1559; John Leslie, *A Defence of the Honour of the Right Highe, Mighty and Nobles Princess Marie Queene of Scotland and Dowager of France*, London: Diczophile, 1569. See also *Half Humankind*, eds Katherine Usher Henderson and Barbara F. McManus, Urbana, 1975, and Amanda Shephard, *Gender and Authority in Sixteenth-Century England: The Knox Debate*, Keele, 1994. Fundamental to all study is Maclean, *Renaissance Notion*.

'Renaissance gynecocracy' (a modern anachronism) have focused on the relation of these texts to an inchoate or sophisticated – as the case may be – political theory.[69] That may be a worthwhile project, but for Howard's text, and its immediate model, to describe the task as the construction of a given political theory is already a little unhistorical. Given the large number of *ad hominem* (in the technical sense of an argument which concedes one of your opponent's presuppositions) arguments that the texts rely on, what is going on in both Howard's text and its closest model, the work of Mary's ambassador, John Leslie, is the skilled demonstration Howard's work would only be politically effective if it managed to give a good account of his arts course procedures of proof and persuasion.[70] This is not to suggest that both Howard and, even more strongly, Leslie were not anxious to influence the march of events by their pen, but it is simply to recognize the centrality of the hermeneutic and rhetorical sphere in deciding the claims. Nor is it to deny that these texts are evidence for changes in the notion of law itself; it is simply a question of emphasis and addressing recent scholarly imbalance. As earlier parts of this book have explored the influence of grammar, rhetoric and dialectic on various of Howard's works, so we now consider the influence of the rules of legal interpretation, drawn from both the common law and civil law traditions, which both serve and are served by Howard's broader political and patronage purposes. These texts, in other words, belong as much to the history of displays of legal hermeneutics as to that sporadically insightful invention of the last thirty years, Renaissance feminism. To separate out the interpretative scope and the political aim of law in the Renaissance and to focus on the form rather than the content of the argumentation is, let us admit straightaway, a difficult task in the Renaissance (and indeed a fraught question for today's legal theorists) since the expansive definition of law (*Digest* 1.1.10.2 and *Institutes* 1.1.1: 'Jurisprudence is the knowledge of things both human and divine, the knowledge of good and bad') created a space for law that straddled both theology, natural philosophy and morality, as well as purely 'instrumen-

---

[69] This is the focus of the well-known book by Constance Jordan, *Renaissance Feminism. Literary Texts and Political Models*, Ithaca: NY, 1990, though she shows herself slightly more adept than some others to the rhetorical construction of the texts she studies.

[70] 'Arts course' because instruction in civil law was sometimes included as part of the arts course, rather than being only available to students of the BCL or LLD degrees at Oxford and Cambridge respectively.

tal' or 'formal' rules of argument and evidence, along with some notions of 'legal rights'.[71]

Howard's legal education has already been touched upon.[72] A possible, but unproven, reason for his transfer to Trinity Hall may have been the prospect of a strong training in civil law. After all, civil law was still used in the ecclesiastical and admiralty courts, and (a more plausible attraction for Howard) it was the base of international law, with its ambassadorial disputes, and of the *lex mercatoria*, although it would appear that, from what we know of actual teaching practice, such practical topics were rare birds at the universities. Alberico Gentilis, Regius Professor of Civil Law at Oxford, wrote on embassies, and Sir Richard Swale, a distinguished civilian, was sent in 1600 to Emden, along with Richard Bancroft and Sir Christopher Perkins, to negotiate in a Danish trade dispute.[73] Although Trinity Hall was a civilian stronghold, there is no reason not to think that during his time at King's Howard could not have been introduced to, at least, the *Institutes* of Justinian (based largely on the earlier *Institutes* of Gaius), an ABC of the civil law.[74] Civil law permeated common law in various ways, a topic that itself proved of much interest and controversy in the early years of the seventeenth century, though there has also been work done for the sixteenth century. Ever since F. W. Maitland's famous 1901 Rede lecture, 'English Law and the Renaissance', it has been customary to downgrade the importance of the civil law tradition, treating civil law as a 'threat' (real or imagined, depending on one's interpretation of the evidence) against which the bulwark of the common lawyers stood firm.[75] F. W. Maitland was not as care-

---

[71] For a (somewhat Olympian) overview of the contribution of lawyers to political thought at the time, see Donald R. Kelley, 'Elizabethan Political Thought', in *The Varieties of British Political Thought, 1500–1800*, eds J. G. A. Pocock, Gordon S. Schochet and Lois G. Shwoerer, 1993, Cambridge, 1993, pp. 47–79, in which there is great emphasis, perhaps too much, on the competing welter of political 'vocabularies'; Brian P. Levack, *The Civil Lawyers in England, 1603–1641: A Political Study*, Oxford, 1973, is an excellent survey, but does not help one get at the bread and butter of legal argumentation.

[72] See Chapter Two, pp. 35–6. See also A. Shepard, 'Legal Learning and the Cambridge University Courts, 1560–1640', *Journal of Legal History*, 1998.

[73] See *ODNB*, sub nomine, 'Swale, Richard' (Levack); G. Van der Molen, *Alberico Gentili and the Development of International Law*, 1968, pp. 197–257, and Diego Panizza, *Alberico Gentili, Giurista ideologo nell'Inghilterra elisabettiana*, Padua, 1981.

[74] Ross, Richard J., 'The Commoning of English Common Law. The Renaissance Debate about Printing English Law 1520–1640', *University of Pennsylvania Law Review*, 146, 1998, pp. 323–461.

[75] F. W. Maitland, 'English Law and the Renaissance', in idem, *Selected Historical Essays of F. W. Maitland*, ed. Helen M. Cam, Cambridge, 1957. On the supposed insularity of English law, see Donald Kelley, 'History, English Law and the Renaissance', *Past and Present*, 1974, pp. 24–51.

ful a reader, perhaps, of Lord Scrutton, whose lucid and forthright survey of the topic had been published sixteen years earlier.[76] The picture will not now stand; even 'internalist' histories of law are clear that in the attempt to win cases away from the Admiralty court the common lawyers were (so to speak) at sea.[77] Louis Knafla has pointed out that it became increasingly common from 1570 for lawyers trained at the Inns of Court to also have matriculated at Oxford and Cambridge, with the greater exposure to civil law.[78] That is what one might call, to some extent, an institutional picture, but we have also come to see a degree of interpenetration of common law and civil law maxims and argumentation.[79] The English civilians themselves, especially in the light of the humanist conjunction of custom with history, were familiar with common law material.[80] The revisionist picture which has been drawn has focused around such figures as Sir Henry Spelman, Francis Bacon, William West, Sir John Davies and Howard's fellow student at Kings, John Cowell: in other words, figures who (for Cowell turned later to the study of civil law under pressure from Richard Bancroft) belong predominantly to a slightly later period than that of Howard's intellectual formation and date of the 'gynecocracy' manuscript.[81]

Previous scholarship, however, has not usually shown specific connections between early modern English texts and various passages from the *Pandects*, the *Institutions* and the *Novells* (as the main parts of the *Corpus iuris civilis* were known), for the civil law was a transformation of the law

---

[76] Thomas Scrutton, *The Influence of Roman Law on the Law of England*, Cambridge, 1885. Like so many of the Victorian judges, Scrutton's economy with language and precision with words make his academic work as readable as his judicial pronouncements.

[77] J. P. Dawson, *A History of Lay Judges*, Cambridge: MA, 1960, pp. 167–8.

[78] L. Knafla, 'The Matriculation Revolution and Education at the Inns of Court in Renaissance England', in *Tudor Men and Institutions*, ed. A. Slavin, Baton Rouge, 1972, pp. 251–5.

[79] See Christopher Brooks and Kevin Sharpe, 'Debate. History, English Law and the Renaissance', *Past and Present*, 1976, pp. 133–42; and, more recently, the brisk, elegant pages in Ian Maclean, *Interpretation and Meaning in the Renaissance: The Case of Law*, Cambridge, 1992, pp. 181–6.

[80] The growth of humanism, historicity and law is the large point of Donald Kelley, *Foundations of Modern Historical Scholarship: Language, Law and History in the French Renaissance*, New York, 1970.

[81] See, e.g., Sir Henry Spelman, 'Of the original of the four law terms of the year', in idem, *English Works*, London, 1723, p. 102; Francis Bacon, 'Maxims of the Law', (Spedding, Ellis, Heath VII. 319); William West, *Symboleograhia*, London, 1590; Sir John Davies, 'A Discourse on Law and Lawyers', in *The Complete Works…*, ed. A. B. Grosart, London, 1869–76, III.255. Scholarship now benefits from the well-documented work of D. Coquillette, *The Civilian Writers of Doctors Commons*, Berlin, 1988. Note also the chronologically apposite article of P. G. Stein, 'Thomas Legge. A Sixteenth-Century Civilian and his Books', in *Satura Roberto Feenstra oblata*, Fribourg, 1985, pp. 545–56.

of the Roman Empire.[82] It is hard to understand why. Admittedly, the *Digest* (an alternative name for the *Pandects*) is a vast, unwieldy text which accreted considerable commentary, and it is very hard to keep large chunks in one's head (hence the vogue in the sixteenth century for legal dictionaries), and yet there is no alternative if one is to trace in more precise fashion the styles of argumentation that these texts deploy. Since 1985 there has been a helpful four-volume edition of Theodor Momsen's Latin text with a facing English translation.[83] Furthermore, Justinian's *Institutes* is a very manageable text, available with a number of short helpful early modern commentaries. The following pages represent a small contribution to this difficult heuristic task and they are heavily reliant on the work of scholars such as Gerhard Otte, Ian Maclean and Vincenzo Piano Mortari; they aim to provide a more nuanced reading of the influence of civil law in Elizabethan England, and mildy to diminish the importance of 'Renaissance feminism' as a useful tool for the texts studied.[84]

A starting point for this study may be made with a work whose author was well-known to Howard: Mary's ambassador, John Leslie. Leslie's legal education was, like Howard's, wholly civilian in formation.[85] At first sight, however, it could appear that Leslie's work dismissed the relevance of the civil law.[86] Leslie does indeed say that the objections to Mary's rule are for the most part based on the civil law (*A Treatise*, sig. D3^r) and that

---

[82] See *The Roman Law Tradition*, eds A. Lewis and D. Ibbetson, Oxford, 1994. For more general works on Renaissance humanism and law, see H. E Troje, *Humanistische Jurisprudenz*, Goldbach, 1993, and (with caution) *Rhetoric and Law in Early Modern Europe*, eds Lorna Hutson and Victoria Kahn, New York, 1994. Only a very basic knowledge of Roman law has been assumed throughout this section – for a preliminary overview of the main issues, there is no better introduction than to read *The Elements of Roman Law*, ed. R. W. Lee, London, 1956 (superior in clarity of purpose and execution to the later editions of the same work), which contains a full translation of Justinian's *Institutes*, as well as more discursive introductory material and glossaries. It is the *Institutes*, indeed, whence Howard appears to derive his knowledge of the law.

[83] *The Digest of Justinian*, ed. A. Watson, Philadelphia, 1985. There is, furthermore, a useful website dedicated to the publication of corrections to Watson's translation: www.iuscivile.com/materials/digest.

[84] Vincenzo Piano Mortari, *Diritto, logica, metodo nel secolo XVI*, Naples, 1978; and idem, *Gli inizi del diritto moderno in Europa*, Naples, 1986.

[85] Leslie studied law at Poitiers, Tolouse and Paris in the 1540s and 1550s. References are to *A Treatise touchcing the Right, Title and Interest Aswell of the Most Excellent Princesse, marye Queene of Scotland, as of the most noble Kyng James, her Graces sonne, to the succession of the Croune of England*, London, 1584.

[86] So Caney (reliant on Shephard, *Gender and Authority*, p. 144), 'Let he who objects', p. 47, writes: "Aylmer and Leslie both denied that the civil law had any relevance in the English system."

Justinian's *Institutes* and the *Digest* deal with private persons and not state figures (sig. D2^v), but we should not always take him at his word. He is in fact dependent on the norms of civil law argumentation. What counted as a legitimate argumentative move in the discourse of law was the object of particular humanist enthusiasm in the wake of Andrea Alciato's *De verborum significatione* (1530), strictly speaking a commentary on *Digest* 50.16.[87] It is this section of the *Digest* that Leslie refers to in making an argument about succession that the word *filius* 'contains' the word *nepos*.[88] Or when he writes (sig. E5^r): 'We stand upon the interpretation of the common law recited and declared by statute, & how shal we better understand, what the law is therein, then by the use and practise of the said law? For the best interpretation of the law, is custome' [= *Digest* 1.3.37], Leslie is in fact quoting the *Digest* again, albeit in English vernacular clothing. Again, when discussing the common law of England, he is adroit in his language of rule, law and exception. He discusses 'many rules of the lawe' (thereby suggesting the civil law distinction between rule and law: *Digest* 50.17.1[89]), then continues that even if there were such a rule, then there it is not so general as to not admit of an exception (sig. D3^v), drawing on a body of legal learning which made room for the exception and did not thereby call into question the general rule, a very effective strategy rhetorically given that Leslie is interpreting the great authority of English statute.[90]

> For it doth plainely appeare by the statute of the 25 E. 3 (being a declaration of the lawe, which I suppose they meane in terming it a Maxime) that this rule [above which, Leslie implies, stands the law, of which he is the expositor]
>
> extendeth not unto the Kinges children. Whereby it most evidently appeareth, that it extendeth not generally to all. And if it extende not to binde the Kinges children in respect of any inheritance descended unto them from any of their Auncestors: it is an argument a fortiori, that it doth not extende to binde the king or his Croune.[91]

---

[87] Maclean, *Meaning and Interpretation*, esp. pp. 87–178.
[88] Leslie, *A Treatise*, sig. E3^v.
[89] 'Regula est, quae rem quae est breviter enarrat. Non ex regula ius sumitur, sed ex iure, quod est regula, fiat. Per regulam igitur brevis rerum narration traditur, et, ut ait Sabinus, quasi causae coniectio est, quae simul in aliquo vitiata est, perdidit officium suum'. This was a very frequently studied introductory part of the *Digest*.
[90] Maclean, Ian, 'Evidence, Logic, the Rule and the Exception in Early Modern Law and Medicine', *Early Science and Medicine*, 5, 2000, pp. 227–256.
[91] Ibid., sig. D3^v.

The repeated usage of the word 'extendeth' calls to mind the disputed practice of 'interpretatio extensiva', which is a catch-all term for hermeneutic excess, defined sometimes as what *other* jurists do. Similarly, he glances at the civil law rules about 'interpretatio restrictiva':

> The most principal cause of all is, for that in the said statute, whereupon the said supposed rule or Maxime is gathered, the children descendants and descended of the blood royall by the wordes of Infantes de Roy are expressly excepted out of the sayd supposed rule or Maxime. Which wordes the adversaries do much abuse, in restraining and construing them, to extende but to the first degree onely; whereas the same wordes may very well beare a more large & ample interpretation.[92]

Sometimes, to be fair, Leslie's logical manoeuvres seem to have derived as much from class logic as from traditions of civil law, as when he claims that even if it were true that cases argued involved (as Mary was) 'a Denizon' and not 'of an Alien borne', then 'yea, a more general rule' existed (sig. D4ʳ). This is a logical manoeuvre that owes as much to the tree of Porphyry (with its classification, variously elaborated, as the Middle Ages drew to a close, of the different ways in which one thing may be predicated of another), and hence arts course logic, than a particular civil law maxim (though the Whitmanesque *Digest* may contradict). There is, furthermore, a degree of crossover between some of the Ciceronian topics, studied so well by Gerhard Otte, which makes specification of influence tricky. Since, furthermore, Leslie is not writing purely as a legal theoretician, he can draw arguments from a wider range of sources:

> And therefore if the adversaries would go about, to restrine and withdraw from the Croune that privilege, which the law geveth to kings children for the Crounes sake: they should doo therein contrarie to al reason, & against the rules of the Arte of Reasoning, which saith, that: Propter quod unumquodque & illud magis [= *Summa Theologiae*, I.LXXXVII. q. 2, art. 2.3].

Leslie's emphasis on custom lends itself toward the argumentative force of the 'exemplum', and here is the opportunity for Leslie to display considerable historical acumen in dealing with the evidence about sources (in particular a fascinating passage about how to deal with the will of Henry VII: sig. E5ᵛ–H3ᵛ). This 'humanist' interest, let Donald Kelley take note, was to find a ready audience in Howard.

---

[92] Ibid., sig. E3ᵛ.

Considerations of rhetoric, perhaps, should account for the mismatch between the apparent and the substantive usage of civil law material in Leslie's work. He is arguing on the basis of the laws of England. This makes Henry Howard's treatise all the more notable, for it has an entire section devoted to arguments drawn from the civil law.[93] Certainly, the tripartite structure of Howard's work (with one section devoted to natural law, one to civil law and one to sacred law) was cued by Leslie, but the extent of the civil law treatment is unusual.[94] Only David Chambers, who wrote anyway in French and for a French audience, can be fairly compared in the context of the authors who derive inspiration from John Knox's assault on the idea of female regency.[95] Indeed, Chambers' work is more closely a work of civilian argumentation than Howard's, which modulates, as we shall see, across more and less rhetorical modes. This modulation was the corollary of the 'expansive' conception of law in the Renaissance, with its porous argumentative modes seeping into philosophy and rhetoric.

The main issue that civil law could resolve in the dispute was whether or not women had a right to inherit property, and hence office. The slide between property and office in Howard's work is prepared for in the civil law. The definition of property needed to be property 'per universitatem' rather than the acquisition of individual things (*Institutes*, II.9.6): such 'universal' property was property with all rights and obligations attached (D. 50.17.62). Howard then noted that there was no division between the sexes with respect to inheritance in the civil law (e.g., *Institutes*, III.7).[96] Here Howard rings an interesting change on his civilian sources. The *Digest* and Justinian's *Institutes* justified this gender blindness in a number of ways: for example, the emphasis on degrees of succession and hence the inferior position of adoptive children (*Institutes*, 1.3.11), but the argument in Justinian that Howard picks up and expands is the reference to 'nature', in some ways unsurprisingly given the growth of the phenomenon of 'natural law' in the sixteenth century (though the story is extremely murky in Elizabethan England until, and to some extent

---

[93] BL Lansdowne MS 813, ff. 125–55.
[94] Leslie, *A Treatise*, sig. D1ʳ: 'But since God, nature and the law doth call a person …'. Howard is purportedly writing against Knox, who makes only very slight use of civil law material – Knox had no civilian training.
[95] David Chambers, *Discours de la legitime succession des femmes aux possessions de leur parents et du gouvernement aux empires et royaumes*, Paris, 1579.
[96] Howard, 'Dutiful Defence', BL Lansdowne MS 813, f. 126ᵛ.

including, Hooker).⁹⁷ Justinian's *Institutes* had already referred to a gender difference in succession; under the old law, the succession to status of 'sui heredes' (full heirs) was limited to grandchildren of sons, with grandchildren of daughters being barred (so *Institutes*, III.1.15) from this status. There was a conflict of laws scenario already in the appropriate passage of the *Institutes* (between the old and new codes), and the way in which this conflict is by emphasising the role of direction succession at the expense of agnatic relations. At one point the old law is referred to as an 'affront to nature (ibid.), and it is this reference to nature that Howard expands.⁹⁸

Knox had, rather vaguely, employed Justinian's *Institutes* to prove the legal inferiority of women.⁹⁹ Knox, however, was not a trained lawyer, and it was enough for him to cite 'the Digestes' as a mere authority. This led the way open to later authors, better trained in the civil law, to exercise their hermeneutic skills in refuting Knox's intemperate attack. At one point, Howard deals with the objection that 'since the civil lawes forbidde weomen to adopte heires when by nature they have none yt is not like that the same lawes will admit them to inheritance of crownes'.¹⁰⁰ Howard continues

> this limitation is particuler rather then general rather *secundum quid* as the logicians use to distinguish then *simpliciter*

This is a mix of trivium logic (*secundum quid* = relatively, and *simpliciter* = without qualification) and civilian hermeneutic (*interpretatio limitativa*). Then he goes on to point out that there are occasions when women may adopt. There is an unstated debt here to Justinian's *Institutes*. For when Howard writes 'we must interpret that bit of the lawe according to the former reason that it is not all one to supplie defecte and to overrule ympossibilities', this is drawn out from Justininan, *Institutes* 1.XI.9 (where the distinction is made between adoption by persons naturally impotent and adoption by persons who have been castrated). He then needs to deal with 1.XI.10, which noted that women cannot adopt because even natural chil-

---

[97] There is a tangled mess of concepts such as 'fundamental law', 'fairness', 'basic rights', 'equity' and 'natural law', all of which intersect in complex ways, with competing vocabularies. A start may be made with J. W. Gough, *Fundamental Law in English Constitutional History*, Oxford, 1955, who makes the dispiriting but still accurate comment (p. 12) that 'we do not yet know, at least with any clarity, what it [sc. fundamental law] stood for'. A basic starting point for scholarship would be an analysis of the section on natural law in Howard's 'Dutiful Defence'.

[98] Howard, 'Dutiful Defence', BL Lansdowne MS 813, f. 128ᵛ.

[99] Knox, *First Blast*, p. 13.

[100] Howard, 'Dutiful Defence', BL Lansdowne MS 813, f. 152ᵛ.

dren are not in their power ('in potestate'): this Howard recognizes as an assumption, and therefore does not use legal argumentation per se to argue against it, but simply uses rhetorical arguments.[101] This was already prepared for in the text of Justinian, *Institutes* 1.XI.10, where a factual exception to the principle about adoption is mentioned: 'but by imperial clemency they are allowed to adopt as a solace for loss of natural children'. Howard simply expands the authority by which exceptions are created from one local historical to a series of broader historical instances, together with the comment on the self-interest of male legislators: viri erant qui hanc tulerunt legem ('it was men that made this law').[102] Throughout the 'Dutiful Defence', then, Howard's usage of legal material notably expanded the range and styles of argumentation that could be used to legitimate the female rule debate. The very large number of manuscript copies of the work suggests that this expansion found a ready audience and yet, as before with his tract on the Presbyterianism dispute, there appears to be no immediate intellectual reception. On the other hand, the practice of legal argumentation, to the extent that it was shaped by the university exercises apposite for such display, was often a mixed genre, closely related to rhetoric.

As we will see, Howard's progress from conspirator to kingmaker was a sluggish one. He remained humiliatingly dependent on state payments for financial maintenance. Even that appears to have been a low priority for Burghley, to whom Howard wrote (29 October 1589) with a plangent request that his annuity be restored, following a period of thirteen months in which it had been stopped. The same letter requested further protection against Sir Roger Townshend (who appears to have been his principle creditor).[103] Yet again, however, Howard survived. He had kept his eye on the succession. He, more clearly than most, favoured the claim of Mary to the throne, though with her death (and, perhaps, his manuscript on female rule), it was easier for him to play loyalist. Mary's death, however, opened up the question of the succession in other ways. The taint of suspicion, moreover, long remained with Howard, and it was many years before the brilliant light of courtly power would shine upon him again.

---

[101] Ibid., ff. 150–153.
[102] Ibid., f. 150. Cf. Shephard, *Gender and Authority*, pp. 143–55.
[103] BL Cotton MS, Titus C vi f. 41ᵛ. See p. 113.

Chapter 8

'AN NOBILITAS PERDATUR PER INFAMIAM?'
FROM CONSPIRATOR TO KINGMAKER

THE LONG autobiographical sketch with which Howard prefaced his 'Dutiful Defence' leaves the reader in no doubt of the low pitch of disfavour to which he felt himself to have sunk: 'my reason [is] like a flash of lightning in a winters night, which serveth not so much to guide my steppes as to manifest my miserye'.[1] His plight was made worse by his sense of entitlement and nobility. In one of his discussions on the topic of nobility, Howard asked 'Can it [sc. 'nobility'] be lost through *infamia*?'[2] The word *infamia* should be lingered over. As the context suggests, Howard is referring to something more precise than what we would today call 'infamy' or 'poor reputation'. Once again, a knowledge of the Renaissance curriculum assists us with pinning down the meaning here. *Infamia* was a clearly defined term in the civil law, with two passages of Justinian in particular being the object of early modern commentary (D. 3. 2 *De his qui notantur Infamia*, and in Cod. 2.12 *Ex quibus causis Infamia irrogatur*). In the Roman period, this was something which had consequences for one's ability to hold office.[3] It was defined and controlled by the Censor rather than the courts. It was, furthermore (and this is of relevance to Howard, and his dealings with the Earl of Essex), developed in connection with administrative functions. *Infamia* was a sort of precursor to or substitute for legal action, and so neatly fitted the myth of self-regulation that was an

---

[1] BL Lansdowne MS 813, f. 5r.
[2] DUL Howard MS 2, f. 58: 'An perdatur per infamiam'.
[3] See the solid overview of A. H. J Greenidge, *Infamia: Its Place in Roman Public and Private Law*, Oxford, 1894 (= 2005, Kessinger reprint). Somebody interested in the political theory of the Renaissance would do well to write a study of the learned interpretation of this concept.

important constituent of the ideology of nobility to which Howard (along with others) strongly attached himself in the last years of Elizabeth's reign. For alternative polities (or at least, new political groupings) were in the air, though Elizabeth remained a central symbolic node for the practices of politics focused around the court.[4]

Nothing would change immediately. Certainly, in 1590 (the year of the scribal publication of the 'Dutiful Defence') and for most of the last decade of his life, Burghley remained crucial to Howard, though it was clear that he too, like his queen, would not live forever. Howard was far from a central courtier: a letter from Howard (probably written in January 1591) makes it clear that he is reliant on contacts such as his nephew for information about Burghley.[5] Hints, however, of a slight increase in Howard's credit may be found in the role he played, or attempted to play, with the Spaniard Don Lewes, a man who wished to settle in England having been cast here by the fallout from the war with Spain. Howard (who was in personal contact with Don Lewes) weighed in by writing (in a letter to Burghley dated 15 January 1591) with a defence of his character and his religious opinions, the terms of which recall Howard's attempt to cultivate a liturgical 'third way' in his prayer book preface to Burghley.[6] Early signs of the importance to Howard of cultivating Burghley's son, Sir Robert Cecil, also appear: from this period (to judge by palaeographical evidence and its position with the normally chronologically ordered manuscript) comes a letter from Howard to Cecil *fils*, enclosing a now-lost manuscript collection of passages culled from Howard's reading.[7] The emergence of Robert Cecil was, however, only the first of several important changes to the political landscape of the 1590s.

Soon after his tract of the defence of female rulership, Howard penned his last significant work to be addressed to Elizabeth, one that may be seen as drawing to a close one style of humanist address in Howard's career. It was a variant on the 'advice to princes' genre, in which humanists had proved themselves particularly adept.[8] A manuscript which purported to

---

[4] See *The Reign of Elizabeth I: Court and Culture in the Last Decade*, ed. John Guy, Cambridge, 1995, emphasizing the decade as one of crisis.
[5] BL Cotton MS, Titus C vi f. 44^r.
[6] See BL Cotton MS, Titus C vi ff. 44 and 46–7. There is an important clarification letter at 48^r (dated 29 January 1591).
[7] See BL Cotton MS, Titus C vi f. 52^r, where Howard describes his compilation: 'theas flowers grewe in the gardens of invention of learned men'.
[8] See most recently the two complementary works: Peter Stacey, *Roman Monarchy and the Renaissance Prince*, Cambridge, 2007, and A. Pollnitz, 'Princely Education in Tudor and Stuart Britain', unpublished PhD dissertation, University of Cambridge, 2005.

be the last instructions of the Holy Roman Emperor Charles V to his son Philip on the event of Charles' withdrawal to the private life in the monastery on 16 Jaunary 1556 circulated widely throughout late sixteenth-century Europe. It was this manuscript that Howard chose to translate into English.[9] At first sight it may seem tactless, a failure of the 'politics of address', to give a monarch in the last years of her life so obvious a reminder of both her own death and, more particularly, the fact that (unlike Charles V) the issue of the succession was far from settled. The long dedicatory letter that Howard prefaces to his translation skirts round these issues, but beyond the internal rhetoric of the piece, there is one further scrap of evidence that may suggest a reason (and a more definite assistance with dating). Giacomo Castelvetro, brother of the more famous translator of Aristotle's *Poetics*, Lodovico Castelvetro, arrived in London in 1591 and, like several other of his (usually Reform-minded) fellow émigrés, made a living from his language, writing a grammar for Cambridge students and undertaking commercial translations.[10] Somewhere between 1592 and 1594, when in Edinburgh, he presented James VI of Scotland with a manuscript translation of the Charles V tract.[11] If this dating is correct, it accords well with what Howard himself says in his preface, namely, that twelve years have passed since the time of his disfavour with the queen (1583), giving a date of 1595, and it would suggest an earlier degree of contact, however tangential, between Howard and James' circle. The considerations of tact mentioned above required careful rhetoric, though the second edition of Spenser's *Faerie Queene* perhaps shows how quickly power, if not position, was ebbing away from Elizabeth. Howard's stated reason is to demonstrate that Philip, who by now had been safely trounced following the English victory at the Armada in 1588, had fallen far short of the noble precepts which his father had given him.[12]

In 1594, Howard decided to have his portrait painted in the fashionable

---

[9] BL King's MS 166. There were very many other copies, proving this Howard's most popular work: see now Woudhuysen, *Sir Philip Sidney*, p. 102. I have not investigated the issue of which version of the original Howard was translating.

[10] See Paolo Ottolenghi, *Giacomo Castelvetro. Un esile modenese nell' Inghilterra di Shakespeare*, Pisa, 1982, and for the background the wide-ranging and scholarly study of J. Tedeschi, 'I contributi culturali degli Riformatori italiani del tardo Rinascimento', *Italica*, 1987, pp. 19–61 (at n. 134 for Castelvetro). See now Sonia Massai, *Shakespeare and the Rise of the Editor*, Cambridge, 2007, p. 76, for an argument that Castelvetro is Britain's first professional editor.

[11] The manuscript is National Library of Scotland, MS Adv. 23.I.6: see *The Works of William Fowler*, eds H.W. Meckle, James Craigie and John Purves, Edinburgh, 1940, pp. cxxvii–cxxx, and *The Basilikon Doron of King James VI*, ed. James Craigie, Edinburgh, 1950, pp. 63–9.

[12] BL MS Sloane 792, f .1^v.

style promulgated by Hieronimo Custodis.[13] He was represented as a scholar, holding an armillary sphere, with the word 'scientia' written thereon (strictly speaking, the word appears to be 'santia' – thereby suggesting both the absence of Howard as 'humanist adviser' to his clearly not very educated painter and the likely Elizabethan pronunciation of the word *scientia* with a silent 'c').[14] In the background, there is picture of a flower blasted by a stormy snow cloud, an image for the relation of youth and age familiar from, for example, Shakespeare's fifth sonnet.[15] It is a nice question to ask how seriously at this point in Howard's life the self-identification as scholar should be taken. After all, we have observed that both for the *Defensative* and the 'Dutiful Defence' Howard wrote less as an internalist explicator of the disciplines, respectively, of astrology and law than as an accomplished rhetorician, drawing more widely on techniques of proof and persuasion. The importance of Howard's continuing distance from the University of Cambridge has been emphasized. It would, however, be wrong wholly to reduce Howard's intellectual interests to questions of prudential self-service. It should, furthermore, be emphasized how important the thrust and parry of scholarly argument was to state service, or at least so Howard thought. This is the conclusion suggested to us by some letters written in 1594.

Howard was, so the first letter says, invited to the Commencement proceedings at Cambridge University 'by an olde frende'.[16] Howard took notes because of 'the pleasure I tooke in those kindes of exercise'. Although we should tarry over the past tense 'tooke', it is clear that Howard took these Commencement disputations sufficiently seriously to note down the arguments ('the swifte passage of reasons and denialls') and then to write them up ('at lengthe with much adoo I pieced together many slivers of a broken

---

[13] See frontispiece. For more on Custodis and his influence, see Christopher Brown, 'British Painting and the Low Countries, 1530–1630', in *Dynasties. Painting in Tudor and Jacobean England*, ed. K. Hearn, New York, 1995.

[14] For a recent discussion of the armillary sphere's various significances, including mastery of the world (though perhaps here most relevant the association with the 'scientiae' of the arts course), see A. Mosley, 'Objects of Knowledge: Mathematics and Models in Sixteenth-Century Cosmology and Astronomy', in *Transmitting Knowledge: Words, Images and Instruments in Early Modern Europe*, eds I. Maclean and S. Kusukawa, Oxford, 2006, pp. 193–216.

[15] Peck, *Northampton*, p. 13, suggests that the iconography is an image of the Howard family's reverses of fortune. The accompanying motto, however, surely argues against this ('ut flosulus [for 'flosculus'] nive sic senect. Iuventus'), making it clear that this is a comment about vigour in age (for Howard was already, by Elizabethan standards, of relatively advanced age at the time of the portrait): Shakespeare, *Sonnets*, V.8 and 13–14: 'Beauty o'er snowed' and 'But flowers distilled, though they with winter meet/Leese but their show; their substance still lives sweet' (with the commentators ad loc.).

[16] BL Cotton MS, Titus C vi f. 54^r.

glass'). In an interesting aside, he compared the writing-down of arguments to the different ways in which musical voices 'hold' tunes: 'for whear the base and treble holde one tune the base is ever notwithstanding the more audible'. He sent this fair copy of the disputation on to his correspondent (presumably Burghley) and another 'brefe copy' in a further letter.[17] A similar such transcription of Commencement exercises Howard sends to Robert Cecil, in response to some unspecified good service.[18] The letter's (non-autograph) date, if correct, on the Robert Cecil material (26 February 1594) is particularly interesting: it suggests that Howard (recognizing his 'longe disgrace') spent some considerable time in making this manuscript a good presentation copy for Cecil, since Commencement proceedings took place in the summer: we know, for example, that he paid for scribal publication of these 'engrossed wares ... of philosophie' because a note at the end of the letter craves Robert Cecil's indulgence for any of the 'scriveners faults', since Howard had insufficient time to look over the piece.

Howard did not, however, confine his political interests, if the Charles V piece may be interpreted in the way suggested, to James or to the Cecils, father and son. A new star had been moving erratically (who should perhaps then be called planet for such wandering) in the Elizabethan political firmament: Robert Devereux, the Earl of Essex. The rapidly changing landscape of the political culture of the 1590s was created by both the gradual elimination of Elizabeth from power, if not role, and the increasingly obvious differences in culture and political stance of the two main factions at court: the Cecils and Essex.[19] To the latter clique belonged Sir Edward Dyer, Fulke Greville, Antonio Perez, the Bacon brothers, Anthony Standen, Sir Christopher Blount, the Earl of Worcester and Henry Howard. In other words, only a handful of people, and none of the most influential at court, though by his birth he remained very well-connected. What then, for Howard, was the appeal of Essex? Youth, intellectual accomplishment, nobility and a convenient distaste for Cecil, father and son, all played a part. Although the Essex circle, Classical and militaristic in ethos, had no explicit engagement in religious debate, we cannot exclude the possibility that Howard saw therein a chance for a regime more tolerant of conservative religious sentiment.[20]

---

[17] Ibid., f. 53ʳ.
[18] Ibid., f. 55.
[19] I rely here on the excellent work of Paul Hammer, *Polarisation*.
[20] I register gentle disagreement with Hammer, *Polarisation*, p. 288, where he says that Howard distanced himself from Essex in later years; the evidence does not quite support so active a term as distancing, though Howard had perhaps always been a more circumspect Essexian than some others from the start: see the evidence of DUL Howard MS 2 (and we might weigh the evidence of *HMCD*, II, p. 397, perhaps more carefully than Hammer does).

Howard continued attendance on Essex. When Queen Elizabeth permitted the earl to spend time in Oxfordshire at a family residence, Sir Robert Cecil wrote to Sir George Carew in August 1600 that the queen had given Essex to understand that this did not mean that she was any less angry with him. Such obvious disfavour made 'very few resort to him but those who are of his blood, amongst which I imagine you think Lord Henry Howard will not be long from him'.[21] The dating of the last full-scale manuscript that Howard wrote while Elizabeth was still on the throne is significant. In 1597, Essex was made Earl Marshal.[22] The strong interest in rank is attested to already in his first year at Cambridge, when we know that he purchased Gerard Legh's *The Accedens of Armory*, a manual on heraldy.[23] This was an office also with strong personal associations for Howard, since thirty years earlier we have an *Orders to be observed and kept by the Officers of Armes made by the high and mighty Prince Thomas Duke of Norfolke*.[24] Linda Levy Peck dates Howard's work on this office to around 1597, against the dating of the library catalogue, which is 'c. 1600'.[25] The question is how long it would have taken Howard to write this elaborate and lengthy work. We have seen that longish periods of composition are appropriate for both Howard's work on astrology and the defence of female rule. This is relevant because the later that Howard's presentation of the Earl Marshall manuscript can be pushed, the more plausible is the picture of Howard as an Essex loyalist, rather than someone who abandoned him the moment it appeared advantageous to do so. It was, after all, precisely for such a failing (characteristically expressed in the Essexian language of honour) that Howard was to upbraid Francis Bacon in a letter that has frequently been quoted in the secondary literature:

> The travail of the worthy gentleman in your behalf, when you stood for a place of credit; the delight which he hath ever taken in your company; the grief that he should not seal up assurance of his love by fruits, effects and offices proportionable to his infinite desire; his study in my knowledge to

---

[21] LPL Carew papers, MS 604 (letter dated 29 August 1600). Reference cited from J. Maclean, ed. *Letters from Robert Cecil to Sir George Carew*, London, 1864, p. 23.

[22] De Maisse, *A Journal of All that was Accomplished by Monsieur de Maisse Ambassador in England from Henri IV to Queen Elizabeth*, eds G. B. Harrison and R. A. Jones, London, 1931, p. 75.

[23] This information comes from Hammer, *Polarisation*, p. 29, citing BL Lansdowne MS 25, f. 107. Hammer also (p. 311) mentions that Howard's work was not alone, for 'heralds searched old records for [Essex]' in connection with the office.

[24] See the fascinating collection *Munimenta Heraldica 1484–1984*, ed. G. D. Squibb, London, 1985.

[25] Peck, *Northampton*, p. 14 n. 38.

engage your love by the best meanss he could devise, are forcible reasons and instances to make iudge that a gentleman so well born, a wise gentleman, so well learned, a gentleman so highly valued by a person of his virtue, worth, and quality, will rather hunt after all occasions of expressing thankfulness (so far as duty doth permit) than either omit opportunity or increase indignation.[26]

Howard's loyalty came at a time of worsening prospects for Essex. The grant of the Earl Marshall position was accepted with spectacularly bad grace by Essex, and he infuriated the queen, again. It is all the more significant that Howard's devotion to Essex carried with it, at least in 1597, the risk of alienating his own clan. Queen Elizabeth had attributed victory at Cadiz not to Essex but to that deft survivalist Charles Howard, with whom Essex was now on venomous terms, even if it be objected that Henry Howard's relations with Charles Howard had never been very warm (though, as we have seen, Henry Howard depended on him for his Greenwich lodgings for some time).

A further piece of evidence shows us how important attending to the language of honour is in understanding Howard's involvement with the Essex circle.[27] Fragments of a masque in Howard's show 'pilgrims' appearing on an island (perhaps shipwrecked); they journey to the location of a shrine where a figure offers (or is made to offer) to transmute them into shadows. At some point prior to this, there is an interlude of dancing nymphs. Then we have one long fragment of a speech by a Merlin-like figure. It is safe to assume that the speech came close to the end of the piece; Merlin's description of his speech as an 'offering' and his address to the nymphs 'Virgines that beginne with invocation must *end* with offeringe' strengthens this assumption.[28] The masque continues with a metaphor of the queen as a sea or with sea attributes, variously describing her as a gale of wind, a mighty ocean and 'an encouragement to all faithfull and humbel spirites to embarke but under caution'.[29] The Merlin figure then takes it upon himself to offer advice

> to all devoute pilgrims, that are yet in appetitt, and have freedome of election to sette saile ore to caste anchore, to steppe forwarde, or drawe back,

---

[26] Peck, *Northampton*, p. 16 with p. 221 n. 49 (for copies).
[27] For a detailed account of this masque, with arguments on dating and context, see D. C. Andersson, 'Embarke but under caution. Fragments of a New Elizabethan Masque', *Notes and Queries*, 55, 2008, pp. 171–5.
[28] BL Cotton MS, Titus C vi ff. 205ʳ.
[29] Ibid., f. 203ʳ.

that theie will be thoroughlie advised before theie begin this hopeful viage, leste by pursuing over hastilie the bright blasis of encouragement (with Petrackes flie) theie be scorchid in the flames of their folly. For presumption is ever apte to drawe comforte from the vase ocean of appetite, but discrecion from the sweete springes of opportunity[30]

Taking the ocean-going metaphor literally, we can suggest that the masque functions as a piece of political advice to a young nobleman or military leader who is about to undertake a journey. If these young men 'ende in seking honor', says the speaker, they thereby indicate a key ideological term of the 1590s, particularly associated with the Essex circle.[31] Another recently rediscovered work of Howard (DUL Howard MS 2), also written, it would seem, for Essex, affords us very close parallels to this masque fragment's manipulation of the vocabulary of honour, thereby corroborating my suggestion of authorship and establishing a more precise context in the political culture of the time.[32] Howard's draft manuscript of advice to a young nobleman cannot be dated certainly, and probably reflects several chronological layers of composition, as with most of the other manuscripts with which DUL 2 was found (all of them probably dating from the middle of the 1580s to the middle of the 1590s).[33] Honour and virtue and the importance of both in setting the political course of the addressee's actions form the bedrock of the advice given in DUL 2, but there are clear signs of Howard's cautious tone throughout. The key section here runs from about ff. 117^r to f. 124^v, which is replete with admonitions about the virtues of patience and caution.[34] Essex, Howard writes, is the object of suspicion at court for his 'verie politick insinuation into the good will of forain states that in the Queens service have had occasion to deal with him'.[35] One should note here the emphasis on how Essex has arrived at his position of power: through the queen's service, underlining the point that the masque made.[36] Loyalty to the queen might be thought of as really being careful

---

[30] Ibid.
[31] See Bryson, *From Courtesy to Civility*, pp. 248–9.
[32] DUL Howard MS 2 (hereafter DUL 2). This has been the object of a recent article by Paul Hammer, 'Lord Henry Howard, the Earl of Essex and the Politics of Friendship', *English Manuscript Studies*, 13, 2007, pp. 1–34, whose article provides greater precision and depth of argument on the dating and context of DUL 2 than I can rehearse here.
[33] It contains many crossings out, for example.
[34] I differ slightly from Hammer, 'Lord Henry Howard', here, who sees the key section as running from f. 120 onwards; the passages at f. 115^v 'electio amicorum' and f. 118^r 'his carriage in the place ever since his coming thither' are also highly relevant.
[35] DUL 2, f. 120^v.
[36] For other comments on the queen, and the importance of her role in the state, see f. 124r.

dealing with the Cecil alliance. The centrality of the queen in this masque, however, suggests it would be wrong to strip out the queen entirely from this ideological picture, unless one inclines to an entirely cynical view of Essex's approach to one source of his virtue.[37]

The masque shows how keenly aware this 'invisibile Merline' was of the delicacy of Essex's situation in advance of the Atlantic expeditions and of the threat to the body politic that they posed, but it is a clear protestation of loyalty as well. Howard had written a letter to Essex in August 1596 in which he pledged his fidelity:

> if ever I find change wher I desir most to establish permanent contente the last wordes that I to you shall utter I shall conclude with that brefe sentence of Philotas at his end:
>> O simplex et singularis amor
>> o nimuim sincera fides
>> o veri consilii periculosa libertas,
>>   vos me perdidistis.[38]

Loyalty is not something associated with Howard, but it was crucial to the ideology of Roman honour which animated Essex. Howard's loyalty was genuine (and he was to be gratifying venomous toward those whom he considered to have 'betrayed' Essex), but he began to cultivate Robert Cecil as an alternative means to securing royal favour. Similar unfashionable loyalty to clan manifested itself in a letter on behalf of Anne Dacre, wife of Philip Howard, who was then languishing in the Tower (if the dating proposed here is correct).[39]

The end of the 1590s saw a slow separation of favour between Howard

---

[37] The emphasis on the more cynical and Machiavellian atmosphere of late Elizabethan and early Jacobean politics, with political concepts being emptied of content and becoming mere ciphers for self-interest, is still influential: see Scott Mandelbrote, 'The Religion of Thomas Harriot', in *Thomas Harriot: An Elizabethan Man of Science*, ed. Robert Fox, Aldershot, 2000, pp. 247–79, at 262–3.

[38] LPL MS 661, f. 238ᵛ. It is extremely unlikely that these words are (*pace* Hugh Gazzard, 'Those Grave Presentiments of Antiquitie: Samuel Daniel's Philotas and the Earl of Essex', *Review of English Studies*, 51, 2000, pp. 423–50) a quotation from the lost Latin drama of Richard Latewar: firstly, they are unmetrical; secondly, given how few non-university copies of such drama survive it seems unlikely that Howard would have had access to this performance or a recording; thirdly, the words are in fact an adaptation of Quintus Curtius VI.10: 'Fides amicitiae, veri consilii periculosa libertas, me decepistis'.

[39] BL Cotton MS, Titus C vi f. 57ᵛ. The letter is dated 13 May 1596, which may be an error. The letter is concerned with interceding on behalf of a ladie, who is worried about 'her Lorde', who is in turn described as a 'stem' of Howard's family. The alternative dating suggested here must be 1595, since Philip Howard was dead in 1596. Other identifications may be possible, of course.

and Essex. In 1597 Howard was finally brought into Elizabeth's presence. In September 1600 he was at the 'palace of Oatlands, where Elizabeth demonstrated her regard by ordering his bed to be removed from the tented accommodation into the council chamber'.[40] By 1600 Essex had no access to Elizabeth, and he was forced into sequestration. By the time of Essex's rebellion – a sort of militarised love letter to Elizabeth – and his death, Howard had prudently built up connections with Sir Robert Cecil. By contrast, Howard's position looked ever more secure: in 1601, he was one of a commission of officials (of noble birth) who attempted some reform of the heralds office, a topic close to Howard's heart, and which drew on the new model of scholarly service that such figures as Sir Robert Cotton in the Jacobean period would emulate. The final step in Howard's transformation from conspirator to kingmaker was taken through, once again, the medium of letters. There remained continuing uncertainty about the succession, since Elizabeth refused to have her apparent freedom of action circumscribed by naming the next monarch. There was, furthermore, a plethora of candidates. A 'secrete correspodence' began in May 1601 between Howard and James' agents Robert Bruce and the Earl of Mar. The ultimate selection of Mary Stuart's son, James VI of Scotland, secured the establishment 'of a new patronage relationship and Cecil, and Howard, too. Both Cecil and Howard sought to reinforce James's belief that Cecil provided the only means to the throne'.[41] The 'great wheel of the horologue' had turned and Howard finally occupied a key position of influence.[42]

The route, however, from college to court, from arts course accomplishment to political power, had involved many detours. Long distant from Cambridge and the more scholarly life that he had once pursued, but finally within reach of power, Howard could look back on his career under Elizabeth, with its many humiliations and failures, its numerous attempts at scholarly and political accomplishment. Its successes do not appear to have been brought about by the smooth functioning of the model of humanist counsellor, in its various English incarnations. There is, furthermore, no evidence that James selected Howard to be a member of inner circle for his learning. It was rather the long history of association between Mary and Howard that appears to have been the key factor. His Jacobean years of wealth and influence were marked by a total absence of any inter-

---

[40] *ODNB*, sub nomine 'Howard, Henry' (Croft).
[41] Peck, *Northampton*, p. 19.
[42] *Correspondence of King James VI of Scotland with Sir Robert Cecil and Others in England During the Reign of Queen Elizabeth...*, ed. J. Bruce, London, 1848, p. 49 (adapted), from a letter from Bruce to Howard.

est in the writing of texts, other than his political oratory in the House of Lords and the brief tract 'Duello foil'd'.[43] He was, however, some years later to return in glory to the academic environment where he had spent so much of his youth. In 1610, Cambridge elected him Chancellor. This, too, was a recognition of his governmental and courtly position rather than any tribute to his learning. The peculiarly Elizabethan inflection of humanism which resulted in the indissoluble compact of courtly influence and humanist career was, in any case, being broken in the first decades of the seventeenth century by a profusion of alternative career routes for the public intellectual: private academies of useful knowledge, the emergence of the public schoolteacher, the professionalization of the 'lower' medical practitioners, the provision of libraries and the profusion of philological think tanks all transformed the scholarly landscape.[44] One may describe the first half of the seventeenth century as being characterized, at least in comparison with the Elizabethan period, by a certain intellectual pluralism. By the time of his greatest influence, Howard's politics of learning were already a splendid but empty throwback to an earlier age.

---

[43] See M. Peltonen, *The Duel in Early Modern England: Civility, Politeness and Honour*, Cambridge, 2003.

[44] See D. C. Andersson, 'Andrew Downes and his Pupils' (forthcoming). Angus Gowland, *The Worlds of Renaissance Melancholy: Robert Burton in Context*, Cambridge, 2008, pp. 205–44, has argued that we should view Robert Burton's anatomy within a political context of the reduced opportunities for the model of the 'humanist counsellor' beloved of the century before.

CONCLUSION

HOWARD found himself in a difficult position throughout Elizabeth's reign. The ideology of self-assertion and free speech that characterized some aspects of his father's noble inheritance conflicted with the more prosaic and humiliating need to write begging letters and the fact of his frequent surveillance by the state.[1] There was the possibility, too, that the position of a regent master, teaching or otherwise, at a university was not, despite the changes wrought in the self-image of the aristocracy, a proper occupation for the scion of the noblest family in England. After all, no one else of Howard's rank had pursued this career. His sexual leanings may have contributed to a certain sympathy with what to later generations can look like the dissimulations of rhetoric in general, and his own 'Asiatic' volumes of flattery in particular.[2] There were, however, distinct continuities throughout his life. As we have seen, clear limits to his religious conformity (as the letter to Walsingham about private mass and the devotional offices addressed to Burghley show) may be discerned.[3] He was a notably loyal friend, and seemingly genuinely devoted to his clan, especially his ill-starred nephew, Philip Howard. Under James, it has been observed that he pursued consistent 'if unpopular' social and foreign policy goals.[4]

Perhaps, however, asking for this kind of political and personal consistency is already a misreading. Especially for his years under Elizabeth, an important articulation of consistency is better sought in the construction,

---

[1] By suggesting the connection between free speech and the nobility, I do not underestimate the extent to which freedom of speech was one of the values that the culture produced more broadly (such as in manuals of rhetoric), as the learned work of Colclough, *Freedom of Speech*, demonstrates. The situation may, however, be slightly more restricted for the Tudor period, though only further research will confirm.
[2] See *DNB* for this reference.
[3] See pp. 100 (Walsingham) and 150–54 (offices).
[4] Peck, *Northampton*, p. 213. Howard was also to become, with power, an implacable enemy, as Sir Walter Raleigh would attest.

development and gradual dissolution of the model of the humanist courtier, with a particularly well-stocked storehouse of argumentative techniques culled from his time studying the arts course at Cambridge. His was an attempt to domesticate an imaginary Italy of civil conversation, a cultural geography of the universities and the wider political stage that has long been influential in England.[5] That at least has been in part the argument of this book. And at this point, we rather reach a historiographical fork in the road.

Casting a somewhat dyspeptic retrospective eye over his first book, an elegant if crude interpretation of Archbishop Laud, Hugh Trevor-Roper opined that tyro historians should not choose to write a biography as their first scholarly work.[6] It is certainly true that such a decision may encourage a narrowness of perspective, thereby fostering a tendency to see the world in a grain of biographical sand. For all that, intellectual history differs from more expansive historiographical regimes in being first and foremost the history of intellectuals, individual men and women with their own trajectories and local explanatory contexts. Ideas, of course, have their own trajectories at a certain level, but it does not make sense to be simply 'for' the one style of history and 'against' the other, as if it were a matter of faith. It is the evidence that will determine on a case-by-case basis the likely success or failure of an intellectual biography. The depth of precision that a richly documented intellectual biography can bring to the particular local causal matrices that inform historical change is extremely satisfying; where evidence for any biographical specifics is sparse, biographical explanation will appear crude and lacking in sophistication, over-reliant on generalisations. We know a great deal of Thomas Hobbes' immediate contexts.[7] Conversely, not for nothing are there few truly satisfying intellectual biographies of medieval scholars and philosophers.

The traces of Howard's life and activities preserved in archives and libraries suggest that he falls somewhere between these two poles. There is certainly enough in the way of context, both political and institutional, to have illuminated not only the course of his career and his policy goals (to adopt a slightly old-fashioned register), but also to assess his deployment of

---

[5] See Warren Boutcher, 'Pilgrimage to Parnassus: Local Intellectual Traditions, Humanist Education and the Cultural Geography of Sixteenth-Century England' in *Pedagogy and Power: Rhetorics of Ancient Learning*, eds Niall Livingstone and Yun Lee Too, Cambridge, pp. 110–24.

[6] Hugh Trevor-Roper, *Archbishop Laud 1573–1642*, revised edition, London, 1965, p. ix et seq.

[7] See Thomas Hobbes, *The Correspondence of Thomas Hobbes, II, 1660–1679*, ed. Noel Malcolm, Oxford, 1994.

Conclusion

rhetorical, dialectical and legal norms of argumentation, presentation and interpretation. Howard was not a genius, and that is precisely wherein lies the value of a close study of him. Not only do we have a clearer view of how one important noble tried, failed and then succeeded ('a cautious pilot') in navigating a voyage from college to court, but we have in the process learnt to understand something of the mechanics of discourse (to use anachronistic language) that were widely shared throughout the period.[8] Naturally, as we emphasized in our above remarks on the history of reading, being interested in the mechanics themselves at the expense of the circumstances of deployment raises a number of worries about how contentful these mechanics are. (Though in this worry, we are replicating, at another level, a late Renaissance dispute over the instrumentality of the discipline of logic.) On the other hand, there is no doubt that by closer attention to the styles of argumentation and the shaping of persuasion in particular institutional and political contexts we will better understand the culture of intellectual debate that depended thereon. To the history of this distinctive culture, the current book hopes to have made a modest contribution.

---

[8] The comment (Howard's own) is used by Peck, *Northampton*, p. 21, to whom the reference is owed.

APPENDIX I
HENRY HOWARD'S EPICEDION FOR NICHOLAS CARR

D.[1] Henricus Howardus, frater illu-
strissimi Principis Domini Thomae
Howardi, Ducis Norfolciae, &c
In obitum Nicolai Carri, Medecinae
Doctoris, Philosophi & Oratoris
praestantissimi[2]

Optima ni raperent, subiti vis improba[3] fati,
    Sol sine nube bonis, mel sine felle foret.
Sed pater omnipotens, commiscuit utile dulci,[4]
    Loeta facit memorem, sors, peracerba pium.
Quid repetam vario mutatas ordine formas?[5]
    Fata ciere deus, sistere fata potest.
Vita quid est hominis nisi vasto[6] in gurgite navis,[7]
    Quam lacerent venti, fluctus & unda premant.
Forte subit portum, sed mille[8] elapsa periclis,
    Forte refert merces, saepius icta perit.[9]

---

[1] 'D.' stands for the Latin version of Howard's courtesy title, Dominus.
[2] Nicholas Carr, *Demosthenis…Olynthiacae orations tres*, London: Henry Denham, 1571, sigs Vi[r]–Vii[v].
[3] For the phrase, see Claudian, *De raptu Prosperinae*, III.109: 'vis improba ferri'. This is the only occurrence of the phrase in classical Latin poetry.
[4] Cf. Horace, *Ars poetica*, 343 'qui tulit omne punctum, miscuit utile dulci'.
[5] See the anonymous *Epicedion Drusi*, lines 15–16: 'prisca quid huc repeto?' See Ovid, *Metamorphoses*, I.1: 'in nova fert mutatas animus formas corpora'.
[6] Mimetic elision.
[7] See perhaps the anonymous, but well-diffused because often bound with editions of Vergil, *Elegiae in Maecenatem*, 5–8: 'inreligata ratis, numquam defessa carina, | it redit in vastos semper onusta lacus| illa iuvenes prima florente iuventa| non oblita tamen sed repetitque senes' (text quoted from the OCT).
[8] Mimetic elision.
[9] See Caspar Barlaeus, *Elegiarum liber* I. 10. 11–2: 'percussa bipennibus ilex/ perstet, ad extremum saepius icta ruit'. This suggests a common, if untraced, source in humanist poetry.

Appendix I: Henry Howard's Epicedion for Nicholas Carr

Nullus adest fessis portus, requiesve malorum,[10]
    Incolumnis primus, bella secunda timet.
Exitus incertus rerum est, ac fata vacillant,
    Cum deus unus obest, fert Deus alter opem.[11]
Umbra diem sequitur, solis nox lumina condit,
    Temperat alternis cursibus ista Deus.
Sera manus carpit, primis quod floret in annis
    Vix seges est hodie, quod cito messis erit.
Hanc[12] ubi maturo resecarint tempore falces,
    Fundet arator humum, fruge carebit ager.[13]
Hora rapit subito multos congesta per annos
    Sic dominis favos, non sibi fingit apis.
Quicquid amat mundus, nostro Deus invidet orbi,
    Quod fugimus, sequitur, quod sequimurque, fugit.
Fallor? An hic niveo requiescit marmore Carrus
    Vir sine fraude bonus, vir sine labe pius?
Ipse est. Accedam, violis tua funera spargam,
    Nuper Hamadryadum spesque, decusque[14] gregis.
Laurea cur viridis simulachri tempora cingit?
    Aonidum celebri praefuit iste scholae.
Cur hederae firmus complexus funera vincit?
    Talis erat Carri, cum moreretur amor.
At placide morti venienti arride[n]t imago,
    Nec metuit rapidos laeta subire rogos.
Miles erat Christi, frangit spes summa timorem,
    Institit angustae, quam docet ipse, viae.
Unde frequent templo nitidarum turba sororum?
    Odas quia plectro dulce sonante canit?

---

[10] See, e.g., Lotichius, *Elegiae*, III.2: 'Ad Erasmum Neustetter Elegia', 'requiesque malorum': a fairly obvious ending, however, for a hexameter.

[11] See Ovid, *Tristia*, I.2.4: 'saepe premente deo fert deus alter opem'. Given that the context of the original passage in Ovid deals with the image of a shipwrecked boat, the source is near certain. For the 'unus ... alter' construction (rather than the normal 'alter ... alter') see Ovid, *Tristia*, I.3.16. There seems to be no point in the differing capitalization of the two instances of the word 'deus'.

[12] 'Quam' would be a more Classical and tighter form of connection at the beginning of the sentence.

[13] This couplet, with its threefold asyndeton, is an extreme example of the generally asyndetic character of Howard's poem. This feature is brought about by the high quantity of sententious material it incorporates.

[14] The double -que belongs to the poetic register.

Miraris Carri Musas celebrare sepulchrum?
    Sertaque delitiis pulchra tulisse suis?
Caelicolis certe est domus haec devota Camoenis,
    Et sedet in medio clarus Apollo choro.
At capiti chartae cur cervicalia praebent?[15]
    Laudis habent lapides haec monumenta suae.
Sed color hic cineri, sparsaeque ad busta cupressi
    Non bene conveniunt. Occupat ista dolor.
Tam cito vita perit, misera praecisa senecta,
    Quam rosa, dum perdet, quam tulit una dies.
Cur cineres laurus ramorum protegit umbra?
    Quod referat sortem laurus, & umbra suam.
Si quod onus summis crescentis partibus obstet,
    Fortius insurgit, tollit ad astra caput.
Invidus, & Carrum quamvis compresserit orbis,
    Integriore sui parte superstes erit.
Quam neque discruciat praereptae gloria palmae,
    Nec labor impellet, nec feret arma dolor.
En sacros veneror manes, cineresque sepultos,
    Qui fueris memini, sed meminisse dolet.
Ingemit amissum literarum Granta decorum,
    Moestaque suffuso lumina rore madent.
Hei mihi, quod durae praecidant fila sorores,
    Teque mori iubeant, quam[16] deus ipse dedit.
Ampla tuae laudis, vel me reticente, supersunt
    Signa, memor studii te tamen ore canam.
Velle meum satis est, superest modo carmina virtus,
    Mens mea splendoris victa nitore stupet.
Vincit amor vires, teneros perstringit ocellos,[17]
    Obruta quae parvo cespite forma latet.
Non modo plebeios superas, quae gloria parva est,
    Praevertis summos laude labore viros.
Ego cum domintam plebem praenomina monstrent,
    Plebis eris princeps, Aonidum comes.

---

[15] See Pliny the Younger, *Ep.*, VI.6.16: 'cervicalia capitibus imposita linteis constringunt; id munimentum adversus incidentia fuit.' The word cervicalia is very rare and the conjunction with caput makes it likely that this is the immediate source (the letter is, after all, the famous eyewitness account of Vesuvius).

[16] Sc. *vitam?*

[17] 'Perstringit oculos' (e.g. Psalm 63.4 Vulgate; Petrarch, *De secretu*, 1.1) appears to have been a common phrase, which Howard alters by employing the diminutive.

Appendix I: Henry Howard's Epicedion for Nicholas Carr

Ad metam cursu celeri tum Carre volabas,
    Cum celebris tergum est turba secuta tuum.[18]
Saepe mihi ante oculos tua commentatis imago[19]
    Obvolitat,[20] vultusque aemula larva tui.
Advoco, discedit fugientis more Creusae,
    Alloquor, effari fata, deusque vetant.
Nunc aciem[21] fregit lethum,[22] vox faucibus haesit,
    Nescio,[23] quis nobis invidet ista deus.
Lingua silet, sermoque leves tenuescit in auras,
    ἡδυέπει Graius non fluit ore lepos.[24]
Labra tibi Divum perfudarat aureus imber,
    Solus adhuc nostris cum deus ipse fores.
Artis opem ferro Parcarum scita refellunt,
    Prima trahit filum, tertia falce secit.
Accipe supremos cinerem praeceptor honores,
    Carmine flagrantes persequar usque rogos.
Intimus ipse tibi fueram, dum fata tulerunt,
    Atque manet cineri nostra Thalia comes.
Perge bonis avibus, non te Rhadamanthus habebit,
    Quique Charon Stygiis naufragus haeret aquis.
Aurea perpetui decurrent tempora regni,
    Vita manet fati non resecanda manu,
Notus erit forsan laetis Chrysostomus oris,
    Moxque dabit facilem turba Latina manum.
Sic cumulata[25] tibi Christus promissa refundet,
    Lucida sic firmo tu pede signa premes.
Charior[26] ut nostris fueris vix hospes in orbe,
    Caelicolis gratus quam modo civis eris.
Spes tamen una subest, quae me solatur[27] amantem,
    Quod mihi te iungent tempora meque tibi.

---

[18] Note the considerable alliteration of 'c' in this line.
[19] These lines contain several allusions to Vergil, *Aeneid* II, 768–84 (see further Chapter Two, p. 000 above).
[20] Rare non-Classical word.
[21] The word is used in the sense of 'line of sight'.
[22] A Renaissance spelling of 'letum'.
[23] This comma is reproduced from the printed text, but it impedes the sense.
[24] The implicit contrast is between Howard's incapacity to speak and Carr's eloquence in Greek.
[25] See Vergil, *Aeneid* IV.474.
[26] This, too, may be a pun (Charior > Carrus).
[27] This word highlights the closural section of the traditional epicedion, 'consolatio'.

APPENDIX II
A NOTE ON EDIFICATION

AN AREA where it is possible to trace some degree of difference between Howard and his Conformist collaborator in the Presbyterian polemic is in the treatment of edification.[1] Its centrality in the English Reformation is underlined by its presence in the Thirty-Nine Articles; even more significantly, it occurs there within the ecclesiological context of which ceremonies could and could not be legitimately abrogated.[2] Its semantic connection to building makes it all the more apposite in ecclesiological contexts. Indeed, it is no accident that the culminating words of an anonymous dramatic interlude called *New Custome* published in the year before Howard's piece connects edification with the construction of an international Church:

> Edification: Defend thy Church, O Christ, and thy holy congregation
> Bothe here in England and in every other nation.[3]

---

[1] I should like to thank an audience at the Institut de l'Histoire de la Reformation for their comments on and criticisms of an oral presentation of this material on edification. Edification has been central to recent historiography on the Presbyterian debate (see J. S. Coolidge, *The Pauline Renaissance in England*, Oxford, 1970, esp. 20–71; P. Lake, *Anglicans or Puritans?* ch. 2; Diarmaid MacCulloch, *The Later English Reformation 1547-1603*, London, 2001, pp. 71–3 and 75).

[2] Article 34: 'De traditionibus ecclesiasticis ... Quaelibet ecclesia particularis sive nationalis autoritatem habet instituendi mutandi aut abrogandi caeremonias aut ritus ecclesiasticos, humana tantum autoritate institutos, modo omnia ad aedificationem fiant'. It was also present in the earlier version of the Articles.

[3] Anon., *A New Enterlude No Lesse Wittie then Pleasant Entituled New Custome Devised of Late*, London: Abraham Veale, 1573, sig. D4ᵛ. (The prologue to this work interesting adapts philosophical topoi on the prevalence of error in the formation of judgements to a religious register.) Note that 'Edification' was not normally one of the characters of these dramatic interludes, and the appearance of the name suggests how firm a hold the concept had obtained upon members of the London audience for interludes in the early 1570s. Edification appears also in that 'official' epitome of Elizabethan belief, the *Homilies*.

Appendix II: A Note on Edification

This key item in dispute between the two camps came with an undoubtedly Pauline heritage.[4] Rather like the phrase 'and pitched his tent amongst us', the original Greek word (οἰκοδομέω) captured in its metaphorical grasp both the divine and the social, the celestial and the architectural.[5] The word was translated (not unnaturally) in the Vulgate by *aedificare*.[6] This connotational instability presented for Cartwright and Whitgift a range of problems. It also provided, as we shall see, Howard with the material for a joke. A good idea of the differences between the Puritan and Conformist camps in relation to edification may be obtained from a comparison of their diverse approaches to the topic when discussing ministerial apparel.[7] 'They serve not to edification' is Cartwright's comment. Whitgift replies 'I say they do not edifie of themselves: for only the holy Ghost on this sort doth edifie, by the ministerie of the worde.' And Whitgift again: 'Peter Martyr in his epistle written unto M. Hooper thinketh that they do edifie after a sort as other ceremonies, and so doth M. Bucer in his epistle written to M. Lasco.' Howard, as we shall see, is untroubled by these doubts in his usage of the term. Finally, Whitgift connects edification with the notion of the lawful magistracy, drawing on the link to authority that Luther had already made: 'Furthermore that they do edify it is manifest first because they are by a lawfull magistrat, by lawfull authoritie.' However, Cartwright does not simply reject the connection between the lawful external ecclesiological structure and edification. Rather, he rejects the claim, saying 'as though the lawful magistrate does nothing at any time unlawfully'. This gives a good starting point for discussion of edification in the Presbyterian crisis. The meaning and status of this concept had changed over time, however. I shall note the variety of the term, and how its latent association with authority became stronger in the sixteenth century.

Thomas Aquinas discusses the topic in his *Summa theologica*. In one discussion of prophecy, he stresses that while it deals with cognition, it

---

[4] E.g. Ephesians, 2.20 and 22; 4.12; Romans 14.9.
[5] John 1.14: 'καὶ ἐσκήνωσεν ἐν ἡμῖν'.
[6] Similarly, 'edificato' and its cognates were used in Italian in the transferred sense by the *spirituali*: see, e.g., Benedetto da Mantova, *Beneficio di Cristo*, ed. Salvatore Caponetto, Florence, 1972, IV, 151–2: a definition of faith as 'la pietra, sopra la quale la conscienza edificata non teme alcune tempeste …' (underscore mine).
[7] All the following quotations are taken from Whitgift, *Defense*, pp. 286–7.

also has an important role in edification.[8] The state of edification is not a form of knowledge and therefore should be kept within the pastoral framework of *utilitas*. When St Paul says of prophecy, 'qui prophetat, hominibus loquitur ad aedificationem, exortationem et consolationem' (I Corinthians 14.3), we can clearly see the rhetorical imprint of his affective ministry. Thomas Aquinas notes that 'edification makes the people devout', which shows again the role of edification in the social church. There is also a pronounced consolatory, uplifting and healing character to the concept in medieval usage.[9] Edification is not something one can do by oneself. In contrast to the popular understanding of the term in the later seventeenth and eighteenth centuries (where edification is regularly private and frequently female), for the late medieval mind it was something which arose from a relationship.[10] Luther emphasized the intersubjective nature of the concept.[11] Like his medieval forebears, he goes on to stress its consolatory

---

[8] Thomas Aquinas, *Summa theologica*, Leonine edition, Quaestio 171a. 1 arg 2: '*qui prophetat, hominibus loquitur ad aedificationem*. Sed locutio est effectus cognitionis, non autem est ipsa cognitio. Ergo videtur quod prophetia non est cognoscitive perfectio'; and again, Quaestio 171a. 1 co.: 'respondeo dicendum quod prophetia primo et principaliter consistit in cognitione, quia videlicet cognsocunt quaedam quae sunt procul remota ab hominum cognitione … Unde et gentilitas eos appellabat vates, a vi mentis. Sed quia, ut dicitur I ad Cor XII, unicuique datur manifestatio spiritus ad utilitatem; et infra XIV, dicitur, *ad aedificationem Ecclesiae quaerite ut abundetis*, inde est quod prophetia secundario consistit in locutione, prout prophetae ea quae … aedificationem aliorum annuntiant.'

[9] See W. Burger, *Aedificatio, utilitas, fructus. Jean Gerson als Professor der Theologie und Kanzler der Universität Paris*, Tübingen, 1986, pp. 40–55. This was a natural reading; consider Ambrose's words in his commentary on Romans 14.9 (*Opera*, ed. Erasmus: Basel: Froben, 1555, p. 236): 'Quoniam disceptatio discordiam parit, ideo ut pacisci esse possumus, ab intentione edendi aut non edendi dissimulare nos docet. Aedificationis autem viam sequi hortatur, ut cum pace ea conferamus, per quae invicem nos aedificemus, ab iis quae infructuosa sunt & magis contraria declinantes. Collatio enim potest prodesse. Est enim excitans mentem, si tamen vincendi studium contemnatur.'

[10] This is an exaggeration, since we are aware of the medieval practice of edifying reading (Gillian Rosemary Evans, '*Sententiola ad aedificationem*. The dicta of St. Anslem and St. Bernard', *Révue Benedictine*, 92, 1982, pp. 159–71). For some of the private associations of edification, see J. Kettlewell, *A Discourse Explaining the Nature of Edification*, London: Kettlewell, 1684, esp. his discussion of the 'edification of Particular Men and Private Christians, and that is in any Growth or Improvement, either in Faith or in Manners', p. 3. See also the notion of 'private' edification (and the growth of the transitive usage of the verb with 'men' rather than solely being used with – in a fashion akin to the cognate accusative – of 'the church') at Anon., *A Discourse about Edification*, London: Gardiner, 1683, sig. A2ᵛ.

[11] Martin Luther, 'Commentary on Paul's Letter to the Romans', in *Werke*, Weimar, 1938, LVI, p. 134, Romans 14.19: '**et que** quae [sic] **edificationis** ad mutuam salutem promotionis **sunt invicem** [et melius est, Ut illud invicem ad edificationem et mutuam salutem sectemur] <custodiamus>. Non est in Greco.' Luther's comment 'Non est in Greco' refers to the word 'custodiamus' which translates the φυλάξομεν present in some inferior manuscripts.

Appendix II: A Note on Edification

qualities.[12] He departs, however, from his forebears when he goes on to link the concept with that of authority: 'there is no authority in the Church but edification'.[13] This connection of edification with ecclesiological legitimacy was to have its bitterest fruit in the Presbyterian dispute of the 1570s, but another key connection, that with hermeneutics, is also foreshadowed in a debate between Luther and the Catholic apologist Ambrosius Catharinus, a Dominican theologian born Lanceloto Politi (c.1484–1553). Catharinus charges Luther with confusing the function of edification; it is not, Catharinus asserts, a tool for the correct understanding of Scripture, but rather one for generating a particular effect on others.[14] For Calvin, the concept is less connected with authority and closer to the task of practical divinity, though he does mention that even psalms intoned in the church were capable of edifying.[15] But what, one may ask, is this state of edification, more usually adverted to than defined?[16] Clearly, it is a state of heightened religiosity occasioned by some verbal, not necessarily homiletic, transaction. The increased philological awareness of the sixteenth century caused confusion as to what, precisely, was being built. This generated fur-

---

[12] Ibid., p. 136, Romans 15.2: 'ad **aedificationem**. Non ad vanam iactantiam vel carnalem consolationem.'

[13] Luther, 'Letter to the Christian Nobility of the German Nation', in *Werke*, Weimar, 1888, VI, p. 414. The passage continues with the assertion that if the pope were to order a council for which he had no authority, he would thereby become a hindrance to the edification of the church.

[14] Ambrosius Catharinus Politus, O. P. R., *Apologia pro veritate catholicae et apostolicae fidei ac doctrinae adversus impia ac valde pestifera Martini Lutheri dogmata*, ed. Josef Schweizer, Münster, 1956, p. 101: 'Origenes: Ad alios igitur non dixi, quod "vere esset dictum" quid dictum "vere" idest litteraliter non erat, sed quod videtur dictum, quia verba illa ad omnium doctrinam (ut Paulus ait <Rom. 15.4>) et commodum dicta sunt, et in sensu mysterii et sacramenti et in sensu etiam vago et morali ad aedifcationem nostram, quem potissimum ibi meo more sum secutus ... Intellgis, Martine, ubi sit error tuus? Nam quod in sensu vago et morali ad nostram aedificationem pro more suo aptavit Origenes, tu ad litteralem trahis.' The Pauline reference in pointed brackets is not in the original text but has been supplied from a footnote in Schweizer's edition. I am endebted to Irena Backus for drawing my attention to the fascinating Politi.

[15] Jean Calvin, *Homilia in primum librum Samuelis*, Geneva: Carterius, 1604, sig. Gg2: 'lucre fideles hortatur eo loco ut Deum precantes, et ipsi psallentes, et precentur et psallant intelligentia, non lingua peregrina, sed vulgari et intelligibili, ut sit in ecclesia aedifcatio'. Calvin elsewhere stressed the consolatory and 'mutually accommodating' character of the term: see further the stunning work of J. Bohatec, *Calvins Lehre von Staat und Kirche*, Breslau, 1937, pp. 514–15, with footnotes.

[16] See 'Aedificatio – Der Bau der Kirche', in *Zucht und Ordnung. Reformierte Kirchenverfassungen im 16 und 17 Jahrhundert (Nassau-Dillenburg, Kurpfalz, Hessen-Kassel)*, ed. P. Münch, Tübingen, section. 4.2.

ther conceptual dispute in England of the 1570s as to the scope of the figural and the literal.

So central a concept was edification that one finds its presence continually in the Cartwright and Whitgift. Howard, by contrast, hardly mentions the concept. What he does do is sneer at the users of the term by referring to them punningly as 'these builders' and, in discussing the presbytery, he says one may justly take exception to this 'groundworke and foundation of this popular buylding', emphasizing the problems of policing the borders between the literal and figural.[17] Howard thus draws attention to his opponent's inability to construe the meanings of Scripture correctly since he regularly accuses them of conflating the metaphorical (what he terms in one place 'allegorical') meanings with literal ones.[18] Even more remarkable, however, is one of Howard's very few usages of the term.[19] Howard is defending the use of music in church in his chapter 'Of Singing'. Such a section is an innovation, since it did feature as an independent item for discussion in the previous works.[20]

> But seing that both himselfe [Cartwright] doth thinke it greatly for his credite & somewhat for the furderance of his cause, wherein he travayleth to decke his tale with floures and ornaments of Rhethoricke, sithe cunninge sayinge and cunning singing are al in one effect, & Aaron is commended for using the one in his legal ministerie, I find no warrant to reprove the other in the ministerie of the gospel. Such ought the singing to be in the Church as may be well heard and conceived by the people, which limitation being well observed, it maketh no matter how many lavish tongues utter their venime agaynst so laudable & godly an exercise. The best is nothing is usually song in the Church but what the people have by rote & therefore neede we lesse to feare their wante of edification, so long as the scriptures are distinctly read & the Psalms tretably and in good order sounded ... Musicam non impedies.'[21]

---

[17] Howard, *A Defense*, p. 122
[18] Howard, *A Defense*, pp. 150–1, where Howard accuses Cartwright of understanding one of St Paul's metaphors in too literal a fashion.
[19] There are three further rather general and vague uses of the term earlier on in the work: Howard, *A Defense*, p. 25: 'now omitting questions of pluralities, presentations, and suche like which rather make a noyse upon the stage than serve to edification'. See also p. 32 and p. 65.
[20] E.g.: Whitgift, *Defense*, 1574, p. 606: 'Synging I am sure you do not disallowe, beeing used in all reformed Churches.' There is an additional mention of singing the psalms at p. 741, but there Whitgift's emphasis is wholly on them being clearly pronounced and understood: 'the Psalmes being sung may as well be understanded as being sayde, and better too.'
[21] Howard, A *Defense*, pp. 177–8.

Appendix II: A Note on Edification

This is quite different from the Puritan conception of edification, and, one might add, it is rather a strange example to choose even for a Conformist. A convinced Puritan who read this passage would surely be shocked to discover that the slogan for the construction of the new Jerusalem was being used in this way. Note, too, the implications of Howard's usage of the phrase 'heard and conceived', which suggests passive listening to a skilled choir rather than the congregational intoning of the psalms. Howard's phraseology is careful not to exclude the use of Latin – contrast Calvin's *non lingua peregrina*. This difference in opinion over a single, though important, word shows that it was in reality differences in temperament and in religious experience that distinguished the participants, and it is for this reason that the dialectical arguments that both sides use are so often wide of the mark, albeit, especially in the Conformists' hands, so correct. A knowledge of arts course dialectic is an indispensable tool for interpreting these texts, but it is not a magic bullet and it does not free us of the need to be sensitive and informed readers of other aspects of the debate.

BIBLIOGRAPHY

Manuscript sources

BL Additional 15841
BL Additional MS 2724
BL Additional MS 6928, f. 285
BL Additional MS 10344
BL Additional MS 45716 A
BL Additional MS 46367
BL Additional MS 48029
BL Additional MS 52585
BL Cotton Caligula C vii
BL Cotton MS B I f. 94^v
BL Cotton Titus C vi
BL Harleian 1582
BL Harleian 6035
BL Harleian MS 7031
BL Harley MS 2178
BL Lansdowne 8
BL Lansdowne MS 18
BL Lansdowne MS 388
BL Lansdowne MS 860
BL Lansdowne 891
BL Lansdowne MS 980
BL MS Royal 12 B. XIX
BL MS Royal 12 F V
BL MS Royal 15 A XXV
BLO Bodley MS 616
BLO Malone MS 23
BLO MS Rawlinson D 985
Corpus Christi College, Cambridge, MS 119
DUL Howard MS 1
DUL Howard MS 5
King's College Archive, Cambridge, Commons Books, vol. 17 (1562–1564, 1566–7)
King's College Archive, Cambridge, Miscellaneous Collections 18/3
King's College Archive, Mundum Books, vol. 15
LPL Carew papers, MS 604
St John's College Archive, Cambridge, the Thin Red Book
Stonyhurst College Library, Robert Southwell Stonyhurst manuscript

TNA: PRO LR 2/115 and 2/117
TNA: PRO Prob 11/37/14
TNA: PRO SP 12/85/11
TNA: PRO SP 12/147/6
TNA: PRO SP 12/150/51
TNA: PRO SP12/151/46
TNA: PRO SP 12/151/47
TNA: PRO SP 12/168
TNA: PRO SP 53/10/78
TNA: PRO SP 53/10/79
TNA: PRO SP 53/10/81
TNA: PRO SP 53/10/82
TNA: PRO SP 53/10/84
TNA: PRO SP 53/10/87
TNA: PRO SP 53/10/89
TNA: PRO SP 53/10/90
TNA: PRO SP 53/10/91
TNA: PRO SP 53/10/92
TNA: PRO SP 53/10/103
TNA: PRO SP 53/12/62

An annotated handlist of the Elizabethan works of Henry Howard

This list excludes the many partial witnesses to the text of the 'Dutiful Defence', in the main later seventeenth-century copies often associated with the 'Feathery Scribe', all of which were generously drawn to my attention by Peter Beal, who was also solely responsible for the American witnesses to the Charles V translation. Professor Beal will publish a more codicologically detailed list of Howard's manuscripts in the near future, as part of the Census of English Literary Manuscripts, a draft of which he generously shared with me.

A speculative word on the diffusion of these manuscripts is perhaps in order. There are far more manuscripts surviving from later on in Howard's career than earlier. It may be that in the various arrests, searches and other changes of location, several manuscripts were lost. Furthermore, scribes were not cheap, and Howard in the 1560s and 1570s seems to have been short of money to a greater extent than in the 1590s.

1569: Natural Philosophy treatise
BLO Bodley MS 616, natural philosophy manuscript
Presentation copy of treatise, prefaced by dedication to Howard's sister (ff. 1–12^v); secretary script by Howard's Cambridge scribe; 1569; Normandy pot watermark; luxurious calf binding tooled in gilt

1571: Epicedion for Nicholas Carr
Demosthenis, Grecorum oratorum principis, Olynthiacae orationes tres, & Philippicae quattuor, e greco in latinum conversae a Nicolao Carro, Novocastrensi, doctore medico,

& Grecarum literarum in Cantabrigiensi Academia professore regio. Addita est etiam epistola de vita & obitu Nicolai Carri & carmina, cum greca, tum Latina in eundem conscripta. /apud Henricum Denham: Londini anno 1571
Physical description: [12], 83, [1] pages. Quarto. 20cm x 18cm
Signatures: A–Y, 2A–2B
Number of extant copies: 8
Location of copies: BL; CUL (x4); St John's College, Cambridge; BLO (x2)

1574: Polemic against Thomas Cartwright

A Defense of the Ecclesiasticall Regiment in Englande Defaced by T. C. in his Replie Agaynst D. VVhitgifte. Seene and allowed according to the order appoynted in the Queenes Maiesties iniunctions / Imprinted at London : By Henry Bynneman, for Humfrey Toy, Anno. 1574
Physical description: [4], 194, [2] pages. Octavo. 14 x 15cm
Signatures: [par.]², A–M, N²
Number of extant copies: 14
Location of copies: M; BL (x5, one of which omits a title page); LPL, owned by Richard Bancroft; Beinecke; Huntington, owned by William Lambarde; CUL (x3, one of which omits the title page); BLO (x2)

c.1576: 'Regina fortunata'

BL Egerton MS 944
Presentation copy, autograph throughout in Howard's square italic script; with dedication to Queen Elizabeth, gilt-edged paper; illustration of Elizabeth; Normandy pot watermark; c.1576

1580: Anjou marriage tract

BL Additional MS 48027
Fair copy, secretary script; unknown scribe; this ms came into the possession, it would appear, of Robert Beale; late 16th century

BL Additional MS 34216
Copy in a (?) scribe's hand; unknown scribe; bound with similar documents; early 17th century

BL Cotton MS Titus C. XVIII
Copy in a neat predominantly italic script, untitled, on 29 quarto leaves; the first page signed Ro. Cotton Bruceus; early 17th century

BL Harley MS 180
Copy, entitled 'The Lord Henry Howard after Earle of Northampton his defence Of the ffrench Monsieurs desiring Queene Elizabeth in marriage written in Ao. 22o. Eliz. Ao.Do. 1580, in Answare To Mr. Stubbs treatyse foregoeing which was intitled The Discouerie of a gapeing Gulfe. &c.'; mixed script; bound with similar documents; dated (2 April 1627) annotation by Sir Simonds D'Ewes (1602–50); ? early 17th century

Bibliography

1583: Astrological polemic

A Defensative Against the Poyson of Supposed Prophecies: not hitherto confuted by the penne of any man, which being grounded, eyther uppon the warrant and authority of olde paynted bookes, expositions of dreames, oracles, revelations, invocations of damned spirites, iudicialles of astrologie, or any other kinde of pretended knowledge whatsoeuer, de futuris contingentibus: have beene causes of great disorder in the common wealth, cheefly among the simple and unlearned people: very needefull to be published at this time, considering the late offence which grew by most palpable and grosse errours in astrology / At London : printed by Iohn Charlewood, printer to the right Honourable Earle of Arundell, 1583
Physical description: 332 pages. Quarto. 20 x 18cm
Signatures: [par.]4 *4 [sec.]2, A–Y, 2A–2R [A1 and E4 are cancels in all reported copies]

c.1580s–1589 Devotional Centos and Offices

BL Arundel MS 300
Fair (? presentation) copy, autograph throughout; devotional offices are closely related in content to Additional MS 78414, but lacking the dedicatory epistle and illustrations; contemporary foliation throughout

BL Additional MS 78414
Presentation copy, autograph throughout. Devotional offices are prefaced by dedicatory epistle to Lord Burghley (ff. 1–68); a number of illustrations throughout, no indication of the artist. Paper continuous throughout manuscript; contemporary foliation throughout

DUL Howard MS 1
Preliminary 'rough draft', autograph throughout. In two sections. First section runs from f. 54 to f. 64; the second from f. 66 to f. 75. The two sections were composed at different times, as is suggested by the different paper with different watermarks used for each section; contemporary foliation throughout

DUL Howard MS 5
Preliminary rough drafts of devotional materials; autograph throughout. Contemporary foliation of both prayers and a letter dated in 1584 suggests that date of this manuscript is earlier than the other manuscripts

Rare Book School, Virginia, USA, Collections ID number 4876: "A book of Devotions"
Fair copy, autograph throughout in Howard's square italic; ruled margin in red throughout. Devotional offices preceded (ff.1-15, though the preface is unfoliated) by 'The Preface', in which he calls the works 'the roote of private prayer'. Preface signed 'from Howarde howse this 16 of julye'.

c.1590 Charles V translation

BL King's MS 166
Fair (? presentation) copy; non-autograph, apart from signature at f. 9; with dedication to Elizabeth (ff. 2^r–9^r); the scribe could be the same as the one used for the Dutiful Defence presentation manuscripts; c.1590

BL Lansdowne MS 792
Fair (? presentation) copy; non-autograph; with dedication to Elizabeth (ff. 2ʳ–9ʳ); the scribe could be the same as the one used for the Dutiful Defence presentation manuscripts; c.1590

BLO MS Eng Misc. d. 239
Presentation copy; non-autograph; non-professional scribe; secretary script throughout; the scribe appears to be Paul Thompson (as marginalium makes clear on f. 5) but he was not a professional scribe; ? late 16th century

BL Additional MS 61728
Copy of the main text, lacking the Dedication to the queen, in a professional hand, untitled; in a quarto volume of military and state tracts and extracts; later owned by John Rider; sold at Christie's, 30 January 1980, lot 102; early 17th century

BL Harley MS 836
Copy of main text, lacking the dedication to Elizabeth

BL Harley MS 1506
Copy in two hands, untitled, with Dedication to the queen, incomplete, torn in half down the pages and lacking the ending, in a composite folio volume of heraldic and antiquarian MSS; late 16th-/early 17th-century

BL Sloane MS 1432
Copy of the main text, lacking the Dedication to the queen, in italic script throughout; unknown scribe; c.1630

BL Stowe MS 95, ff. 3–25
Copy, complete with Dedication 'To the Queenes moste excellente Matie:', headed 'A memoriall of a discourse vsed by the late worthy Emperour Charles the vth vppon the resignemt of his gouermente, and stats to his sonne, the now kinge of Spaine', on 45 folio pages; name on f. 1ᵛ of 'John Gybbon'; inscription on f. 2ʳ 'Lent to Mr Gunton. Feb. 16. 1648 ...'; early 17th century

BL Stowe MS 161
Copy of the main text (ff. 3ʳ–23ʳ), followed by the Dedication to Elizabeth; italic script throughout, hand of a professional scribe; c.1630

CUL MS Mm. I. 26
Copy, complete with Dedication 'To the Queenes most Excellent Majestie', headed 'The Memoriall of a Discourse used by the late worthie Emperor Charles the Vth vpon the Resignement of his Government & State to his Sonne, Philip .II. King of Spaine', on 110 quarto pages; from the library of George I; c.1630

CUL MS Mm. VI. 58, ff. 273–88v
Copy of about two-thirds of the main text, incomplete and omitting the Dedication, untitled, in a composite folio volume of legal and historical tracts; early–mid-17th century

Huntington, EL 1612, pp. 87–140
Copy in a single hand, complete with Dedication 'To the Quenes most excellent Matie' (pp. 87–93); in a small folio volume of state letters and tracts, among the Ellesmere papers; early 17th century

Bibliography

Huntington, HAP Box 15/8A
Fragment of a copy, lacking Dedication and ending, on six unbound folio leaves (ff. 4^r–9^v), among the Hastings papers; early 17th century

Huntington, HA 6909
Copy of the Dedication 'To the Queenes most excellent Ma*jestie*' only, in a single secretary hand, on six folio pages; among the Hastings papers; 17th century

LPL MS 711, ff. 213^r–96^v
Copy, complete with dedication to the queen (ff. 215–25^v); 17th-century copy

TNA: PRO SP 12/146/1
Copy, complete with dedication to the queen, on 66 folio pages; late 16th–early 17th century

Yale, Osborn Collection b 31
Copy, *non vidi*

Yale, Osborn Collection fb 27
Copy, *non vidi*

1590 'Dutiful Defence of the Lawful Regiment of Women'

BLO MS Bodley 903
Presentation copy for (?) Sir John Stanhope; secretary and italic script; introduction written in italic script but not Howard's hand; otherwise secretary script, in a hand of a scribe Howard was to use again, but deliberate marginalia in Howard's square italic; with dedication to Elizabeth (ff. 1–20); c.1590 (on the assumption that presentation copies should, in the absence of other evidence, often be dated contemporaneously with initial publication)

BL Additional MS 24652
Presentation copy to (?) Thomas Heneage; secretary script; chiefly written by the same scribe as the other presentation copies of this work, but deliberate marginalia in Howard's square italic; with dedication to Elizabeth; c.1590 (Heneage died in 1595)

BL Harley MS 6257
Presentation copy to Sir Robert Cotton; secretary script; chiefly written by a scribe, but with marginalia in Howard's square italic; with dedication to Elizabeth; early 17th century

BL Lansdowne 813
Presentation copy to Sir George Carey; secretary script; same as other presentation copies of this work, but with marginalia in Howard's square italic hand; with dedication to Elizabeth (ff. 1–27); c.1590

Harvard fMS 826
Presentation copy for Earl of Essex; *non vidi*

Magdalene College, Cambridge, Pepys Library MS 2191
Presentation copy to William Cecil, later Lord Burghley; secretary script; same scribe as the other presentation copies of this work, but with marginalia in Howard's square italic hand; with dedication to Elizabeth (f. 2–27); c.1590

University College, London, MS Ogden 16
Presentation copy to a member of the Trumbull family; autograph dedication to Elizabeth; secretary script; same scribe as the other presentation copies of this work, but with marginalia in Howard's square italic hand; with dedication to Elizabeth (ff. 2–27); c.1590s

Newberry Library, Chicago, Case MS FJ 5452.634
Copy; *non vidi*

General bibliography

Adams, Simon, 'Favourites and Factions at the Elizabethan Court', in *Princes, Patronage and the Nobility: The Court at the Beginning of the Modern Age: c.1450–1650*, eds R. G. Asche and A. M. Birke, Oxford, 1991, pp. 265–88
Addison, W., *Audley End*, London, 1953
Agricola, R., *De inventione dialectica*, ed. Alardus Aemsteledamus, Cologne: J. Gymnicus, 1539
Agricola, R., *De inventione dialectica*, ed. L. Mundt, Tübingen, 1992
Airs, Malcolm, *The Tudor and Jacobean Country House*, London, 1995
Alford, Stephen, *The Early Elizabethan Polity: William Cecil and the British Succession Crisis 1558–1569*, Cambridge, 1998
Allen, Don Cameron, *Francis Meres' Treatise on 'Poetrie'*, Chicago, 1933
Allen, Don Cameron, *The Star-Crossed Renaissance*, Durham: NC, 1941
Ambrose, *Opera*, ed. Erasmus, Basel: Froben, 1555
Andersson, D. C., review of John Bossy, *Under The Molehill*, *Notes and Queries*, 49, 2002, 178–9
Andersson, D. C., 'Th'Expense of Spirit in a Waste of Shame. Aristotelian Exposures in Montaigne', in *Exposures. Revealing Bodies, Unveiling Representations*, eds K. Banks and J. Harris, Geneva, 2004, pp. 61–75
Andersson, D. C., 'Embarke but under caution. New Fragments of an Elizabethan Masque', *Notes and Queries*, 55, 2008, pp. 171–75
Andersson, D. C., 'Humanism and Natural Philosophy in Renaissance Cambridge: Bodley Ms. 616', *History of Universities* (forthcoming)
Andersson, D. C., 'Dialectic and the Church: Experience, Ecclesiology and the Limits of Argument in the Presbyterian Controversy', *Renaissance and Reformation* (forthcoming)
Anon., *Salutem in Christo: Good Men and Evil Delight in Contraries*, London: Richard Grafton, 1571
Anon., *A Treatise of Treasons*, Louvain: John Fowler, 1572
Anon., *A New Enterlude No Lesse Wittie then Pleasant Entituled New Custome Devised of Late*, London: Abraham Veale, 1573
Anon., *A True Reporte of a Conference had betwixt Doctour Fulke, and the Papists, being at Wisbiche Castle, Doctour Fulke beeyng sent thither by the bishope of Ely, the 4 of October*, 1580
Anon., *A Discoverie of the Treasons Practiced and Attempted by Francis Throckmorton*, London [1584]
Anon., *A Historicall Narration of the First Fourteen Years of King James*, London, 1651

Bibliography

Anon., *A Discourse about Edification*, London: Gardiner, 1683
Anstruther, G., *The Seminary Priests*, Durham, n.d.
Arber, Edward, *A Transcript of the Registers of the Company of Stationers of London, 1554–1640 AD*, 5 vols, London [and Birmingham], 1875–1894
Arfé, Pasquale, 'The Annotations of Nicolaus Cusanus and Giovanni Andrea Bussi on the *Asclepius*', *JWCI*, 62, 1999, pp. 25–59
Ariew, Roger, *Descartes and the Last Scholastics*, Ithaca: NY, 1999
Armstrong, G., 'The Political Theory of the Huguenots', *English Historical Review*, 4, 1889, pp. 13–40
Ascham, *The Scholemaster*, London: John Day, 1570
Ascham, Roger, *The Schoolmaster*, ed. L. Ryan, New York, 1967
Ashworth, E. J., 'The Libelli Sophistarum and the Use of Medieval Logic Texts at Oxford and Cambridge in the Early Sixteenth Century', *Vivarium*, 17, 1979, pp. 134–58
Aston, M., *The King's Bedpost*, Cambridge, 1993
Axton, Marie, *The Queen's Two Bodies: Drama and the Elizabethan Succession*, London, 1977
Aylmer, John, *An Harborowe for Faithfull and Trewe Subjects*, London: Day, 1559
Bacon, Francis, *The Advancement of Learning*, ed. M. Kiernan, Oxford, 2000
Baldwin, T. W., *Shakesperes Small Latine and Lesse Greek*, Chicago, 1965
Baldwin, William, *A Treatise of Morrall Philosophie*, edited with additional material by Thomas Palfreyman, London: Thomas Snodham, 1605
Barber, Bruno, and Christopher Thomas, *The London Charterhouse*, Museum of London Archeology Service 10, London, 2002
Barker, Nicholas, 'The Books of Henry Howard, Earl of Northampton', *Bodleian Library Record*, 13, 1990, pp. 376–8
Barnes, K., 'John Stubbe: The French Ambassador's Account 1579', *Historical Journal*, 34, 1991, pp. 421–6
Basile, Bruno 'Tasso e le "Sententiae" di Stobeo', *Filologia e critica*, 7, 1981, pp. 34–41
Bauer, Karl, *Die Wittenberger Universitäts Theologie und die Anfänge der deutschen Reformation*, Tübingen, 1928
Beales, A. C. F., *Education Under Penalty: English Catholic Education From the Reformation to the Fall of James II*, Oxford, 1963
Bedouelle, G. and Roussel, B., *Le Temps des Reformes et la Bible*, Paris, 1989
Bell, G. M., 'John Man: The Last Elizabethan Resident Ambassador in Spain', *Sixteenth-Century Journal*, 2, 1976, pp. 75–93
Bellany, Alistair, *The Politics of Court Scandal in Early Modern England: News Culture and the Overbury Affair, 1603–1660*, London, 2002
du Bellay, Jean, *Les Regrets*, ed. S. de Sasy, Paris, 1967
Bentley, J. H., 'New Testament Scholarship at Louvain in the Early Sixteenth Century', *Studies in Medieval and Renaissance History*, II, 1979, pp. 53–79
Besley, W. T., 'St. Leonard's Priory, Norwich', *Norfolk Archaeology*, 12, 1895, pp. 190–233
Bianchi, L., *Studi sull'Aristotelismo del Rinascimento*, Padua, 2003
Binns, J. W., *Intellectual Culture in Elzabethan England*, Leeds, 1990
A Biographical Register of the University of Cambridge, ed. A. B. Emden, Cambridge,

1963
Blayney, Peter, *The Bookshops in Paul's Cross Churchyard*, Cambridge, 1990
Blundeville, Thomas, *The True Order and Method of Wryting and Reading Hystories*, London, 1574
Bohatec, Josef, *Calvins Lehre von Staat und Kirche*, Breslau, 1937
Bossy, John, *Giordano Bruno and the Embassy Affair*, London, 1994
Bossy, John, *Under the Molehill: An Elizabethan Spy Story*, London, 2001
Bossy, John, 'Rome and the Elizabethan Catholics: A Question of Geography', *Historical Journal*, 7, 1964, pp. 135–49
Bossy, John, 'William Byrd Investigated 1583/4', *Annual Byrd Newsletter*, pp. 5–7 in *Early Music Review*, 2002
Botley, Paul, *Latin Translation in the Renaissance*, Cambridge, 2004
Bourgeon, Jean-Louis, *Charles IX devant la Saint-Barthélemy*, Geneva, 1995
Boutcher, W., 'Vernacular Humanism in the Sixteenth Century', in *The Cambridge Companion to Renaissance Humanism*, ed. Jill Kraye, Cambridge, 1996
Boutcher, Warren, 'Pilgrimage to Parnassus: Local Intellectual Traditions, Humanist Education and the Cultural Geography of Sixteenth-Century England', in *Pedagogy and Power: Rhetorics of Ancient Learning*, eds Niall Livingstone and Yun Lee Too, Cambridge, 1998, pp. 110–24
Bracciolini, Poggio, *Les facecies de Poge*, eds F. Duval and S. Hériche-Pradeau, Geneva, 2003
Bradshaw, Henry, 'An Inventory of the Stuff in the College Chambers (King's College) 1598', *Cambridge Archaeological Society Commentaries*, 1879, III, pp. 181–98
Bray, Roger, 'Music and the Quadrivium in Early Tudor England', *Music and Letters*, 76, 2000, pp. 1–18
Brigden, Susan, *New Worlds, Lost Worlds*, London, 2000
Brooke, C., 'Allocating Rooms In Sixteenth-Century Cambridge', *The Caian*, 1987, pp. 56–7
Brooks, Christopher and Kevin Sharpe, 'Debate. History, English Law and the Renaissance', *Past and Present*, 1976, pp. 133–42
Broomhall, Susan, *Women and the Book Trade in Sixteenth-Century France*, Aldershot, 2002
Brown, Christopher, 'British Painting and the Low Countries, 1530–1630', in *Dynasties. Painting in Tudor and Jacobean England*, ed. K. Hearn, New York, 1995
Bruni, Francesco, 'Sperone Speroni e la Academia degli Infiammati', *Filologia e letteratura*, Naples, 1967, pp. 27–71
Bryson, A., *From Courtesy to Civility: Changing Codes of Conduct in Early Modern England*, Oxford, 1998
Bull, Malcolm, *The Mirror of the Gods: Classical Mythology in Renaissance Art*, London, 2005
Burger, W., *Aedificatio, utilitas, fructus. Jean Gerson als Professor der Theologie und Kanzler der Universität Paris*, Tübingen, 1986
Burke, Peter, *The Fortunes of the Courtier*, London, 1996
Burrows, Mark S., 'Jean Gerson on the Traditioned Sense of Scripture as an

Argument for an Ecclesial Hermeneutic,' in *Biblical Hermeneutics in Historical Perspective*, eds Mark S. Burrows and Paul Rorem, Grand Rapids: MI, 1991, pp. 152–72
Buzzi, Franco, *Teologia e cultura cristiana tra xv e xvi secolo*, Genoa, 2000
Cairns, F., 'The Metrical and Stylistic Competence of Latin Poetry in the Second Half of the Fifteenth Century', in *Homo Sapiens, Homo Humanus*, ed. G. Taurigi, Florence, 1990, pp. 33–40
Calvin, Jean, *Sermons de Jean Calvin sur les epistres de Sainct Paul a Timonthee et sur l'epistre a Tite*, Geneva: Jean Bonnefoy, 1563
Calvin, Jean, *Advertissement contre l'astrologie qu'on appelle judiciare, et autres curiosités qui règnent aujourdhuis dans le monde*, ed. O. Millet, Geneva, 1985
Calvin, Jean, *Homilia in primum librum Samuelis*, Geneva: Carterius, 1604
Camden, William, *The Historie of the Moste Renowned and Victorious Princesse Elizabeth*, London: Benjamin Fisher, 1630
Camporeale, Salvatore, *Lorenzo Valla: umanesimo e teologia*, Florence, 1972
Capp, B., *Astrology and the Popular Press: English Almanacs 1500–1800*, London, 1979
Cardano, Girolamo, *De subtilitate*, ed. Elio Nenci, Milan, 2004
Carpenter, Christopher, *The Wars of the Roses*, Cambridge, 1997
Cartwright, Thomas, *A Replye Made to an Answere Made of Doctor Whitegifte*, London, [1573]
Castiglione, Baldassare, *Il libro del cortegiano*, Venice: Aldus Manutius, 1541
Castiglione, Baldassare, *The Book of the Courtier*, ed. W. H. D. Rouse, London, 1959
Cataneo, Arturo, *L'ideale umanistico: Henry Howard, Earl of Surrey*, Bari, 1991
Catharinus Politus, O. P. R., Ambrosius, *Apologia pro veritate catholicae et apostolicae fidei ac doctrinae adversus impia ac valde pestifera Marthini Lutheri dogmata*, ed. Josef Schweizer, Münster, 1956
Cave, Terence, *The Cornucopian Text: Problems of Writing in the French Renaissance*, Oxford, 1979
Cerreta, Florindo Vincent, *Alessandro Piccolomini: letterato a filosofo senese del cinquecento*, Siena, 1960
Chamber, John, *A Discourse against Judicial Astrologie*, London: John Harison, 1601
Chambers, David, *Discours de la legitime succession des femmes aux possessions de leur parents et du gouvernement aux empires et royaumes*, Paris, 1579
Chomorat, Jacques, 'Erasme lecteur des *Elegantiae* de Valla', in *Acta neolatini conventus Amstelodamnesis*, eds J. Tuynman, G. Kuiper and E. Kessler, Munich, 1979, pp. 203–46
Churchyard, Thomas, *A Discourse of the Queene's Majesties Entertainment in Norfolk and Suffolk*, London: Henry Bynneman, 1578
Clegg, Susan Cyndia, *Press Censorship in Elizabethan England*, Cambridge, 1997
Clucas, Stephen, 'Thomas Harriot and the Field of Renaissance Science', in *Thomas Harriot: An Elizabethan Man of Science*, ed. R. Fox, London, 2002, pp. 93–106
Clucas, Stephen and Gordon Batho, *The Wizard Earl's Advices to His Son*, The Roxburghe Club, 2002
Colclough, David, *Freedom of Speech in Early Stuart England*, Cambridge, 2005
Coleridge, Samuel Taylor, *Biographia Literaria*, ed. G. Watson, London, 1906

A Collection of Letters, Documents, Statutes Illustrative of the History of the University of Cambridge, ed. J. Lamb, London, 1838
Collinson, Patrick, *The Elizabethan Puritan Movement*, London, 1968
Collinson, Patrick, *Edmund Grindal 1519–1583: The Struggle for a Reformed Church*, London, 1979
Collinson, Patrick, *The English Captivity of Mary, Queen of Scots*, Sheffield, 1987
Collinson, Patrick, *Elizabethan Essays*, London, 1994
Collinson, Patrick, 'The Elizabethan Exclusion Crisis and the Elizabethan Polity', *Proceedings of the British Academy*, 84, 1993, pp. 51–92
Collinson, Patrick, 'Biblical Rhetoric: The English Nation and National Sentiment in the Prophetic Mode', in *Religion and Culture in the English Renaissance*, eds C. McEachern and D. Shuger, Cambridge, 1997, pp. 27–45
Colomer, J. L., 'Translation and Imitation: Amplification as a Means of Adapting the Spanish Picaresque Novel', *Révue de la literature comparée*, 67, 1989, pp. 369–76
Commentaria in Isagogen Porphyrii, et in omnes libros de dialectica Aristotelis, Louvain, 1535
Coolidge, J. S., *The Pauline Renaissance in England*, Oxford, 1970
Cooper, J., *Annals of Cambridge*, 3 vols, Cambridge, 1842–1853
Copenhaver, Brian, 'Translation, Terminology and Style in Philosophical Discourse', in *The Cambridge History of Renaissance Philosophy*, ed. E. Kessler, C. B. Schmitt and Q. Skinner with J. Kraye, Cambridge, 1988, pp. 76–90
Coquillette, D., *The Civilian Writers of Doctors Commons*, Berlin, 1988
Correspondence of King James VI of Scotland with Sir Robert Cecil and Others in England During the Reign of Queen Elizabeth…, ed. J. Bruce, London, 1848
Covell, William, *Polimanteia*, Cambridge: John Legate, 1595
Cowell, John, *Institutiones iuris anglicani*, Cambridge: John Legate, 1605
Craig, John, 'Erasmus' *Paraphrases* in English Parishes, 1547–1666', in *Holy Scripture Speaks: the Production and Reception of Erasmus's Paraphrases on the New Testament*, eds Hilmar M. Pabel and Mark Vessey, Toronto, 2002, pp. 313–59
Cranefield, P., 'On the Origin of the Phrase, "Nihil est in intellectu quod non prius fuerit in sensu"', *Journal of the History of Medicine and Allied Sciences*, 25, 1970, pp. 36–47
Crawley, Charles, *Trinity Hall*, Cambridge, 1976
Cressy, David, *Birth, Marriage and Death: Ritual, Religion and the Life Cycle in Tudor and Stuart England*, Oxford, 1997
Croft, Pauline, 'Trading with the Enemy, 1585–1604', *Historical Journal*, 32, 1989, pp. 281–303
Curry, Patrick, *Prophecy and Power: Astrology in Early Modern England*, Cambridge, 1989
Curtis, Mark H., *Oxford and Cambridge in Transition: 1558–1642*, Oxford, 1959
Cusa, Nicholas, *De pace fidei*, eds R. Klibansky and H. Bascour, O. S. B., Hamburg,
Cyprian, *Opera*, ed. Erasmus Rotterdamus, Paris: Gryphius, 1569
Cyprian, *Opera*, ed. G. Pamelius, Paris: Sebastian Nivelle, 1574
Daston, Lorraine, 'The Nature of Early Modern Nature', *Configurations*, 6, 1998, pp. 149–72
Davies, Sir John, 'A Discourse on Law and Lawyers', in *The Complete Works…*, ed.

A. B. Grosart, London, 1869–1876

Dawson, J. P., *A History of Lay Judges*, Cambridge: MA, 1960

Des Chene, Denis, *Physiologia: Natural Philosophy in Late Aristotelian and Cartesian Philosophy*, Ithaca: NY, 1996

The Diary of Sir John Manningham, of the Middle Temple, and of Bradbourne, Kent, Barrister at Law, 1602–3, ed. J. Bruce, Westminster, 1868

The Digest of Justinian, ed. A. Watson, Philadelphia, 1985

Dionysius Areopagita, *Opera*, Paris: Rovilius, 1585

Divination et controverse religeuse en France au XVIe siècle, ed. N. Cazauran, Paris, 1987, republished 2002

The Divine Office in the Latin Middle Ages. Methodology, Source Studies, Regional Developments, Hagiography, eds. Margot Elisbeth Fassler and Rebecca A. Balzer, Oxford, 2000

Doran, Susan, *Monarchy and Matrimony: The Courtships of Elizabeth I*, London, 1996

van Dorsten, J. A., *The Radical Arts*, Leiden, 1970

D'Oyly Bayly, Walter, 'An Account of the Family of Hodilow', *Topographer and Genealogist*, 1853, pp. 28–72

Dreizel, Horst, *Protestantischer Aristotelismus und absoluter Staat*, Wiesbaden, 1970

Duke, Alistair, *Reformation and Revolt in the Low Countries*, London, 2003

Dunant, David N., *Bess of Hardwick: Portrait of an Elizabethan Dynast*, London, 1999

Duncan-Jones, Katherine, *Sir Philip Sidney: Courtier Poet*, 1991

Duncan-Jones, Katherine, '*Christ's Teares*: Nashe's Forsaken Extremities', *Review of English Studies*, 1998, pp. 167–80

Dynasties. Painting in Tudor and Jacobean England, ed. Karen Hearn, New York, 1995

Edward VI, *Chronicle*, ed. W. K. Jordan, London, 1966

Edwards, Francis, *The Marvellous Chance, Thomas Howard, Fourth Duke of Norfolk, and the Ridolfi Plot, 1570–1572*, London, 1968

Edwards, Francis, 'Sir Robert Cecil, Edward Squier and the Poisoned Pommel', *Recusant History*, 25, 2001, pp. 377–414

Eguiluz, Federico, *Robert Persons: El Architraidor. Su Vida y su Obra*, Madrid, 1990

The Elements of Roman Law, ed. R. W. Lee, London, 1956

Elyot, Thomas, *Dictionary*, London: Thomas Berthelet, 1538

England, Spain and the Gran Armada, 1585–1604, eds S. Adams and M. J. Rodriguez-Salgado, Edinburgh, 1991

Erasmus, Desiderius, *De duplici copia rerum et verborum*, Paris, 1512

Erasmus, Desiderius, *Opus epistolarum*, ed. P. S. Allen, 12 vols, Oxford, 1906–1958

Erasmus, Desiderius, *Opera omnia Desiderii Erasmi Roterodami: recognita et adnotatione critica instructa notisque illustrate*, Amsterdam, 1965–, [abbreviated to ASD]

Erastus, Thomas, *Defensio libelli Hieronymi Savonarolae in astrologiam divinatricem adversus Christophorum Stathmionem* [Paris]: Jean Le Preux, 1569

Erastus, Thomas, *De astrologia diviniatrice epistole*, Basel: Grynaeus, 1580

Evans, G. R., *Old Arts and New Theology: The Beginnings of Theology as an Academic Discipline*, Oxford, 1980

Evans, Gillian Rosemary, '*Sententiola ad aedificationem*. The dicta of St. Anslem and

St. Bernard', *Révue Benedictine*, 92, 1982, pp. 159–71
Facultas S[anctae] Theologiae Lovaniensis 1432-1797, eds E. M. Ejil and Anthony Black, Louvain, 1977
Fairbank, Alfred J. and Bruce Dickins, *The Italic Hand in Tudor Cambridge*, London, 1962
Faulkner, Robert K., *Richard Hooker and the Politics of a Christian England*, London, 1981
Feingold, Mordechai, 'The Occult Tradition at English Universities', in *Occult and Scientific Mentalities in the Renaissance*, ed. Brian Vickers, London, 1984, pp. 73–94
Fichter, Paula Sutter, *Emperor Maximilian II*, New Haven, 2001
Fine Bindings from Oxford Libraries: Catalogue of an Exhibition, Oxford, 1968
Finé, Oronce, *The Rules and Ryghte Ample Documents Touching the Use and Practise of the Common Almanackes which are named Ephemerides*, tr. Humfrey Baker, London: Thomas Marshe, 1555
Forster, Richard, *Ephemerides meteographicae*, London: John Kyngston, 1575
Fortuna di Michelangelo nell'incisione: catalogo della mostra, ed. Mario Rotili with the assistance of Maria Catelli Isola and Elio Galasso, Benevento, 1964
Fowler, Alistair, *Kinds of Literature*, Cambridge: MA, 1982
Fowler, Alistair, 'The Formation of Genres in the Renaissance and After', *New Literary History*, 34, 2003, pp. 185–200
Fox, Adam, *Oral and Literate Culture in England 1500-1700*, Oxford, 2000
Froehlich, K., 'Walafrid Strabo and the *Glossa Ordinaria*: The Making of a Myth', *Studia Patristica*, 28, 1993, pp. 192–6
Froehlich, K., 'The Fate of the Gloss Ordinaria in the Sixteenth Century', in *Die Patristik in die Bibelexegese des 16. Jahuhunderts*, ed. David C. Steimnetz, Wiesbaden, 1999, pp. 19–49
Fulke, William, *A Goodlye Gallerye*, London: William Griffith, 1563
Fulke, William, *A Goodlye Gallerye*, ed. Theodore Hornberger, Philadelphia, 1979
Gazzard, Hugh, 'Those Grave Presentiments of Antiquitie: Samuel Daniel's Philotas and the Earl of Essex', *Review of English Studies*, 51, 2000, pp. 423–50
Gelli, Giovanbattista, *Circe*, Florence: Lorenzo Torrentino, 1549
[Gelli, Giovanbattista], *Circes of G B Gello, Florentyne, Translated out of Italyon into Englishe, by H Iden, B. L.*, London: J. Cawoode, 1557
Gerson, Jean, *Liber de vita spirituali animae*, in *Oeuvres*, ed. Mgr. P. Glorieux, Paris, 1962
Gillingham, John, 'From Civilitas to Courtesy: Codes of Manners in Medieval and Early Modern England', *Transactions of the Royal Historical Society*, 12, 2002, pp. 267–89
Glomski, Jacqueline, 'Careerism at Cracow', in *Self-Presentation and Social Identification: The Rhetoric and Pragmatics of Letter Writing in Early Modern Times*, eds T. Van Houdt, J. Papy and G. Tournoy, Leuven, 2002, pp. 165–82
Goclenius, Rudolph, *Lexicon philosophicum*, Frankfurt, 1615 (reprinted Hildesheim, 1980)
The Gospel of Thomas, ed. M. Meyer, San Francisco, 1992
Gosselin, Edward A., 'A Listing of the Printed Editions of Nicholas of Lyra', *Traditio*,

Bibliography

26, 1970

Gough, J. W., *Fundamental Law in English Constitutional History*, Oxford, 1955

Gowland, Angus, *The Worlds of Renaissance Melancholy: Robert Burton in Context*, Cambridge, 2008

Grace Book Δ, Containing the Records of the University of Cambridge for the years 1542–1589, ed. J. Venn, Cambridge, 1910

Grafton, A., *Joseph Scaliger: A Study in the History of the Classical Tradition. I: Textual Criticism and Exegesis*, Oxford, 1983

Grafton, A. T., *Defenders of the Text: The Traditions of Scholarship in an Age of Science: 1450–1800*, Cambridge: MA, 1994

Grafton, A., *Cardano's Cosmos*, London, 1999

Grant, Leonard W., *Neo-Latin Literature and Pastoral*, Chapel Hill: NC, 1965

Grassby, R., 'The Decline of Falconry in Early Modern England', *Past and Present*, 157, 1997, pp. 37–62

Graves, Michael, *Thomas Norton*, Oxford, 1999

Greengrass, Mark, 'Informal Networks in French Protestantism', in *Society and Culture in the Huguenot World, 1559–1685*, eds Raymond A. Mentzer and Andrew Spicer, Cambridge, 2007, pp. 78–96

Greenidge, A. H. J., *Infamia: Its Place in Roman Public and Private Law*, Oxford, 1894 (= 2005, Kessinger reprint)

Gregg, W. W., *A Companion to Arber*, Oxford, 1967

Greville, Fulke, *The Prose Works of Fulke Greville, Lord Brooke*, ed. J. Gouws, Oxford, 1986

Gross, G., 'Les rééditions du *Livre des Marchans* de 1541 et 1544: un livre à double enjeu', *Bulletin de l'Insitut d;Histoire de la Réformation*, 2004–5, pp. 45–58

Gualdo Rosa, L., *La fede nella 'paideia': aspetti della fortuna europea di Isocrate negli xv e xvi secoli*, Rome, 1984

Guggisberg, Hans Rudis, *Sebastian Casteillo: Humanist und Verteidiger der religioesen Toleranz im konfessioneller Zeitalter*, Goettingen, 1997

Guy, John, 'The Rhetoric of Counsel', in *Tudor Political Culture*, ed. Dale Hoak, Cambridge, 1995, pp. 292–311

Guy-Bray, Stephen, *Homoerotic Space: The Poetics of Loss in Renaissance Literature*, Toronto, 2002

Haar, James, 'Lasso as Historicist: the *Cantus Firmus* Motets', in *Hearing the Motet: Essays on the Motet in the Middle Ages and the Renaissance*, ed. D. Pesce, St. Louis, 1994

Haar, James, 'Palestrina as Historicist: The *L'homme armé* masses', *Journal of the Royal Music Association*, 121, 1996, pp. 191–205

Hackett, M. B., *The Original Statutes of Cambridge University. The Text and its History*, Cambridge, 1970

Hacking, Ian, *The Emergence of Probability*, Cambridge, 1975

Half Humankind, eds Katherine Usher Henderson and Barbara F. McManus, Urbana, 1975

Halpern, Richard, *The Poetics of Primitive Accumulation: English Renaissance Culture and the Genealogy of Capital*, Ithaca: NY, 1991

Hammer, Paul, *The Polarisation of Elizabethan Politics: The Political Career of Robert*

Devereux, 2nd Earl of Essex 1585–1597, Cambridge, 1999

Hammer, Paul E. J., *Elizabeth's Wars: Society, Government and Military Reformation in Tudor England, 1558–1604*, London, 2003

Hammer, Paul E. J., 'Lord Henry Howard, the Earl of Essex, and the Politics of Friendship', *English Manuscript Studies*, 13, 2007, pp. 1–34

Hannay, M. P., *Silent but for the Word: Tudor Women as Patrons, Translators and Writers of Religious Works*, Kent: OH, 1985 [Not in current version]

Hardison, O. B., *The Enduring Monument: A Study of the Idea of Praise in Renaissance Literary Theory and Practice*, Chapel Hill: NC, 1962

Harris, Jason, 'The Practice of Community: Humanist Friendship During the Dutch Revolt', *Texas Studies in Language and Literature*, 2005, pp. 299–325

Harvey, Gabriel, *Rhetor*, London: Henry Bynneman, 1574

Harvey, Gabriel, *Graulationum Valdinensium libri quattuor*, London: Henry Bynneman, 1578

Harvey, John, *An Astrologicall Addition or Supplement to be annexed to the late Discourse upon the Great Conjunction of Saturne, and Jupiter*, London: Richard Watkins, 1583

Harvey, Richard, *An Astrological Discourse upon the Conjunction of Saturne & Jupiter*, London: Bynneman, 1583

Hasse, Nikolaus Dag, 'Die humanistische polemik gegen arabischen Authoritäten', *Neulateinisches Jahrbuch*, 3, 2001, pp. 65–79

Hathaway, N., '*Compilatio*: From Plagiarism to Composition', *Viator*, 20, 1989, pp. 19–44

Haynes, Alan, *Invisible Power: The Elizabeth Secret Services 1570–1603*, Stroud, 1992

Head, David M., *The Ebbs and Flows of Fortune: The Life of Thomas Howard, Second Duke of Norfolk*, Athens: OH and London, 1995

Heidegger, Martin, *Phänomenologie des religiösen Lebens*, Gesammtausgabe, LX, ed. M. Jung, Frankfurt am Main, 1995

Heydon, Christopher, *A Defence of Judicial Astrologie*, Cambridge: John Legat, 1603

Hicks, Leo, *An Elizabethan Problem: Some Aspects of the Careers of Two Exile Adventurers*, London, 1964

Hill, Christopher, 'The Definition of a Puritan', in his *Society and Puritanism in Prerevolutionary England*, London, 1964, pp. 15–30

L'Histoire de l'édition française, eds H.-J. Martin, R. Chartier and J.-P. Vivet, Paris, 1989

Hobbes, Thomas, *The Correspondence of Thomas Hobbes II. 1660–1679*, ed. Noel Malcolm, Oxford, 1994

Hoenen, M. J. F., 'Late-Mediaeval Schools of Thought in the Mirror of University Text-Books', in *Philosophy and Learning: Universities in the Middle Ages*, eds M. J. F. M. Hoenen, J. H. Josef Schneider and Georg Wieland, Leiden, 1995, pp. 329–69

Honan, Michael, *Christopher Marlowe*, London, 2005

Houelebecq, Michel, *Les éléments particuliers*, Paris, 2001

Howard, Henry, *A True and Perfect Relation of the Whole Proceedings Against the Late Most Barbarous Traitors*, London, 1605

Howard, Henry, *The Poems of Henry Howard Earl of Surrey and of Sir Thomas Wyatt the Elder*, ed. G. F. Nott, 2 vols, New York, 1965

Huizinga, J., *Erasmus*, Basel, 1928

Bibliography

Hunter, George K., 'The Marking of *Sententiae* in Elizabethan Plays, Poems and Romances', *The Library*, series V, 6, 1951, pp. 151–88

[I.B.], *The Merchants Avizo*, London: Richard Whittaker, 1604

Idea, eds M. Fattori and L. Bianchi, Rome, 1990

Jardine, L., 'Dialectic Teaching in Sixteenth-Century Cambridge', *Studies in the Renaissance*, 21, 1974

Jardine, Lisa, 'Humanism and the Arts Course in Sixteenth-Century Cambridge', *History of Education*, 4, 1975, pp. 16–31

Jardine, L. and W. Sherman, 'Pragmatic Readers: Knowledge Transactions and Scholarly Services in Late Elizabethan England', in *Religion, Culture and Society in Early Modern Britain: Essays in Honour of Patrick Collinson*, eds A. Fletcher and P. Roberts, Cambridge, 1994, pp. 113–24

Jardine, L. and A. Stewart, *Hostage to Fortune: The Troubled Life of Francis Bacon 1561–1626*, London, 1998

Javitch, Daniel, 'The Assimilation of Aristotle's *Poetics* in Sixteenth-Century Italy', in *Cambridge History of Literary Criticism, 3: Renaissance Criticism*, ed. G. Norton, Cambridge, 1999, pp. 53–65

Javitch, Daniel, 'On the Rise of Genre-Specific Poetics in the Sixteenth Century', in *Making Sense of Aristotle: Essays in Poetics*, eds O. Andersen and J. Haarberg, London, 2001, pp. 127–44

Jensen, Kristian, 'The Humanist Reform of Latin and Latin Teaching', in *The Cambridge Companion to Renaissance Humanism*, ed. J. Kraye, Cambridge, 1996, pp. 63–81

Jongh, H. de, *L'ancienne faculté de la theologie de Louvain au premier siècle de son existence*, Louvain, 1911

Jordan, Constance, *Renaissance Feminism. Literary Texts and Political Models*, Ithaca: NY, 1990

Junius, Hadrianus, *Epistolae*, Dordrecht: Vincent Cairnax, 1652

Kallendorf, Craig, 'Marginalia and the Rise of Early Modern Subjectivity', in *On Renaissance Commentaries*, ed. M. Pade, Hildesheim, 2005, pp. 110–29

Kanas, Nick, 'Alessandro Piccolomini and the First Printed Star Atlas (1540)', *Imago Mundi*, 58, 2006, pp. 70–7

Kassell, Lauren, *Medicine and Magic in Elizabethan England*, Oxford, 2005

Kay, Dennis, *Melodious Tears: The Funeral Elegy from Spenser to Milton*, Oxford, 1990

Kearney, H., *Scholars and Gentleman: Universities and Society in Pre-Industrial England, 1500–1700*, London, 1970

Kelley, Donald, *Foundations of Modern Historical Scholarship: Language, Law and History in the French Renaissance*, New York, 1970

Kelley, Donald, 'Elizabethan Political Thought', in *The Varieties of British Political Thought, 1500–1800*, eds J. G. A. Pocock, Gordon S. Schochet and Lois G. Shwoerer, Cambridge, 1993, pp. 47–79

Kelsey, Harry, *Sir John Hawkins: Queen Elizabeth's Slave Trader*, New Haven, 2003

Kettlewell, J., *A Discourse Explaining the Nature of Edification*, London: Kettlewell, 1684

King, John, 'Representations of the Virgin', *Renaissance Quarterly*, 42, 1990, pp. 34–49

Knafla, Louis, *Law and Politics in Jacobean England: The Tracts of Lord Chancellor*

Ellesmere, Cambridge, 1977

Knafla, Louis, 'The Matriculation Revolution and Education at the Inns of Court in Renaissance England', in *Tudor Men and Institutions*, ed. A. Slavin, Baton Rouge, 1972, pp. 251–5

Knox, D., 'Erasmus *De civilitate* and the Religious Origins of Civility in Protestant Europe', *Archiv für Reformationsgeschichte*, 86, 1995, pp. 7–55

Knox, John, *The First Blast of the Trumpet against the Monstrous Regiment of Women*, Geneva: n.p., 1558

Krausman Ben-Amos, Ilana, *Adolescence and Youth in Early Modern England*, New Haven, 1994

Kraye, Jill, 'Like Father, Like Son: Aristotle, Nicomachus and the *Nicomachean Ethics*', in *Aristotelica et Lulliana magistro doctissimo Charles H. Lohr septuagesimum annum feliciter agenti dedicata*, eds R. Imbach, F. Dominguez, T. Pindl-Büchel and P. Walter, Turnhout, 1995, pp. 155–80

Kraye, Jill, review of Bossy, *Giordano Bossy and The Embassy Affair*, in *The Heythrop Journal*, 33, 1992, pp. 324–7

Kristeller, P. O., 'The Modern System of the Arts', in his *Renaissance Thought II: Papers on Humanism and the Arts*, New York, 1965, pp. 163–227

Kroll, B. M., *Henry Peacham's 'The Garden of Eloquence' (1593): historische-kritische Einleitung mit einer Kommentar*, Frankfurt am Main, 1996

Kusukawa, Sachiko, 'The Reception of Melanchthon in Sixteenth-Century Cambridge and Oxford', in *Melanchthon und Europa*, ed. K. Meerhof, Stuttgart, 2002, pp. 233–54

Lake, Peter, *Anglicans or Puritans? English Conformist Thought from Whitgift to Hooker*, London, 1986

Leader, D. R., 'Philosophy at Oxford and Cambridge in the Fifteenth Century', *History of Universities*, 4, 1984, pp. 25–46

Ledegant, F., *Mysterium Ecclesiae: Beelden voor de Kerk in de Leden bij Origines*, Leuven, 2001

Leedham-Green, Elizabeth, *Book From Cambridge Inventories: Books Lists from the Vice Chancellor's Court Probate Records From the Tudor and Stuart Periods*, 2 vols, Cambridge, 1986

Lehmberg, Stanford, 'The Musicians of Westminster Abbey, 1540–1640', in *Westminster Abbey Reformed 1540–1640*, eds C. S. Knighton and Richard Mortiner, Aldershot, 2002, pp. 94–113

Leijenhoorst, C., *The Mechanization of Aristotelianism*, Leiden, 2002

Leslie, John, *A Defence of the Honour of the Right Highe, Mighty and Nobles Princess Marie Queene of Scoatland and Dowager of France*, London: Diczophile, 1569

Leslie, John, *A Treatise Touching the Right, Title and Interest as well of the most Excellent Princesse, Marye Queene of Scotland, as of the most noble Kyng James, her Graces sonne, to the succession of the Croune of England*, London, 1584

The Letters of Stephen Gardiner, ed. J. A. Muller, London, 1933

Levack, Brian P., *The Civil Lawyers in England, 1603–1641: A Political Study*, Oxford, 1973

Lindroth, S., *Uppsala Universitet, 1477–1977*, Uppsala, 1976

Lindsay, David, *An Dialogue betwixt Experience and ane couteour off the miserabill estait of the warld*, Paris: [Petit], 1558

Locatelli, A., 'The Land of "Plenty": Erasmus' *De copia* and English Renaissance Rhetoric', in *Silenos: Erasmus in Elizabethan Literature*, ed. C. Corti, Pisa, 1995, pp. 41–57

Long, A. A., 'Stoic Readings of Homer', in *Homer's Ancient Readers*, ed. Robert Lamberton and John J. Keaney, Princeton, 1992, pp. 41–66

Lord Morley: Triumphs of English, Henry Parker, Lord Morley, eds J. P. Carley and M. Axton, London, 2000

Lorenzetti, Stefano, *Musica e identità nobilare nell'Italia del rinascimento*, Florence, 2002, esp. pp. 65–118

Lotichius, Petrus, *Poemata*, Leipzig: Iohannes Steinmann, 1576

Lubac, Henri, *Exegèse medieval: Les Quatre sens de l'écriture*, Paris, 1959–1964

Ludwig, Walter, 'Die Epikedien des Lotichius für Stilbar, Micyllus und Melanchthon', in *Lotichius und die Römische Elegie*, ed. Ulrike Auhagen, Tübingen, 2001, pp. 153–84

Luther, Martin, *Werke*, Weimar, 1938–1966

Lysias, *Eratosthenes, hoc est brevis et luculenta defensio Lysiae pro caede Eratosthenis*, Cambridge: John Legatt, 1593

MacCaffrey, W., *Queen Elizabeth and the Making of Policy, 1572–1588*, Princeton, 1981

McConica, James, 'Humanism and Aristotle in Tudor Oxford', *English Historical Review*, 94, 1979, pp. 291–317

McConica, James, 'The Collegiate Society', *History of the University of Oxford*, III, pp. 669–75

MacCulloch, Diarmaid, *Suffolk under the Tudors. Politics and Religion in an English County 1500–1600*, Oxford, 1988

MacCulloch, Diarmaid, *Thomas Cranmer*, London, 1998

MacCulloch, Diarmaid, *The Tudor Church Militant*, London, 2000

MacCulloch, Diarmaid, *The Later English Reformation 1547–1603*, London, 2001

Mack, Peter, *Elizabethan Rhetoric*, Cambridge, 2002

Mack, Peter, 'Ramus Reading: The Commentaries on Cicero's Consular Orations and Vergil's *Eclogues* and *Georgics*', *JWCI*, 61, 1998, LXI, pp. 111–41

Maclean, Ian, 'Evidence, Logic, the Rule and the Exception in Early Modern Law and Medicine', *Early Science and Medicine*, 5, 2000, pp. 227–256

Maclean, Ian, *Interpreation and Meaning in the Renaissance: The Case of Law*, Cambridge,1992

Maclean, Ian, *The Renaissance Notion of Woman: A Study in the Fortunes of Scholasticism and Medical Science in European Intellectual Life*, Cambridge, 1980

MacPhail, Eric, 'The Mosaic of Speech: A Classical Topos in Renaissance Aesthetics', *JWCI*, 66, 2003, pp. 249–63

de Maisse, André Hurault, *A Journal of All that was Accomplished by Monsieur de Maisse Ambassador in England from Henri IV to Queen Elizabeth*, tr. G. B. Harrison and R. A Jones, London, 1931

Maitland, F. W., 'English Law and the Renaissance', in idem, *Selected Historical Essays of F. W. Maitland*, ed. Helen M. Cam, Cambridge, 1957

Maltby, W. S., *Alba: A Biography of Fernando Alvarez de Toledo, Third Duke of Alba,*

Berkeley, 1982

Mandelbrote, Scott, 'The Religion of Thomas Harriot', in *Thomas Harriot: An Elizabethan Man of Science*, ed. Robert Fox, Aldershot, 2000

Mantova, Benedetto da, *Beneficio di Cristo*, ed. Salvatore Caponetto, Florence, 1972

Marotti, Arthur F., *Manuscript Circulation and the English Renaissance Lyric*, Chicago, 1996

Marotti, Arthur F., 'Love is not Love: Elizabethan Sonnet Sequences and the Social Order', *English Literary History*, 49, 1982, pp. 296–328

Massai, Sonia, *Shakespeare and the Rise of the Editor*, Cambridge, 2007

May, Steve, 'Tudor Aristocrats and the Mythical Stigma of Print', *Renaissance Papers*, 10, 1980, pp. 11–18

Meerhof, Kees, *Entre logique et literature: Autour de Melanchthon*, Paris, 2001

Melton, John, *Astrologaster: or the Figure-Caster*, ed. Hugh G. Dick, Los Angeles, 1975

Memoirs of the Life and Times of Sir Christopher Hatton KG, ed. H. Nicolas, London, 1847

Menander Rhetor, eds D. A. Russell and M. Winterbottom, Oxford, 1981

Milham, Mary E., 'The Manuscripts of Platina's *De honesta voluptate* and its source', *Scriptorium*, 26, 1972, pp. 127–9

Milham, Mary E., 'The Latin Editions of Platina's *De honesta voluptate*', *Gutenburg Jahrbuch*, 52, 1976, pp. 57–63

Milward, Peter, *Religious Controversies of the Elizabethan Age: a Survey of Printed Sources*, London, 1977

Minnis, Anthony J., '*Quadruplex sensus, multiplex modus*: Scriptural Sense and Mode in Medieval Scholastic Exegesis', in *Interpretation and Allegory*, ed. J. Whitman, Leiden, 2000, pp. 231–56

Momigliano, A., *The Classical Foundations of Modern Historiography*, Berkeley, 1990

Mondin, Battista, *Il problema del linguagio teologico dalle origini ad oggi*, Brescia, 1971

Monfassani, John, *George of Trebizond: A Study of his Logic and Rhetoric*, Leiden, 1976

Moore, Peter R., 'Hamlet and Surrey's Psalm 8', *Neophilologus*, 82, 1998, pp. 487–98

Moore, Peter R., 'The Heraldic Charge against the Earl of Surrey', *English Historical Review*, 116, 2001, pp. 557–83

Morgan, Victor, 'Cambridge University and "the Country"', in *The University in Society*, ed. L. Stone, 2 vols, Princeton, 1974, II, pp. 183–245

Mortari, Vincenzo Piano, *Diritto, logica, metodo nel secolo XVI*, Naples, 1978

Mortari, Vincenzo Piano, *Gli inizi del diritto moderno in Europa*, Naples, 1986

Morzillo, Sebastian Fox, *De naturae philosophia*, Louvain: Colonaeus, 1554

Morzillo, Sebastian Fox, *In Platonis Timaeum seu de universo commentarii*, Basel: Oporin, 1554

Mosley, A., 'Objects of Knowledge: Mathematics and Models in Sixteenth-Century Cosmology and Astronomy', in *Transmitting Knowledge: Words, Images and Instruments in Early Modern Europe*, eds I. Maclean and S. Kusukawa, Oxford, 2006, pp. 193–216

Moss, Anne, *Printed Commonplace Books and the Structuring of Renaissance Thought*,

Oxford, 1996
Mowl, Timothy, *Elizabethan and Jacobean Style*, London, 1993
Munimenta Heraldica, ed. G. D. Squibb, London, 1985
Murdin, William, *A Collection of State Papers Relating to Affairs in the Reign of Elizabeth from the Years 1571 to 1596*, London: William Bowyer, 1759
Muret, Marc-Antoine, *Variae lectiones*, Paris: Guillaume Rovillé, 1594
Muret, Marc-Antoine, *Opera omnia*, ed. D. Ruhnken, 4 vols, Leiden, 1794
Murphy, Beverley A., *Bastard Prince: The Lost Son of Henry VIII*, Thrupp, 2001
Muslow, Martin, 'Ambiguities of the Prisca Sapientia in Late Renaissance Humanism,' *Journal of the History of Ideas*, 65, 2004, pp. 1–13
Nashe, Thomas, *The Unfortunate Traveller*, London, 1968
Nelson, Alan, *Monstrous Adversary: The Life of Edward de Vere, Seventeenth Earl of Oxford*, Liverpool, 2003
Neubauer, Hans-Joachim, *The Rumour: A Cultural History*, tr. C. Brown, London, 1999
Nisbet, R. G. and Margaret Hubbard, *A Commentary on Horace Odes II*, Oxford, 1978
Nuttall, J. F., *The Holy Spirit in Puritan Faith and Experience*, ed. Peter Lake, Princeton, 1992
Oakley, Francis, *Natural Law, Laws of Nature, Natural Rights*, London, 2005
Oecolampadius, Johannes, *In Hieremiam commentariorum libri tres*, Strassburg: Apiarius, 1530
Officium B. Mariae virginis nuper reformatum et Pii pontificis maximi editum, Antwerp: Plantin, 1575
Osborne, James, *Young Philip Sidney, 1572-1577*, New Haven and London, 1972
Ottolenghi, Paolo, *Giacomo Castelvetro. Un esile modenese nell' Inghilterra di Shakespeare*, Pisa, 1982
Palliser, D. M., *Tudor York*, London, 1979, p. 244
The Papers of Nathaniel Bacon of Stiffkey, eds A. Hassell Smith and Gillian Baker, 2 vols, Norwich, 1983
Panowsky, Erwin, *Idea: A Concept in Art Theory*, London, 1968
Pantin, Isabelle, 'Alessandro Piccolomini en France: La question de la langue scientifique et l'evolution de genre du traité de la sphère', in *La réception des écrits italiens en France à la Renaissance*, ed Alfredo Perifano, Paris, 2000, pp. 9–28
Park, K. D., 'The Organic Soul', in the *Cambridge History of Renaissance Philosophy*, eds Q. Skinner, E. Kessler and C. B. Schmitt, Cambridge, 1988, pp. 464–84
Parker, G., 'David or Goliath? Philip II and his World in the 1580s', in his *Empire, Warfare and Faith in Early Modern Europe*, London, 2002
Parker, G., 'The Place of Tudor England in the Messianic Vision of Phiip II of Spain', *Transactions of the Royal Historical Society*, 12, 2002, pp. 167–221
Parkes, M. B., 'The Influence of the Concepts of *Ordinatio* and *Compilatio* on the Development of the Book', in *Medieval Learning and Literature: Essays Presented to Richard William Hunt*, eds J. J. G. Alexander and M. T. Gibson, Oxford, 1976, pp. 115–41
Pearson, David, *English Bookbinding Styles: A Handbook 1450-1800*, London, 2003
Peck, D. C., *Leicester's Commonwealth: The Copy of a Letter Written by a Master of*

Art at Cambridge (1584) and Related Documents, Athens: OH, 1985
Peck, Linda Levy, *Northampton. Patronage and Policy at the Court of James I*, London, 1982
Peck, Linda Levy, 'The Mentality of a Jacobean Grandee', in *The Mental World of the Jacobean Court*, ed. Linda Levy Peck, Cambridge, 1998, pp. 148–68
Peck, Linda Levy, 'Uncovering the Arundel Library at the Royal Society: Changing Meanings of Science and the Fate of the Norfolk Donation', *Notes and Records of the Royal Society*, 52, 1998, pp. 3–26
Peltonen, Markku, *The Duel in Early Modern England: Civility, Politeness and Honour*, Cambridge, 2003
Pettegree, Andrew, 'Nicodemism and the English Reformation', in his *Marian Protestantism: Six Studies*, Aldershot, 1996, pp. 86–117
Philip, I. G., *Gold-Tooled Bookbindings*, Oxford, 1951
Philipson, Martin, *Ein Ministerium unter Philipp II: Kardinale Granvalle am Spanische Hofe, 1579–1586*, Berlin, 1895
Piccolomini, Alessandro, *La sfera del mondo*, Venice: Giovanni Guarisco, 1579
Pico della Mirandola, Giovanni, *Disputationes adversus astrologiam divinatricem*, ed. E. Garin, 2 vols, Florence, 1946–1952
Pigman III, G. W., *Grief and Renaissance Elegy*, Cambridge, 1985
Pincombe, Michael, *Elizabethan Humanism: Literature and Learning in the Later Sixteenth Century*, London, 2001
Plaisance, M., 'Iacopo Corbinelli de l'exclusion e l'exil, la rupture avec la France', in *L'Exil et l'exclusion dans la culture italienne*, ed. G. Ulysse, Aix-en-Provence, 1991, pp. 67–76
Platina, *On Right Pleasure and Good Health*, ed. M. E. Milham, Tempe, 1998
Plutarch, *De placitis philosophorum libri a Guilelmo Budeo latini facti*, Paris: Iehan Petit, 1505
Plutarch, *Bruta animalia ratione utantur*, Cologne, 1522
Polman, Pontien, *L'élément historique dans la controverse religieuse du 16ème siècle*, Gembloux, 1932
Pon, Lisa, *Raphael, Dürer and Marcantonio Raimondi: Copying and the Italian Renaissance Print*, New Haven, 2004
Pontano, Giovanni, *Opera omnia*, 3 vols, Venice: Aldus Manutius, 1518
Popper, Nicholas, 'The English Polydaedali: How Gabriel Harvey Read late Tudor London', *JHI*, 66, 2005, pp. 351–81
Porter, H. C., *Reformation and Reaction in Tudor Cambridge*, Cambridge, 1958
Das Problem der Sprache in Theologie und Kirche, ed. W. Schneemelcher, Berlin, 1959
Przypkowski, Samuel, *Dissertatio de pace et concordia ecclesiae*, ed. M. Brozek, Warsaw, 1981
Pucci, Francesco, *De praedestinatione*, ed. M. Biagioni, Florence, 2000
Pumfrey, Stephen, 'Science and Patronage in Early Modern England 1570–1625', *History of Science*, 2004, pp. 137–88
Pustianaz, Marco, *Per una letteratura giustificata: scritura e lettertura nella prima riforma in Inghilterra 1525–1550*, Florence, 1995
Puttenham, George, *The Arte of Englishe Poesie*, London: Richard Field, 1589
[Q. Z.], *A Discoverie of the Treasons Practiced and Attempted Against the Queenes*

Bibliography

Maiestie by Francis Throckmorton, [London], [1584]
Rambuss, Richard, *Spenser's Secret Career*, Cambridge, 1998
Ramsay, G. D., *The Queen's Merchants and the Revolt of the Netherlands*, 2 vols, Manchester, 1986
Ravisius Textor, Johannes, *Epitheta*, Geneva, 1640
Read, Conyers, *Mr. Secretary Cecil and Queen Elizabeth*, London, 1955
Read, Conyers, *Lord Burghley and Queen Elizabeth*, London, 1960
Registrum annalium collegii Mertonensis, 1521–1567, ed. J. Fletcher, Oxford, 1974
The Reign of Elizabeth I: Court and Culture in the Last Decade, ed. John Guy, Cambridge, 1995
Renaissance Genres, ed. B. Lewalski, Cambridge, 1986
Reusens, E., *Documents relatifs à l'histoire de l'université de Louvain*, Louvain, 1893–1903
Rhetoric and Law in Early Modern Europe, eds Lorna Hutson and Victoria Kahn, New York, 1994
Richards, Jennifer, 'Assumed Simplicity and the Critique of Nobility: Or, How Castiglione read Cicero', *Renaissance Quarterly*, 53, 2001, pp. 212–32
Roberts, Julian and Andrew G. Watson, *John Dee's Library Catalogue*, London, 1990
Rodriguez-Salgado, M. J., 'Paz ruidosa, guerra sorda', in *La monarquia de Felipe II a debate*, ed. L. Ribot Garcia, Madrid, 2000, pp. 63–119
The Roman Law Tradition, eds A. Lewis and D. Ibbetson, Oxford, 1994
del Rosso, Paolo, *La fisica*, Paris: Pierre le Voirrier, 1578
Ross, Richard J., 'The Commoning of English Common Law. The Renaissance Debate about Printing English Law 1520–1640', *University of Pennsylvania Law Review*, 146, 1998, pp. 323–461
Roth, C., 'Roberto Ridolfi e la sua congiura', *Rivista storica degli archivi toscani*, 2, 1930, pp. 119–32
Rowe, Joy, 'The Lopped Tree: The Re-formation of the Suffolk Catholic Community', in *England's Long Reformation 1500–1800*, ed. N. Tyacke, London, 1998, pp. 167–93
Rummel, Erika, *Erasmus'* Annotationes *on the New Testament*, Toronto, 1986
'The Ryalle Booke', ed. F. Grose, in *The Antiquarian Repertory*, 4 vols, London, 1807–1809
Rye, Walter, 'Surrey House and St. Leonard's Priory, Norwich', *Norfolk Archaeology*, 15, 1903–4, pp. 194–5
Sabinus, Georgius, 'De carminibus ad veterum imitationem artificiose componendis', in idem, *Poemata*, Leipzig: Iohannes Steinman, 1581, pp. 486–514
Saltmarsh, J., *King's College: A Short History*, Cambridge, 1958
Sanderson, Robert, *Logicae artis compendium*, ed. E. J. Ashworth, Bologna, 1985
Sasso, G., *Machiavelli e gli antichi*, 3 vols, Milan, 1988
Saunders, J. W., 'The Stigma of Print: A Note of the Social Bases of Tudor Poetry', *Essays in Criticism*, I, 1951, pp. 139–64
Savonarola, Girolamo, *Contro gli astrologi*, ed. C. Pompeo Faracovi, Rome, 2000
Scaliger, Julius Caesar, *Poetices libri VII* [Heidelberg]: Petrus Santandareus, 1581
Scaliger, Julius Caesar, *Poetices libri septem. Sieben Bücher über die Dichtkunst*, ed. L. Deitz, 5 vols, Stuttgart, 1992–2003
Scarisbrick, J. J., *Henry VIII*, New Haven, 1968

Schurink, Fred, 'Like a hand in the margine of a booke: William Blount's Marginalia and the Politics of Sidney's Arcadia', *Review of English Studies*, 59, 2008, pp. 1–24

Schütze, Ingo, *Die Naturphilosophie in Giralomo Cardanos De subtilitate*, Munich, 2000

Screech, M. A., *Clement Marot: A Renaissance Poet Discovers the Gospel*, Leiden, 1994

Scrutton, Thomas, *The Influence of Roman Law on the Law of England*, Cambridge, 1885

Seifert, Arno, 'Der Humanismus an der Artistenfakultaeten des katholischen Deutschland', in *Humanismus im Bildungswegen des 15 und 16 Jahrhunderts*, ed. W. Reinhard, Weinheim, 1996, pp. 133–54

Self-Presentation and Social Identification: The Rhetoric and Pragmatics of Letter Writing in Early Modern Times, eds T. Van Houdt, J. Papy and G. Tournoy, Leuven, 2002

Seneca, *Opera omnia*, ed. Marc-Antoine Muret [Heidelberg]: Hieronymus Commelinus, 1594

Serjeantson, R. W., 'Testimony and Proof in Early Modern England', *Studies in the History and Philosophy of Science*, 30, 1999, pp. 195–236

Sessions, William, *Henry Howard: The Poet Earl of Surrey. A Life*, Oxford, 1999

Shapiro, Barbara J., *A Culture of Fact: England 1550–1720*, Ithaca: NY, 2000

Sharpe, Kevin, *Reading Revolutions in Early Modern England*, Yale, 2001

Shephard, Amanda, *Gender and Authority in Sixteenth-Century England: The Knox Debate*, Keele, 1994

Sherman, W., *John Dee: the Politics of Reading and Writing in the English Renaissance*, Amherst, 1995

Shipley, E. J., 'An Inventory of the Effects of Henry Howard KG, Earl of Northampton, taken on his death in 1614, together with a transcript of his will', *Archaeologia*, 42, 1869, pp. 347–78

Shrank, Cathy, 'These Few Scribbled Rules: Representing Scribal Intimacy in Early Modern Print', *Huntington Literary Quarterly*, 67, 2004, pp. 295–314

Sidney, Philip 'A Defence of Poetry', in *English Renaissance Literary Criticism*, ed. B. Vickers, Oxford, 1999, pp. 340–68

Sidney, Sir Philip, *The Countess of Pembroke's Arcadia (The New Arcadia)*, ed. Victor Skretkowtcz, Oxford, 1988

Simoncelli, P., *Il cavaliere demezzato. Paolo del Rosso 'fiorentino e letterato'*, Milan, 1990

Skinner, Quentin, *The Foundations of Modern Political Thought*, 2 vols, Cambridge, 1978

Skinner, Quentin, *Reason and Rhetoric in the Philosophy of Thomas Hobbes*, Cambridge, 1996

Slights, William W. E., *Managing Readers: Printed Marginalia in English Renaissance Books*, Michigan, 2001

Smalley, Beryl, 'Glossa ordinaria', *Theologische Realenzynkopaedie*, 13, p. 456

Smith, Alan, *Servant of the Cecils – The Life of Sir Michael Hickes*, London, 1977

Smith, Charles George, *Shakespeare's Proverb Lore: His Use of Leonard Culman and Pubilius Syrus*, Cambridge: MA, 1963

Somerset, Anne, *Unnatural Murder: Poison at the Court of James I*, London, 1997

Bibliography

[Sparke, Michael], *A Historicall Narration of the First Fourteen Years of King James*, London: Richard Cotes, 1651

Stacey, Peter, *Roman Monarchy and the Renaissance Prince*, Cambridge, 2007

Stadter, Philip A., 'Arrianus, Flavius' in *Catalogus Translationum et Commentariorum*, eds F. E. Cranz and P. O. Kristeller, Washington DC, 1960, III, pp. 1–20

Stanihurst, Richard, *Harmonia*, London: Wolf, 1570

Starkey, David, *The Reign of Henry VIII: Politics and Personalities*, London, 1985

Starkey, David, *Elizabeth*, London, 2000

Steel, Carlos, 'Nature as an Object of Science', in *Nature in Medieval Thought. Some Approaches East and West*, ed. Chumaru Koyama, Leiden, 2000, pp. 125–52

Steimnetz, David C., *Luther and Staupitz: An Essay in the Intellectual Origins of the Protestant Reformation*, Durham: NC, 1980

Stein, P. G., 'Thomas Legge. A Sixteenth-Century Civilian and his Books', in *Satura Roberto Feenstra oblata*, Fribourg, 1985, pp. 545–56

Stern, Virginia F., *Gabriel Harvey: His Life, Marginalia and Library*, Oxford, 1979

Stewart, Alan, *Close Readers: Humanism and Sodomy in Early Modern England*, Princeton, 1997

Stone, Lawrence, *The Crisis of the Aristocracy 1558–1641*, London, 1967

Stone, Lawrence, *Fortune and Family: Studies in Aristocratic Finances in the Sixteenth and Seventeenth Centuries*, Oxford, 1973

Stone, Martin, 'Protestant Casuistry', in *Humanism and Early Modern Philosophy*, eds Jill Kraye and Martin Stone, 1999, pp. 59–90

Ström, Annika, *Lachrymae Catharinae. Five Collections of Funeral Poetry from 1628*, Stockholm, 1994

Strype, John, *The History of Edmund Grindal*, London, 1710

Strype, John, *Life of Matthew Parker, Archbishop of Canterbury*, London, 1711

Strype, John, *Life of Matthew Parker*, London, 1845

Süss, W., *Ethos*, Berlin, 1911

Swynnerton, Thomas, *A Reformation Rhetoric*, ed. R. Rex, Cambridge, 1999

Taylor, E. G. R., *Mathematical Practitioners of Tudor and Stuart England*, Cambridge, 1954

Thomas, Keith, *Religion and the Decline of Magic*, London, 1987

Thomas, Max, 'Reading and Writing the Renaissance Commonplace Book: A Question of Authorship?', in *The Construction of Authorship: Textual Appropriation in Law and Literature*, eds Martha Woodmansee and Peter Jaszi, Durham: NC, 1994, pp. 401–15

Thomas Thomas, *Dictionarium linguae latinae et anglicae*, Cambridge: Thomas, 1587

Trevor-Roper, Hugh, *Archbishop Laud 1573–1642*, revised edition, London, 1965

Trinkaus, Charles, *In Our Image and Likeness: Humanity and Divinity in Italian Renaissance Thought*, 2 vols, Chicago, 1970

Troje, H. E., *Humanistische Jurisprudenz*, Goldbach, 1993

[Tudor], Elizabeth, *Collected Works*, eds Leah S. Marcus et al., New York, 1998

Two Tudor Subsidy Rolls for the City of London, 1541 and 1582, ed. R. G. Lang, London, 1993

Tyacke, Nicholas, 'Introduction', in idem, *England's Long Reformation 1500–1800*,

London, 1998, pp. 1–32
Unguerer, Gustav, *A Spaniard in Elizabethan England: The Correspondence of Antonioz Perez' Exile*, London, 1988
Urkundenbuch der Universität Wittenberg (1502–1611), ed. W. Friedensburg, Magdeburg, 1926
Usher, Bert, 'Edward Brocklesby: "The First Put Out of his Living for the Surplice"', in *From Cranmer to Davidson: A Church of England Miscellany*, ed. S. Taylor, Woodbridge, 1999, pp. 47–67
Van Miert, Dirk, 'The Religious Beliefs of Hadrianus Junius (1511–1575)', in *Acta Conventus Neolatini Cantabrigiensis, Proceedings of the Eleventh International Congress of Neo-Latin Studies*, ed. R. Schnur, Tempe: AZ, 2003, pp. 583–94
Velcurio, Johannes, 'Commentarius studiosae iuventuti utilissimus in Copiam Erasmi', in Erasmus, *De copia*, London: Sibertus Roedius, 1556
Velcurio, Johannes, 'Commentarius studiosae iuventuti utilissimus in Copiam Erasmi', in Erasmus, *De copia*, Antwerp, 1565, pp. 333–416
Venn, John and Venn, J. A., *Alumni Cantabrigienses, a biographical list of all known students, graduates and holders of office at the University of Cambridge, from the earliest times to 1751*, 4 vols (1922–27)
Verkamp, Bernard J., *The Indifferent Mean: Adiaphorism in the English Reformation to 1554*, Athens: OH, 1977
Vine, A. E., 'Franis Bacon's Commonplace Books', *Transactions of the Cambridge Bibliographical Society*, 13, 2008
Wakelin, Daniel, *Humanism, Reading and English Literature, 1430–1530*, Oxford, 2007
Walsham, Alexandra, *Church Papists: Catholicism, Conformity and Confessional Polemic in Early Modern England*, Woodbridge, 1996
Walsham, Alexandra, *Providence in Early Modern England*, Oxford, 1999
Warren's Book, ed. A. W. W. Dale, Cambridge, 1911
Wells-Cole, A., *Art and Decoration in Elizabethan and Jacobean England: The Influence of Continental Prints 1558–1625*, New Haven, 2004
Wels, Volkhard, *Triviale Künste: Die humanistische Reform der grammatischen, dialektischen und rhetorischen Ausbildung an der Wende zum 16. Jahrhundert*, Berlin, 2000
White, John, *Diacosio-Martyrion id est...*, London: Cuthbert Cale, 1553
Wijffels, A., 'Law Book in Cambridge Libraries, 1500–1640', *Transactions of the Cambridge Bibliographical Society*, 10, 1993, pp. 359–412
Williams, Neville, *Captains Outrageous: Seven Centuries of Piracy*, London, 1961
Williams, Neville, *Thomas Howard, Fourth Duke of Norfolk*, London, 1964
Willis Clark, J. and Gary, A., *Old Plans of Cambridge*, Cambridge, 1921
Wills, R., and Clark, J. W., *The Architectural History of the University of Cambridge and of the Colleges of Cambridge and Eton*, with a new introduction by D. Watkin, Cambridge, 1988
Wilson, Thomas, *The Rule of Reason*, London: Richard Grafton, 1551
Wissowatius, Andreas, *Religio rationalis*, ed. Z. Ogonowski, Wolfenbüttel, 1982
Woolton, John, *A Treatise of the Immortalitie of the Soule*, London: John Sheppard, 1576
Wooding, Lucy, *Rethinking Catholicism in Reformation England*, Oxford, 2000

Bibliography

Woolfson, Jonathan, *Padua and the Tudors: English Students in Italy 1485–1603*, London, 1999
Woolfson, Jonathan, 'Between Bruni and Hobbes: Aristotle's Politics in Tudor Intellectual Culture', in *Reassessing Tudor Humanism*, ed. J. Woolfson, London, 2002, ch. 10
Word, Church and State: Tyndale Quincentanry Essays, eds John T. Day, Erik Lund and Anne M. O'Donnell, Washington, 1998
Worden, Blair, *The Sound of Virtue: Sir Philip Sidney's Arcadia and Elizabethan Politics*, London, 1998
Worden, Blair, 'Court Centred [sic] Politics and the Uses of Roman Historians, 1590–1620', in *Culture and Politics in Early Stuart England*, eds K. Sharpe and P. Lake, Basingstoke, 1994, pp. 21–43
Woudhuysen, Henry, *Sir Philip Sidney and the Circulation of Manuscripts 1558–1642*, Oxford, 1998
Wright, Louis B., *Advice to a Son: Precepts of Lord Burghley, Sir Walter Raleigh, and Francis Osborne*, Ithaca: NY, 1962
Wyclif, John, *Tracts and Treatises of John de Wycliffe*, ed. R. Vaughan, London, 1845
Zanier, Giancarlo, *La medicina astrologica e la sua teoria: Marsilio Ficino e i suoi critici contemporanei*, Rome, 1977
Zucht und Ordnung. Reformierte Kirchenverfassungen im 16 und 17 Jahrhundert (Nassau-Dillenburg, Kurpfalz, Hessen-Kassel), ed. P. Münch, Tübingen, 1978

Unpublished dissertations

Adam, Robyn, 'Both Diligent and Secret: The Intelligence Letters of William Herle', unpublished PhD dissertation, University of London, 2004
Caney, Anna Christine, 'Let He Who Objects Produce Sound Evidence: Henry Howard and the Sixteenth Century [sic] Gynecocracy Debate', unpublished MA dissertation, Florida State University, 2005
Doran, S., 'Thomas Radcliffe, 3rd Earl of Sussex, ?1526–1583', unpublished PhD dissertation, London University, 1979
Dunn, R. S., 'The Status of Astrology in Elizabethan England', unpublished PhD dissertation, University of Cambridge, 1988
Gibbons, Katy, 'The Experience of Exile and English Catholics: Paris in the 1580s', unpublished PhD dissertation, University of York, 2004
Guerci, Manolo, 'The Strand Palaces of the Early Seventeenth Century: Northumberland House and Salisbury House', unpublished PhD dissertation, University of Cambridge, 2007

INDEX

There is no entry for Henry Howard. See rather under, for example, 'Catholicism' or 'Homosexuality' and so on.

Agrippa, Cornelius 151
Alcantara, battle of 114
Alciato, Andrea 163
Aldridge, Robert 29 n. 91
Antwerp 56 n. 8
Aphthonius 135 n. 41
Architecture 17–8, 18 n. 31, 18 n. 33
Arras, Union of 115
Aristotle 40ff, 50, 137, 140, 141
Arundell, Charles 2, 109, 115, 116, 123, 128, 148, 156
Astrology 15 n. 21, 130–42
Audley End 106, 107
Augustine, St. 141

Babington, Anthony 158
Bacon, Anne (Lady) 82 n. 5
Bacon, Anthony 47 n. 71, 155
Bacon, Francis 173
Bacon, Nathaniel 155
Bailly, Charles 56
Baker, Philip 26, 44
Ballard, John 157
Bancroft, Richard 160, 161
Bannister, Lawrence 55, 58
Berkeley, Henry Lord 16
Biographical history 180
Bonatti, Guido 132
Brancpeth Park 16 n. 23
Breviary, Pius V 152, 154 n. 51
Bromley, Sir Thomas 54, 123
Bruno, Giordano 129 n. 10, 148 n. 21
Byrd, William 153
Buxton, Robert 113

Caius, John 131
Calvin, Jean 137, 191
Cambridge University 23–9, 30–53, 178
   Arts Course 26–9, 34–5
   Dialectic 87–92
   Exegesis 29, 88
   Grammar 59–61, 78, 144
   Hermeneutics 88–9
   Legal study in 34, 35, 159 n. 70
   Lecture system 44 n. 64,
   Natural Philosophy 40–6
   Regency 32, 46
   Rhetoric 34, 92, 93, 134–6, 140
   'Commencement' 83, n. 7, 171–2
   Fellow-commoners 24–5
   King's College 24–9
      Curriculum 28–9
      Commons Books 25–6
      Dining system 26
      Lectures 29
      Mundum books 26
   Trinity College 29 n. 93 and n. 94
   Trinity Hall 16 n. 26, 30–53, 59 n. 21
      Legal study at 36–7
      Library 37
      Tutorial system 24, 44 n. 62
Camden, William 47, 132
Campion, Edmund 2, 44 n. 63
Carey, Henry 144
Careerism 106–8
Carr, Nicholas 44, 46–7
Castelnau (the French Ambassador) 100–1, 118, 120, 145–6
Castiglione, Baldassare 67ff
Castelvetro, Giacomo 170
Catharinus (Lanceloto Politi) 189
Catholicism 6, 17, 22, 27, 31, 47, 100, 109–10, 115–9, 122, 124, 149, 150–54, 179

Index

Carew, Sir George 173
Cartwright, Thomas 84, 117, 187–90
Cecil, Sir Robert 168, 173, 176, 177
Cecil, Sir William 6, 31, 37–8, 39, 53, 54, 56, 57, 58, 83, 84, 102–3. 106, 108, 109, 113, 117, 122, 149, 153, 155, 158
Chaldeans 14
Chambers, David 165
Charles V, Holy Roman Emperor 170
Charles IX, King of France 94
Charterhouse (London) 106 n. 1
Christening ceremonies 14 n. 19 and n. 20
Churchyard, Thomas 108
Cicero 71–2, 73, 135
Cockyn, Henry 94, 96–99
Consolation 52–3
Cotton, Sir Robert 177
Covell, William 133
Cowell, John 36, 161
Croft, Sir James 82, 109 n. 15, 122
Custodis, Hieronimo 171
Cuttes, Richard 113

Dacre, Anne 176
Dannett, John 150
Dee, John 131
Demosthenes 39
Doget, John 40
'Don Lewes' 169
Dyer, Sir Edward 172

Edification 186–91
Edward VI 18, 19–20, 21
Elizabeth I, Queen 23, 95, 169, 173, 177
Elyot, Thomas Sir 62 n. 37, 64 n. 42
Epicedia 47–9, 47 n. 75, 182–5
Erasmus, Desiderius 10 n. 4, 27 n. 81, 29 n. 81, 50 n. 84,
Erastus, Thomas 136 n. 47, 137
Essex, Earl of (Robert Devereux) 7, 158, 172–77

Fagot, Henri 100–1, 145
Falconry 16
Field, John 84
Fitzalan, Jane 133
Fitzroy, Henry 13
Fletcher, Giles 50 n. 80

Fludd, Robert 131
Forster, Richard 132, 133
Foxe, John 21
Foxe, Simeon 21 n. 49
Fox Morzillo, Sebastian 45, 76
Francois, duc d'Alencon 114–120
Fulke, William 131

Gardiner, Stephen 13, 23
Gelli, Giambattista 135 n. 38,
Gentili, Alberico 27 n. 81, 160
Genre 49 n. 76
Gest, Edmund 39
Gilbert, Humphrey 134
Gilbert, William 132
Good, James 99 n. 74
Grammar (non-university) 21 n. 49
Greek language 10 n. 5, 16, 19 n. 39, 27 n. 81
Greville, Sir Fulke 172
Grindal, Edmund 106

Hart, John 104–5
Harvey, Gabriel 27 n. 81, 30, 65, 102, 107–8, 127
Harvey, John 142
Harvey, Richard 127
Hatton, Sir Christopher 54, 82, 122, 149
Hawford, Edward 88
Hawkins, John 55
Heneage, Sir Thomas 158
Henri III, King of France 94
Herle, William 82, 128, 129, 147–8
Hervey, Henry 30
Heydon, Christopher 131
Hickes, Michael 16 n. 26
History, views of 118–9, 118 n. 49
Hodilow family 26 n. 76
Homer 38, 135
Homosexuality 11 n. 11, 49 n. 79, 129 n. 12
Hood, Sir Thomas 131
Howard, Charles (Lord Admiral) 156, 174
Howard, Henry (Earl of Surrey) 3, 12, 18, 108, 152
Howard, Jane 15
Howard, Katherine 16, 23 n. 61, 40
Howard, Margaret 17
Howard, Philip 101, 102, 113, 176, 179
Howard, Thomas (Third Duke) 21, 23

219

Howard, Thomas (Fourth Duke) 9, 54 n. 3, 55, 57, 58
Humanism 1–2, 4–5, 8, 181

Infamia 167, 168
Italy 180
Ivy Bridge Lane (the Strand) 94 n. 50

James VI, King of Scotland 172, 177, 179
Joinville, Treaty of 157
Junius, Hadrianus 18
Justinian I 160, 162, 163, 166, 167, 168

Knafla, Louis 161
Knollys, Lettice 116
Knox, John 165, 166

Lambarde, William 94
Lambeth Palace 58
Latewar, Richard 176 n. 38
Laud, William 180
Leicester, Earl of 107, 119, 128
Leighton, Sir Thomas 145
Leslie, John 94, 104, 159, 162, 163
Lestrange, Sir Nicholas 113
Letter-writing 37, 81–2, 179
Luther, Martin 188–9

Maitland, F. W. 160
Man, John 55
Marot, Clement 152
Martin, Gregory 105 n. 101
Martyr, Peter 22
Mary Stuart 55, 94, 119–122, 145, 148, 157–8, 177, 167
Melanchthon, Philip 130
Mendoza, Bernardino 82 n. 4, 100, 121, 123 n. 71, 124, 157–8
Merlin 174–6
Metre 22 n. 55, 50–1
Meurer, S. see under 'careerism'
Military pursuits 1, 13, 158 n. 66, 175, 177
Mildmay, Sir Walter 54, 116
Momsen, Theodor 162
Montaigne, Michel 81 n. 1
Montreuil, siege of 13
Morgan, Thomas 95
Muret, Marc-Antoine 67, 74
Mushold Hill, Norwich 83 n. 101

Navarre, Henri 126
Neville, Sir Henry 149
Norton, Thomas 104, 129

Oxford, Earl of 6, 59, 82 n. 4, 102, 123–25

Pace, Richard 25
Paget, Lord William 109, 148
Parker, Matthew 59, 106
Pastoral poetry 49 n. 79, 53
Paulet, Sir Amias 47 n. 71
Pedagogy 1, 9, 18–21
Perez, Antonio 82 n. 5, 172
Phelippes, Thomas 157
Philip II, King of Spain 114–5, 122 n. 64, 126, 158
Pico, Giovanni 142
Piccolomini, Alessandro 75–8
Platina, Bartolomeo 81 n. 1
Prayer 152–54

Radcliffe, Thomas 109, 116
Randolph, Sir Thomas 97 n. 59
Rayleton, Rowland 121
Ridolfi, Roberto 55–7, 128
Ripley, George 151
Russell, Henry 113

St. Paul 86, 187
Sabinus, Georgius 49 n. 78, 51 n. 85
Sadler, Sir Ralph 150
Salisbury Court (the Stand) 145
Sallust 139
Scaliger, Julius Caesar 50
Scientific instruments 16
Scrutton, Lord 161
Shakespeare, William 127 n. 2, 171 n. 15
Shelley, William 146
Sidney, Sir Philip 50, 62, 107, 119, 149, 150
Simier, Jean de 114, 115
Smith, John (clerk to Berkeleys) 16
Sorites 90
Spelman, Sir Henry 132, 161
Spenser, Edmund 170
Stafford, Elizabeth 13
Stafford, Edward 100, 122
Standen, Anthony 172
Stanhope, Sir John 158
Stanihurst, Ricahrd 2, 44 n. 63, 46, 87 n. 20

Index

Steward, John 95
Stoicism 72, 111, 142
Stone, Lawrence 2
Stubbs, John 117
Swale, Sir Richard 160

Tacitus 138–9
Talbot, George, Earl of Shrewsbury 95
Terrail, Pierre 1
Theobalds (Cheshunt) 109
Throckmorton 148
Thucydides 138–9
Townshend, Sir Roger 113
Trithemius, Johannes 152

Utrecht, Union of 115

Valerius, Cornelius 130
de Vere, Frances 15
Vergil 52, 107–8

Walsingham, Francis 54, 95, 108, 109–110, 127, 128, 144–9, 158
West, Sir William 161
White, John 22
Whitgift, John 93
Wilcox, Thomas 74
Wilson, Thomas 91

Young, Thomas 47

Studies in Renaissance Literature

Volume 1: *The Theology of John Donne*
Jeffrey Johnson

Volume 2: *Doctrine and Devotion in Seventeenth-Century Poetry
Studies in Donne, Herbert, Crashaw and Vaughan*
R. V. Young

Volume 3: *The Song of Songs in English Renaissance Literature
Kisses of their Mouths*
Noam Flinker

Volume 4: *King James I and the Religious Culture of England*
James Doelman

Volume 5: *Neo-historicism: Studies in Renaissance Literature,
History and Politics*
edited by Robin Headlam Wells, Glenn Burgess
and Rowland Wymer

Volume 6: *The Uncertain World of* Samson Agonistes
John T. Shawcross

Volume 7: *Milton and the Terms of Liberty*
edited by Graham Parry and Joad Raymond

Volume 8: *George Sandys: Travel, Colonialism and Tolerance
in the Seventeenth Century*
James Ellison

Volume 9: *Shakespeare and Machiavelli*
John Roe

Volume 10: *John Donne's Professional Lives*
Edited by David Colclough

Volume 11: *Chivalry and Romance in the English Renaissance*
Alex Davis

Volume 12: *Shakespearean Tragedy as Chivalric Romance:
Rethinking Macbeth, Hamlet, Othello, and King Lear*
Michael L. Hays

Volume 13: *John Donne and Conformity in Crisis in
the Late Jacobean Pulpit*
Jeanne Shami

Volume 14: *A Pleasing Sinne:*
Drink and Conviviality in Seventeenth-Century England
Adam Smyth

Volume 15: *John Bunyan and the Language of Conviction*
Beth Lynch

Volume 16: *The Making of Restoration Poetry*
Paul Hammond

Volume 17: *Allegory, Space and the Material World in the*
Writings of Edmund Spenser
Christopher Burlinson

Volume 18: *Self-Interpretation in* The Faerie Queene
Paul Suttie

Volume 19: *Devil Theatre: Demonic Possession and Exorcism*
in English Drama, 1558-1642
Jan Frans van Dijkhuizen

Volume 20: *The Heroines of English Pastoral Romance*
Sue P. Starke

Volume 21: *Staging Islam in England: Drama and Culture, 1640-1685*
Matthew Birchwood

Volume 22: *Early Modern Tragicomedy*
Edited by Subha Mukherji and Raphael Lyne

Volume 23: *Spenser's Legal Language: Law and Poetry*
in Early Modern England
Andrew Zurcher

Volume 24: *George Gascoigne*
Gillian Austen

Volume 25: *Empire and Nation*
in Early English Renaissance Literature
Stewart Mottram

Volume 26: *The English Clown Tradition*
from the Middle Ages to Shakespeare
Robert Hornback